FIELD GUIDE TO THE
BIRDS OF
BRITAIN

BIRDS OF BRITAIN

was edited and designed by
The Reader's Digest Association Limited, London.

First edition Copyright © 1981
The Reader's Digest Association Limited,
11 Westferry Circus, Canary Wharf, London E14 4HE

We are committed to both the quality of our products and the service we provide to our customers.
We value your comments, so please feel free to contact us on 08705 113366,
or via our web site at www.readersdigest.co.uk
If you have any comments about the content of our books, you can email
us at gbeditorial@readersdigest.co.uk

Reprinted 2002

Printed in Italy

ISBN 0 276 42504 9

READER'S DIGEST
NATURE LOVER'S LIBRARY

FIELD GUIDE TO THE
BIRDS OF BRITAIN

PUBLISHED BY THE READER'S DIGEST ASSOCIATION LIMITED

LONDON · MONTREAL · NEW YORK · SYDNEY

Contributors

*The publishers wish to express their gratitude to the following people for their
major contributions to the Field Guide to the Birds of Britain*

CONSULTANTS AND AUTHORS

Dr. Philip J.K. Burton
Robert Gillmor
Howard Ginn, M.A.
T.W. Parmenter
John Parslow
Cyril A. Walker
D.I.M. Wallace, B.A.

PHOTOGRAPHERS

For a full list of acknowledgments
to the photographers whose work
appears in this book, see page 320.

CARTOGRAPHY

The distribution maps were based on information
supplied by John Parslow and prepared by Clyde Surveys Ltd.
Revised maps for the 2000 reprint were prepared by
Andrew Thompson from information supplied by John Parslow.

ARTISTS

Stephen Adams
Norman Arlott
Peter Barrett
Trevor Boyer
John Busby
John Francis
Robert Gillmor
Tim Hayward
Hermann Heinzel
Mick Loates
Sean Milne
Robert Morton
D.W. Ovenden
Patrick Oxenham
Jim Russell
Ken Wood

A full list of the plates contributed by each artist appears on page 320.

Contents

Understanding birds

It is a bird's feathers that make it unique. There are other animals which fly, sing, make nests, lay eggs or migrate. But only birds have feathers. The nearest any other creature comes to having feathers is the reptile with its scales. Feathers probably evolved from scales, and birds and reptiles such as crocodiles and dinosaurs, for all their immense differences, shared a common ancestor.

Scientists are unable to tell exactly how the change from scales to feathers took place. Fossils of *Archaeopteryx*, the first known bird, show that 150 million years ago feathers were already the same as they are today. But *Archaeopteryx* was no ordinary bird. Although it had feathers, it still had the teeth and long, bony tail of a reptile. Its breastbone was poorly developed and lacked the deep keel to which the flight muscles of modern birds are anchored. This suggests that at best it could only flap its wings weakly. Probably it relied mostly on gliding.

Their mastery of the air is the main reason why birds have been one of nature's most spectacular successes, evolving into thousands of different species and colonising every corner of the globe. In every aspect of their physiology, they reveal how perfectly they are adapted for flight. Some bones which were separate in their flightless ancestors – including bones in the wings and sections of the backbone – are now fused together, giving greater strength. Others are hollow and strutted, combining strength with lightness. Massive breast muscles power their wings, while their hearts keep pace with their intense energy, beating with fantastic rapidity; in the case of a robin's heart, for instance, more than eight times as fast as a man's. Birds' eyesight is also the most acute in the animal world, adapted to gathering information at the same high speed at which they live.

Speed, infinite mobility and wildness: these are the characteristics common to all birdlife, which make birds so fascinating to watch. Birds rarely remain still, except when they are roosting or incubating their eggs, and they are always on the alert. But their actions are never without meaning; every movement a bird makes has an exact purpose. One of the greatest satisfactions in birdwatching is understanding why birds behave as they do – learning to tell the difference between threat and courtship displays, for instance, or observing how they look after their feathers or build their nests.

Bird classification

It is now established that there are some 9,000 different kinds of birds in the world. At one time the number was put as high as 25,000, partly because the same bird had different names in different parts of the world. This was before the modern system of classification had been developed, which groups birds according to their evolutionary relationship with one another, and gives each of them a set of scientific names.

The basic unit of the modern system is the species, an interbreeding group of individuals. The next, larger division is the genus, a group of closely related species of birds, usually showing obvious similarities. The black-headed gull, for instance, is one of many species belonging to the gull genus. A bird's scientific name always states the genus first, then the species. The black-headed gull is called *Larus ridibundus* – translated literally, the name means 'Gull, laughing'.

When one genus closely resembles another, they are grouped together to make a family. Gulls are similar in many ways to terns, and both belong to the family *Laridae*, named after the Greek word for a gull; in some schemes of classification they are separated into sub-families, *Larinae* (gulls) and *Sterninae* (terns). The families are grouped into 27 different orders. The family of gulls and terns belongs, together with a great variety of other sea and shore birds, in the order *Charadriiformes*, after the Greek for 'plover'. All the orders together make up the zoological class *Aves* – 'Birds'.

The birds of Britain

More than 550 different species of bird have been recorded in Britain, but many of them have been seen on only a very few occasions, after being swept from their proper homes or migration routes by freak winds or weather conditions. Naturalists call these very rare species 'accidentals'. The 'true' British birds – those which live here all year round – number closer to 130 species. However, many other species are regular visitors, either coming here every summer to breed after spending the winter in Africa or the Mediterranean countries; or flying in from their breeding grounds in the Arctic, northern Europe and even parts of Siberia, to take advantage of the relatively mild, snow-free British winter. Other species occur regularly as passage migrants in spring or autumn, using Britain as a stopping-off point on the long journey between their breeding and wintering grounds. Both in variety and numbers, more birds can be seen in Britain than almost anywhere else in Europe.

The birds described and illustrated in this book include all the resident British birds, together with the summer and winter visitors and passage migrants, and some of the most frequently seen 'accidentals'.

How to use this book

The birds described in this book are arranged in their family groups, starting with the more primitive families and ending with the most advanced species – the passerines, or perching birds. Familiarity with the family groups is the first step towards proficiency as a birdwatcher. In 'How birds are grouped' (pp. 18–23), all the major families are listed and described, and one or more birds from each group are illustrated. These are the first pages to turn to when you spot an unfamiliar bird. Check through the descriptions and illustrations, to establish in which group the bird belongs. Then turn to the relevant pages in the main part of the book to complete the identification.

For beginners to birdwatching, 'How to identify birds' (pp. 8–17) explains the basic techniques of bird identification. By looking at these pages you can quickly train your eye to spot the essential characteristics of different species. For further information about birdwatching, turn to 'Birdwatching as a hobby' (pp. 298–314).

Sometimes there are marked differences between the plumages of males and females of the same species, or between their winter and summer or adult and juvenile plumages. All the main plumage variations which occur during a bird's stay in Britain are illustrated on the page dealing with that species in the main part of the book.

How to read the maps

Distribution maps in the main part of the book show when and where you are most likely to see each species. The time of year when you see a bird, or the part of Britain where you see it, can be useful clues to its identity.

Red dots show the sites of breeding colonies

Red shows the usual breeding range of summer visitors

Green shows the areas where a resident species breeds and remains all year round

Blue shows the areas where a species is found in winter

Shading indicates where passage migrants occur

The winter range of birds and the range of passage migrants are less precise than the breeding range of resident birds or summer visitors for they depend on factors such as the severity of the weather. Of course any bird, particularly a passage migrant, may sometimes be seen outside its usual range.

How to identify birds

Knowing what to look for is the key to success in identifying birds. The size, shape and colouring of a bird are the first and most obvious clues to its identity. But how it stands or moves, how it swims or flies, how it sings, feeds or approaches its mate – these and other aspects of its behaviour may be just as distinctive as its plumage. The time of year, and the place where the bird is seen, are also identification points. Some birds only visit Britain at particular times of the year, coming from breeding or wintering grounds that may be thousands of miles away. Other birds are so well adapted to life in a particular habitat that they are only rarely encountered outside it.

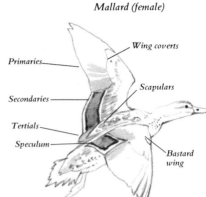

Mallard (female)

Primaries
Secondaries
Tertials
Speculum
Wing coverts
Scapulars
Bastard wing

Oystercatcher
Wing-bar
Rump
Terminal band

House sparrow (male)
Crown
Forehead
Ear coverts
Bill
Nape
Chin
Back
Throat
Breast

Rump
Upper tail coverts
Tail
Under tail coverts
Hind claw
Belly
Flanks
Tarsus
Toes

Supercilium
Eye-ring
Moustachial stripe

Reed bunting (female)

Naming the parts

Putting the right name to the parts of a bird is almost as important as naming the bird itself. For it provides a language in which to discuss birds with other birdwatchers, and it makes for quick and simple note-taking in the field.

What size is it?

When an unfamiliar bird is seen, the first point to note is its size. The easiest way to fix this is by comparing it with a bird that is known. Measured from its bill tip to the tip of its tail, for instance, a house sparrow is 5¾ in. (14·5 cm), while a blackbird is nearly twice as long, at 10 in. (25 cm). The familiar mallard is twice as long again, at 23 in. (58 cm), while its frequent companion on the waters of rivers and lakes, the mute swan, is the largest of all British birds, at 60 in. (152 cm) in length. The shape of a bird can also be very distinctive. For instance, it may be slim and delicate like a wagtail, or plump and stocky like a wood-pigeon.

House sparrow
5¾ in. (14·5 cm)
Heavily built,
with thick bill.

Blackbird
10 in. (25 cm)
Sturdy; adult
male's bill yellow.

Pied wagtail
7 in. (18 cm)
Long and slender.

Black-headed gull
15 in. (38 cm)
Long, pointed wings.

Wood-pigeon
16 in. (40 cm)
Heavy bodied;
broad wings.

Mallard
23 in. (58 cm)
Stout bodied;
long wings.

Mute swan
60 in. (152 cm)
Long neck, curved
when not in flight.

Dunnock
Shuffles or creeps slowly along the ground, with body held almost horizontal.

Starling
Usually seen in flocks feeding on the ground – walking, running, probing for grubs and incessantly squabbling.

House sparrow
Moves on the ground by short hops, feeding in noisy groups and frequently taking dust baths.

Dipper
Plunges or wades into the water in search of food, often becoming entirely submerged.

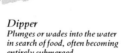

Nuthatch
Moves in quick jerks up, down or sideways on tree-trunks. Woodpeckers, by contrast, only climb upwards.

How does it behave?

Some birds run, some walk, some hop, some shuffle. Some perch high in trees, some stay close to the ground, some cling to tree-trunks or climb straight up them. There are birds which are only ever seen singly or in pairs, and others which invariably feed, roost or travel in large flocks. Observing a bird's behaviour and habits may give important clues to its identity.

Little grebe
Sometimes jumps with a splash before diving, or hides in the water by lowering its body until only its head still shows.

Sandwich tern

Gannet
Dives seawards with wings half closed, then closes them completely just before hitting the water.

Arctic skua
Skuas often feed piratically, chasing other seabirds such as terns or gulls until they drop or disgorge their food.

Arctic skua

Moorhen
Swims high in the water, and patters along the surface before taking off. In water, constantly flicks its tail, showing white tail-patch.

Mallard
Flies up almost vertically from the surface when alarmed; occasionally dives for food, but more often simply dabbles and up-ends.

11

Birds in flight

To identify a bird in the air, observe whether its flight is fast and direct, or slow and laboured; whether it zigzags or climbs and falls in an undulating pattern; whether it flaps, glides, soars or hovers. The angle at which it holds its wings, and the wings' shape and size, are also important. Other points to look for include whether the bird shows any distinctive wing or tail markings, and how it holds its head and legs.

Swift
Very fast flight with rapid beats of long, scimitar-shaped wings; frequently twists and turns in the air, and alternates between flapping and gliding.

Swallow
Swoops and wheels in the air with easy, flowing wing-beats, catching insects on the wing.

Kestrel
Hovers with tail fanned out and long, pointed wings holding it motionless against the wind; then dives on its prey.

Rook
Direct and regular flight, with occasional gliding, often in loose, straggling flocks; wings are broad with deeply slotted tips.

Heron
Flies slowly on down-curved wings, with head drawn well back and legs trailing behind.

Green woodpecker
Highly distinctive undulating flight; the bird alternately rises and falls in the air, as it flaps then closes its broad wings.

Collared dove
Climbs high in the air then falls in spring display flight; easily told from other doves by black and white pattern on tail.

Short-eared owl
Flight slow and silent on long, barred wings; sometimes glides, jinks and wheels as it searches the ground for prey.

Tufted duck
In flight both male and female show a highly distinctive broad white wing-bar.

Female

Male

13

Fieldmarks and other features

The shape of a bird's tail is often a useful recognition feature, and its tail, like its wings, head, neck and rump, may show distinctive patches of colour; these are what ornithologists call the bird's fieldmarks or field characters. Wing markings may take the form of stripes, bars or patches. The tail may be deeply forked, notched, wedge-shaped, rounded or square; and it may have white outer feathers, a white base, bars across it, or a terminal band. The length of a bird's legs and the shape of its bill may also help identification, and give information about how the bird feeds.

House martin

Swallow

Sand martin

Swallows and martins
In flight one of the swallow's most distinctive identification features is its deeply forked tail. The house martin can be told from the sand martin by its white rump.

Pied wagtail
The slim, delicate body and long, wagging tail are typical of all wagtails. The black and white plumage belongs uniquely to the pied wagtail.

Whinchat

Wheatear

Whinchat and wheatear
Its pure white rump and base of tail make the wheatear easy to identify. Equally distinctive are the white patches on the whinchat's wings and tail.

Male

Female

Redstart
The constantly quivering, vivid orange tail instantly identifies a redstart. The male's black mask contrasts with the female's paler face.

Ringed plovers
Little ringed plovers have less black on their foreheads than ringed plovers, and a white line running across the crown. The legs and bills of the two species are also different in colour.

Ringed plover

Little
ringed plover

Treecreeper
No other small British bird has a long, down-curved bill – an adaptation for picking insects from behind bark.

Sparrowhawk
Its strong, hooked bill is designed for tearing apart the flesh of its prey. Its talons are for seizing and gripping.

Reed warbler
These acrobats of the reed-beds are rarely seen out in the open. The long, thin bill is typical of insect-eaters.

Avocet
Its slender, upcurved bill is adapted for skimming insects from mud or shallow water. Its long, leaden-blue legs are suitable for wading at the water's edge.

Bullfinch
The stout bill and grey, pink, black and white plumage are unmistakable. The white rump identifies the bird in flight. The bill is adapted for cracking seeds.

Shelduck
The bill is adapted for sieving marine organisms from the water, or for shearing grass. The webbed feet are adapted for swimming.

15

The variety of plumages

In many species males are more brightly coloured than females; the females need camouflage when nesting, and males have to defend territory and attract a mate. Young birds may have several colourings before acquiring adult plumage. Adults of many species have colourful breeding plumage and more subdued winter plumage.

Blackcap
Only adult males have truly black caps – the female's cap is a distinctive red–brown, and there is also brown in many young males.

Male

Female

Black-headed gull
Plumage changes as birds grow older, and also between summer and winter.

Adult in winter.

Juvenile

First winter

First summer

Adult in summer.

Ptarmigan
Three distinct plumages range from white in winter to mostly grey in autumn and mottled brown in summer.

Winter

Autumn

Summer

16

Identifying birds by song

Some birds which look almost identical turn out, when they sing, to be quite different species. Even professional ornithologists find it hard to distinguish between a chiffchaff and a willow warbler, for instance, except by listening to their songs. Song is a bird's way of advertising its presence and identity, whether to attract a mate, to defend its territory, or for some other reason. For the birdwatcher it gives the opportunity to identify birds without even seeing them.

Lapwing
Males deliver their spring song in twisting, tumbling display flight, mostly between March and May.

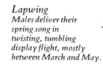

Skylark
Song, usually delivered high in the air, may last uninterrupted for five minutes or more.

White-fronted geese
Huge flocks of birds, often flying in formation, arrive in Britain in October and stay until April.

Time of sighting

Some birds visit Britain in the summer to breed, then fly south to Africa or the Mediterranean before the winter comes. At the same time as the summer visitors are leaving, millions of other birds are flying out of their nesting grounds in the far north, from the Arctic to Siberia, and coming south to Britain to take advantage of the relatively mild winter weather. There are other birds which pass through Britain on migration, on their way between their breeding and wintering grounds. So the time when a bird is seen may be a clue to its identity. The distribution maps in the main part of this book indicate by their colouring whether birds are resident in Britain, summer visitors, winter visitors or passage migrants (see How to read the maps, page 7).

Where birds live

The kind of countryside where a bird is seen may help to identify it, for different birds are adapted to feeding, nesting, roosting and so on in different ways, and are usually only seen in the habitat which suits them best. The birds which live in broad-leaved woodland, such as jays, great and lesser spotted woodpeckers, treecreepers and wood warblers, occur only very rarely in coniferous woods; mountain and moorland birds are unlikely to be seen beside estuaries or the sea. In the identification key to the birds described in this book – How birds are grouped, pages 18–23 – details are given about the habitats in which the birds occur most frequently.

17

How birds are grouped

Shape and size are the first clues to a bird's identity, whether you catch only a quick glimpse of the bird, or have time to study it in detail. Even if you cannot instantly put a name to the bird, its general appearance may at least suggest the family group to which it belongs. In this identification key, all the major families of British birds are described, and one or more species from each family are illustrated. The information given about each family includes the habitat where the birds are most likely to be seen, and the size range of the species in each family. To complete an identification, or for further information, refer to the main descriptions of birds on the pages indicated in the key.

Divers and grebes   Pages 26–33

Divers are large, streamlined swimming and diving birds, with stout necks, short tails and sharply pointed bills. Grebes are smaller, with longer, thinner necks. Both families are clumsy on land, but expert in the water. Flight is fast and direct.

Divers
Gaviidae
21–33 in. (53–84 cm).
Coastal and inland water.

Red-throated diver

Grebes
Podicipedidae
10–19 in. (25–48 cm).
Coastal and inland water.

Slavonian grebe

Petrels and shearwaters   Pages 34–37

Shearwaters are ocean-going birds with long, narrow wings and short tails. They often glide close to the water, and dive for small fish, squid and crustaceans. Petrels are also birds of the open ocean, occasionally seen inland after gales. They flutter over the water, searching for plankton and other small marine organisms.

Manx shearwater

Storm petrel

Shearwaters
Procellariidae
14–18½ in. (36–47 cm).
Offshore.

Petrels
Hydrobatidae
6–8 in. (15–20 cm).
Offshore.

Gannets and cormorants   Pages 38–41

Gannets are large seabirds, often seen diving from the air for fish. On migration, they sometimes fly in line, low over the water. Cormorants dive from the surface, chasing fish under water. Sometimes they fly in V-formations, and often sit on rocks with their wings half open, drying out their feathers.

Gannet

Cormorant

Gannets
Sulidae
36 in. (90 cm).
Offshore.

Cormorants
Phalacrocoracidae
To 36 in. (90 cm).
Coastal and inland water.

Herons and storks   Pages 42–45

Large wading birds with long necks and legs and sharp, pointed bills. Their wings are broad and rounded. Flight is slow, with legs trailing behind.

Bitterns, herons, egrets
Ardeidae
14–36 in. (36–90 cm).
Marshes, tidal flats.

Heron

Wildfowl   Pages 46–81

Swans are the largest of the wildfowl, graceful in the water and powerful in the air. Geese are also large, full-bodied birds, with long necks and short legs. In all species of ducks, males are more brightly coloured than females. All wildfowl fly fast and powerfully, frequently maintaining formation.

Mute swan

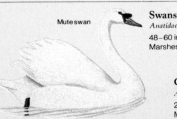

Swans
Anatidae
48–60 in. (120–152 cm).
Marshes, lakes, rivers.

Greylag goose

Geese
Anatidae
22–40 in. (55–100 cm).
Marshes, crops.

Mallard

Ducks
Anatidae
14–26 in. (36–66 cm).
Coastal and inland water such as ponds and lakes, marshes.

Birds of prey   Pages 82–99

All birds of prey have sharp, hooked bills and strong, curved talons, for holding and tearing meat. They are masters of flight: some soar, some hover, some stoop or dive on their prey, some fly their prey down. In most species females are larger than males.

Kestrel

Buzzard

Buzzards
Accipitridae
20–23 in. (50–58 cm).
Woods, marshes, fields.

Falcons
Falconidae
10½–19 in. (27–48 cm).
Woods, mountains, fields, urban areas.

Hen harrier

Harriers
Accipitridae
16–20 in. (40–50 cm).
Marshes, heaths, fields.

Golden eagle

Eagles
Accipitridae
30–35 in. (76–89 cm).
Mountains, moors.

Sparrowhawk

Hawks
Accipitridae
12–24 in. (30–60 cm).
Woods, heaths, hedgerows.

Kites
Accipitridae
22–24 in. (55–60 cm).
Wooded valleys.

Kite

Game birds   Pages 100–8

Heavy-bodied land birds, with stout, short bills, stubby, rounded wings, strong legs and feet adapted for scratching the ground for food. Game birds often run in preference to flying. Flight is usually fast and laboured, with very rapid wing-beats.

Pheasant

Pheasants
Phasianidae
21–84 in. (53–210 cm).
Fields, woods.

Partridge

Partridges and quail
Phasianidae
7–13½ in. (18–34 cm).
Farmland, heaths.

Grouse

Grouse
Tetraonidae
14–34 in. (36–86 cm).
Mountains, moors, woods.

Crakes and rails
Pages 109–13

Medium-sized or small long-legged birds, usually living in or near water. They are frequently secretive, preferring running or swimming to flying. Flight is laboured, with legs trailing behind.

Moorhen

Water rail

Moorhens and coots
Rallidae
13–15 in. (33–38 cm).
Swamps, freshwater lakes, rivers.

Crakes and rails *Rallidae*
9–11 in. (23–28 cm).
Swamps, fields.

Waders   Pages 114–55

Generally plump shore birds, with long legs and bills and pointed wings. In most species males and females are alike. Flight is strong and swift. Most waders are highly migratory, travelling together in huge flocks sometimes many thousands strong.

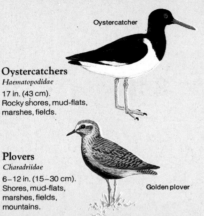

Oystercatcher

Oystercatchers
Haematopodidae
17 in. (43 cm).
Rocky shores, mud-flats, marshes, fields.

Plovers
Charadriidae
6–12 in. (15–30 cm).
Shores, mud-flats, marshes, fields, mountains.

Golden plover

Curlews
Scolopacidae
16–22 in. (40–55 cm).
Marshes, mud-flats, moors.

Curlew

Snipe

Snipe and woodcock
Scolopacidae
7½–14 in. (19–36 cm).
Marshes, woods.

Shanks
Scolopacidae
11–12 in. (28–30 cm).
Marshes, mud-flats.

Redshank

Black-tailed godwit

Godwits
Scolopacidae
15–16 in. (38–40 cm).
Estuaries, marshes, mud-flats.

Sandpipers
Scolopacidae
5–12 in. (12·5–30 cm).
Shores, mud-flats, marshes, streams, moors.

Dunlin

Phalaropes
Phalaropodidae
8 in. (20 cm).
Offshore, coasts, inland water.

Grey phalarope

Skuas   Pages 156–9

Seabirds closely related to gulls, terns and waders. They have white flashes on slender, dark wings, webbed feet, and long central tail feathers. Flight is powerful and rapid. They are often seen chasing other seabirds and robbing them of food.

Arctic skua

Skuas
Stercorariidae
18–23 in. (45–58 cm).
Offshore, coasts, moors.

Gulls   Pages 160–71

Very common seabirds, often found scavenging inland, with webbed feet, pointed wings and sturdy tails. Plumage is usually grey, white and black. Males and females are alike; young birds are flecked with brown.

Black-headed gull

Gulls
Laridae
11–31 in. (28–79 cm).
Coasts, inland water, open spaces.

Terns   Pages 172–9

Slim, delicate birds with narrow wings and forked tails. Bills more slender and pointed than those of gulls. Plumage is usually pale grey or black, and white; caps black in summer. They fly lightly over the water, sometimes hovering, before diving for fish.

Common tern

Terns
Laridae
9–16 in. (23–40 cm).
Coasts, open water.

Auks Pages 180–3

Stout, black and white seabirds, with short tails and short, pointed wings. On land their stance is upright; in the water they are expert swimmers and divers, chasing fish under water. Flight is rapid, with fast wing-beats.

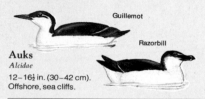

Guillemot

Razorbill

Auks
Alcidae
12–16½ in. (30–42 cm).
Offshore, sea cliffs.

Pigeons Pages 184–7

Stout, rather heavy birds, with small heads and broad, pointed wings, angled at wrist. They often feed in flocks on the ground. Flight is rapid and powerful, with occasional gliding.

Pigeons and doves
Columbidae
11–16 in. (28–40 cm).
Rocky ledges, woods, urban areas.

Wood-pigeon

Cuckoo Pages 188–9

Long-tailed bird with long, pointed wings. Two toes point forwards, two backwards. In flight it can easily be mistaken for bird of prey.

Cuckoo

Cuckoo
Cuculidae
13 in. (33 cm). Heaths, woodland edges, scrub.

Owls Pages 190–5

Mainly night-hunting birds of prey, with round heads, short, hooked beaks and large orange or yellow eyes. They fly silently, hunting for prey, and are most often seen at dusk.

Barn owl

Owls
Tytonidae, Strigidae
8½–24 in. (22–60 cm).
Buildings, marshes, woods.

Nightjar Page 196

Nocturnal insect-eater, with long wings and tail, short bill and large, flat head. Flight is silent, smooth, wheeling.

Nightjar

Nightjar
Caprimulgidae
10½ in. (27 cm).
Heaths, woods.

Swift Page 197

Bird with long, curved wings, which feeds on insects caught in the air. Swifts are often seen in large flocks, alternately flapping wings and gliding.

Swift

Swift
Apodidae
6½ in. (16·5 cm). Open spaces, urban areas.

Kingfisher Pages 198–9

Brightly coloured bird with large head, short tail and long, sharp bill used for catching fish. Dives from perch, or hovers over water before diving. Flight is fast and direct.

Kingfisher

Kingfisher
Alcedinidae
6½ in. (16·5 cm).
Streams, dykes, lakes.

Woodpeckers Pages 202–5

Colourful, broad-winged birds, with strong, sharp bills adapted for chipping and boring into tree trunks. Short, stiff tail is used for support when climbing trees. Flight is undulating.

Great spotted woodpecker

Woodpeckers
Picidae
5½–12½ in. (14·5–32 cm).
Woods, hedgerows.

Swallows Pages 206–9

Small birds with long, pointed wings, forked tails, short legs and small feet. They are fast and graceful in flight, and use their wide mouths to catch insects in the air. Plumage is dark above and pale below.

Swallow

Swallows and martins
Hirundinidae
4¾–7½ in. (12–19 cm).
Open spaces, sand pits, buildings.

Larks Pages 210–11

Streaky, brown birds of open country, which nest and feed on the ground. Songs are usually delivered in flight. They often gather in flocks when the breeding season is over.

Skylark

Larks
Alaudidae
6–7 in. (15–18 cm).
Coasts, marshes, heaths, fields.

Pipits and wagtails Pages 212–17

Delicate, slender, long-tailed birds, with fine pointed bills adapted for catching insects. They feed mostly on the ground, running or walking. Flight is undulating.

Pipits and wagtails
Motacillidae
5¾–7 in. (14·5–18 cm).
Open spaces, shorelines, rivers, mountains.

Pied wagtail

Shrikes Pages 218–19

Medium-sized perching birds, with hooked bills suitable for catching small birds, rodents and insects. Tails are long and rounded, wings broad. Flight is undulating. Occasionally they hover.

Great grey shrike

Shrikes
Laniidae
6¾–9½ in. (17–24 cm).
Heaths.

Starling Page 220

Very common, medium-sized perching bird, with speckled, dark plumage, long, yellow bill and short tail. Flight is rapid and direct. Flies, roosts and feeds in large flocks.

Starling

Starling
Sturnidae
8½ in. (22 cm).
Urban areas, woods, pastures.

Crows Pages 221–7

Largest of the perching birds, with broad wings and strong bills, legs and feet. Plumage is mostly black. They walk or hop on the ground, often feeding in flocks.

Jay

Carrion crow

Chough

Magpie

Crows
Corvidae
13–25 in. (33–64 cm).
Cliffs, woods, fields, marshes.

Waxwing Page 228

Short-tailed, fruit-eating bird, with highly distinctive crest on head. They are usually seen in flocks. Flight is fast and direct, similar to the flight of starlings.

Waxwing
Bombycillidae
7 in. (18 cm).
Hedgerows, woods, gardens.

Waxwing

Dipper Page 229

Plump, short-tailed bird, with white throat and breast. Usually perches on rocks in streams, walking and diving into the water to catch insects.

Dipper

Dipper
Cinclidae
7 in. (18 cm).
Mountain and moorland streams; may visit coast in winter.

Wren Page 230

Small, very active bird, with short, barred brown tail usually held tilted upwards. Flight is rapid and direct, on short, rounded wings.

Wren

Wren
Troglodytidae
3¾ in. (9·5 cm).
Rocky areas, moors, woods, gardens.

Dunnock Page 231

Streaked, grey and brown bird, with sharp, thin insect-eater's bill. It usually feeds on the ground and sings from an exposed perch.

Dunnock
Prunellidae
5¾ in. (14·5 cm). Gardens, woods.

Dunnock

Warblers Pages 232–47

All warblers are slim, active, insect-eating birds, mostly with rather dull, brown plumage. Many species are shy and secretive, more likely to be heard than seen. Their wide variety of songs helps to distinguish the different species.

Reed warbler

Chiffchaff

Whitethroat

Swamp warblers
Sylviidae
5–5½ in. (12·5–14 cm). Reed-beds, thickets.

Leaf warblers, goldcrests
Sylviidae
3½–5½ in. (9–14 cm). Gardens, woods, hedgerows.

Scrub warblers
Sylviidae
5–6 in. (12·5–15 cm). Heaths, woods, hedgerows.

Flycatchers Pages 248–9

Small birds with rather flat, pointed bills, adapted for catching insects in the air. They perch very upright watching for insects, then dart to catch them.

Flycatchers
Muscicapidae
5–5½ in. (12·5–14 cm). Woods.

Pied flycatcher

Thrushes Pages 250–63

A highly variegated group of birds, ranging from small, warbler-like birds such as the chats, to the plump, long-legged thrushes. They feed mainly on the ground, eating worms, insects and fruit.

Blackbird

Thrushes
Turdidae
5½–10½ in. (14–27 cm). Moors, mountains, woods, marshes, urban areas.

Whinchat

Chats and redstarts
Turdidae
5–5½ in. (12·5–14 cm). Heaths, woods.

Wheatears
Turdidae
5¾–6 in. (14·5–15 cm). Open spaces.

Wheatear

Tits Pages 264–71

Small, very lively and acrobatic birds, many of them brightly coloured. In winter, they often fly and feed in mixed flocks.

Tits, Reedling
Paridae, Timaliidae
4½–6½ in. (12–16·5 cm). Woods, hedgerows, gardens, reed-beds.

Blue tit

Nuthatch Page 272

A bird with a long, sharp bill for picking insects from the bark of trees. It can run down tree trunks as well as up them.

Nuthatch
Sittidae
5½ in. (14 cm). Woods and gardens.

Nuthatch

Treecreeper Page 273

Small, brown-backed bird with a fine, down-curved bill. It climbs spirally up tree trunks, probing the bark for insects, and is usually seen singly.

Treecreeper
Certhiidae
5 in. (12·5 cm). Woods.

Treecreeper

Sparrows Pages 274–5

Small, sturdy perching birds, with stout, strong bills for cracking seeds. They hop along the ground when feeding, and are highly gregarious.

Sparrows
Ploceidae
5½–5¾ in. (14–14·5 cm). Urban areas, fields.

House sparrow

Finches Pages 276–86

Mostly small seed-eating birds, with stout, heavy bills. Males are usually more brightly coloured than females. Often flock outside breeding season.

Finches
Fringillidae
4½–7 in. (12–18 cm). Woods, fields, gardens.

Chaffinch

Buntings Pages 287–95

Similar to finches, with strong, stout bills; but feed mainly on ground instead of in trees. Males are usually more brightly coloured than females.

Buntings
Emberizidae
6–7 in. (15–18 cm). Coasts, swamps, heaths, fields.

Yellowhammer

BIRDS OF BRITAIN

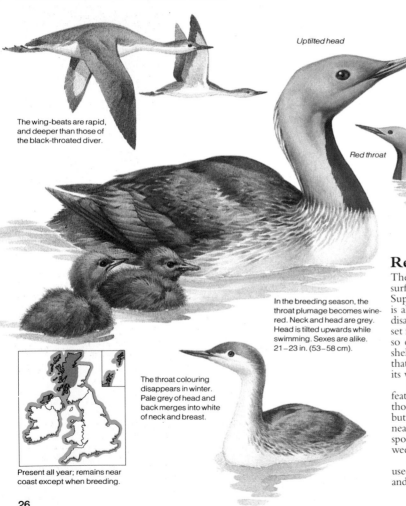

Uptilted head

The wing-beats are rapid, and deeper than those of the black-throated diver.

Red throat

A bird on the alert swims low in the water. Its throat-patch looks dark unless seen in a bright light.

Nests are heaps of moss or water plants, usually on smaller lochs than those used by the black-throated diver.

In the breeding season, the throat plumage becomes wine-red. Neck and head are grey. Head is tilted upwards while swimming. Sexes are alike. 21–23 in. (53–58 cm).

The throat colouring disappears in winter. Pale grey of head and back merges into white of neck and breast.

Present all year; remains near coast except when breeding.

Red-throated diver *Gavia stellata*

The red-throated diver is a good swimmer both on or below the surface, and one of only five species of diver in the world. Superbly streamlined, neck outstretched and legs tucked back, it is also graceful in flight. Alas, like all divers, it is somewhat at a disadvantage on land: its legs, so well adapted for swimming, are set far back on its body, giving the bird a most awkward gait. But so efficient is it under water that it can chase fish or scoop up shellfish as deep as 30 ft (9 m). And so fast is it on the surface that a courting bird may 'run' on the water, beating up spray with its wings.

Like other divers, the red-throated species loses its flight feathers in late summer, and is grounded until new ones grow – though it can still dive for food. It takes to the coast in winter but breeds on small Highland lochs, nesting in shallow water or near the shoreline, and usually laying two dark olive eggs, spotted or blotched blackish-brown. Chicks hatch in about four weeks, swim within 24 hours and fly at around six weeks.

A reedy cooing is the bird's most musical call. Country folk used to think the mewing wail of a courting bird heralded rain, and named it the 'rain goose'.

Black and white neck and back

Wing-beats are slightly slower and shallower than those of red-throated diver.

Downy young, uniform grey and similar to red-throated diver, sometimes ride on back of adult.

The nest is usually a heap of moss or water plants, in offshore shallows or on land at the water's edge.

Present all year; in winter mainly on coasts.

Adult in breeding plumage shows striking black and white patterns. Head is more rounded than red-throated diver's. Divers are ungainly on land, as legs are set back for underwater swimming. Sexes are alike. 23–27 in. (58–68 cm).

Winter plumage is darker than that of red-throated diver, with sharper demarcation between dark and light areas on head and neck.

Black-throated diver *Gavia arctica*

A big dark bird seen swimming out into a large freshwater loch in Scotland is likely to be a black-throated diver. This species has a definite preference for the bigger stretches of water which its slightly smaller cousin, the red-throated diver, shuns. One of the most haunting sounds of the north-western highlands of Scotland and the outer isles is the wailing cry of the black-throated diver, echoing against the mountains as it asserts ownership of its territory. Its call in flight is a sharp 'kwuk-kwuk-kwuk'.

The bird feeds on fish of all sizes from cod to sprats, and also on shellfish. The eggs normally number two, though one or three are occasionally laid. They are slightly glossy, olive-green or orange-brown in colour, with black speckles and blotches. They hatch after just under a month of incubation.

The chicks return to the nest for their first few nights, but subsequently sleep under the adults' wings, 'riding' on the backs of the swimming birds. The chicks start catching some of their own food within eight to ten weeks of hatching, by which time they are starting to fly. They do not become fully independent until they have left the breeding loch.

27

Wing-beats are slower and more powerful than those of smaller divers. In silhouette it is heavier and more goose-like, with drooping neck.

Brilliant white underparts show as the bird rolls in the water to preen itself.

Heavy bill

Neck-patches

Adult bird's large, bulky form and powerful dark bill are distinctive at all seasons. Neck-patches and spotted back show vividly in summer. Sexes are alike. 30–33 in. (76–84 cm).

Spotted back

Great northern divers are usually seen around coastal waters in winter, seldom venturing inland.

Oct.–May visitor to coasts; a few have bred.

In winter, steep forehead and bill carried horizontally distinguish great northern diver.

White-billed diver
Gavia adamsii

Largest of the divers, the white-billed diver is a rare vagrant from the Arctic. It is paler than the great northern and holds its bill up like the red-throated diver

Great northern diver *Gavia immer*

The wailing call of the great northern diver has no doubt sent shivers up the spines of many a film audience. Directors dub recordings of its plaintive moans and howls on to scenes of suspense or the supernatural to heighten the tension. In fact the bird's eerie calls, echoing across the lonely waters of its Arctic breeding grounds, are simply asserting territorial claims.

Almost all the great northern divers seen off British coasts are visitors, seen only in their dull winter plumage. A few spend summer north and west of Scotland, and it was long suspected that some might breed there. That theory was confirmed for the first time in 1970, when a pair with two chicks were seen swimming in a loch in Wester Ross. However, the bird's usual homelands are North America – where it is known as the common loon – and Iceland and Greenland.

This bird is larger than Britain's black-throated and red-throated divers, but its average size is slightly less than that of the white-billed diver, a much rarer visitor from the Arctic. Like all divers the great northern is most at home in or under water, where it feeds, and is ungainly on land. Its wings are small, so although a strong flyer, it cannot take off without great effort.

Little grebes take to the wing more than other grebes, often flying low over water.

Adult in breeding plumage has a red neck and a pale patch at inner end of bill. Female is duller than male. Young are very small, with striped head and back. 10–12 in. (25–30 cm).

Pale patch

Red neck

Winter plumage is much paler; dull brown above, buff and white below.

Present all year; on fresh water with vegetation.

In summer adults often puff themselves up, both at rest and in some display postures.

When alarmed, the little grebe submerges, with only its head showing.

The nest is a heap of water plants built up from the surface or supported by a fallen branch, in shallow water.

Little grebe *Tachybaptus ruficollis*

From Buckingham Palace lake to the humblest farm pond, the little grebe – often called the dabchick – is the most widespread of its family in Britain as well as the smallest. It is at home in any still or slow-flowing fresh water that has a lush growth of vegetation. On large lakes it spends much of its time in the more sheltered, shallow bays with a thick growth of underwater plants.

If observed during its busy search for small fish or water insects, the bird looks like a small ball of feathers, diving frequently and bobbing up again. Sometimes, to make a deeper dive, it jumps up first and enters the water with a splash. The little grebe is more often identified by its trilling call, something like the whinny of a horse and rising and falling in volume and pitch over the space of a few seconds. Pairs prefer to keep to themselves, but on their favourite stretches of water the population may be so dense that they virtually breed in colonies.

Two, or sometimes three, clutches of four to six eggs are laid during the long breeding season. They are white, but soon stained by water-weed. Chicks hatch in about a month and quickly leave the nest, often carried on the parents' backs.

29

In flight, bold white wing-patches are visible. Fast-beating wings seem almost unable to support the long, drooping neck and body.

Double crest

Ruff

Courting birds present vegetation and shake heads breast to breast.

Present all year; large lakes, also coasts in winter.

Adult bird in breeding plumage has double crest, ear-tufts, ruff and contrasting light and dark colouring. Boldly marked chicks are often carried by either parent. Sexes are alike. 19 in. (48 cm).

In winter plumage, white face and neck are conspicuous.

Juvenile has white head and neck, with black-brown streaks. Plumage is gradually moulted to winter plumage similar to that of adult.

The nest is often a floating platform of weeds, anchored among the reeds at the edge of a freshwater lake.

Great crested grebe *Podiceps cristatus*

Few British birds have a more elaborate and fascinating courtship display than the great crested grebe. Before the breeding season both sexes acquire conspicuous and beautiful dark head-plumes which are erected during the height of the courting display. This involves head-shaking, diving, fluffing out the plumage in the so-called 'cat' display, and presenting each other with water plants while rising from the water breast to breast. A century ago the fashion for ladies' grebe-feather hats meant that the birds were almost lost to Britain forever; but protection has since produced a large, healthy population.

The nest, like that of other grebes, is a simple heap of water plants built up from the bottom of shallows, or else supported by or tethered to a fallen branch or submerged stems. The shallow cup of the nest is surrounded by fine vegetable material which is used to cover the eggs when they are unattended.

The elongated, whitish eggs – usually four in number – take three and a half to four weeks to hatch into distinctively striped chicks. These squeak shrilly to the adults as they swim towards them to be fed on insects or fish. The chicks are dependent on the parents for at least ten weeks.

Yellow bill base

Reddish neck

Adult is smaller and stockier than great crested grebe, and generally darker. In summer, the pale cheeks contrast with black cap and reddish neck. Sexes are alike. 17 in. (43 cm).

In flight the bird appears more compact than the great crested grebe, and its forewing shows less white.

Great crested grebe

Red-necked grebe

In winter plumage, the red-necked grebe can be distinguished from the great crested species by its shorter, thicker and greyer neck.

The young bird has much the same pattern as an adult but is duller in colour. Soon it will develop head-tufts.

The bird's winter plumage, unlike that of great crested grebe, shows no white above eye.

Mainly Oct.– Apr. visitor to coasts and inland waters.

Red-necked grebe *Podiceps grisegena*

Summer travellers to the lakes of Denmark, Finland or western Germany may see the red-necked grebe in its handsome breeding plumage – a treat that is all too rare in Britain. On its annual migrations to these shores it is usually seen in drab winter garb, and from a distance is not easily distinguished from the native great crested grebe.

The red-necked species, however, favours smaller and shallower stretches of water, with more vegetation growing above the surface. Although it nests and breeds on fresh water, when it visits Britain it may make for estuaries or coastal lagoons. Insects and their larvae are its favourite food, taken from the water or from plants. Fish are also caught, either by shallow diving or by swimming with only the head submerged. Small fish are swallowed live; larger fish are killed before they are eaten, by crushing or a violent shaking.

Red-necked grebes are seldom seen in flight because they make their major journeys by night. Their take-off is slow and awkward, so when they are under attack they are more likely to dive. At home in the breeding season they are the most vocal of European grebes, but they are usually silent in Britain.

Golden tufts

Chestnut neck

White patch on front of wing, near shoulder, is distinctive. Less white on back of wing than black-necked grebe.

The nest is an anchored mat of floating weed, built in sheltered shallows but with easy access to open water.

Adult in breeding plumage has horn-like golden tufts; neck and flanks are chestnut. Chicks, paler and more striped than young of black-necked grebe, often ride on parent's back. Sexes are alike. 13 in. (33 cm).

Mainly winter visitor to coasts, but nowhere common.

In winter plumage, cheeks are whiter than those of black-necked grebe, and head shape is flatter.

Slavonian grebe *Podiceps auritus*

Progress has been slow and uncertain for this eye-catching bird since the first breeding pair were seen in Scotland in 1908. They presumably came from Scandinavia or Iceland, the nearest foreign breeding grounds. Even today there are fewer than 60 pairs, concentrated on shallow freshwater lochs in remoter parts of Scotland. They seem more vulnerable than other grebes to human disturbance and still suffer, because of their rarity, from the illegal activities of egg collectors.

After wintering on coastal waters, paired birds return to their breeding grounds and take part in an elaborate ritual of display ceremonies before they mate. Their nests of floating water-weed, sometimes only a few feet apart, are hidden among rocks or under drooping tree branches, and are anchored to plants growing from the lake bottom.

Egg numbers vary widely, but the usual clutch is four or five. The chicks hatch in three to three and a half weeks and quickly leave the nest. Although they can dive well after ten days, they rely on their parents for food almost until the time they can fly, at about two months. Slavonian grebes' main food is water insects, grubs and small fish.

The wings are narrow. The bird takes to the air less frequently than other species of grebe.

Ear-tuft

Black neck

Black neck and golden ear-tufts identify adult in breeding plumage. Head feathers are raised in a crest in displays. Sexes are alike. 12 in. (30 cm).

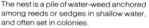

The nest is a pile of water-weed anchored among reeds or sedges in shallow water, and often set in colonies.

Black-necked grebe *Podiceps nigricollis*

Most grebes require extensive areas of open water for successful breeding, but the black-necked grebe is an exception. This attractive little bird, not much bigger than the little grebe, requires pools with a rich growth of water plants both fringing the water and submerged and floating in it; often such pools have very limited open water. Only a few such sites exist in Britain, and this is probably the main reason why the species is scarce in this country. A few central Scottish lochs provide the black-necked grebe's only reliable breeding areas, though elsewhere it may choose a spot for just one season before moving on and sometimes it may take to man-made stretches of water such as reservoirs and sewage farms.

Outside the breeding season the black-necked grebe makes for open waters, including estuaries or sea channels. It is a capable diver and eats small fish, but prefers insects, grubs and other food taken from the surface or from vegetation.

Springtime courtship involves a variety of paired displays, including a water dance similar to that of the great crested grebe, in which two birds rear up breast to breast or side by side. The nest contains three or four eggs, hatched in three weeks.

Present all year; now also nests locally in England.

Steep forehead and slightly upturned point of bill distinguish bird in winter plumage from Slavonian grebe.

Wings are held stiffly outstretched as the bird glides low over the sea.

White underparts catch the light as the birds bank. Their long, narrow wings are well adapted for sustained fast gliding.

Grey back

Birds with dark-coloured heads and underparts are found in Arctic waters.

White head

The fulmar's build is bulky, with a heavy bill and thick neck. Sexes are alike. 18½ in. (47 cm).

Courting pairs cackle and croon. Clumsy on land, they squat on their lower legs.

Present all year; at nest sites in most months.

The fulmar can be identified at close range by prominent tubular nostrils set on top of the bill.

The fulmar usually nests on cliff sides, its single egg being laid on the bare ledge. The chick flies at about seven weeks.

Fulmar *Fulmarus glacialis*

Intruders on the nesting territory of the fulmar meet with an unusually hostile reception. The fulmar brings up a stinking oil, produced from its stomach, and squirts it over the enemy in an accurately aimed jet. Even a young fulmar chick can defend itself in this way.

The fulmar population has increased astonishingly in the last two centuries. Fulmars were first noted in Iceland around 1750, and pairs had settled in the Faeroes by 1820 and in the Shetlands by 1878. By 1970 these few pioneers had increased to more than 300,000 pairs around the coasts of Britain and Ireland. This increase in population is the more remarkable in that the birds do not breed until they are six or more years old – and even then lay only one egg a year. A factor that may have helped them is the vast expansion of fishing, the fish offal thrown overboard providing large quantities of food for seabirds.

A single egg is laid in any convenient depression on a cliff ledge or offshore rock pillar. Incubation takes about 50 days, the parents sharing the task in shifts. During the seven weeks before the hatched chick can fly, they give it food regurgitated from their own stomachs.

Black crown

White chin, throat

A bird with sharply contrasting plumage: its upper parts are black, its underparts white or greyish-white. Sexes are alike. 14 in. (36 cm).

Birds assemble in huge flocks near their nesting colonies at dusk.

Flight alternates between gliding and rapid flapping, both with stiff wings.

Feb.–Oct. visitor, breeding on west coast islands.

A skilful and buoyant swimmer, the bird keeps its head and tail well up.

The chick has dense down; it does not leave its burrow until it flies, at about ten weeks old.

Birds nest in burrows in cliff tops of islands, and occasionally of the mainland. Burrows are close and often collapse.

Manx shearwater *Puffinus puffinus*

After an absence of 150 years, this remarkable bird has returned in strength to breed on the Isle of Man from which its name is derived. There are thriving colonies on other islands off Britain's western coast. Manx shearwaters come to land only to breed; when the breeding season is over many cross the Atlantic to spend the winter at sea off the coast of South America.

Manx shearwaters fly with powerful wing beats, interspersed with long glides in which they skim the surface of the water, appearing even to 'shear' the waves. The bird is one of nature's most brilliant navigators. One bird from the Welsh island of Skokholm was taken to Massachusetts, over 3,000 miles across the North Atlantic and outside its normal range. It was released there, and took only 12 days to return to its chick.

Icelandic sagas of the early 11th century refer to the eerie, unnerving din that these birds set up as the adults come back to their nests from feeding at sea, particularly in the hour before midnight. The Manx shearwater builds its nest in a burrow, and the parents take turns to incubate the single egg. About 60 days after hatching, the chicks are deserted, and a week or ten days later they make their way to the sea.

35

Seen from below in flight, white patches under wings are conspicuous. Tail is square and black.

Pale wing-bar

Storm petrel is sooty black, except for white rump and pale wing-bar. Sexes are alike. 6 in. (15 cm).

White rump

Leach's petrel

Wilson's petrel

The storm petrel is Europe's smallest sea-bird. It comes ashore only in the breeding season, to nest under rocks or walls.

Two rarer petrels

Leach's petrel (*Oceanodroma leucorrhoa*) is blackish-brown with a white rump and a forked tail. The inner wing shows a paler brown diagonal band on top. Under-wings are dark. Even rarer is Wilson's petrel (*Oceanites oceanicus*), which can be distinguished by its long legs and yellow-webbed feet that may extend beyond the tail; the tail is not forked.

Storm petrel *Hydrobates pelagicus*

When the storm or stormy petrel followed the wake of a vessel, it was believed to forecast the coming of a storm. In fact the bird probably follows ships in order to feed on the marine life brought to the surface in the disturbance of their passage. The name 'petrel' is said to be a diminutive of Peter: when feeding, the bird flits and hovers just above the water, often with feet pattering on the surface, appearing to 'walk on the water' as St Peter did in the Bible story. The storm petrel is also called Mother Carey's chicken, a name that may be a corruption of *Mater Cara*, 'Dear Mother', the name formerly given by sailors in the eastern Mediterranean to the Virgin Mary.

The storm petrel spends its entire life on the open sea except when breeding, when it comes ashore at night to remote and lonely islands off the western shores of the British Isles. Colonies may vary in size from a few pairs to many thousands. A single, dull white egg is laid. The chick is at first covered thickly in greyish-brown down, but grows a second plumage of darker down before the flight feathers develop.

The larger Leach's petrel does not customarily follow ships, but the very similar Wilson's petrel has this habit.

Cory's shearwater
Calonectris diomedea

Cory's shearwater is grey-brown above and lacks distinctive markings. The bill is large and pale yellow. Sexes are alike. 18 in. (45 cm).

Little shearwater
Puffinus assimilis

The little shearwater has white cheeks, its black crown extending no further than the eye. Sexes are alike. 15½ in. (39 cm).

Great shearwater
Puffinus gravis

The great shearwater's dark cap is emphasised by the contrasting pale collar. Sexes are alike. 18 in. (45 cm).

Sooty shearwater
Puffinus griseus

The sooty shearwater is dark and mostly sooty-grey. Its wings are narrow. Sexes are alike. 16 in. (40 cm).

West Mediterranean shearwater
Puffinus mauretanicus

This cousin of the Manx shearwater has dirty white lower parts and dark flanks. Sexes alike. 15 in. (38 cm).

Rare shearwaters

When they are not nesting, most shearwaters are only seen passing along the coast. The exception is the Manx shearwater, which breeds in Britain. Tipping from side to side, shearwaters glide gracefully over the surface of the ocean with a few leisurely wing-beats every now and then.

Cory's shearwater arrives from islands in the Mediterranean and off the coast of Africa; the great shearwater comes from the southern Atlantic, and the sooty shearwater from Antarctic or Pacific waters. The western Mediterranean shearwater breeds in the Balearics, and rare little shearwaters come all the way from islands off Australia and New Zealand and in the south Atlantic.

Skypointing

Gannets plunge vertically down on fish from as high as 100 ft (30 m).

Adult's wings are swept back as it performs its spectacular dive for fish, its main food.

In flight, the gannet shows long, narrow wings and a pointed, streamlined tail.

Adult in flight

Immature, third year, in flight.

Bowing display

Social behaviour among gannets includes a greeting ceremony between pairs, known as 'mutual fencing'; a bowing display which is vital to territorial defence; and a 'skypointing' display which indicates intention to take flight.

Mutual fencing

Immature gannets have all-dark plumage with white speckles. They become whiter gradually as they reach maturity.

Immature, second year

Immature, first year

Gannets nest in densely packed colonies which are usually sited on rocky islands and rock stacks. The young grow a woolly looking coat of down.

Immature, second year, in flight.

Adult gannet's plumage is white, except for a buff head and nape and black wingtips. Winter and summer plumages are similar. Legs are black; the large, pointed bill turns down at the tip. The bird has a wing-span of up to 6 ft (1·8 m). Sexes are alike. 36 in. (90 cm).

Present all year; most common in north and west.

Gannet *Sula bassana*

When crowds of gannets nest in an offshore colony, or gannetry, they are at their most aggressive. The nests are evenly spaced on sloping rocks or wide ledges, and the birds keep just out of pecking distance of each other. But if an adult lands in the wrong place, or a chick strays from its nest, the offender is mercilessly attacked and is sometimes pecked to death.

A gannetry may contain as many as 60,000 pairs of birds. The air above such a colony is usually full of birds. Some of them hang on motionless wings in the strong updraught at the side of a rock, while others fly in from fishing trips on 6 ft (1·8 m) wing-spans. Their calls are loud, bark-like 'urrahs' and 'aarrhs', and the collective sound of many thousands of gannets in a large colony is almost deafening.

The nests consist of large heaps of seaweed and other plants, and materials such as feathers. The clutch is nearly always a single egg; two-egg clutches are very rare. The egg is rather elongated with an irregular chalky coating, so thin in places that the pale blue shell can be seen through it. The parents take turns at incubation, for which they use their overlapping, webbed feet. The chick hatches after 43–45 days.

39

Non-breeding plumage lacks the white thigh-patch.

Nestling has thick black down and a bare face.

Upright, spreading-wing stance is a characteristic posture.

Present all year; inland breeding only recently established.

White cheeks

Thigh-patch

Adult in breeding plumage is identified by white cheeks and chin and white patch on thigh. Sexes are alike. 36 in. (90 cm).

Immature bird is brownish, but paler underparts distinguish it from an immature shag. Flight is goose-like, with head held up.

Bird swims low in water with head held high and tilted upwards.

Cormorants breed in close colonies, building their nests mainly of twigs and seaweed. Cliff ledges are favourite sites.

Cormorant *Phalacrocorax carbo*

Fishermen have tended to persecute the cormorant in the belief, perhaps unfair, that its combination of fishing skill and large appetite depleted stocks – especially in rivers, where it was said to favour trout, young salmon and eels. Researches show, however, that cormorants seem to favour flat fish and eels, taking only a small proportion of marketable fish. Enterprising Japanese and Chinese make use of the cormorant's expertise by training one species to dive and catch fish for them.

Cormorants are members of the pelican family, with all four toes on each foot webbed, which aids them in swimming and pursuing fish under water. Emerging from the waves, they are often seen standing on a rock or jetty with wings outstretched, apparently drying them; but why a bird that spends so much time in the sea should not have evolved efficient waterproofing like other marine birds remains a mystery.

Some cormorant colonies have hundreds, or even thousands, of birds. They build large nests on cliff tops and rocky islets, sometimes by rivers and lakes – even in trees. Three or four eggs are laid; the chicks hatch in about a month, and are fed once a day by each parent with regurgitated food.

Short crest

Yellow mouth

Immature birds are dark brown and lack the pale belly of the immature cormorant.

Adult males give throw-back displays during courtship.

Nestlings have thick brown down.

At the beginning of the breeding season adult shags are glossy, greenish-black, with a short crest. Their mouths are yellow, tapering to a slender bill. Sexes are alike. 30 in. (76 cm).

Present all year; coastal, found inland only rarely.

Like cormorants, shags often spread out their wings to dry; but shags usually perch on rocks rather than man-made objects.

When not breeding, adults have duller plumage, no crest and paler chin.

Because they feed in deeper water than cormorants, shags nest in places that are less accessible, including sea caves.

Shag *Phalacrocorax aristotelis*

Shags are notably vigorous defenders of their nests and young, refusing to leave the nest during attacks and thrusting their beaks forward menacingly at intruders. All but the most determined of their enemies are driven off.

The nest is of sticks and seaweed, grass-lined. The eggs laid vary from one to six and are pale blue with a chalky white coating – rather like those of their larger cousin, the cormorant. They hatch after a month, the chicks remaining on the nest seven or eight weeks more, fed by both parents. By then they can fly, but may still return to the nest for another three weeks or longer.

During the first part of this century the shag increased around British coasts and is still doing so in some areas. There seem to be five or six times as many shags as there are cormorants. Most recent figures put the British population at 38,500 pairs, against 7,000 pairs of cormorants – despite shags being more difficult to count because their nests are not so accessible. This boom in population has probably been aided by a decrease in man's persecution; but on occasions many shags die as a result of a poison produced by a tiny pinkish sea creature so numerous that it can colour the water in a 'red tide'.

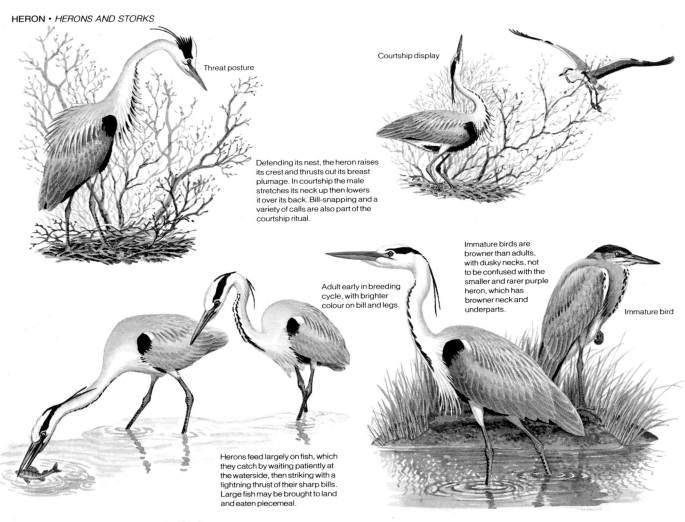

Threat posture

Courtship display

Defending its nest, the heron raises its crest and thrusts out its breast plumage. In courtship the male stretches its neck up then lowers it over its back. Bill-snapping and a variety of calls are also part of the courtship ritual.

Adult early in breeding cycle, with brighter colour on bill and legs.

Immature birds are browner than adults, with dusky necks, not to be confused with the smaller and rarer purple heron, which has browner neck and underparts.

Immature bird

Herons feed largely on fish, which they catch by waiting patiently at the waterside, then striking with a lightning thrust of their sharp bills. Large fish may be brought to land and eaten piecemeal.

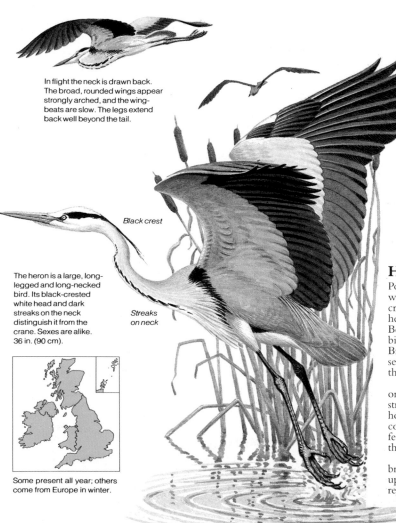

In flight the neck is drawn back. The broad, rounded wings appear strongly arched, and the wing-beats are slow. The legs extend back well beyond the tail.

Black crest

The heron is a large, long-legged and long-necked bird. Its black-crested white head and dark streaks on the neck distinguish it from the crane. Sexes are alike. 36 in. (90 cm).

Streaks on neck

Some present all year; others come from Europe in winter.

Herons breed in colonies, usually nesting on stick platforms high in trees, but in northern regions they often choose cliffs or reed-beds.

Heron *Ardea cinerea*

Poised, alert or motionless, in or beside shallow water, the watchful heron waits patiently for a fish or some other small creature to come within range of its dagger-sharp bill. Then the heron strikes, stabbing the prey and swallowing it whole. Besides fish, herons readily take small mammals and amphibians, reptiles, insects and even birds. The heron population of Britain fluctuates around 10,000 to 12,000 pairs, but falls after severe winters when frozen rivers and lakes deprive the birds of their main food.

Herons nest in colonies, or heronries, building in large trees or bushes, in reed-beds or on cliff edges. The nest is a large structure of sticks and twigs with a shallow, saucer-shaped hollow in the top. The same nest is used year after year, and consequently grows in size until it is several feet across. The female usually builds the nest and lays three, four or five eggs that are a pale greenish-blue in colour.

The chicks which emerge are clad in long, sparse down, bristly on the crown, giving a comical crest-like effect. Keeping up an incessant, begging 'agagagagag' call, they are fed by regurgitation by both parents.

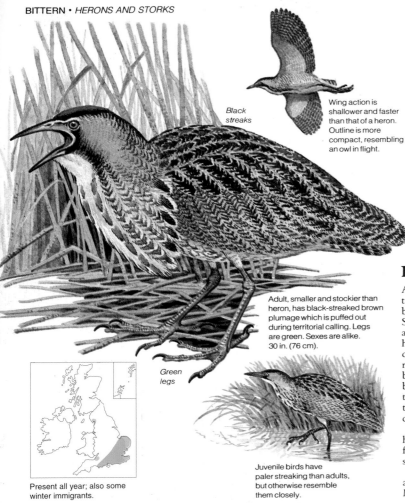

Black streaks

Wing action is shallower and faster than that of a heron. Outline is more compact, resembling an owl in flight.

Adult, smaller and stockier than heron, has black-streaked brown plumage which is puffed out during territorial calling. Legs are green. Sexes are alike. 30 in. (76 cm).

Green legs

Juvenile birds have paler streaking than adults, but otherwise resemble them closely.

Bitterns can climb tall reeds by grasping several at a time.

The bittern's nest is built among reeds or sedge. It consists of fragments of water-side vegetation lined with finer matter.

Bittern *Botaurus stellaris*

At the beginning of the 19th century, bitterns were regarded as a table delicacy and special shoots were organised in the fens and broadlands of eastern England – as well as in Wales, southern Scotland and Ireland. The bird was then quite common in those areas. By the middle of the century, however, the population had collapsed as a result of the shoots, the activity of egg-collectors and drainage of the marshes. The last breeding was recorded in Norfolk in 1868. Then, at the start of this century, bitterns from the Continent began to recolonise Britain, and breeding recommenced in 1911. Despite some severe winters, the bittern population steadily increased and reached a peak in the 1950s. Since then a decline has set in, because of further destruction of suitable habitats.

The bittern's call is a deep, resonant 'boom', which may be heard as far as 1 mile away. Its generic name *Botaurus* is derived from the Latin *boatum tauri*, 'the bellowing of a bull', and in the spring its call resembles the distant lowing of a cow.

In the breeding season, four to six olive-brown eggs are laid at two to three day intervals and are incubated by the hen. Meanwhile, the cock sometimes mates with another female.

Spoonbill
Platalea leucorodia

All-white plumage and a stout bill, flattened and yellow at the tip, identify this occasional visitor, usually seen on estuaries or coastal lagoons. 34 in. (86 cm).

Little egret
Egretta garzetta

Long head plumes, black legs and yellow feet distinguish this bird. It occurs mainly on south-coast estuaries where it has now begun to breed. 22 in. (55 cm).

Crane
Grus grus

This rare passage migrant from Scandinavia is sometimes seen on its way to southern Spain and North Africa. It is larger than the heron. A pair or two now nest in Norfolk. 45 in. (114 cm).

White stork
Ciconia ciconia

This rare stray from mainland Europe can be distinguished by its contrasting black and white plumage. In spite of its long legs it is mainly a bird of grassy marshland rather than a wader. 40 in. (100 cm).

Little bittern
Ixobrychus minutus

Adult male in breeding plumage. A bird of skulking habits, hiding among reeds and emerging only at dusk, except in the breeding season. It breeds in Europe, Asia and North Africa and is an irregular visitor to Britain in early summer and autumn, mostly in the south. 14 in. (36 cm).

Rare heron-like birds

Nearly all the rare herons and heron-like birds seen in the wild today are visitors or strays from continental Europe, although some used to nest in Britain before the once-extensive lowland marshes were drained. The secretive little bittern may still do so now, unobserved. More conspicuous is the little egret, which feeds in shallow, open waters and has recently begun to nest on the south coast of England.

The tall, ash-grey crane, striding across grassland and open marshes, is found mainly when winds divert it westwards, and dislikes being approached closely. White storks are conspicuous, less-shy birds that also favour open ground, usually by water; while the spoonbill is seen chiefly on the brackish, muddy waters in which it feeds with broad sweeps of its bill.

The whooper flies on slow, powerful wing-beats, without the mute swan's 'wing music'.

Whoopers frequently graze in fields, remaining in family groups all winter. Head and neck often have 'rusty' staining from feeding in shallow, iron-rich waters.

The yellow patch on the bill of the whooper swan is more angular than that on Bewick's swan.

The nest is a mound of reeds and sedges with a depression in the top, sited on a snow-free bank near water.

Adult

Adult whooper swan has a triangular head, and carries its neck straight. The juvenile is generally paler than the juvenile Bewick's swan. Sexes alike. 60 in. (152 cm).

Juvenile

Oct.–Apr. visitor; but occasionally nests in Scotland.

Whooper swan *Cygnus cygnus*

Both the whooper swan and Bewick's swan are noisier birds than the more familiar mute swan; but the whooper swan has a loud trumpeting call more assertive than that of Bewick's swan, which accounts for its name. In flight, on the other hand, the whooper swan and Bewick's swan are relatively quiet: their wing-beats make a swishing sound, rather than the loud twanging buzz of the mute swan.

Most whooper swans wintering in Britain are from Iceland, and they return there in spring to breed. The odd pair – which may sometimes involve an injured individual too weak to migrate – may stay behind to nest beside moorland tarns and desolate lochs in northern Britain.

In late May or early June a clutch of three to five eggs is laid, and incubated for four and a half to five weeks by the female. The cygnets, silver-grey and white at first, develop greyish-brown head plumage and white, grey-tipped feathers on the body. They fly after about eight weeks. In summer the whooper swan finds plentiful underwater plants, molluscs and insects on which to feed. As the cold closes in it will forage on stubble fields, unlike the fussier Bewick's swan.

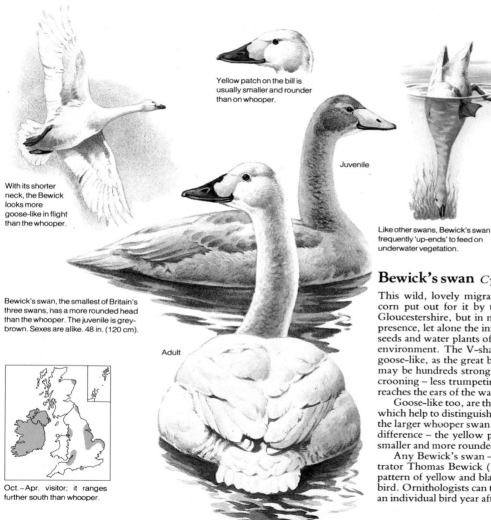

Yellow patch on the bill is usually smaller and rounder than on whooper.

Juvenile

With its shorter neck, the Bewick looks more goose-like in flight than the whooper.

Bewick's swan, the smallest of Britain's three swans, has a more rounded head than the whooper. The juvenile is grey-brown. Sexes are alike. 48 in. (120 cm).

Adult

Oct.–Apr. visitor; it ranges further south than whooper.

Like other swans, Bewick's swan frequently 'up-ends' to feed on underwater vegetation.

Each individual has a distinctive bill pattern, enabling birdwatchers to recognise it in successive years.

Bewick's swan *Cygnus bewickii*

This wild, lovely migrant from Arctic Siberia, may take the corn put out for it by the Wildfowl Trust at Slimbridge in Gloucestershire, but in no other way does it acknowledge the presence, let alone the influence, of man. Best of all it likes the seeds and water plants of the lakes and pools that are its natural environment. The V-shaped skeins against the winter sky are goose-like, as the great birds wing across Britain in flocks that may be hundreds strong. A distant high-pitched honking and crooning – less trumpeting than the call of the whooper swan – reaches the ears of the watcher.

Goose-like too, are this swan's short neck and rounded head, which help to distinguish Bewick's swan from its close relative, the larger whooper swan. Close observation reveals yet another difference – the yellow patch on the Bewick's bill is generally smaller and more rounded than that of the whooper.

Any Bewick's swan – named after the celebrated bird illustrator Thomas Bewick (1753–1828) – can be identified by the pattern of yellow and black on its bill, which is peculiar to each bird. Ornithologists can therefore build up a picture of the life of an individual bird year after year.

47

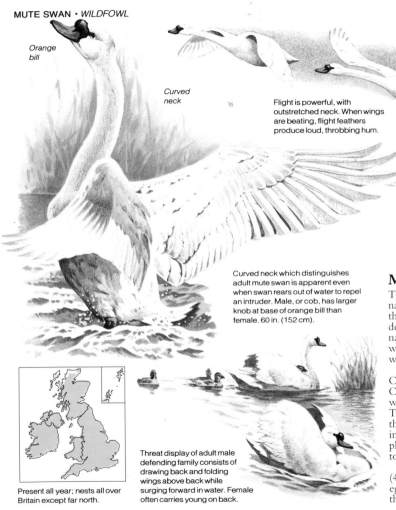

Orange bill

Curved neck

Flight is powerful, with outstretched neck. When wings are beating, flight feathers produce loud, throbbing hum.

Cygnets (chicks) are pale grey above and white below; about six to a brood.

Curved neck which distinguishes adult mute swan is apparent even when swan rears out of water to repel an intruder. Male, or cob, has larger knob at base of orange bill than female. 60 in. (152 cm).

Present all year; nests all over Britain except far north.

Threat display of adult male defending family consists of drawing back and folding wings above back while surging forward in water. Female often carries young on back.

Mute swans like still or sluggish waters with a supply of aquatic vegetation for food. Young birds are light brown.

Mute swan *Cygnus olor*

This graceful bird's placid, decorative appearance belies its nature; it is extremely quarrelsome, and bullies smaller species. In the breeding season the male stakes out a large area of water and defends this territory aggressively against all-comers. The bird's name, too, is deceptive, for although quieter than Britain's two wild swans, the whooper and Bewick's, it hisses and snorts when angry, and may trumpet feebly.

All mute swans on the River Thames belong either to the Crown or to one of two London livery companies: the Vintners' Company and the Dyers' Company. Until recently, many birds were rounded up in late July during a 'swan-upping' ceremony. Those owned by the livery companies were marked by having their bills notched; the rest belonged to the Crown. Today, instead of bill marking, the ceremony involves leg rings being placed on a token number of swans. The ceremony dates back to the Middle Ages when swans were valued as a table delicacy.

The nest is an enormous mound of water plants up to 13 ft (4 m) across and 30 in. (76 cm) high. Normally four to seven eggs are laid, and they are incubated for 34–38 days, mainly by the female, or pen. The young fly in four and a half months.

Immature white form

Snow geese of blue form are mainly grey and black, but head and most of neck are white. Immature white-form birds have ash-grey plumage.

Adult blue form

Black wingtips of white-form snow goose are conspicuous in flight.

Black wingtips

Adult snow goose of white form is entirely white, except for black wingtips and some pale grey on back. Sexes are alike. 25–30 in. (64–76 cm).

Snow geese are usually only seen singly in flocks of other wild geese – particularly the white-fronted species.

Red-breasted goose
Branta ruficollis

This very rare wanderer from Siberia, with distinctive black, chestnut and white markings, is at 22 in. (55 cm) the smallest goose ever seen in Britain.

The sturdy snow goose is a lone traveller and may sometimes be seen in Ireland or in Scotland in winter.

Snow Goose *Anser caerulescens*

Sometimes in a flock of geese one bird will stand out because of the contrast between its snow-white plumage and the greys and browns of its companions. It is likely to be that rare visitor to these islands, the snow goose. Its visits may occur more by accident than by design, perhaps as a result of cross-winds that blow the bird off-course while making its autumn migration from the Arctic down the east coast of North America.

There are two distinct races of snow goose, the greater and lesser, and the lesser divides into two forms – white and blue. Both birds are readily identifiable by their red bills which have black cutting edges on each side, giving the appearance of a supercilious grin.

The red-breasted goose (*Branta ruficollis*) is another rare vagrant in winter, a visitor from Siberia whose main wintering area is in Romania. Its markings are distinctive, and its call unusually high-pitched – a varied and musical two-syllable sound of 'kee-kwa' or 'kee-kwit'. Both the red-breasted goose and the snow goose are kept in waterfowl collections in this country, so that it is usually impossible to tell whether those seen are genuine visitors or birds that have escaped from captivity.

49

In flight, adult bird is distinguishable from pink-footed goose by long dark neck and head, and lack of pale forewing.

Juvenile bird has duller legs and feet, and its plumage is usually more mottled than that of adult bird.

When feeding, bean geese appear long-necked and bulky.

White on base of bill

The stout black and yellow bill identifies the bean goose. It often nests in forests in a hollowed-out heap of vegetation.

Dark plumage

Orange feet

Adult goose is a large, upstanding bird with mottled dark brown plumage, a long neck and head, and yellow-orange legs and feet. Long black and yellow bill sometimes has white feathers at base. Sexes are alike. 28–35 in. (70–89 cm).

Oct.–Apr. visitor; not widespread, uncommon.

Bean goose *Anser fabalis*

On marshy grassland in East Anglia or central Scotland in winter, a scattered flock of large geese, all grazing, may sometimes appear. At first sight they resemble greyish-brown farmyard geese, but a closer look will reveal the much browner plumage, longer necks and black and yellow bills of bean geese, scarce visitors from northern Scandinavia and Russia. A mere 300–500 birds winter regularly in Britain.

The type of bean goose occurring in northern Europe is unique among our geese in that it frequently nests in birch or conifer regions instead of on open ground. The four to six eggs in a clutch are an off-white colour when laid, but they quickly become stained as incubation proceeds. As with most waterfowl and waders, the female begins incubating only when all, or nearly all, her eggs have been laid, covering them with down whenever she leaves to feed. This means that after about four weeks, all hatch together.

The gander, which guards the nest throughout incubation, accompanies the brood when it leaves. The goslings feed themselves and can fly after about six or seven weeks, but remain with their parents until the following spring.

In flight, the adult bird is distinguishable from the bean goose by its shorter neck, rounder head and pale grey forewings.

Grey back

Adult bird is smaller than bean goose, and distinguished by its pink feet and pale grey back. Sexes are alike. 24–30 in. (60–76 cm).

Pink feet

Pink-footed geese often fly in large, noisy flocks. Their dark heads and pale bodies, and the musical calls, help to distinguish them in flight.

Juvenile bird is browner than adult, with yellow legs and feet.

Birds often 'whiffle' as they approach feeding grounds, dropping vertically or tumbling and twisting in mid-flight.

Sept.–Apr. visitor; Icelandic population winters here.

Families stay together throughout the winter in their north European feeding grounds, picking over the stubble after the harvest is in.

Pink-footed goose *Anser brachyrhynchus*

To the wildfowl enthusiast, the sound of an approaching flock of these large, wild and wary creatures is thrilling music. The cries of individual pink-footed geese vary widely in pitch between 'ang-ang' and 'wink-wink', creating a chorus that leads some experts to call them the most musical of grey geese.

There are two distinct populations of these birds. One breeds in Spitsbergen and winters in Denmark, Germany and the Low Countries. The other breeds in Iceland and Greenland and winters in Britain, roosting on estuaries and large lakes and feeding by day or moonlight on stubble and post-harvest root crops. On arrival in autumn, most are found in east Scotland but many then disperse into England, especially to Lancashire and, increasingly, to Norfolk. More than 200,000 spend the winter in Britain.

The goose breeds in June in spots where the snow has thawed, and where ground predators such as Arctic foxes are unlikely to reach. The nest is a low mound of vegetation lined with down. Three to five eggs are laid, and are incubated by the female for about a month. The goslings fly after about eight weeks. They stay with the adults until the following spring.

51

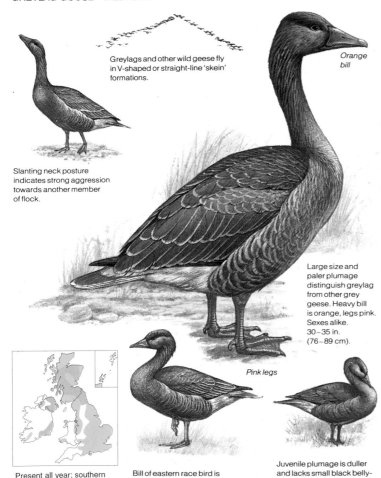

Greylags and other wild geese fly in V-shaped or straight-line 'skein' formations.

Slanting neck posture indicates strong aggression towards another member of flock.

Orange bill

Large size and paler plumage distinguish greylag from other grey geese. Heavy bill is orange, legs pink. Sexes alike. 30–35 in. (76–89 cm).

Pink legs

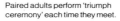

Present all year; southern birds naturalised.

Bill of eastern race bird is pink, not orange.

Juvenile plumage is duller and lacks small black belly-marks of adult bird.

Paired adults perform 'triumph ceremony' each time they meet.

Goslings take to water within hours of hatching. Nests are built of heather, grass or moss, on the ground near water.

Greylag goose *Anser anser*

Greylags mate for life – and give their partners no chance to forget it. Every time they meet after any loss of contact, goose and gander go through a complicated ritual of posturing and calling that re-enacts their original courtship.

The greylag was once the only goose that bred in Britain, and may have earned its name by lagging behind when other species migrated. It was the ancestor of the familiar white farmyard goose, and its cackles and 'aang-ang-ang' honk in flight are similar to the sounds of the domestic bird. The greylag was once found as far south as the Fens, but was driven back to the remoter parts of Scotland when agricultural development destroyed its breeding grounds. In recent times, however, the bird has been re-introduced to many of its old areas, and new ones as far south as Kent.

Hilly Scottish heather moors, with a scattering of lochs, provide the greylag's most natural breeding ground. Unusually for a goose, it also inhabits sea islets. The descendants of re-introduced birds take readily to man-made freshwater sites. Goslings hatch after a month and fly after about two months, but stay in the family party until the following spring.

In flight, the darker forewing of the white-front distinguishes it from the pink-footed goose.

Adult bird has white forehead and black-barred underparts. Sexes are alike. 26–30 in. (66–76 cm).

White forehead

Flocks feed at night if moon is bright. They graze on pastures, plant shoots and grain.

Black bars

White-fronted geese favour freshwater marshes and water-meadows during their winter stay in Britain.

Lesser white-fronted goose
Anser erythropus

This species, a rare visitor, is more slender, with a higher white face-patch and yellow eye-ring.

Oct.–Apr. visitor from Greenland and Siberia.

Bill of Greenland race is orange-yellow, not pink.

Immature bird's plumage shows fewer contrasts than adult's, and it lacks a white forehead. Orange legs and paler chest distinguish it from pink-footed goose.

White-fronted goose *Anser albifrons*

The white-fronted goose, or 'white front', is perhaps the most easily recognised of the grey geese, with its white forehead 'blaze' and its transverse black belly markings. White-fronts flock in from their Arctic breeding grounds in late September or early October. Those that come to western Scotland or Ireland are from Greenland, and have orange-yellow bills. Visitors to England breed in the far north of Russia; they have pinkish bills. Like greylags, mating white-fronts are paired for life, and reinforce their bond by repeating a similar courtship 'triumph ceremony' whenever they meet.

In flight, white-fronts may be distinguished by their call, which is higher pitched than that of other common geese. Even shriller in its call is the lesser white-fronted goose, which is classed as an 'accidental': flocks do not habitually migrate to Britain, but a few arrive among other species almost every year. It breeds in Arctic Scandinavia and Russia, and normally winters in the Balkans and south-west Asia.

The nest of both white-fronts is little more than a depression in the ground, lined with grass and down. Incubation takes up to four weeks, and the young fledge after five to six weeks.

Flocks of barnacle geese often fly in irregular, ragged packs with a chain stringing out behind – but never in regular formation. Stragglers are sometimes found in flocks of grey geese.

White face and light belly of adult contrast strikingly with other plumage in flight.

White face

Black neck

A white face contrasting with black crown, neck and breast make the adult barnacle goose unmistakable. Upper parts are grey with white-edged black bars. Sexes are alike. 23–27 in. (58–68 cm).

Mating displays include a characteristic wing-flicking action as paired birds rush about, calling loudly.

Pale brown and downy white goslings can fly after seven weeks, but remain with their parents throughout the winter.

Juvenile bird has duller head and neck plumage than adult.

Oct.–Apr. visitor, mainly to west Scotland, Ireland.

Barnacle goose *Branta leucopsis*

In the air or on the ground, family groups of barnacle geese bicker continually with a noise like yapping, yelping small dogs. Rarely silent for long, they produce the loudest clamour of all when taking flight. Coastal grass that is periodically flooded by high tides is their favourite food, but if none is available they graze on pastureland – leading to occasional complaints from farmers that they foul it with their droppings.

Family bonds are strong: although goslings can soon look after themselves, they stay with their parents until the next breeding season. For their annual migrations, family groups join together in larger travelling parties.

Wintering flocks come to the British Isles from two separate homelands, and they stay apart. Those that visit the Solway Firth area breed on the Arctic island of Spitsbergen. Birds seen in western Scotland and Ireland are from Greenland. Before the Arctic was explored and the nesting grounds found, people thought that the birds grew on trees. They also believed that the barnacles seen on floating timber were the embryos of the birds, and so came to apply the same name to both the bird and the crustacean.

Brent geese fly in long wavering lines, usually low above water or ground.

In flight, birds are identified by dark plumage and white stern.

Black head and neck

White neck-patch

Pale-bellied race has whitish underparts.

Dark-bellied race from Russia has slate-grey underparts.

Young goose has white edges to the wing coverts, and lacks white neck-patch.

Excellent swimmers, brent geese spend much of their time afloat, feeding on eel-grass and seaweed.

Oct.–Apr. visitors to estuaries and coastal fields.

A dark, black and grey goose with a noticeable white stern. It is only slightly larger than the mallard. Adult has a black head, neck and breast with a small white patch on the neck, and dark grey-brown back. The bill is short and the head narrow. Sexes are alike. 22–24 in. (55–60 cm).

Brent goose *Branta bernicla*

Small, dark brent geese, winter visitors to Britain from the Arctic tundra, all but died out in the 1930s. One reason for this decline was that disease struck their main winter food plant, the eel-grass that grows on tidal flats in estuaries around the North Sea. The number dropped by three-quarters, but under strict protection the species has recovered. Flocks, flying low in straggly but disciplined formation or roosting on the water, are no longer a rare sight off the east and south coasts. The eel-grass appears to be recovering too, but the brent goose now also raids winter cereals to supplement its diet.

Two races of brent geese winter in England. Dark-bellied geese from Arctic Russia visit the south-east and pale-bellied brents from Spitzbergen and Frans Josef Land arrive in north-east England and Denmark, while others of the same race, from Greenland and even Canada, pass the winter in Ireland.

When feeding at sea, brent geese bob like ducks, with their white sterns in the air. In the tundra, the geese begin nesting before the ice and snow have melted. They lay three to five eggs which hatch in three and a half weeks, and within three months the young birds must be ready to fly south.

Birds fly with slow wing-beats and may form lines or wedges. Ducks utter an 'ak-ak-ak' call, drakes a soft whistle.

Red bill

Dark green head

Rusty breast-band

Adult male in breeding plumage. It has a bright red bill, very dark green head, and white body with rust-coloured breast-band. 24 in. (60 cm).

The head-up 'salute' is used between birds that have paired to show they intend to take flight.

The female is distinguished by the lack of a bill knob. Ducklings are white with broad, deep brown stripes.

Present all year; coastal, but increasing inland.

Juveniles have much white about the head and underparts. They are generally duller in colour than adults, with brownish-grey upper parts.

Adult female in duller eclipse plumage. It patters on the mud with its feet to bring prey to the surface.

Broods of young shelducks may join up to form a crèche under the care of a few adults until they are independent.

Shelduck *Tadorna tadorna*

These colourful waterfowl leave Britain each summer, usually in July, for the annual 'moult migration' that follows the breeding season. Thousands gather in the tidal estuaries of the Heligoland Bight off the north German coast, where they become flightless for three to four weeks while their entire plumage is renewed. They return in autumn.

After three to six months, the new, duller eclipse plumage gives way to the handsome breeding plumage. The nest is made by the female and sparsely lined with grass and insulated with down and feathers from the bird's own breast. It is often placed 8–10 ft (2·5–3 m) down a rabbit burrow in sand-dunes, or in a similar hole. The duck lays a single clutch of 8–15 creamy-white eggs, usually in early May, and she does all the sitting while the drake remains near by. The ducklings, which hatch in just under a month, are led to the nearest water by one or both parents. They can dive expertly if threatened, and are independent after about two months. Broods tend to join up in large crèches.

A favourite food of the shelduck is the small marine snail called *hydrobia*. They also eat small shellfish, insects, fish, worms and some vegetable matter.

Flightless like most wildfowl during the post-breeding moult, birds move first to safe waters.

Long neck and deep wing-beats are distinctive in flight.

Present all year; introduced species.

Black head, neck

White chin-patch

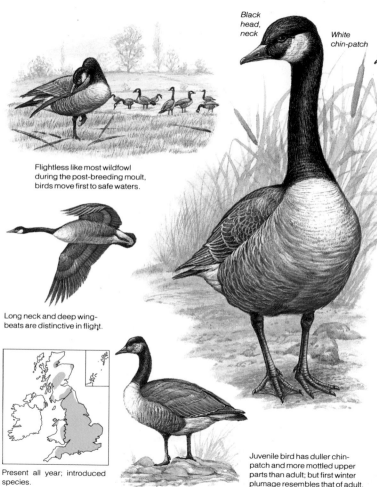

Aggressive displays include a threat posture with head lowered nearly to ground level.

Head and neck have unmistakable pattern. Sexes are alike. 36–40 in. (90–100 cm).

The nest is a ground hollow lined with leaves, grass and down. The gander often stands guard beside his mate.

Juvenile bird has duller chin-patch and more mottled upper parts than adult; but first winter plumage resembles that of adult.

Canada goose *Branta canadensis*

Extreme tameness has saved the Canada goose from becoming a popular target for wildfowlers and probably helped to give it the chance to establish itself as a wild breeding bird in Britain. The first Canada geese were brought across the Atlantic in the 17th century as decorative birds for parkland lakes. Attempts were later made to develop their numbers for shooting, but the bird is too tame, too irregular in its flighting times and flies too low to make it a 'sporting target'. It has now spread out of its parkland homes and recent countrywide counts revealed a population of more than 60,000 birds.

Although a large bird, the Canada goose can be unobtrusive when resting or feeding. Suddenly, however, a party may start calling with a trumpet-like honking. The noise builds up and the geese take wing, continuing their calls as they make for a neighbouring stretch of water.

The nest of the Canada goose consists of plant material at the water's edge or on an island. The female lays five or six creamy-white eggs in April or May. From these are hatched greenish-yellow or brown goslings. They can fly after nine weeks but remain as a family until the following spring.

57

Male

Male

Egyptian goose
Alopochen aegyptiacus

This large bird has buff-brown body and pink legs. In flight, its large, white wing-patches with narrow, black bar are prominent; the under-wing also shows a white patch. A grey-backed form also occurs; immatures lack the neck ring. Sexes are alike. 27 in. (68 cm).

Ruddy shelduck
Tadorna ferruginea

The bird's orange-brown body and pale head are distinctive both on the ground and in flight. The black-tipped wings show a similar pattern to those of the Egyptian goose, but lack the narrow, black bar. Females lack the black neck band. 25 in. (64 cm).

Introduced wildfowl

Many species of wildfowl have been introduced to Britain, and those that manage to flourish usually occupy a niche in the wild that is not fully exploited by native birds, so avoiding competition. The Egyptian goose is a goose-like grazing shelduck of moist grassy places, nesting in cavities and trees. The ruddy shelduck is also a grazing duck but is more ground-loving; it comes from the drier, warmer regions of Europe and Asia.

The mandarin duck, an introduction from China, prefers streams and overgrown lakesides in broad-leaved woodland, and nests in tree cavities. The wood duck, or Carolina duck, has similar preferences, but the ruddy duck, another native of North America, is a diving duck that prefers more open waters.

Female

Male

Male

Female

Male

Female

Ruddy duck
Oxyura jamaicensis

The male has dark cap, white face
and blue bill. Female is much
darker. Birds often swim with
their tails stiff and cocked. In
flight, the head pattern, brown
wings and pointed tail are prominent. 16 in. (40 cm).

Wood duck
Aix sponsa

Male in summer has green
head with violet-black
cheeks and two narrow
white stripes. Females and
eclipse males resemble
female mandarin ducks.
17 in. (43 cm).

Female

Male

Female

Male

Male

Female

Male

Mandarin duck
Aix galericulata

The male bird has variegated
breeding plumage, with very
distinctive chestnut-orange
wing-fans. When moulted, it resembles the female. In flight,
green wing-patches are conspicuous. 17 in. (43 cm).

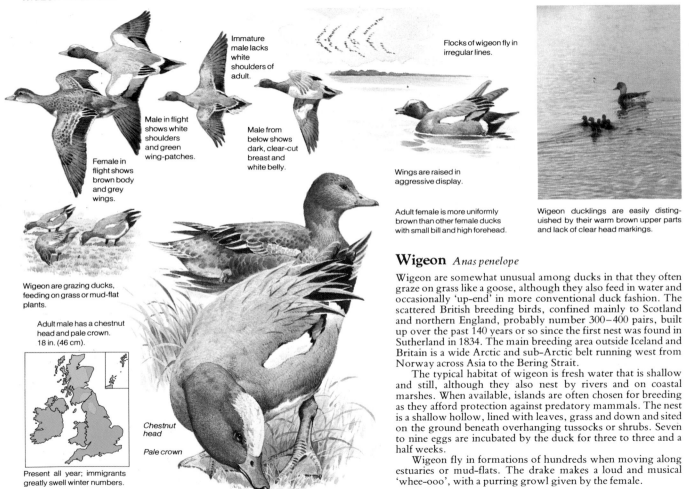

Immature male lacks white shoulders of adult.

Male in flight shows white shoulders and green wing-patches.

Female in flight shows brown body and grey wings.

Male from below shows dark, clear-cut breast and white belly.

Flocks of wigeon fly in irregular lines.

Wings are raised in aggressive display.

Adult female is more uniformly brown than other female ducks with small bill and high forehead.

Wigeon ducklings are easily distinguished by their warm brown upper parts and lack of clear head markings.

Wigeon are grazing ducks, feeding on grass or mud-flat plants.

Adult male has a chestnut head and pale crown. 18 in. (46 cm).

Chestnut head

Pale crown

Present all year; immigrants greatly swell winter numbers.

Wigeon *Anas penelope*

Wigeon are somewhat unusual among ducks in that they often graze on grass like a goose, although they also feed in water and occasionally 'up-end' in more conventional duck fashion. The scattered British breeding birds, confined mainly to Scotland and northern England, probably number 300–400 pairs, built up over the past 140 years or so since the first nest was found in Sutherland in 1834. The main breeding area outside Iceland and Britain is a wide Arctic and sub-Arctic belt running west from Norway across Asia to the Bering Strait.

The typical habitat of wigeon is fresh water that is shallow and still, although they also nest by rivers and on coastal marshes. When available, islands are often chosen for breeding as they afford protection against predatory mammals. The nest is a shallow hollow, lined with leaves, grass and down and sited on the ground beneath overhanging tussocks or shrubs. Seven to nine eggs are incubated by the duck for three to three and a half weeks.

Wigeon fly in formations of hundreds when moving along estuaries or mud-flats. The drake makes a loud and musical 'whee-ooo', with a purring growl given by the female.

Gadwalls 'up-end' often, like all dabbling ducks.

Female

Male

Sharp-pointed wings and wing-patches are conspicuous in flight.

Swimming posture is high, with wing and tail raised.

Male

Male courtship display emphasises wing and tail colour contrasts.

The duckling is like a young mallard, but with more contrast in colouring, bigger back-patches and pinkish bill-sides.

Wing-patches distinguish female gadwall from female mallard.

Black coverts

Present all year, but rather thinly distributed.

Adult male's most prominent features are black tail coverts and red-brown, black and white wing-patches. 20 in. (50 cm).

Gadwall *Anas strepera*

Language experts offer no clue as to how the gadwall got its name which, centuries ago, was written as 'gadwell' or 'gaddel'. But before 1850, when a visiting pair was trapped and wing-clipped, this duck was known only as a winter immigrant. Today a few breed in Scotland but, after a huge recent increase, most of the 1,000 or so pairs that breed in Britain are found in East Anglia and south-east England.

The drake of this species, whose true homelands are central and western Asia and western North America, is rather drab. The bird's voice is unremarkable too: various grunts and whistles from the male and a mallard-like quack from the female.

Eggs are laid from early May in a ground hollow, lined with grass or leaves, insulated with down pulled from the duck's breast and well hidden in thick vegetation. They are covered if unattended during the month-long incubation period, and the hatched ducklings are shepherded out of the nest as soon as their down dries. Easy prey for predators, they stand a better chance by keeping on the move. Gadwalls are vegetarians for all but the first weeks of life, when the ducklings feed themselves on protein-rich insects, snails and worms.

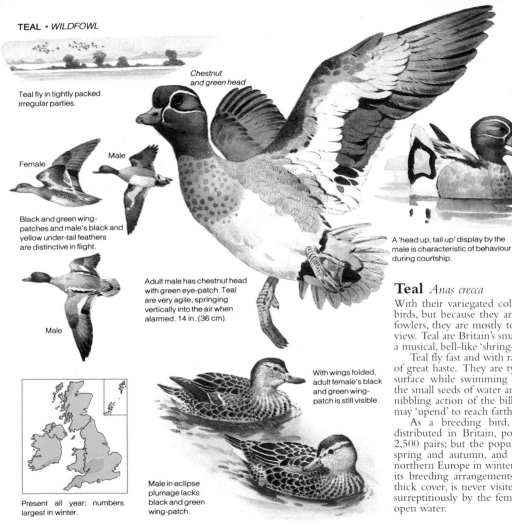

Teal fly in tightly packed irregular parties.

Chestnut and green head

Female

Male

Black and green wing-patches and male's black and yellow under-tail feathers are distinctive in flight.

Male

Adult male has chestnut head with green eye-patch. Teal are very agile, springing vertically into the air when alarmed. 14 in. (36 cm).

With wings folded, adult female's black and green wing-patch is still visible.

Male in eclipse plumage lacks black and green wing-patch.

Present all year; numbers largest in winter.

A 'head up, tail up' display by the male is characteristic of behaviour during courtship.

The small ponds that teal like to frequent are often the first to freeze over in hard weather.

Teal *Anas crecca*

With their variegated colouring, teal drakes are attractive little birds, but because they are a favourite winter quarry for wild-fowlers, they are mostly too wary to allow birdwatchers a close view. Teal are Britain's smallest ducks, and the call of the drake – a musical, bell-like 'shring-shring' – is distinctive.

Teal fly fast and with rapid wing-beats, giving the impression of great haste. They are typical 'dabbling' ducks, feeding on the surface while swimming or walking in the shallows, straining the small seeds of water and marsh plants from the water with a nibbling action of the bill. Occasionally, in deeper water, they may 'upend' to reach farther below the surface.

As a breeding bird, the teal is widespread but thinly distributed in Britain, possibly numbering as few as 1,500 – 2,500 pairs; but the population is increased by passage birds in spring and autumn, and by a large migrant population from northern Europe in winter. The teal is extremely secretive about its breeding arrangements. The nest, which is well hidden in thick cover, is never visited by the conspicuous male, and only surreptitiously by the female. Teal ducklings rarely venture into open water.

Blue forewing of male can be seen in flight. Females have grey-brown wings with duller patches of colour.

Male

Female

Adult male has distinctive pale eye-stripe on a mottled brown head. The head-back courtship display of the male is unique among dabbling ducks. 15 in. (38 cm).

Pale eye-stripe

Reed-fringed pools on fresh-water marshes are favoured by garganey.

Agile like the teal, the garganey shows its blue forewings as it rises from the water.

Ducklings are distinguished by the line from the lower bill that runs back to the eye-stripe in front of the eye.

Garganey, like shovelers but with shorter bills, often swim with bills immersed to pick up food.

Mar.–Oct. visitor; sometimes nests in other counties.

Female has less prominent eye-stripe and greyer plumage than male. Male in eclipse plumage resembles female.

Garganey *Anas querquedula*

A birdwatcher's first glimpse of a garganey may well be a pair of small ducks springing in alarm from a pool in a freshwater marsh, the drake showing a pale blue-grey forewing, white belly and a broad, pale eye-stripe on a mottled brown head. The drake's call, a grating sound like the rapid clicking of a tiny ratchet or a fisherman's reel, will confirm the identification. But both the sight and the sound are rare: numbers probably never exceed 150 pairs for the whole of Britain, and may fluctuate from year to year.

The bird feeds by swimming with its bill or whole head submerged, by 'upending', or sometimes by picking individual items of food from the surface. The garganey's food consists of insects and their larvae, water beetles, caddis flies, midges, water snails, worms and the spawn of fish and frogs; it also eats roots, buds, leaves and fruits of pondweed and water lilies.

The eight or nine brownish-white eggs hatch after three weeks, and the ducklings can fly at five or six weeks old. The drake becomes flightless for three or four weeks during its post-breeding moult, when it adopts 'eclipse' plumage. The female does not moult until the young are almost independent.

Male mallards are often seen in pursuit of a female in flight.

In communal courtship displays, males pull their necks well back and often flick water with their bills.

When moulting, July–Sept., the flightless male resembles female, except for yellow bill.

The adult female has a greenish-yellow bill and violet-blue wing-patch.

The search for food continues throughout the winter. These males have found a hole in the ice on their home water.

Pairs often nest high in a waterside tree. Newly hatched ducklings have to drop to the ground.

Green head

Maroon breast

Present all year; many from west Europe winter in Britain.

Adult male has glossy green head, white collar, maroon breast and curly black tail-feathers. The mallard is the biggest of the surface-feeding ducks in the British Isles. 23 in. (58 cm).

Mallard *Anas platyrhynchos*

In both town and country, the mallard is the most familiar duck in the British Isles. It is as much at home on a park lake or city canal as it is on a quiet country backwater or remote reservoir. Mallards living near towns have learned to live side by side with man, often relying on him to supplement their diet with bread and other scraps of food. Country-dwelling birds, however, have learned to fear humans, because of the activities of wildfowlers.

The mallard is typical of the 'dabbling' ducks in that it feeds on the surface of the water and can spring straight up into the air with a powerful whirring of wings. Its broad, flattened bill is adapted for filtering from the water a wide range of tiny plant and animal matter. The webbed, paddle-like feet are placed well back on the mallard's body so that it walks with a rolling waddle from side to side.

The female mallard makes the quacking sound that people associate with ducks. The drake, however, also gives an occasional subdued, hoarse-sounding 'raarb' call, especially when suspicious or alarmed. Nests are made from leaves and grass, and lined with down. They are generally well-concealed.

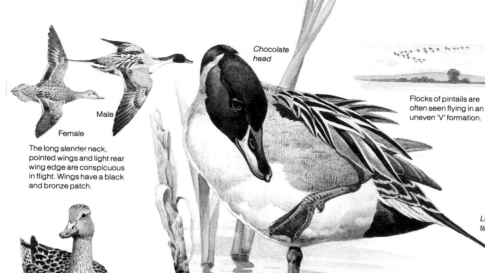

Chocolate head

Male

Female

The long slender neck, pointed wings and light rear wing edge are conspicuous in flight. Wings have a black and bronze patch.

Flocks of pintails are often seen flying in an uneven 'V' formation.

Long tail

Pintails form dense flocks over large expanses of inland water, though more usually they gather in smaller groups.

Adult female is pale brown and, like the male, slim and rakish in build.

Present all year; rare as breeding bird.

Adult male has chocolate and white head pattern and a long pointed tail. The tail feathers can add an extra 8 in. (20 cm) to the bird's body length of 22 in. (55 cm).

In moult, drake resembles female, but upper parts more uniform in colour.

Communal courtship displays by males include a head-stretching posture, with a burping call.

Pintail *Anas acuta*

Both on the ground and in the air, this is the most elegant of the British ducks. Its long slender neck, wings and tail, combined with its subtle colouring, make it easy to recognise and attractive to watch. A flock passing high overhead makes a beautiful picture. The watcher can also hear the drakes' faint wheezing 'geeeee' calls and the ducks' rattling sounds.

Most pintails spend only the winter in Britain. None was known to breed in the British Isles before 1869, and even now the breeding population probably rarely reaches 50 pairs. They rarely nest on the same site for more than a couple of years, so it is difficult to make an accurate count, even though the nest is often less camouflaged than that of other ducks.

Breeding begins in mid-April in southern Britain, but not until two months later in the north. Usually there are seven or eight eggs, varying in colour from creamy-yellow to pale green or blue. As is usual in waterfowl, the duck incubates the eggs, camouflaged by her dull colouring, and defends the nest and the ducklings with distraction displays. The ducklings – brown with white stripes and greyish-white underparts – take to the water as soon as they are hatched; they fly after seven weeks.

65

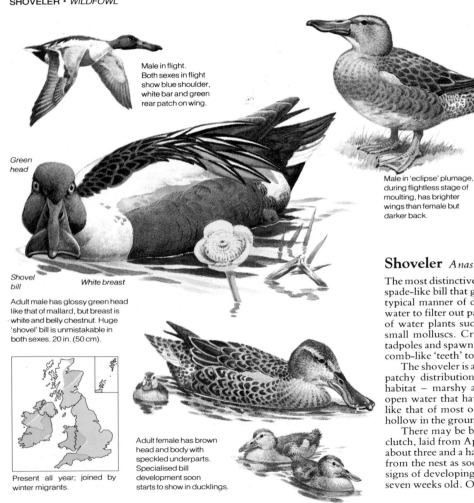

Male in flight. Both sexes in flight show blue shoulder, white bar and green rear patch on wing.

Green head

Shovel bill

White breast

Adult male has glossy green head like that of mallard, but breast is white and belly chestnut. Huge 'shovel' bill is unmistakable in both sexes. 20 in. (50 cm).

Male in 'eclipse' plumage, during flightless stage of moulting, has brighter wings than female but darker back.

The nest is a feather or grass-lined hollow in the ground, often in relatively open country but usually close to water.

Present all year; joined by winter migrants.

Adult female has brown head and body with speckled underparts. Specialised bill development soon starts to show in ducklings.

Shoveler *Anas clypeata*

The most distinctive feature of the shoveler is the long, rounded, spade-like bill that gives the bird its name. The bill is used in the typical manner of dabbling ducks for sifting large volumes of water to filter out particles of food. This includes buds and seeds of water plants such as reeds and sedges, as well as algae and small molluscs. Crustaceans and insects are eaten, and so are tadpoles and spawn. The inside edges of the bill have numerous comb-like 'teeth' to trap food as water is forced through them.

The shoveler is a handsome but uncommon bird, with a very patchy distribution governed partly by the availability of its habitat – marshy areas with pools, ditches and other areas of open water that have muddy shallows rich in food. The nest, like that of most of the shoveler's close relatives, is a shallow hollow in the ground lined with grass, feathers and down.

There may be between seven and 14 pale greenish eggs in a clutch, laid from April onwards. The female incubates them for about three and a half weeks. The ducklings, which are led away from the nest as soon as all have hatched and dried, soon show signs of developing outsize bills, and can fly when about six to seven weeks old. Only one brood is reared each year.

In courtship, the male bird may jerk head onto back while emitting a soft, wheezing whistle.

Adult female is dull brown, with pale face markings and light streaks on back and flanks.

Feeding dive starts with a small jump.

Take-off is laborious, with a pattering run across the water. Once launched, the bird's flight is fast.

Present all year; joined by winter migrants.

Red head

Grey back

Black breast

Adult male's brick-red head, black breast and grey back are distinctive. Both sexes have grey wing-bars. 18 in. (45 cm).

The pochard's young are blackish-brown above and greenish-yellow beneath. They take about eight weeks to fledge.

Pochard *Aythya ferina*

Like its close relative the tufted duck, the pochard habitually nests in reed-beds and other vegetation around inland stretches of fresh water. Unlike the tufted duck, however, the pochard has not yet bred to any great extent on the vast acreage of wetland created in recent years by man – sand pits, gravel pits and reservoirs.

The pochard chooses its nesting site carefully, requiring an area of open water free from floating plants but rich in the submerged vegetation that provides food – seeds, leaves, tubers, crustaceans, molluscs, worms and insects. This food the pochard gathers by diving down to about 3–8 ft (1–2·5 m). The pochard particularly favours lakes with tall vegetation fringing them, and sheltered islands with cover, in which the nest will be safe from most mammal predators.

The nest is either a shallow cup in the ground, lined with reeds and leaves, or a platform with a cup built up from the bottom in shallow water. In either case, it is lined with down. The eggs are greenish-grey, and a typical clutch numbers from 6–12 eggs. The pochard is rather a silent species: the most frequent call is a harsh, purring 'kerrr' uttered by the female.

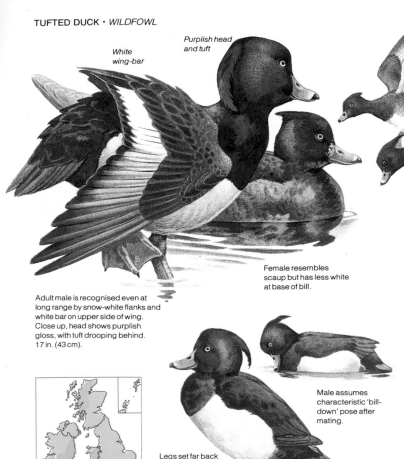

White wing-bar

Purplish head and tuft

In flight, both sexes show longer and more pointed wings than those of pochard.

Ducklings take to water within hours of hatching. Their nest is a pile of vegetation, well hidden near the water's edge.

Female resembles scaup but has less white at base of bill.

Adult male is recognised even at long range by snow-white flanks and white bar on upper side of wing. Close up, head shows purplish gloss, with tuft drooping behind. 17 in. (43 cm).

Male assumes characteristic 'bill-down' pose after mating.

Legs set far back on body make bird clumsy on land.

Present all year; joined by winter migrants.

Tufted duck *Aythya fuligula*

The tufted duck has made a special place for itself on the lakes and ponds of city parks and gardens, where it has become one of the main contenders in daily scrambles for scraps of stale bread and biscuit, and is often almost completely tame. A stranger to Britain before 1849, the tufted duck is now our commonest diving duck and can be found bobbing over the waves of suitable stretches of water almost anywhere in Britain. In the British Isles as a whole there are probably more than 10,000 pairs of tufted duck. One reason for its rapid spread has been the development of lakes from disused gravel pits and of reservoirs.

Another reason for the rapid spread of the tufted duck was the introduction, and wildfire expansion, of the zebra mussel, a native of southern Russia first discovered in the London docks in 1824. These freshwater molluscs are a favourite food of the tufted duck, along with small fish, frogs, insects and spawn. Occasionally tufted duck also dive for water plants.

The tufted duck is aptly named. The drake has a long tuft of feathers down the back of its head, a particularly striking feature when blowing in the wind. The drake's cry is a soft whistle, the duck's a growling purr.

Both sexes show a broad white wing-bar in flight.

Male

Female

Grey back

Scaup feed at sea, often in dense flocks.

Sand-banks serve as resting places. Scaup are rarely seen inland.

At close range the male's head has a green gloss, as distinct from the purple gloss of the tufted species.

Male has blackish head and breast, white underparts and grey bill like the tufted duck, but is distinguished by pale grey back and lack of crest.
19 in. (48 cm).

Mainly Sept.– Apr. visitor; rarely breeds.

Female has brown head and upper parts. A large white patch at base of bill distinguishes it from the tufted duck. Ducklings are tended by the female and led to water almost as soon as their down is dry.

Scaup *Aythya marila*

This bird's odd name was thought by the ornithologist George Montagu (1751–1815) to be derived from its habit of feeding on broken shells, called scaup. Its diet is largely made up of molluscs, especially mussels; it also eats crustaceans such as crabs, and various insects and worms.

Species that breed very rarely in Britain are protected by law, and the scaup, or scaup-duck as it used to be known, is one of these. In the breeding season scaup frequent inland waters such as lakes and rivers, but in winter they mostly take to the sea, often gathering in large feeding flocks off the coasts.

In its courtship display the male swims towards the female with head stretched up and bill pointing steeply upwards. It also displays with a quick stretching-up of the head and a cooing call. Scaup often breed in spread-out colonies on islands in lakes. The nest is a scrape or hollow, frequently in an open situation but occasionally protected by a tussock of grass. It is lined with vegetation and insulated with down from the female's breast. The eggs, laid from late May onwards, usually number 6–12 or sometimes more. They take three to four weeks to hatch, and the chicks become independent at about six weeks old.

69

Male

Male in flight shows black rump, tail and flight feathers, with rest of body white. Female is mainly brown.

Female

Adult female is mottled brown and has a low, sloping head with the bill extending back to the forehead.

Male, eclipse phase

Black cap

Bill-tossing and neck-jerking are features of the male's courtship display.

Adult male has black cap and belly, the rest of its plumage appearing white; at close quarters the breast is pinkish and the nape of the neck green. When flight feathers moult, other plumage darkens in a less conspicuous 'eclipse' phase. 23 in. (58 cm).

Black belly

Groups of eiders often gather on offshore rocks and islets around the coast to feed on molluscs and to rest and sleep.

Present all year on north coasts, local visitor in south.

Eider *Somateria mollissima*

Bedding manufacturers have found no better insulating material for the traditional eiderdown than the soft breast down of the female eider, which she grows specially to protect the clutch of eggs in the nest. Duck-down farmers remove it in carefully limited quantities for commercial use.

The call of the drake eider is a cooing 'ooo-ooo-ooo', with the middle syllable slightly higher in pitch than the rest. The eider often breeds in colonies on offshore islands or along the shores of rocky or sandy coasts, generally in rather exposed sites. Eiders are thoroughly at home in rough seas, swimming easily through the surf round rocky coasts and islets while diving for molluscs.

The breeding season begins early in April in northern England, and some six weeks later in northern Scotland. One clutch of three to ten eggs is produced each year. The female, crouching close to the ground, incubates her eggs for long, unbroken spells for a period of about a month. The ducklings, mainly blackish-brown in colour, are led down to the water soon after hatching. They are able to look after themselves at about 9–11 weeks old.

Hollow trees are favourite nesting places.

Bill-raising and water-splashing are courtship gestures. The 'threat crouch' is a characteristic aggressive display.

On the water the male appears mainly white, its black head showing a green sheen. It has a white spot on each cheek.

Female has brown and white plumage.

High forehead, short bill

Wing-patches

Adult male has black and white plumage. Both sexes are distinguished in flight by rectangular white wing-patches, high foreheads and short bills. 18 in. (45 cm).

Large winter flocks form, mainly of one sex in most cases. They stay mostly on the water, rarely coming ashore.

Goldeneye *Bucephala clangula*

In 1970 a goldeneye duck and four large ducklings were spotted swimming on a small loch in central Scotland. This was the first proof that the goldeneye had bred successfully in the British Isles. It is now expanding rapidly in Scotland. Normally the goldeneye is a winter visitor that breeds in northern Scandinavia and northern Asia. It prefers to nest in tree-holes near a lake or a river, but also uses rabbit burrows and specially provided nest-boxes. On the Continent, goldeneye have often taken over the old nest holes of black woodpeckers.

The bottom of the goldeneye's nesting cavity is unlined, but simply insulated with some greyish-white down and a few feathers. A typical clutch numbers 6–12 smooth, greenish-blue eggs. The young scramble out of the hole and fall to the ground, often a considerable drop; those that survive unharmed (as most do) take about eight weeks fully to develop their flight feathers. Goldeneye in flight have the fast wing-beats typical of diving ducks, but they take off more easily than most, and the wings produce a pronounced whistling sound which is quite unmistakable. In winter many goldeneye take to coastal waters, but some flocks may be found on larger stretches of inland water.

Both sexes are recognised in flight by the absence of bars on their wings and by their unusual flying action, with shallow wing upstrokes but deep downstrokes.

Male, winter

Female, winter

Male, winter

Long tail

Adult male in winter plumage. Males are distinguished at all times by their long tail; only the pintail, differently marked, has one like it. The female has dark cheek-patches. Male 21 in. (53 cm); female 16 in. (40 cm).

The male moults gradually throughout the year; by midsummer its head and neck are dark but the face remains white.

Courtship features head-tossing and 'rear end' displays.

These ducks usually keep well out to sea and leave in May for breeding grounds in northern Europe.

Sept.–Apr. visitor, but has bred in Scotland.

Long-tailed duck *Clangula hyemalis*

The voice of the male long-tailed duck is extraordinary among ducks for its melodious, resonant and far-carrying quality. The variety of its calls, too, is remarkable: the calls of a displaying flock have been likened by some ornithologists to the sound of distant bagpipes.

The period from the end of September to the end of October sees the arrival in British waters of the wintering population of long-tailed ducks from their northern breeding grounds. The nest, a mere scrape in the ground sparsely lined with plant material and down, is usually sited in thick vegetation not far from water; occasionally it is in a rock crevice. The duck incubates its six to nine olive–buff eggs for about three and a half weeks. The ducklings' down is brown tipped with gold above and greyish-white below. Occasionally several broods may join together in a *crèche* – a phenomenon found in several species of waterfowl, for example eider and shelduck. The young become independent after about five weeks.

This bird's food consists predominantly of animal life such as molluscs and crustaceans, which it gathers by diving, but it also enjoys seeds, leaves and other vegetable matter.

Female

Male in flight appears mainly white with black wingtips and back. In both sexes the double white wing-bar stands out against darker plumage.

Male

Dense flocks may fish together, those in the front ranks diving while the others fly to catch up.

The male's courtship display includes head gestures.

Black eye-patches

Female has white cheeks, chestnut cap and grey upper parts. It is smaller than the male.

Black breast lines

Nov.– Mar. visitor, mainly to East Anglia and south-east.

Adult male's unique plumage is white with white crest and black nape band, eye-patches and breast lines, 16 in. (40 cm).

Wintering smews favour reservoirs and harbours, but they are hardy and will dive below ice for fish and shellfish.

Smew *Mergellus albellus*

There is no mistaking the drake smew, one of Britain's most handsome winter visitors; its snow-white and jet-black feathers contrast strikingly, and are set off by a drooping crest. In flight, more black plumage shows, adding to the pied effect.

Though distinctive in appearance, the smew is not easily or often seen. It comes to Britain every year, when the freshwater lakes and rivers of its forest breeding grounds in northern Scandinavia and Russia freeze up, but it does not do so in large numbers. Moreover, the smew is a very shy, fast-flying, elusive bird, and does not reveal itself in the noisy manner of so many ducks: outside the breeding season the only sound likely to be heard is the female's occasional harsh, rattling call.

The smew will sometimes eat vegetable matter, but its food consists mainly of fish, molluscs and crustaceans. Its saw-edged bill is especially well adapted to grasping and holding slippery fish. At seasons when they are plentiful, the bird will also take quantities of insects. Most of its food is found by diving below the surface. Usually, its dives are short, lasting for less than 30 seconds, and they are shallow, rarely exceeding 13 ft (4 m). The prey is usually brought to the surface for swallowing.

73

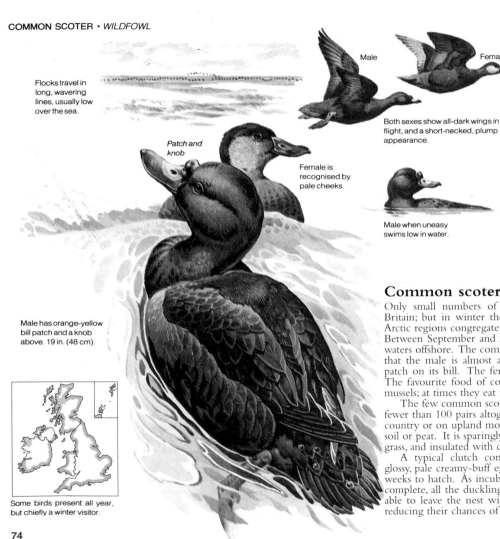

Flocks travel in long, wavering lines, usually low over the sea.

Male

Female

Both sexes show all-dark wings in flight, and a short-necked, plump appearance.

Female is recognised by pale cheeks.

Patch and knob

Male when uneasy swims low in water.

Male has orange-yellow bill patch and a knob above. 19 in. (48 cm).

Some birds present all year, but chiefly a winter visitor.

The nest of the common scoter is usually sited in heather or other dense vegetation, generally close to water.

Common scoter *Melanitta nigra*

Only small numbers of common scoters regularly breed in Britain; but in winter these visitors from the Arctic and sub-Arctic regions congregate in large flocks around Britain's coasts. Between September and April they form 'rafts' of birds on the waters offshore. The common scoter is unusual among ducks in that the male is almost all black, with only an orange-yellow patch on its bill. The female is dark brown with pale cheeks. The favourite food of common scoters is shellfish, particularly mussels; at times they eat insects and vegetable matter.

The few common scoters that do breed in the British Isles – fewer than 100 pairs altogether – nest beside lochs in mountain country or on upland moors. The nest is a shallow scrape in the soil or peat. It is sparingly lined with scraps of lichen, moss and grass, and insulated with down.

A typical clutch consists of five to ten smooth, slightly glossy, pale creamy-buff eggs which take four to four and a half weeks to hatch. As incubation does not start until the clutch is complete, all the ducklings emerge within a short time and are able to leave the nest with their mother with little delay, thus reducing their chances of falling victim to predators.

Both sexes are easily identified in flight by white wing-patches.

Female

Male

Orange-yellow bill sides

Female has two pale face-patches, and darker face than common scoter.

Wing-patch

Male velvet scoter has a white spot behind the eye, visible at close quarters. Scoters prefer calm waters.

Surf scoter
Melanitta perspicillata

This rare visitor is distinguished by a more massive bill shape and by head and neck-patches – white on the male, greyish on the female.

Mainly a winter coastal visitor. Rarely seen inland.

Male is distinguished from common scoter by orange-yellow bill sides and only slight thickening of bill base, and also by its white wing-patch. Red legs show in flight. 22 in. (55 cm).

Wings are slightly open under water. Mussels are a favourite food.

Velvet scoter *Melanitta fusca*

If a few of the birds in a flock of scoters look slightly larger than the rest, and have white patches on their faces and wings, then some velvet scoters have mingled with common scoters. In other respects they are unobtrusive and silent birds. It has been claimed that velvet scoters have bred in the British Isles, but they usually only winter in Britain, around the coasts, far from their Arctic and sub-Arctic breeding grounds. The young are virtually independent at about five weeks old, but may remain in the breeding area for some weeks before migrating.

Flocks do not generally number more than 12–20 birds. In this the velvet scoter differs from the common scoter, which may be seen in flocks of hundreds or even thousands. Molluscs such as mussels form the bulk of the velvet scoter's food, which it obtains by diving to the bottom – which may be 20 ft (6 m) down. Feeding birds usually remain submerged for 20–40 seconds, but longer dives up to about a minute in length have been recorded.

The surf scoter, which breeds in North America, is a rare winter visitor, for it usually winters on the eastern or western coasts of Canada and the United States.

Bufflehead
Bucephala albeola

Male has large white patch on back of dark head; in flight, white wing-patch is visible. Female has smaller patch behind eye. 14 in. (36 cm).

Female

Male

Male

Male

Male

Female

Male

Blue-winged teal
Anas discors

Male has mottled light and dark brown body, with grey neck and bill; female lacks male's white crescent in front of eye. Both sexes show blue forewing in flight.

Female

Male

Hooded merganser
Lophodytes cucullatus

Male's black-bordered white cockade, which can be raised or lowered, is distinctive. Female has red-brown upper parts and breast, and short grey bill. 18 in. (45 cm).

Male

Female

Red-crested pochard
Netta rufina

Male has red-brown head and black breast; white wing-bar shows in flight. Female is brownish. 22 in. (55 cm).

Male

Rare ducks from abroad

Although ducks can fly for considerable distances, most rare foreign species appearing in the British countryside today are likely to have escaped from British wildfowl collections. The hooded merganser is a bird of woodland freshwater ponds and rivers. The same habitat is favoured in summer by the little bufflehead, though it prefers estuaries in winter. The American wigeon grazes on estuaries and coastal marshes, while the blue-winged teal seeks small, sheltered stretches of fresh or brackish water. All these are North American birds, as is the ring-necked duck, which is found with other divers on the deeper lakes and reservoirs. The red-crested pochard, a native of warmer European regions, prefers large stretches of fresh water; the ferruginous duck from the same areas favours swamps.

Male

Ring-necked duck

Aythya collaris

Male has contrasting dark upper parts and white underparts, an indistinct, brownish collar that gives it its name and two white bands on bill. A short crest gives it a peaked head shape. Duller female has white eye-ring. 19 in. (48 cm).

Male

Female

Female

Female

Male

Male

Female

Ferruginous duck

Aythya nyroca

Male has white eyes; both sexes have brown plumage, with distinctive white under-tail feathers, and show striking white wing-bar. 16 in. (40 cm).

Male

Male

American wigeon

Anas americana

Male bird can be distinguished by white forehead, mottled grey and white face and neck, and green stripe running from behind eye to nape. Female has greyer head and white under-wing.

77

Female

Male

Flight is fast and direct, with neck and body outstretched to produce a long, narrow shape. White wing-patch is more extensive on male.

Double crest

Red-brown breast

Adult female in breeding plumage has shorter crest than the male. The brown colouring of the head merges into neck and breast.

Fishing birds often swim with head under water before submerging totally to dive on prey.

During its moult the male resembles the female, but back is darker and forewing whiter.

The female alone tends the ducklings. Nests are built near rivers or lakes and only one brood is reared each year.

Present all year; mainly on estuaries in winter.

Downy young are generally dark above and pale below, with white spots on their wings and backs.

Adult male has dark green head and reddish-brown breast and neck. Double crest and darker colouring distinguish it from goosander. 23 in. (58 cm).

Red-breasted merganser *Mergus serrator*

These ducks have a bad reputation among trout and salmon fishermen because of their taste for the young of the two fish. Defenders of the red-breasted merganser argue, however, that they also eat many non–game species, including eels, perch and pike which compete with or prey on the eggs or the young of salmon and trout.

The red-breasted merganser and the goosander are the only two species of sawbill duck that breed in the British Isles. They have finely serrated cutting edges to their bills that enable them to grasp slippery fish. The red-breasted merganser has a long history of residence in Scotland and Ireland. Since about 1950, however, in spite of some persecution, birds have spread into England, breeding as far south as Derbyshire, and also into Wales.

The nest is a shallow depression in the ground lined with grass, leaves and down. Thick vegetation usually makes it hard to find. From late April to early July the female lays and incubates eight to ten pale buff eggs that take a month to hatch. When the female leaves the nest, she camouflages the eggs with down. The ducklings can fly about two months after hatching.

Female

Male

Flight is rapid and powerful; the wing-beats produce a pronounced whistle. Long neck and slim bill are noticeable. Female has brown head and grey back.

Male

Narrow red bill

Adult female in breeding plumage has flatter crest than female merganser. Brown head is sharply divided from white chin and throat.

Adult male in breeding plumage, with dark green head and pinky-white body. Larger, more buoyant than merganser. 26 in. (66 cm).

Dark green head

Present all year; breeding range spreading south.

Goosanders nest in holes, usually in hollow trees or crevices in rocks.

Male in post-breeding plumage is like female but has white forewing.

Goosanders are frequently seen on reservoirs and lakes during winter. They swim well under water.

Goosander *Mergus merganser*

The goosander is one of the few species of duck that frequently nests in holes in trees. Within two or three days of hatching, the ducklings are encouraged to leave the nest. As this happens eight to ten weeks before the young birds can fly, they face a vertical drop of several feet to the ground below, which they usually survive without injury.

Goosanders sometimes nest in holes in banks and among boulders, as does their close relative the red-breasted merganser. The nest, on a base of leaves, has a plentiful lining of down to keep the clutch of up to 15 creamy-white eggs warm. The drake takes virtually no part in the incubation of the eggs or the raising of the young; instead, the drake congregates with fellow males near by.

As it lives on fish, the goosander suffers the same persecution by conservators of fisheries as its fellow sawbill duck, the red-breasted merganser. Since the goosander is more of a freshwater species than the merganser, it is persecuted on an even larger scale. Nevertheless, since it first nested in Perthshire in 1871, it has colonised much of Scotland and spread into England, Wales and Ireland.

79

FEMALE DUCKS IN FLIGHT

Most male ducks advertise their presence with bold plumage patterns in the breeding season, losing them only when they are moulting. Females, however, do not need to advertise to attract a mate, and when they are incubating eggs they must remain as inconspicuous as possible to avoid the attentions of predators. In general, therefore, they have dull brown, streaky plumage, making them difficult to tell apart. The best means of identification is often the speculum – a bright patch of colour on the secondary feathers on the trailing edge of the wing, which usually differs in colour from one species to another.

Most ducks fly fast and silently, making identification in flight still harder. Head shape may provide a clue, and occasionally behaviour may help, as in the almost vertical take-off of the teal and the straggling lines of eiders low over the sea.

White wing-bar

Dark head

Green and black wing-patches

Teal
Anas crecca
Page 62

Tufted duck
Aythya fuligula
Page 68

Grey wing-bar

Pale chin and bill base

Pochard
Aythya ferina
Page 67

Head more striped than teal's

Orange-yellow bill sides

White wing-patches

Huge bill

Blue-grey shoulder

Green and black wing-patches

Shoveler
Anas clypeata
Page 66

Wing-patches less distinct than teal's

Garganey
Anas querquedula
Page 63

Gadwall
Anas strepera
Page 61

Green and black wing-patches

Short bill

Pointed tail

Long neck

Bronze wing-patches

White belly

Wigeon
Anas penelope
Page 60

Large violet wing-patches

Yellowish bill

Mallard
Anas platyrhynchos
Page 64

Pintail
Anas acuta
Page 65

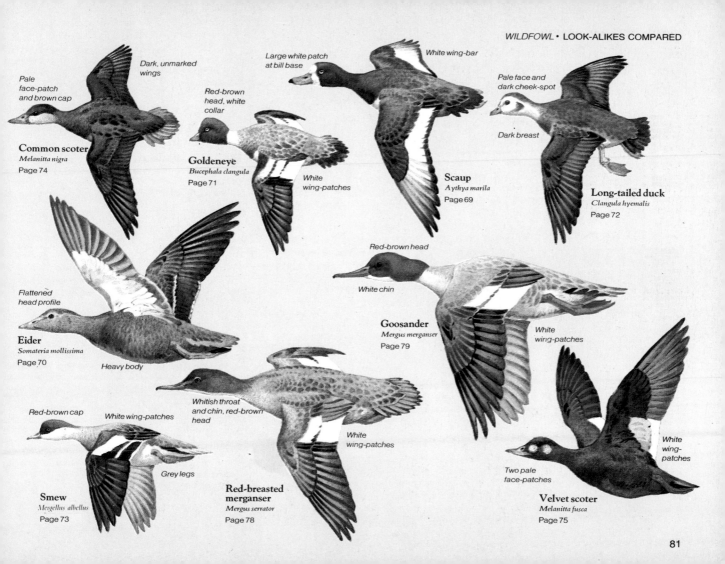

Pale face-patch and brown cap

Dark, unmarked wings

Large white patch at bill base

White wing-bar

Pale face and dark cheek-spot

Common scoter
Melanitta nigra
Page 74

Red-brown head, white collar

Dark breast

Goldeneye
Bucephala clangula
Page 71

White wing-patches

Scaup
Aythya marila
Page 69

Long-tailed duck
Clangula hyemalis
Page 72

Red-brown head

White chin

Flattened head profile

Goosander
Mergus merganser
Page 79

White wing-patches

Eider
Somateria mollissima
Page 70

Heavy body

Red-brown cap

White wing-patches

Whitish throat and chin, red-brown head

White wing-patches

White wing-patches

Grey legs

Smew
Mergellus albellus
Page 73

Red-breasted merganser
Mergus serrator
Page 78

Two pale face-patches

Velvet scoter
Melanitta fusca
Page 75

81

Pale head

When soaring with tail spread, fork in tail is unobtrusive, but from below, white underwing-patches are distinctive.

Immature bird has darker head and duller, more uniform plumage than adult bird.

Although the kite is usually seen over open ground it makes its nest in the shelter of deciduous woodland.

Black kite
Milvus migrans

This rare kite is dark brown, with less deeply forked tail. In flight it is more compact, with paler wing coverts. 22 in. (55 cm).

Present all year; re-introduced England and Scotland.

Adult male has a pale head, brownish-red upper parts with pale bordered feathers and a long, deeply forked tail. Female is slightly duller. 24 in. (60 cm).

Long forked tail

Kite *Milvus milvus*

The kite helped to clear Tudor London's garbage – it flew everywhere in the city's unsavoury streets, scavenging among the offal and carrion that lay about. Nowadays it has vanished from our cities, its food supply gone, though its relative the black kite, very rare in Britain, still frequents many cities around the Mediterranean and in Asia and Africa.

The child's toy kite was named after the bird because of its habit of hovering or gliding slowly over rural hillsides. By about 1900, gamekeepers – wrongly believing the kite to be a threat to their birds – had slaughtered the kite almost to extinction. A mere handful of pairs survived in the remote hills of central Wales. Helped by strict protection, numbers have recovered, and re-introductions are in progress in England and Scotland.

Apart from carrion, the kite eats mainly small mammals, birds and insects. In Wales the drop in rabbit numbers, due to the disease myxomatosis, reduced the number of breeding pairs of kites; those that remained survived on dead sheep in the hills.

The kite's nest is built of sticks, mud and miscellaneous rubbish such as paper and bones. Two or three white eggs with very variable reddish-brown markings are laid.

The female is the biggest of all harriers, dark brown with a pale crown, throat and forewing. 23 in. (58 cm).

Young are coloured like the female but have no yellow on the forewing.

The older male has pale colouring under the wings. The head is also pale and the underparts are reddish-streaked. 20 in. (50 cm).

Pale head

Reddish underparts

Pale shoulders of female are distinctive. In the marsh harrier's flight, slow, steady flaps alternate with glides.

A substantial nest of reeds is built among marsh plants. The young may leave it before they are fully fledged.

The male is unique among harriers in having a dark back, grey tail and pale head.

Wings are held in a shallow V when gliding or soaring.

Present all year; the young move south in winter.

Marsh harrier *Circus aeruginosus*

Once quite common, this powerful hawk is today one of Britain's rarest birds. Increasing use of pesticides, drainage of the fens and, not least, persecution by man probably contributed to the bird's decline. Recently, however, there has been a steady increase in numbers with birds prospecting many new areas for nest sites.

The female is larger than the male and is almost as big as a buzzard, though not so heavily built. Both male and female birds, in common with other harriers, have face feathers arranged to give them an owl-like appearance. This probably serves to funnel sound into the ears – a great advantage to a bird that hunts its prey in dense reeds or grass.

In Britain, some marsh harriers remain near the breeding grounds all winter. At the approach of spring, the pairs begin their display ritual. They fly up to a height of several thousand feet before diving and somersaulting downwards, swooping upwards again as they near the ground. The male often passes food to the female during these displays, and this must help to nourish her in preparation for egg-laying. Four to five bluish-white eggs make up the average clutch.

Adult male is pale grey above and white below. It is larger and bulkier than Montagu's harrier. 17 in. (43 cm).

Dark wingtips

Male in flight shows white rump and dark wingtips.

White rump

Adult female is brown above and brown-and-white streaked below, with black bars on its wings. It is larger than the male. 20 in. (50 cm).

The female builds a nest of grass, heather and bracken on the ground, usually among moorland heather.

Female is called from nest by male to catch prey that he drops to her; she rolls over as she catches it.

Adult female in flight shows white rump and barred tail.

Present all year; breeding range spreading south.

Hen harrier *Circus cyaneus*

Pouncing from a low-level hunting glide, this moorland marauder is far from particular about its prey. Almost any creature up to the size of a hare or a duck is fair game for its powerful talons. Small mammals and birds, including the chicks of other birds of prey, make up most of the hen harrier's diet, but it also eats lizards, snakes, frogs, beetles and the eggs of ground-nesting birds.

Centuries ago, when the bird was more widespread, it preyed on domestic poultry and so obtained its name; today, however, it is considered to be little threat to the farmyard hen. Hen harriers became very rare in the early part of this century, vanishing entirely from mainland Britain by about 1940 and surviving only in the Orkneys and Outer Hebrides. Since all Britain's hawks gained the protection of the law, however, hen harriers have shown a particularly large population increase.

Breeding areas of the hen harrier are now spreading back through England, Wales and Ireland, and birds are nesting in birch and willow scrub, young fir plantations and even among crops, as well as in their traditional moor and marsh areas. Chicks hatch in about five weeks and fly at five weeks old.

Female

The bird's flight is very buoyant, with wings raised in a shallow V.

Black wing-bar

Brown streaks

The male often perches on a post overlooking grassland, watching for prey such as insects and small mammals.

Montagu's harrier nests on the ground among vegetation in most kinds of open country, from farmland to sand-dunes.

Pallid harrier
Circus macrourus

This harrier is a vagrant, slimmer than Montagu's harrier and even rarer. The male is very pale in colour.

Late Apr.– Sept. visitor; only a handful now breed.

Adult male is slighter-built than the hen harrier, with black wing-bar and brown streaks on whitish under-wing and flanks. 16 in. (40 cm).

Immature bird resembles female, but has unstreaked, chestnut underparts.

Adult female is generally similar to the hen harrier but slightly smaller, with a narrower white rump-patch. 18 in. (45 cm).

Montagu's harrier *Circus pygargus*

A Montagu's harrier is so easy to confuse with a hen harrier that it was not until 1802 that George Montagu, the Devon naturalist who compiled an early dictionary of birds, distinguished between them and gave one his name. Only the immature birds, with their chestnut underparts, are distinctive. The two birds differ also in their breeding habits. The hen harrier is a well-established breeding bird in the north and west, while the Montagu's harrier is one of Britain's rarest breeding birds, limited to a few pairs in southern and eastern England.

Migrants arrive from the Mediterranean and tropical Africa in April and settle down in their pairs by the end of May or early June. The eggs are laid at intervals of up to two or three days, and since the female starts to incubate after laying the first egg, the young hatch at similar intervals after four weeks.

The female greets the male as he brings food for her and the chicks. In common with most harriers, the prey is passed from foot to foot in mid-air, or dropped by the male and caught by the female. After about three weeks, the female shares in the hunting to satisfy the appetites of the growing family, which takes wing after about five weeks.

85

Honey buzzards, like buzzards, occur in light and dark colour forms.

Rough-legged buzzard
Buteo lagopus

Adult is usually pale below with dark belly and patches on wing wrists. Legs are feathered right to the toes. Tail is whitish, with black terminal band. Wings are longer and narrower than those of buzzard.

Adult bird has narrower head and longer tail than the buzzard. Tail has narrow regular bars and a broader bar at the tip. Sexes are alike. 20–23 in. (50–58 cm).

The honey buzzard usually frequents small woods or forestry plantations that are surrounded by open country.

Tail bars

May–Sept. breeding visitors; probably increasing.

Honey buzzard *Pernis apivorus*

The main diet of the honey buzzard is extremely unusual for a bird of prey: it consists of wild bees and their honey (hence the bird's name), wasp grubs, hornets, ant pupae and other insects. It does, however, sometimes supplement its diet with the type of food more usually associated with birds of prey – small mammals, nestling birds, lizards and frogs.

The honey buzzard, a summer visitor, is one of the rarest of British breeding species. Even after a recent increase, there are seldom more than 50 pairs breeding in any year. Once restricted to southern England, nesting birds have now reached Scotland and Wales. Its display flight is spectacular: a series of steep earthward dives, each followed by an upward sweep. Sometimes the honey buzzard hovers for a moment, clapping its wings rapidly above its back.

The nest, built of large sticks and lined with leafy twigs, is often the old foundations of a crow's nest or buzzard's nest. Two eggs are usually laid, from late May or early June onwards. They have rich reddish-brown, purplish-brown or chocolate markings that almost obliterate the white base colour. The eggs hatch in 30–35 days, and the young fly at about six weeks old.

Perching buzzard has an upright stance and shows a heavy, rounded build.

In-gliding, wings are held flat with primary feathers turned back and pointed.

Wings are held forward and raised when soaring, with primary feathers turned up and tail widely spread.

Legs are unfeathered, unlike those of the visiting rough-legged buzzard.

Trees and cliff ledges are favoured for nesting. The bulky nest is built of sticks and 'decorated' with greenery.

Short neck

Finely barred tail

Adult in its most frequent colouring. Buzzards range in colour from dark grey or brown to the palest grey. Sexes are alike. 20–22 in. (50–55 cm).

Present all year; breeding range spreading east.

Buzzard *Buteo buteo*

A familiar sound in hilly country in western or northern Britain is the mewing 'kiew' of a buzzard as it sails apparently without effort over a neighbouring hillside, circling in the updraught from the hill or in a rising thermal of hot air. The keen-sighted bird meanwhile scans the ground below for prey. Small mammals are its favourite food, in particular rabbits – so much so that the number of buzzards declined dramatically after myxomatosis almost wiped out Britain's rabbit population in the mid-1950s.

Buzzards prefer open hillsides and wooded valleys like those of South Wales, the Lake District and western Scotland; they are fewer in bare, mountainous regions and moorland. They build large nests of sticks or heather stalks and line them with finer twigs, bracken, grass, moss or seaweed.

The handsome eggs have a white or bluish-white shell decorated with brown spots or blotches. They take about a month to hatch, and since the eggs are laid at intervals of three or four days the young are of variable age. Young birds often die of starvation when food is short, but despite this, buzzards remain the most common of Britain's larger birds of prey.

White streak

White under-tail coverts are conspicuous in flight. Silhouette resembles the sparrowhawk's.

Nests are lined with green leaves or pine needles. If alarmed at the nest, birds utter a harsh, plaintive call.

Wing strokes are usually long and slow in display flight. Hunting birds fly swiftly and surely between trees.

Present all year; population mainly from introductions.

Adult males and females resemble huge female sparrowhawks. A whitish streak runs from eye to the ear coverts. Female 24 in. (60 cm); male 20 in. (50 cm).

Underparts of young birds are streaked, rather than barred.

The nest is a substantial platform of sticks. The goshawk's eggs, sometimes as many as five, are bluish-white.

Goshawk *Accipiter gentilis*

This handsome bird is a very efficient killer. Swift but controlled, it swoops through the trees to take its prey completely unawares, delivering the *coup de grâce* with its powerful claws. It is often trained for falconry.

The goshawk is much larger than the sparrowhawk, which it otherwise closely resembles in both appearance and habits. Probably because of its greater size it feeds on bigger prey: wood-pigeons, crows, game birds, rats and hares constitute its staple diet. The female goshawk is larger than the male.

The bird's main display consists of flights over its woodland breeding territory with very slow, deliberate wing movements. Three to five eggs, rather plain for a bird of prey, are laid, usually in April or May. These are incubated for five to five and a half weeks, almost entirely by the female. At first the downy white chicks are fed by the female on morsels of food torn from prey brought to the nest by the male, but as the family appetite becomes greater both adults provide the food. The goshawk was, until the 1950s, a very rare breeding species in Britain, but since then, aided by escapes from falconry training and deliberate introductions, the population has built up in some areas.

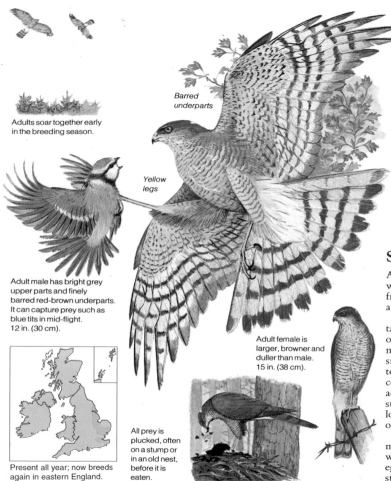

Adults soar together early in the breeding season.

Barred underparts

Yellow legs

Adult male has bright grey upper parts and finely barred red-brown underparts. It can capture prey such as blue tits in mid-flight. 12 in. (30 cm).

Adult female is larger, browner and duller than male. 15 in. (38 cm).

Present all year; now breeds again in eastern England.

All prey is plucked, often on a stump or in an old nest, before it is eaten.

Short, rounded wings and long tail are identifiable in flight.

The sparrowhawk's nest is made of sticks, especially larch. It is lined with down and twigs or pieces of bark.

Sparrowhawk *Accipiter nisus*

Ambush is the sparrowhawk's favourite method of hunting. A watcher must be alert to spot the quick flurry and chorus of frantic alarm calls as the agile, yellow-eyed predator darts down a woodland ride or clearing, scattering terrified small birds.

Although most prey is probably captured with the advantage of surprise, the sparrowhawk is quite capable of outflying or overtaking its quarry with sheer superior power and skill, matching every twist and turn of its fleeing victim. Usually a small bird's only chance of escaping the long, slender yellow toes and their needle-sharp black talons is to dive into very dense cover. The short, rounded wings of the sparrowhawk are clearly adapted to woodland hunting; longer wings would not allow such nimble manoeuvring through the trees. Occasionally, a longer view of a sparrowhawk presents itself as it circles high over a wood – in search, perhaps, of a winter flock of finches.

The nest, a flattish, often bulky platform of sticks, is built mainly by the female. Sometimes the remains of a nest built by a wood-pigeon or crow is used as a foundation. The three to six eggs are rounded and bluish-white, with spots, blotches and streaks of rich chocolate-brown.

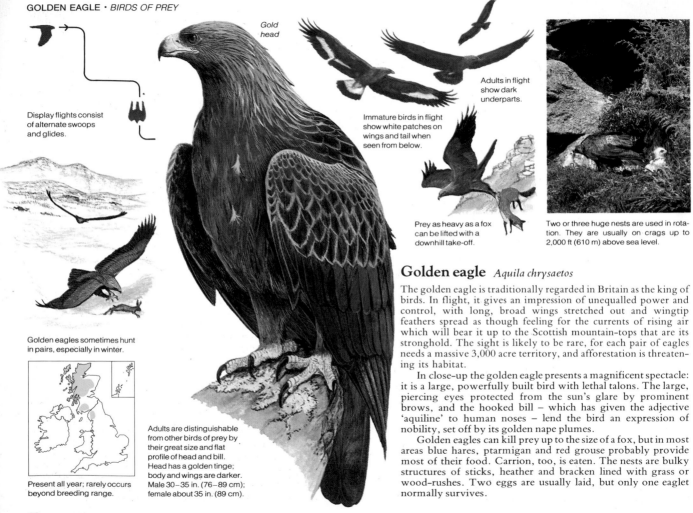

Display flights consist of alternate swoops and glides.

Golden eagles sometimes hunt in pairs, especially in winter.

Present all year; rarely occurs beyond breeding range.

Adults are distinguishable from other birds of prey by their great size and flat profile of head and bill. Head has a golden tinge; body and wings are darker. Male 30–35 in. (76–89 cm); female about 35 in. (89 cm).

Gold head

Immature birds in flight show white patches on wings and tail when seen from below.

Adults in flight show dark underparts.

Prey as heavy as a fox can be lifted with a downhill take-off.

Two or three huge nests are used in rotation. They are usually on crags up to 2,000 ft (610 m) above sea level.

Golden eagle *Aquila chrysaetos*

The golden eagle is traditionally regarded in Britain as the king of birds. In flight, it gives an impression of unequalled power and control, with long, broad wings stretched out and wingtip feathers spread as though feeling for the currents of rising air which will bear it up to the Scottish mountain-tops that are its stronghold. The sight is likely to be rare, for each pair of eagles needs a massive 3,000 acre territory, and afforestation is threatening its habitat.

In close-up the golden eagle presents a magnificent spectacle: it is a large, powerfully built bird with lethal talons. The large, piercing eyes protected from the sun's glare by prominent brows, and the hooked bill – which has given the adjective 'aquiline' to human noses – lend the bird an expression of nobility, set off by its golden nape plumes.

Golden eagles can kill prey up to the size of a fox, but in most areas blue hares, ptarmigan and red grouse probably provide most of their food. Carrion, too, is eaten. The nests are bulky structures of sticks, heather and bracken lined with grass or wood-rushes. Two eggs are usually laid, but only one eaglet normally survives.

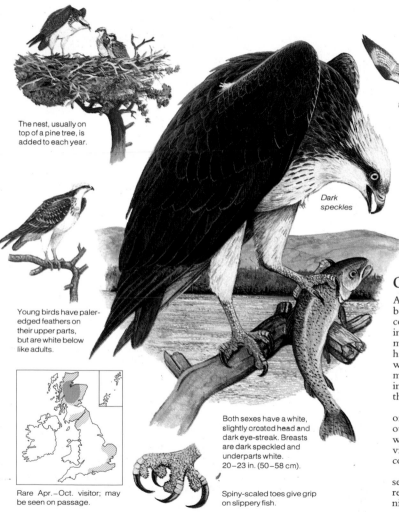

The nest, usually on top of a pine tree, is added to each year.

Young birds have paler-edged feathers on their upper parts, but are white below like adults.

Both sexes have a white, slightly crested head and dark eye-streak. Breasts are dark speckled and underparts white. 20–23 in. (50–58 cm).

Dark speckles

Spiny-scaled toes give grip on slippery fish.

Rare Apr.–Oct. visitor; may be seen on passage.

In flight the wings are sharply angled at the wrist joint.

An adult hovers about 100 ft (30 m) above water, then plunges onto its prey.

An adult osprey can carry fish weighing up to about 4½ lb (2 kg) back to its nest. It is also known as a fish hawk.

Osprey *Pandion haliaetus*

An osprey making a kill is a spectacular sight. Fish make up the bulk of its diet, and a hunting bird flies over the water at a considerable height, with alternate spells of flapping and glid-ing, until it spots a large fish near the surface. It pauses in mid-flight, sometimes hovers momentarily, then turns with half-closed wings and plummets to the water, entering feet first with a large splash and often completely submerging for a moment or two. On surfacing after a successful dive with a fish in its talons, it shakes its plumage violently to remove the water, then carries the fish, often a trout or a pike, back to its nest.

An outstanding success story of recent times was the return of the osprey to its former breeding areas in Scotland. Driven out partly because it competed with anglers for trout, the bird was absent for 50 years. Then, after four years in which they visited but did not breed, one pair raised young in 1959; under constant protection, numbers have built up steadily ever since.

The osprey's large nest, built of sticks, is used for season after season. The eggs are white, with blotches of chocolate or reddish-brown, and are incubated mainly by the hen. Eight or nine weeks may elapse before the young can fly.

91

Kestrels often perch on man-made structures such as telegraph poles.

Pairs can be persuaded to settle in nest-boxes.

For its final pounce, the kestrel half-closes its wings to drop on its prey.

Female

Male

Young male's tail is grey, female's rusty-brown; both have dark bars.

Chestnut back

In level flight the tail appears very long and the wings pointed.

Adult male has chestnut back with grey head and tail. Kestrels hunt by searching while hovering; if no prey is seen the bird flies on, rises slightly, then hovers again. 13½ in. (34 cm).

Grey tail with black band

Present all year; our commonest bird of prey.

The natural sites for kestrels' nests are tree cavities and disused crows' nests, though they also breed in buildings.

Kestrel *Falco tinnunculus*

A medium-sized, brownish bird hovering above the roadside is often a fleeting point of interest to the passing motorist and usually means imminent death for some small creature below. Reduced to low numbers in the late 1950s and 1960s, the kestrel has now largely recovered to become Britain's most widespread bird of prey. Its hovering technique of hunting – which gave rise to the country name of 'windhover' – can be watched in open countryside, along motorway verges and in urban areas. Kestrels have even nested in central London.

Typically, the kestrel flies along until prey or a likely spot for prey is sighted. It then checks and hovers, with occasional deeper wing-beats and tail fanned out and pointing down for stability. In spite of the exertion of hovering, the kestrel can keep its head motionless to pinpoint a possible meal. Lift-like, the bird drops by stages, finally pouncing and grasping with its talons. Small mammals are its staple diet.

Four or five rounded, heavily reddish-speckled eggs are incubated for about four weeks, mainly by the female. The chicks' coats of white down give way to brownish-grey before flight feathers develop. Chicks fly at four to five weeks.

Female and young of both sexes look brown from above when in flight.

Blue-grey upper parts

Adult male has blue-grey upper parts and black tail band. When perched, merlins appear more compact than other falcons. 10½–13 in. (27–33 cm).

Black tail band

Present all year; some birds migrate from Iceland.

The low-flying merlin often takes small birds in level flight; but sometimes the quarry escapes by going to ground under a bush or other vegetation.

In winter, merlins may move to low ground such as marshland to hunt.

The erratic flight is punctuated by short glides. The tail appears shorter than that of the kestrel.

Early in the breeding season, males fly between low perches calling to females.

Females usually lay their clutch of four speckled eggs in a shallow scrape in the ground, but may use an old crow's nest.

Merlin *Falco columbarius*

Flying low, fast and level, with quick, shallow wing-beats, the male merlin, little bigger than a mistle thrush, quarters the heather-clad moors of northern and western Britain in search of its prey – mainly small birds, but sometimes insects, lizards and mice. On sighting its prey, the merlin rises above it, then drops to sink its talons into its victim. The merlin carries its prey off to a so-called 'plucking-post' – a rock outcrop, fence or drystone wall where the bird plucks its prey before presenting it to its mate, who takes it back to the nest.

In the 60 days or so it takes merlins to hatch and learn to fly, the male bird hunts for mate and family. Then, while the offspring are maturing – a process that takes a further six weeks – the female joins the quest for food to satisfy the youngsters.

Merlins, the hunting bird of noblewomen during the Middle Ages, are shy and rare, and declining in numbers. Because they are low-flying and do not engage in the aerobatics of other falcons they are hard to spot. However, anyone who approaches a nest soon becomes aware of the birds' presence – the male darts to the nearest vantage point or circles round, and shrills its 'quik-ik-ik' call.

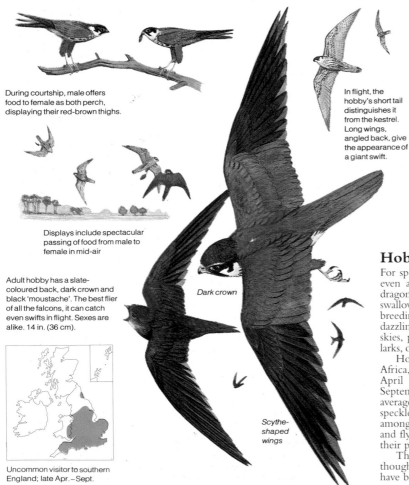

During courtship, male offers food to female as both perch, displaying their red-brown thighs.

Displays include spectacular passing of food from male to female in mid-air

Adult hobby has a slate-coloured back, dark crown and black 'moustache'. The best flier of all the falcons, it can catch even swifts in flight. Sexes are alike. 14 in. (36 cm).

Dark crown

Scythe-shaped wings

In flight, the hobby's short tail distinguishes it from the kestrel. Long wings, angled back, give the appearance of a giant swift.

Adults have clear-cut face pattern, and underparts streaked with black.

Hobbies normally take over a disused nest, such as that of a crow, high up in a tree. The young are fed on insects.

Uncommon visitor to southern England; late Apr.–Sept.

Hobby *Falco subbuteo*

For speed, grace and agility in flight, the hobby has few rivals, even among its fellow falcons. Whether delicately picking a dragonfly out of the sky or swooping down to capture a swallow in full flight, it presents a breath-taking spectacle. In the breeding season, pairs of hobbies soar, hover, dip and loop in dazzling displays of flying skill. These superb hunters of the skies, prized in the days of hawking for their ability to catch larks, often seem to perform their feats for pure joy.

Hobbies are also great travellers. They spend the winter in Africa, south of the Sahara desert, and arrive in Britain in late April and May after a 2,500 mile journey, remaining until September or October to breed. The females produce, on average, one clutch of two or three eggs. The eggs are densely speckled with reddish-rust markings, a feature not uncommon among falcons. The downy young hatch after about a month and fly when four to four and a half weeks old, but depend on their parents for some time afterwards.

The hobby is one of Britain's rarer birds, though it is now thought that the population, reckoned at up to 500 pairs, may have been underestimated previously.

Prey is killed with one blow of the peregrine's talons; the attacker circles back to retrieve the body from the ground.

Courting male 'loops the loop' after mock dive at female.

Dark crown

Cheek 'moustache'

When not attacking, bird flies with series of shallow flaps alternating with glides.

Broad wings make tail look short.

Young bird is brown above and streaked, not barred, below.

Adult bird has dark crown, 'moustache' cheek pattern and grey upper parts. White underparts are barred with black – more strongly in female, which also tends to be larger. 15–19 in. (38–48 cm).

The eyrie of a peregrine falcon is simply a bare rock ledge on a cliff. A slight nesting depression may be scraped out.

Peregrine falcon *Falco peregrinus*

Death is merciful for the peregrine's victim – a single blow out of nowhere. The attacker, a speck in the sky as it keeps a lonely, circling watch for prey, suddenly snaps back its wings and plummets in a wind-whistling 'stoop' that has been estimated as reaching 180 mph (290 km/h). If the attack is successful, a blow from the peregrine's talons instantly breaks the neck or back of the flying prey, typically a pigeon or grouse, although birds up to the size of a Brent goose may be tackled.

The peregrine's appetite for sporting birds led to its long persecution by gamekeepers. In wartime, when homing pigeons were used to carry messages, the destruction of peregrines and their eggs was officially encouraged. Now the bird is specially protected, and there has recently been some recovery in its numbers. Interest has revived in the ancient art of falconry – taming and training the birds to kill for their masters – but enthusiasts have to import most of their hunters from Asia or the Middle East.

Although peregrines occasionally nest on the ledges of high city buildings, their favourite site is a coastal cliff. The eggs take a month to hatch and the chicks fly in five or six weeks.

LARGE BIRDS OF PREY IN FLIGHT

If any group of birds warrants the description 'majestic' it is the larger birds of prey: the eagles, buzzards, kites, larger hawks and vultures. Though varying considerably in their size, shape and hunting techniques, all are masters of the air, and a sight of any of them adds excitement to a birdwatcher's day.

Birds of prey feed mostly on animals, and they have powerful feet and talons with which to seize their prey and carry it off to their nests or other feeding places. There they use their powerful, hooked bills to tear the flesh apart. The forward-looking eyes of a bird of prey give it binocular vision like man's, enabling it to judge distance accurately and pinpoint its prey exactly. Its vision is in many ways greatly superior to that of man, enabling it to spot distant fine detail or movement.

Long, broad, rounded wings are characteristic of the larger birds of prey. The flight feathers at the tips of the wings are 'slotted', or spread like fingers. This feature permits low-speed soaring without the danger of stalling; the feathers are tapered to produce the slotted effect.

Contrasts in size, shape and colour

Most larger birds of prey are seen only as they soar overhead at a great height, borne up by thermals, or rising currents of hot air. Circling in a column of air, the bird can gain height rapidly until it becomes little more than a speck in the sky. When it decides to move off it simply closes its wings and tail and goes into a shallow dive. In this way a bird of prey can cover vast distances with little expenditure of energy.

Because they so often soar high above the ground, the most practical way of distinguishing one species from another is from the features visible from below. These include its overall silhouette; the length, breadth and shape of its wings and tail and their relative proportions; the size of its head and the extent to which head and neck project in front of the wings; the number and thickness of any bars of dark and light colouring on the tail; barring across or streaking along the body; and the pattern of dark and light on the wings.

Apart from its overall shape and colour, each species has characteristics of flight and behaviour which distinguish it from other species. Its flight may be easy and buoyant, or heavy and laboured. It may hold out its wings above, horizontal with or below the level of the body. It may catch its prey by a high-speed chase, by a rapid pounce or by plunging into the water.

Long wings

Entirely dark below

Head pointed and prominent

White on base of tail

White wing-patches

Golden eagle
Aquila chrysaetos
Immature
Page 90

Golden eagle
Aquila chrysaetos
Adult: wing-span
75–90 in.
(190–230 cm).
Page 90

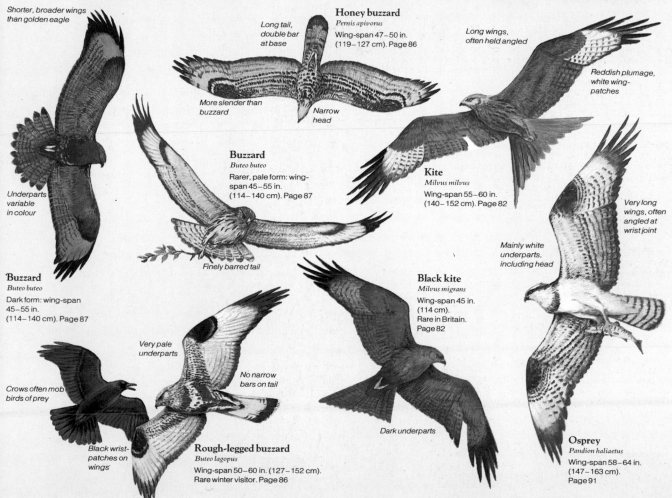

Shorter, broader wings than golden eagle

Honey buzzard
Pernis apivorus
Wing-span 47–50 in.
(119–127 cm). Page 86

Long tail, double bar at base

More slender than buzzard

Narrow head

Long wings, often held angled

Reddish plumage, white wing-patches

Underparts variable in colour

Buzzard
Buteo buteo
Rarer, pale form: wing-span 45–55 in.
(114–140 cm). Page 87

Kite
Milvus milvus
Wing-span 55–60 in.
(140–152 cm). Page 82

Very long wings, often angled at wrist joint

Mainly white underparts, including head

Finely barred tail

Buzzard
Buteo buteo
Dark form: wing-span 45–55 in.
(114–140 cm). Page 87

Black kite
Milvus migrans
Wing-span 45 in.
(114 cm).
Rare in Britain.
Page 82

Very pale underparts

No narrow bars on tail

Crows often mob birds of prey

Black wrist-patches on wings

Rough-legged buzzard
Buteo lagopus
Wing-span 50–60 in. (127–152 cm).
Rare winter visitor. Page 86

Dark underparts

Osprey
Pandion haliaetus
Wing-span 58–64 in.
(147–163 cm).
Page 91

SMALL BIRDS OF PREY IN FLIGHT

Although the smaller birds of prey lack the sheer bulk and power of the larger species, they share the same features of a sharp, hooked bill, long needle-sharp claws on powerful toes, and fierce-looking eyes that face forward to give binocular vision. Their dominance over other bird species gives them an air of majesty which has probably encouraged royalty and noblemen through the ages to pursue the sport of falconry. The birds' imperious qualities were appropriate to their owners' position in life, and lent rulers added nobility in the eyes of their subjects.

The smaller birds of prey fall into two distinct groups or families, the hawks and the falcons. The hawks are members of the same family as the larger birds of prey – the eagles, buzzards and their relatives – but the falcons are grouped in a family of their own. Hawks have short, rounded wings, quite different from the falcons' longer, tapered, sharply pointed wings.

Wings shaped for different habitats

Difference in wing shape is linked to the habitats in which the birds live and to their modes of hunting. Hawks such as the goshawk and sparrowhawk are birds of woodland or countryside with scattered trees; here, long wings would be a disadvantage when darting and manoeuvring between tree trunks and interlacing branches. Within the hawk family, the goshawk can be half as big again as the sparrowhawk and the female is generally larger than the male, but it is not always easy to judge size at a distance. Features such as dark barring of plumage and relative length of tail may then be clues.

Falcons are mainly birds of open country, with long wings designed for high-speed flight and quick acceleration, though some also have the manoeuvrability of the hawks. Habitat, hunting technique and silhouette all help the observer to distinguish between the different falcons. Among the clues are the kestrel's persistent hovering; the merlin's moorland habitat and dashing low-level flight; the hobby's swift-like silhouette, speed and agility; and the peregrine's size, heavy build, short tail and rarely witnessed, breathtaking 'stoop' or dive on to its prey.

Colour and pattern of plumage may also be visible, though immature birds and females often have less striking plumages than adult males. The adult male kestrel is the only British species with a rich reddish-brown back and wings, and a slate-grey tail with a single dark bar near its tip; while the adult hobby has reddish thighs and a streaked breast.

Short wings

Barred underparts

Long tail

Red-brown barred underparts

Sparrowhawk
Accipiter nisus
Adult male: wing-span 24–27 in. (60–68 cm).
Page 89

Sparrowhawk
Accipiter nisus
Adult female: wing-span 28–31 in. (70–79 cm).
Page 89

Long pointed wings

Grey tail with black band at tip

Kestrel
Falco tinnunculus
Adult male: wing-span 28–31 in. (70–79 cm).
Page 92

Kestrel
Falco tinnunculus
Adult female: wing-span 24–27 in. (60–68 cm).
Page 92

Long tail, barred with brown, fanned out while hovering

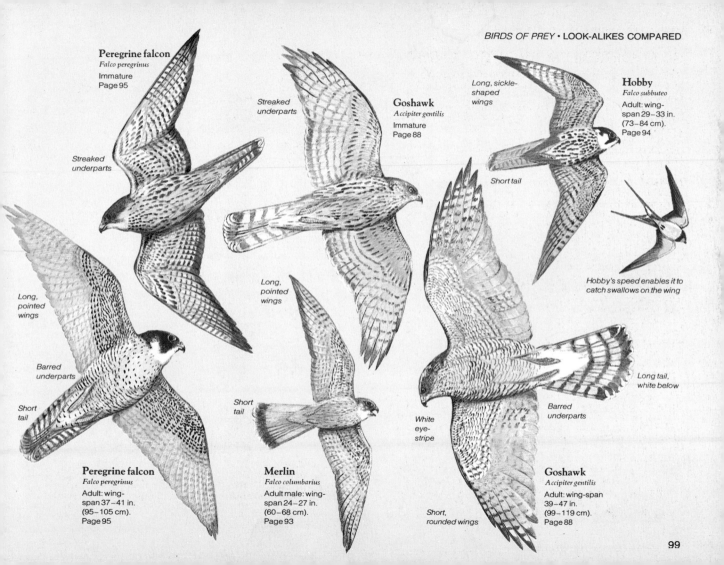

Peregrine falcon
Falco peregrinus
Immature
Page 95

Streaked
underparts

Goshawk
Accipiter gentilis
Immature
Page 88

Long, sickle-
shaped
wings

Hobby
Falco subbuteo
Adult: wing-
span 29–33 in.
(73–84 cm).
Page 94

Streaked
underparts

Short tail

Long,
pointed
wings

*Hobby's speed enables it to
catch swallows on the wing*

Long,
pointed
wings

Barred
underparts

Long,
pointed
wings

Short
tail

Short
tail

Long tail,
white below

White
eye-
stripe

Barred
underparts

Peregrine falcon
Falco peregrinus
Adult: wing-
span 37–41 in.
(95–105 cm).
Page 95

Merlin
Falco columbarius
Adult male: wing-
span 24–27 in.
(60–68 cm).
Page 93

Short,
rounded wings

Goshawk
Accipiter gentilis
Adult: wing-span
39–47 in.
(99–119 cm).
Page 88

In display flight, male springs straight up, then glides down crowing loudly, flapping wings before landing.

Red wattles

Dark wings, body

Seen in flight, bird lacks wing-bar of black grouse.

Adult male has dark reddish-brown plumage, except for red eye-wattles and white legs. 15 in. (38 cm).

Adult female is smaller and paler than male; chicks more deeply coloured than ptarmigan.

Present all year; stays within breeding range.

The nest is a shallow hollow scraped by the female, well concealed among the heather or other moorland vegetation.

Red grouse *Lagopus lagopus*

Exploding into chattering flight out of the moorland heather almost beneath one's feet, a plump and handsome red grouse is an exhilarating sight. A different sighting of the red grouse is that eagerly awaited by the hunter as beaters drive birds towards the waiting guns on August's 'Glorious Twelfth', when the grouse-shooting season opens. Stocks are maintained by managed breeding, and the systematic burning of patches of heather ensures new growth in the variety of stages that the birds need: mature vegetation for cover, young heather shoots for food and clearings where chicks can sun themselves.

The red grouse, with its 'qurrack-rack-rack' bark of an alarm call and the male's 'go-back, go-back' challenge to rivals, used to be considered an exclusively British species. Today it is classified as a 'race' – a slightly different subspecies – of the willow grouse of Europe, Asia and North America.

Six to a dozen eggs are laid in a sparsely lined ground depression, sheltered by heather or a tussock of grass. The eggs, basically creamy but thickly speckled and blotched with dark brown, hatch after three to three and a half weeks. The chicks quickly leave the nest to feed and can fly in less than two weeks.

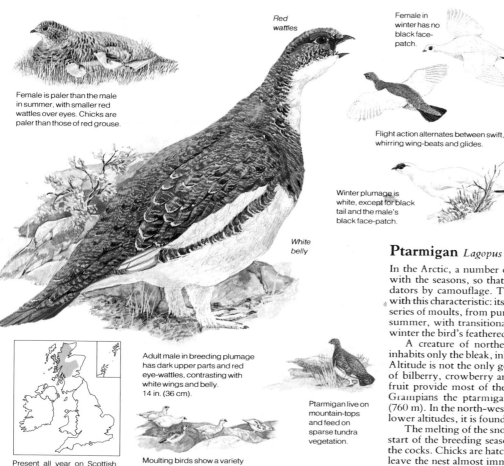

Female is paler than the male in summer, with smaller red wattles over eyes. Chicks are paler than those of red grouse.

Red wattles

Female in winter has no black face-patch.

Flight action alternates between swift, whirring wing-beats and glides.

Winter plumage is white, except for black tail and the male's black face-patch.

White belly

Adult male in breeding plumage has dark upper parts and red eye-wattles, contrasting with white wings and belly. 14 in. (36 cm).

Present all year on Scottish mountain-tops.

Moulting birds show a variety of plumages in the autumn.

Ptarmigan live on mountain-tops and feed on sparse tundra vegetation.

On the barren slopes of its Scottish mountain home, the ptarmigan may let skiers or climbers approach closely.

Ptarmigan *Lagopus mutus*

In the Arctic, a number of birds and mammals change colour with the seasons, so that they are always protected from predators by camouflage. The ptarmigan is the only British bird with this characteristic: its colouring changes through a complex series of moults, from pure white in winter to mottled brown in summer, with transitional stages in the spring and autumn. In winter the bird's feathered feet act as 'snow-shoes'.

A creature of northern climes, the ptarmigan in Britain inhabits only the bleak, inhospitable tops of Scottish mountains. Altitude is not the only governing factor, but also the presence of bilberry, crowberry and heather, whose shoots, leaves and fruit provide most of the bird's food. In the Cairngorms and Grampians the ptarmigan occurs only above about 2,500 ft (760 m). In the north-west of Scotland, where its food grows at lower altitudes, it is found at 500–1,000 ft (150–300 m).

The melting of the snow late in May or early June brings the start of the breeding season and territorial skirmishes between the cocks. Chicks are hatched after three and a half weeks. They leave the nest almost immediately and can fly within ten days, but many are killed by late snowstorms or cold snaps.

Adult male's tail shape and white wing-bar are distinctive in flight.

As immature males moult, their plumage gradually changes from brown to black.

Female in flight is distinguishable from red grouse by notched tail.

Adult males perform communal courtship displays before the female birds. The birds are polygamous.

Lyre-shaped tail

Red wattles

Adult male's black plumage, red head wattles and lyre-shaped tail make it immediately recognisable. 21 in. (53 cm)

Adult female is smaller than male. Her brown-barred plumage is more like that of the red grouse, but it is greyer and the tail is forked.

Present all year; recently extinct in south-west England.

Chicks are tended by the female alone. She leads them out morning and evening to feed on shoots, buds and seeds.

Young grouse have a mottled, reddish-buff crown and upper parts. The nest is scraped in the ground by the mother bird.

Black grouse *Lyrurus tetrix*

In the mating season, male and female black grouse gather early in the morning for a communal courtship display known as a 'lek'. The same site may be used for the display over many years. Each male holds a small area within the site, on which he stands with tail fanned and erect, wings spread and drooped. He faces a rival male and utters a prolonged, bubbling, cooing sound which is occasionally interrupted by a loud, scraping 'tcheway'.

The cock birds adopt threatening postures and frequently jump into the air. During this display, the sombre-plumaged females strut nonchalantly between the males. For most of the time, the aggression is ritualised. But sometimes full-blooded fights take place in which beaks, wings and breasts are used. After a cock bird has vanquished its rival it will turn and take on another bird. Eventually, a female may invite mating by crouching before the victorious male – which circles in front of the hen with its neck and head outstretched.

The nest of the black grouse is well hidden in grass or heather, and six to ten eggs are usually laid. The newly hatched chicks start to grow their flight feathers within three or four days, and can fly well within a month.

In flight, rounded tail distinguishes both male and female from black grouse.

Bushy throat feathers

Adult male makes short display flights during the breeding season.

Adult female resembles female black grouse but is larger – 24 in. (60 cm) – with a chestnut breast. A submissive posture is adopted in courtship.

The capercaillie nests on the ground, often between roots of a tree. Chicks can fly a little by about three weeks old.

Adult male is distinguishable from other game birds by its large size, dark colouring and bushy throat feathers. Its display posture is accompanied by a characteristic gurgling song. 34 in. (86 cm).

Present all year; derived from 1830s re-introduction.

Comb-like projections beneath the toes may help the bird to walk on snow.

Displaying males are very aggressive and may threaten deer, sheep or even humans.

Capercaillie *Tetrao urogallus*

Although the capercaillie was fairly widespread in Scotland and Ireland up to the beginning of the 18th century, it had virtually been exterminated by the 1750s. This was the result of the wholesale clearance of the pine forests in which it lived, and of excessive shooting. In Scotland, the last individual birds were shot in Aberdeenshire in 1785.

It was not until 1837, when a long series of re-introductions started from Sweden, that the species was re-established throughout most of the eastern highlands of central Scotland – especially in the river valleys of the Dee, Don, Spey and Tay. Attempts at introductions into England, and re-introductions into Ireland, have not been successful.

Like the black grouse, the male capercaillie is noted for its flamboyant and aggressive courtship display and extraordinary vocal accompaniment. The call starts with a slow series of clicks which gradually speed up into a rattle; this is quickly followed by a 'klop' rather like a cork being drawn from a bottle, and by a final rustling, hissing sound. The exact derivation of the bird's peculiar name is lost in antiquity; it may come from the Gaelic word *capullcoille*, which means 'horse of the woods'.

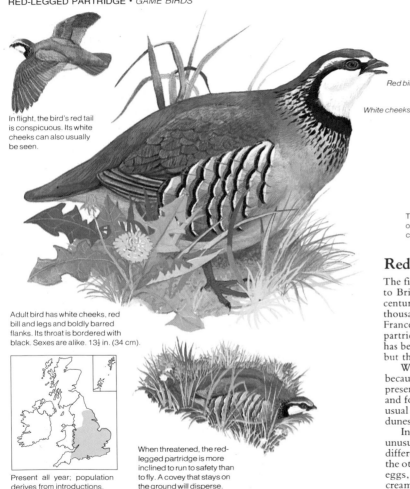

In flight, the bird's red tail is conspicuous. Its white cheeks can also usually be seen.

Red bill

White cheeks

Adult bird has white cheeks, red bill and legs and boldly barred flanks. Its throat is bordered with black. Sexes are alike. 13½ in. (34 cm).

Present all year; population derives from introductions.

When threatened, the red-legged partridge is more inclined to run to safety than to fly. A covey that stays on the ground will disperse.

The bird is fond of perching on a fence post or other convenient object.

The nest of the red-legged partridge is sparsely lined with dried grass. It is usually in long grass or under brambles.

Red-legged partridge *Alectoris rufa*

The first recorded attempt to introduce the red-legged partridge to Britain took place in 1673; but it was not until more than a century later that the species really became established. In 1790 thousands of chicks were reared from eggs imported from France, and the bird is still sometimes known as the French partridge. Recently, the closely related Chukar (*Alectoris chukar*) has been widely released. It interbreeds readily with the red-leg, but the hybrids breed less well in the wild.

When flushed, the bird often runs rather than flies, and because of this, some sportsmen complain that it does not present a good target for their guns. It tends to remain in cover, and for such a colourful bird, it blends remarkably well with its usual habitats, such as ploughed fields, heaths, downs, coastal dunes and open countryside.

In the breeding season, the red-legged partridge has the unusual habit of sometimes laying two clutches of eggs in different nests. One of these is incubated by the female bird, and the other by the male. Each clutch may consist of 10–20 or more eggs, which are laid at 36 hour intervals. The eggs are a pale, creamy-brown with a few reddish-brown speckles.

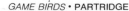

Coveys of birds disturbed
while feeding keep
together even in flight.

*Orange-
brown face*

In flight, the partridge's
red-brown tail is noticeable.

Adult male has distinctive
dark brown horseshoe
mark on lower breast. It has
a grey neck and breast,
and an orange-brown face.
12 in. (30 cm).

Horseshoe mark

A bird incubating its eggs in the well-
hidden nest may blend so well with its
surroundings as to be almost invisible.

Partridge *Perdix perdix*

The partridge is one of the most popular game birds, and
Britain's partridge population has frequently been boosted by
imports from the Continent, particularly from eastern Europe:
hence its alternative name of Hungarian partridge. It is also
known as the common or grey partridge, to distinguish it from
the French, or red-legged, partridge. Shooting starts early in
September, when the birds are gathered together in family
flocks, or coveys.

By February the surviving birds have paired off and the cock
birds spiritedly defend their territory against rivals. Courtship
often takes the form of a running chase, the cock and hen taking
it in turns to pursue each other. The nest is a hollow scrape in the
ground in suitable cover such as under a hedge, growing corn or
tall grass. From 10 to 20 eggs are laid, olive-brown in colour, but
partridges are prolific layers and two or more birds will often lay
eggs in one nest, so that clutches of up to 40 may occur.

The partridge's call is a grating 'karr-wick', repeated at
intervals. When startled they leap into the air with an explosive
'krikrikrik . . .', repeated rapidly at first but slowing down as the
birds escape from danger.

Present all year; has de-
creased in recent decades.

Female's markings are duller than
those of male, and lack clear mark on
underparts. Chicks are marked with
clear bands.

Dark green head

Red face

Some males have a white neck-ring, grey rump and paler flanks; others are dark green.

Though incapable of long-distance flight, pheasants can rise steeply and quickly when danger threatens.

Long, pointed tail

Pheasants forage in cultivated land for seeds and insects, but may also eat lizards, small snakes and mammals.

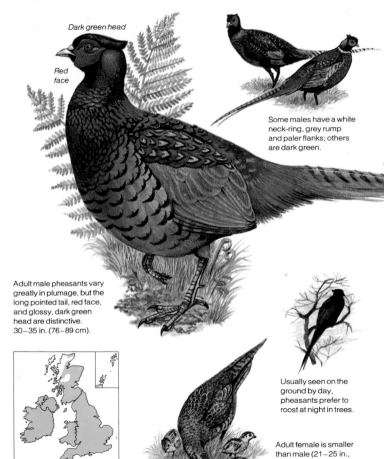

Adult male pheasants vary greatly in plumage, but the long pointed tail, red face, and glossy, dark green head are distinctive. 30–35 in. (76–89 cm).

Resident; breeds in heaths, hedges, reeds and woods.

Usually seen on the ground by day, pheasants prefer to roost at night in trees.

Adult female is smaller than male (21–25 in., 53–64 cm), mottled buff to blackish, and well camouflaged like the chicks.

Pheasant *Phasianus colchicus*

Though this colourful and handsome creature is Britain's most widespread game bird, it is not a native. The pheasant's natural home is in Asia, from the Caucasus eastwards to China. Its eating qualities were appreciated by the English in the early Middle Ages, when birds from the Caucasus were introduced. By the end of the 16th century they were common, and from late in the following century birds from China, distinguished by their white neck-rings, were being brought in.

In modern times, the large-scale rearing of pheasants in captivity for release to the wild has encouraged estate owners to maintain woods and copses on their land. This has brought some benefit to other forms of wildlife; on the other hand it has also led to the trapping and shooting of many species of mammals and birds which are regarded as special enemies of game birds, in spite of the protection given to them by the law.

For nesting, the pheasant favours almost any thick ground vegetation, though it prefers areas with trees as well. The nest, a shallow scrape in the ground, usually contains a clutch of 7–15 pale buff eggs. But the cock has several females in his 'harem', so a nest may contain more than one clutch.

Female

Male

Female

Male

Reeves's pheasant
Syrmaticus reevesi

Tail of male can be up to 66 in. (168 cm) long; male also has distinctive black and white head. Female has chestnut and buff face pattern. Male averages 84 in. (210 cm); female 30 in. (76 cm).

Silver pheasant
Gennaeus nycthemerus

The male's loud whistling call often betrays its presence. The male is identified by its black and white plumage; the female has a dark crest, pinkish skin round eyes, and a shorter tail than other pheasants. Male 47–49 in. (119–125 cm); female 27–28 in. (68–70 cm).

Male

Female

Male

Lady Amherst's pheasant
Chrysolophus amherstiae

The male of this shy species has a dark green head, crimson crest, white underparts, black and white barred tail. The female has blue-grey legs. Male 50–67 in. (127–170 cm); female 26–27 in. (66–68 cm).

Female

Male

Golden pheasant
Chrysolophus pictus

Retiring habits make this a difficult bird to spot in spite of the male's striking gold crown and crest and predominantly red plumage. Female has strongly barred wings. Male 40–43 in. (100–110 cm); female 25–26 in. (64–66 cm).

Ornamental pheasants

These pheasants were introduced into Britain from China and Burma, mainly to grace the parks and gardens of stately homes. Reeves's pheasant is an exception, for it was introduced as a sporting bird; but it proved to fly too high and fast for the guns.

All the introduced pheasants have bred in the wild, but the two most brightly coloured of the species, the golden pheasant and Lady Amherst's pheasant, are shy birds. Their presence is often detected only by the short, harsh call of the male or by a brief glimpse of a pair sprinting across a forest trail. The silver pheasant and the Reeves's are less furtive in their habits.

When flushed from cover, quail flies with whirring flight low over the ground for a short distance.

Streaked back

Mottled neck

Adult male, built like a small partridge, has streaked back and black-and-white pattern on throat and neck. 7 in. (18 cm).

Female   Male

Bobwhite quail

Colinus virginianus

This introduced species is larger – 9¼ in. (24 cm) – more boldly marked and less furtive in behaviour.

May–Oct. visitor; more widespread in some years.

Nest is well hidden in long grass or corn.

Female is drabber than the male, lacking strong throat and neck markings.

Young are rarely seen and have a pattern of stripes which helps them to lie concealed in grass.

Reluctant to fly, quail remain well hidden among tall vegetation and are seen only when flushed from meadows.

Quail *Coturnix coturnix*

In cornfields and hayfields in spring and early summer can sometimes be heard one of the most distinctive calls of any bird: the liquid, three-syllable 'whit-whit-whit' of the quail, sometimes rendered as 'wet-my-lips'. The bird seems to 'throw' its voice like a ventriloquist, for the sound apparently moves about as the bird turns its head. The quail resembles a tiny partridge, only 7 in. (18 cm) long, and is sometimes plentiful and at other times very scarce. Periods of plenty are known as 'quail years', but the reasons for the fluctuations are not fully understood.

Brood numbers also vary greatly, from 6 to 18 or more. The larger clutches are probably produced by two females – for the male quail is often a bigamist. Creamy coloured eggs, spotted or blotched with brown, are incubated for 18–21 days. The chicks, well camouflaged and rarely seen, leave the nest in a few hours and fly at 19 days old.

A larger relative, the North American bobwhite quail, has been introduced at intervals since the early 1800s. It does not migrate and is vulnerable to severe winters and wet springs. In recent years the only bobwhite breeding grounds were in Suffolk and the Isles of Scilly, but they have now died out.

The bird's grating call is uttered with head pointed up and wings drooped.

The nest is a pad of dead grass built on the ground among long grass or weeds. The female alone incubates the 8–12 eggs.

Apr.–Sept. visitor; numbers gradually decreasing.

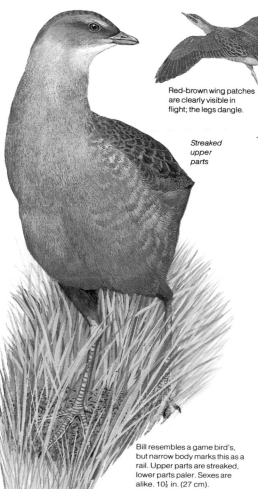

Streaked upper parts

Bill resembles a game bird's, but narrow body marks this as a rail. Upper parts are streaked, lower parts paler. Sexes are alike. 10½ in. (27 cm).

Red-brown wing patches are clearly visible in flight; the legs dangle.

During migration, flight appears stronger and legs are carried more horizontally.

Corncrake nests and young can survive only where unmechanised methods of reaping are used.

Corncrakes commonly build their nests in fields of grass left for hay or silage; only rarely do they nest in cornfields.

Corncrake *Crex crex*

Birdwatchers eager for a sight of this elusive bird sometimes notch a piece of wood or bone with a knife and draw a stick across it near a likely field of growing grass. The rasping sound produced is an acceptable imitation of the bird's distinctive and far-carrying rasping double call, 'aarr-aarr, aarr-aarr', repeated monotonously for long periods by day and night. A male bird that hears the imitation sometimes breaks cover in the belief that the sound comes from a rival male invading its territory.

Although fields of corn are sometimes used for breeding, the common name corncrake is less appropriate than the rarer alternative, landrail. Formerly it nested in large numbers throughout the British Isles, but it is now widespread only in Ireland and the Scottish islands and its range is still contracting in Britain and elsewhere in northern Europe. Mechanical hay-cutting has been blamed as part of the cause of the bird's decline, but it cannot be the only one.

Corncrakes' eggs are incubated mainly by the female. The blackish-brown chicks hatch after about 17 days, leave the nest in a few hours, and feed themselves after two or three days.

109

Flight is usually short and fluttering, with legs dangling.

Migrating flight is stronger, with legs extended.

Red bill

Juvenile colouring is duller, with black barring on breast.

Striped flanks

Adult male has strongly marked upper parts. The long red bill and striped flanks are distinctive in both sexes. 11 in. (28 cm).

Normally secretive, birds when migrating sometimes appear near towns.

Present all year, birds from Europe winter here.

Adult female has duller colouring than male on upper parts. Chicks are black, as with most rails.

The nest, concealed among reeds near a lake or river or on marshy ground, is built of dead stalks and leaves.

Water rail *Rallus aquaticus*

This elusive bird is heard much more often than it is seen. Its call, emanating from some dense bed of reeds or similar waterside thicket, sounds like a young pig squealing with fear. A glimpse, however, is enough to identify the water rail. Its long red bill and its slate-grey underparts, barred with black on the flanks, give it an appearance quite distinct from any other British bird.

The water rail's long legs and toes are adapted for walking on floating plants, and its unusually narrow body enables it to slip quickly between the close-growing stems of the vegetation among which it lives. This also means that it can travel to and from its nest in any direction, without leaving tell-tale tracks.

The nest is a bulky, untidy cup of dead leaves from sedges, reeds and other waterside species. It is concealed by pulling down reed stems to form a canopy. The 6–12 eggs, laid in April–July, have a creamy-white ground colour, with many small speckles and a few bigger blotches of bluish-grey and rusty-brown. They take about three weeks to hatch into jet-black, downy chicks. Two broods are usual. One parent guards the chicks while the other fetches food, until the chicks are independent at seven to eight weeks.

Fluttering flight, with dangling legs, is typical of rails.

Short bill

White spots

Birds have greenish legs, white spotted underparts. Female duller. 9 in. (23 cm).

A rare close-up view of one of the most elusive birds in the British Isles. It is not even known if it breeds here regularly.

When anxious, bird's tail is cocked up showing buff under-tail.

Although a good swimmer when necessary, the spotted crake rarely crosses large stretches of water.

Young bird has duller underparts, like the female.

Mostly non-breeding Apr.– Dec. visitor; a few nest.

Nests are usually sited on tussocks of sedge or grass.

Spotted crake *Porzana porzana*

This elusive bird was probably quite common in parts of the British Isles until extensive land drainage schemes were undertaken in the 18th and 19th centuries. The main evidence that it is still present in the dense, tangled vegetation of the remaining bogs and marshland is its distinctive calls, for it is rarely seen. The spotted crake's loudest identifying call is its 'hwitt hwitt hwitt', a single note repeated at short intervals which sounds like a small whip being cracked regularly.

What is known of the bird's breeding habits is based on scanty records. The nest is a thick, cup-shaped cluster of the leaves and stems of grasses and sedges, lined with finer material and placed on or near the ground. Clutches range from 6 to 15 eggs, but 8–12 seems most usual. The eggs are a greenish-buff in colour, marked with heavy speckles and blobs of grey and purplish-brown.

Parental duties are shared at all stages from building the nest to caring for the young until they are independent. The chicks, which leave the nest soon after hatching, are balls of blackish down, moving around on disproportionately large legs and feet. They fly after about seven and a half weeks.

111

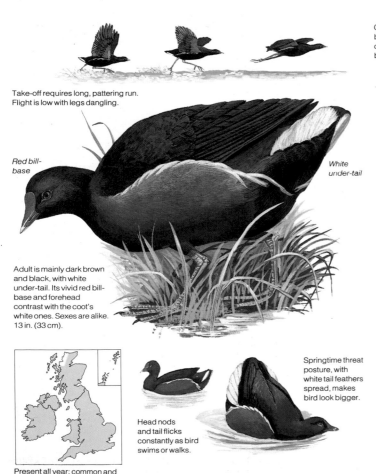

Take-off requires long, pattering run. Flight is low with legs dangling.

Red bill-base

White under-tail

Adult is mainly dark brown and black, with white under-tail. Its vivid red bill-base and forehead contrast with the coot's white ones. Sexes are alike. 13 in. (33 cm).

Head nods and tail flicks constantly as bird swims or walks.

Springtime threat posture, with white tail feathers spread, makes bird look bigger.

Chicks have bare blue crown and black down.

Juvenile is dull brown and pale-faced; tail pattern differs from coot's.

The nest is a platform of dried water plants built among waterside vegetation, usually ashore but sometimes floating.

Moorhen *Gallinula chloropus*

In spite of its name, the moorhen is not a moorland bird; 'moor' comes from the Anglo-Saxon word *mor*, meaning mere or bog. The 16th-century naturalist William Turner called the bird 'mot-hen' because the species frequented 'moats which surround the houses of the great'. In fact, moorhens can be found on almost any stretch of fresh water.

The moorhen's food consists of water plants and their fruits and seeds, insects, spiders, worms and other invertebrates. Like the coot, the moorhen is aggressive in defence of its territory, and boundary disputes often lead to exchanges of blows with bill and feet. The moorhen's toes are particularly long, spreading its weight so that it can walk on floating water plants. There is no webbing between the toes, and perhaps because of this, the moorhen's swimming action seems laboured, the head jerking forward with each stroke like a cyclist toiling uphill. The bird swims readily under water, and when very alarmed stays submerged and motionless with only its bill above the surface.

One bird's clutch of eggs is likely to number five to ten, buff in colour with fine reddish-brown speckles. A nest may contain up to 20 eggs, laid by more than one female.

White bill, forehead

Males fight frequently and fiercely when claiming territory.

Juvenile is greyer than young moorhen, with pale throat and breast.

The large nest of reeds is often raised above the level of the water, with a ramp leading from the top to the water.

Breeding birds often chase away other species.

Lobed toes

Long legs trail in flight after pattering take-off.

Present all year; visitors join winter flocks.

Adult has white bill and frontal shield, contrasting with slate-black plumage. Lobed toes help swimming and diving. Sexes are alike. 15 in. (38 cm).

Feeding bird jump-dives with a splash, popping up again at same spot.

Chicks have brightly coloured bare heads.

Coot *Fulica atra*

A glimpse of this bird explains the origin of the expression 'as bald as a coot'. In striking contrast to their black plumage, both sexes have an area of bare skin on their foreheads called a frontal shield, matching their glistening white bills.

Males squabble frequently over territory, and the shield plays an important part in their aggressive displays. It is held forward, low on the water, with wings and body feathers fluffed up behind to give as menacing an impression as possible. As the two birds approach one another the coot's harsh, unmusical call – rather like a hammer striking a sheet of metal – rings out.

The coot benefits greatly from booms in the building industry, which demand enormous amounts of sand and gravel for making concrete. The quarrying of these materials usually leaves behind flooded pits which provide excellent homes for many British water birds. In winter, the bigger expanses of water may attract large flocks of coots busily diving for the soft submerged plants that form the bulk of their diet. After a dive, the bird, bobbing up like a cork, brings its food to the surface to eat. The eggs are similar to those of the moorhen, but have more and finer markings. Chicks are independent after eight weeks.

113

IDENTIFYING WADERS BY SIZE

Wading birds are confusing to the eye because they are often similar in shape – long-legged, long-necked and thin-billed. They do, however, differ in size, habitat and feeding habits. The waders shown are painted to scale, in their summer plumage.

Among the larger waders, the biggest of all is the curlew, about the size of a mallard overall, but longer and more slender in all parts. Striding across mud-flats it probes deep with curved bill, but on upland grasslands it snatches insects from the surface. The tall black-tailed godwit may wade up to its belly to probe the underwater mud of estuary or coast with its long, straight bill; but it breeds in wet, grassy meadows. Brackish lagoons are the home of the avocet, which sweeps the water with upcurved bill in wide sideways movements to catch tiny creatures. The oystercatcher, stout and noisy, ranges widely from meadows and moors to sea-coasts, probing and digging with its strong orange bill.

Among the middle-sized birds, about as big as jays, are the nervously active redshank, delicately picking food from the surface of mud or water margin, and the slightly larger greenshank that feeds more vigorously, running through puddles with quick sideways movements of its bill. The knot is nearly as big, but stouter and more compact, and feeds in close-packed flocks on estuary mud-flats with a steady downward jabbing of bills. Two very long-billed waders avoid mud-flats: the woodcock keeps to marshy woodland, while the smaller snipe hides in the vegetation of marsh and water's edge.

How smaller waders feed and behave

Smaller waders include the dunlin, which is about two-thirds the size of the knot, similar in build, and also feeds in flocks on mud. In summer it seeks food on wet upland moors. There are three more or less dunlin-sized but more slender species: the common and green sandpipers are seen in summer on the edges of inland waters; and the rare grey phalarope is usually found swimming rather than wading.

The plovers are plump birds with a 'run-and-snatch' method of feeding. The dunlin-sized ringed plover lives on bare sand or gravel by water, while the bigger, pigeon-sized lapwing occupies meadows, fields and marshes; and the golden plover – a bird of similar size – breeds on high moorland and winters on coastal marshes. Smallest of all British waders is the sparrow-sized little stint, which runs about on muddy estuaries.

Curlew
Numenius arquata
The largest wader
22 in. (55 cm) Page 147

Mottled
upper parts

Down-
curved bill

Green sandpiper
Tringa ochropus
9 in. (23 cm)
Page 150

Green legs

Little stint
Calidris minuta
The smallest wader
5¼ in. (13·5 cm)
Page 130

Red-brown
and black back.

Dunlin
Calidris alpina
7 in. (18 cm)
Page 133

Black belly

Grey phalarope
Phalaropus fulicarius
8 in. (20 cm)
Page 153

Brick-red below

White underparts

Common sandpiper
Actitis hypoleucos
7¾ in. (19·5 cm)
Page 151

Dark
breast band

Ringed plover
Charadrius hiaticula
7½ in. (19 cm)
Page 121

Knot
Calidris canutus
10 in. (25 cm)
Page 128

Stout build

Long, straight bill

Orange bill

Black and white plumage

Black cap

Up-curved bill

Avocet
Recurvirosta avosetta
17 in. (43 cm)
Page 117

Oystercatcher
Haematopus ostralegus
17 in. (43 cm)
Page 116

Long crest

Black-tailed godwit
Limosa limosa
16 in. (40 cm)
Page 144

Pale head stripes

Lapwing
Vanellus vanellus
12 in. (30 cm)
Pages 124-5

Snipe
Gallinago gallinago
10½ in. (27 cm)
Page 138

Greenshank
Tringa nebularia
12 in. (30 cm)
Page 141

Grey upper parts

Orange-red legs

Russet plumage

Gold speckles

Redshank
Tringa totanus
11 in. (28 cm)
Page 142

Black belly

Woodcock
Scolopax rusticola
13½ in. (34 cm)
Page 140

Short legs

Greenish legs

Golden plover
Pluvialis apricaria
Northern form,
with more black
than southern form.
11 in. (28 cm)
Page 122

In flight, black tail-band, white rump, and broad white wing-bar are conspicuous.

Long orange bill

Juvenile

Adult

Adult in winter has white throat-patch. Juvenile bird has thin white line at throat, and blackish bill tip.

Adult in summer breeding season. Pied plumage and long, heavy orange bill are unlike those of any other wader. Sexes are alike. 17 in. (43 cm).

The oystercatcher opens mussels that are slightly agape by stabbing its bill through the linking muscle. It hammers a hole in the shell of a closed mussel.

Present all year; mainly coastal, but some nest inland.

Oystercatcher chicks can leave the nest within a few hours of hatching and become independent within five weeks.

Oystercatcher *Haematopus ostralegus*

With its immaculate black and white plumage, orange chisel-like bill and pink legs, the oystercatcher is one of the most handsome of British shorebirds. From late summer through to spring, wintering flocks grace our sandy shores wherever food is plentiful in the form of cockles, mussels, limpets, small crabs, shrimps and worms. But the oystercatcher's feeding habits are considered by some to be damaging to shellfisheries, and limited shooting of the birds is permitted in certain areas.

Breeding takes place after the flocks have broken up, in mid-April in the south and May or June further north. The courtship display is one of the noisiest of any British bird and has been called the 'piping' display. It usually consists of several birds walking around agitatedly, uttering a shrill chorus of 'kleep-kleep-kleep'. In flight, the note is a shorter 'pic-pic'.

Usually one brood is produced each year. Two to four sandy or buff-coloured eggs with bold blotches, fine speckles and streaks of blackish-brown are laid in a shallow depression scraped in the sand or shingle, sometimes sparsely lined with plant fragments, tiny pebbles or rabbit droppings. The eggs are incubated for three and a half to four weeks by both sexes.

In flight, wings show a striking black and white pattern.

Black cap

Upturned bill

Adult bird's white plumage with black cap and wing markings, blue-grey legs and long, upturned bill distinguish it from all other waders. Sexes are alike. 17 in. (43 cm).

The female shelters the eggs with outstretched wings.

Blue-grey legs

In juvenile bird, the black parts have a brownish tinge.

Their sharply contrasting plumage makes even juvenile avocets conspicuous. Birds often rest on one leg.

Avocets swim readily, and often 'up-end' to feed.

Present all year; breeds mainly in East Anglia

Group circle displays are a ritualised form of aggression between pairs of birds.

Avocet *Recurvirostra avosetta*

In recent decades this striking black-and-white bird has re-established itself in Britain. It once bred widely in eastern England but died out in the 19th century. During the Second World War, coastal farmland in Suffolk was flooded as a defence measure and avocets returned to the new pools. They flourished and now thrive in protected colonies from Yorkshire to Kent.

Avocets feed on tiny invertebrates which they strain from the water with sweeping movements of their curving bills. They are quite noisy birds, with a clear, piping call of 'klewit' which they repeat rapidly when excited. When their breeding territory is invaded a call of 'cccrrreewer' or 'kweet kweet' adds threat to their swooping attack on the trespassers.

An unusual feature of avocet behaviour is a ritual form of aggression known as 'grouping'. Pairs of birds gather in groups, often in a circle, with lowered heads. Each pair presses close together and confronts other pairs. Fighting sometimes occurs, but the display involves mainly posturing and threatening. Avocets nest in a hollow in open ground in April or May. The eggs, usually four, are buff blotched with black, and hatch after about three weeks.

117

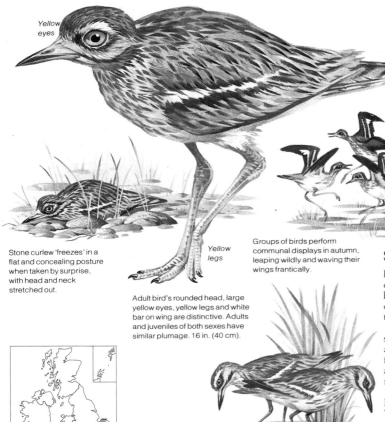

Yellow eyes

In flight, the adult bird's wings show a striking pattern of dark and light bars.

For their breeding grounds, stone curlews favour heaths, downs, stony or sandy areas and open farmland.

Stone curlew 'freezes' in a flat and concealing posture when taken by surprise, with head and neck stretched out.

Yellow legs

Groups of birds perform communal displays in autumn, leaping wildly and waving their wings frantically.

Adult bird's rounded head, large yellow eyes, yellow legs and white bar on wing are distinctive. Adults and juveniles of both sexes have similar plumage. 16 in. (40 cm).

Mar.–Oct. visitor; rare outside breeding areas.

Courting birds perform a stately ritual, facing in opposite directions, with bills pointed downwards.

Stone curlew *Burhinus oedicnemus*

Fluty, wailing and somewhat plaintive, the cry of the stone curlew hangs hauntingly over the chalky downs and sandy heaths of south and east England. The bird owes its name to that call and to its breeding ground; for its 'coooeee' resembles that of the curlew, and it usually nests on stony ground.

Snails, slugs and a variety of insects are the main food of the stone curlew, although it occasionally swallows larger prey such as field-mice and frogs. One reason why the stone curlew favours open country is that it likes to be able to see danger approaching at a distance. Then it usually prefers to run away rather than to fly.

The nest is a shallow scrape on bare ground, at most slightly lined with tiny pebbles, plant oddments or rabbit droppings. The stone curlew arrives on the south coast from March onwards. Breeding begins in April or May, two or rarely three eggs being laid. They are creamy or yellowish-brown, speckled and streaked with brown and grey. Both sexes take turns to incubate the eggs, which hatch after about 26 days. The young are pale buff above and white below, with blackish streaks and speckles on the back, which provide good camouflage.

White breast-band

Adult female, summer

Adult female, summer

Adult, winter

In all plumages, birds in flight show white breast-band from below.

Adult males have duller plumage than females. They assume all parental duties.

The dotterel's nest is a scrape in the ground lined with moss and lichen. The male bird incubates the eggs.

Adult female has a plump body and a small head. Its chestnut underparts and white breast-band are distinctive. 8½ in. (22 cm).

Rare May–Oct. visitor; has bred in Wales.

Juveniles lack the adult's chestnut belly, and have pale-edged feathers on their upper parts.

Adult male uses distraction display to lure predator from the eggs or young birds. It flops to the ground as though its wings are broken.

Dotterel *Eudromias morinellus*

This charming, tame little wader breeds on barren mountain-tops in the north and west of Britain, though in the Arctic it occurs down to sea level and in Holland it has bred on farmland below sea level. Its tameness makes it easy to catch and, before protective legislation was introduced, persecution by humans wanting to eat it or use its feathers to make fishing lures reduced its population to a low level from which it has not completely recovered. The bird's strongholds have been invaded by holiday-makers, but it seems to be more than holding its own.

In the first half of May, as the snows melt above 2,500–3,000 ft (760–900 m), the nesting season gets under way with the making of a shallow scrape in the ground. After laying, the female usually loses almost all interest in her offspring, the male incubating the eggs and, after they hatch, undertaking almost all parental duties.

Dotterels feed mainly on insects such as beetles and flies, but also eat spiders, small snails, earthworms and seeds. When the young are grown, dotterels begin their migration. Small flocks often follow the same routes each year, even turning up each spring in exactly the same group of fields.

White line

Yellow eye-ring

In flight the wings are plain, lacking the white bar of the ringed plover.

Juvenile bird has incomplete black breast-band and mainly brown head, but shows the adult's yellow eye-ring.

In its threat display, the bird exaggerates its size by fluffing out its feathers.

Its smaller size, slimmer build, yellow eye-ring and white line on forehead distinguish adult bird from the ringed plover. The bill is mainly dark. Sexes are alike. 6 in. (15 cm).

Apr.–Sept. visitor; breeds mainly at gravel pits.

Courtship displays include the male's 'umbrella' posture, and a ritual in which the female passes under the male's outspread tail.

The well-camouflaged, downy chicks are slightly browner than those of the ringed plover. Both parents tend them.

Little ringed plover *Charadrius dubius*

Until shortly before the Second World War, the little ringed plover was very seldom seen in Britain, turning up only occasionally on migration. In 1938, a single pair nested at a reservoir at Tring in Hertfordshire. Six years later two more pairs arrived there, and another pair settled in Middlesex. Since that time, hundreds of pairs have made their homes in Britain.

The little ringed plover is attracted by the ideal nesting sites to be found in the wide expanses of shingle in river valleys and other sites adjoining fresh water. Since the end of the war, such places have become far more plentiful, for the expansion of the building industry has created numerous sand and gravel pits which provide waterside sand and shingle ridges. Most of the bird's food is made up of insects and their larvae, supplemented by large spiders, small molluscs and worms.

The bird's nest is a shallow scrape in the ground, lined with small stones or a little plant material. The nest is usually completely exposed, but the four eggs are well camouflaged: they are sandy, stone or buff-coloured, with a sprinkling of fine speckles, some larger and darker spots, and streaks of brown, black or purple. The chicks hatch after three to four weeks.

Juveniles have dull, incomplete breast-bands and pale legs.

Breeding birds deter intruders with threatening postures.

Birds seeking food 'patter' with their feet to make their prey reveal itself.

The white wing-bar shows up in flight.

Females will feign injury to lure predators away from eggs or young.

Black-tipped orange bill

Black breast-band

The nest is a hollow scraped in sand or shingle. The spread of holiday areas is diminishing breeding grounds.

Ringed plover *Charadrius hiaticula*

These handsome birds of sandy shores and shingle ridges have a seemingly vague, faintly comical manner of feeding. They can be seen walking energetically for a few paces, pausing as if lost in thought, then suddenly seizing food from the mud surface with a swift dip of their beaks, which is followed by another pause. When halted, they may indulge in 'foot pattering'. Their diet consists of small shellfish, worms, insects and some plants.

Eggs are laid from April to July, usually in fours, and are a pale stone-buff colour with grey or blackish-brown spots and blotches. Two, or very occasionally three, clutches may be laid in a season. Both parents sit on the eggs, which hatch in 23–26 days, and the chicks can run about as soon as they are dry. They are beautifully marked to merge with their background, and when danger threatens will lie motionless while a parent diverts attention by feigning injury such as a broken wing. Chicks are independent after about three and a half weeks.

Birds often collect in small flocks. In flight, as the flocks turn in unison, they alternately display their white underparts and brown upper parts. They have a clear, fluid 'poo-eep' call, and their song is a series of flute-like 'taweeoo, taweeoo' notes.

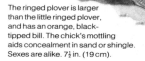

Present all year. Chiefly coastal; inland on passage.

The ringed plover is larger than the little ringed plover, and has an orange, black-tipped bill. The chick's mottling aids concealment in sand or shingle. Sexes are alike. 7½ in. (19 cm).

121

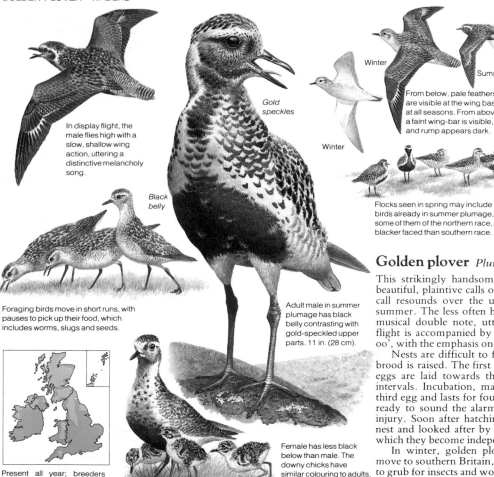

In display flight, the male flies high with a slow, shallow wing action, uttering a distinctive melancholy song.

Gold speckles

Black belly

Foraging birds move in short runs, with pauses to pick up their food, which includes worms, slugs and seeds.

Adult male in summer plumage has black belly contrasting with gold-speckled upper parts. 11 in. (28 cm).

Female has less black below than male. The downy chicks have similar colouring to adults, but show more white.

Present all year; breeders leave high moors in winter.

Winter

Summer

Winter

From below, pale feathers are visible at the wing base at all seasons. From above, a faint wing-bar is visible, and rump appears dark.

Flocks seen in spring may include birds already in summer plumage, some of them of the northern race, blacker faced than southern race.

The nest of the golden plover is a sparsely lined scrape on a bog hummock or grass tussock on moorland.

Golden plover *Pluvialis apricaria*

This strikingly handsome wader produces one of the most beautiful, plaintive calls of any British bird. Its flutey 'klew–ee' call resounds over the upland moors on which it breeds in summer. The less often heard full song is a longer but equally musical double note, uttered repeatedly, 'koo–roo'. Display flight is accompanied by a sad-sounding 'perr–ee-oo, perr–ee-oo', with the emphasis on the middle syllable.

Nests are difficult to find, and so are the chicks. Only one brood is raised. The first clutches of four, or sometimes three, eggs are laid towards the end of April at two to three-day intervals. Incubation, mainly by the female, begins after the third egg and lasts for four weeks. The male remains on guard, ready to sound the alarm and set up a diversion by feigning injury. Soon after hatching, the chicks are led away from the nest and looked after by both adults for about a month, after which they become independent.

In winter, golden plovers from Iceland and Scandinavia move to southern Britain, gathering on farmland in large flocks to grub for insects and worms. In severe weather they are much less inclined to seek food on the coast than the grey plovers.

In winter plumage, flying birds show a faint white wing-bar above, and prominent black spot at base of each wing below. In summer plumage, black underparts are visible.

Winter

Summer

Winter

Birds forage like golden plovers, often catching small crabs.

At high tide plovers at different stages of moult roost in flocks on sand bars or a short distance inland.

Grey plovers are often seen feeding in shallow water, particularly by the sea-shore and mud-flats.

Grey plumage

Adult in winter is mottled grey and white. Bill is heavier than golden plover's. Sexes alike. 11 in. (28 cm).

Winter visitor to estuaries; a few remain in summer.

Adult in summer; chequered black-and-white plumage appears from late spring.

The grey plover's hunched posture contrasts with the golden plover's sprightly, upright stance.

Grey plover *Pluvialis squatarola*

Two medium-sized birds with pale greyish upper parts, white underparts and dark grey legs are feeding near a coastal pool in winter. When disturbed they take off, call with a musical 'pee-oo-ee' and fly with strong, direct flight out over the salt-marsh. The conspicuous black axillaries, or 'arm-pits', remove any doubt that the birds are grey plovers.

Grey plovers breed in the high Arctic tundras of Canada and Russia, and it is only for the autumn and winter that most birds visit Britain, although a few non-breeding birds stay over summer. Usually they are seen in twos and threes or in small groups foraging along the seashore or on estuary mud-flats.

For most of their stay in Britain these birds are dressed in their drab grey winter plumage, but in their Arctic breeding grounds they assume a striking summer plumage in which the entire face, breast and belly are black. As with most waders, grey plovers lay eggs that contain a large reserve of food, permitting the young to hatch out well enough developed to leave the nest quickly. Such species are called nidifugous, unlike nidicolous species which are hatched helpless and remain in the nest for some time.

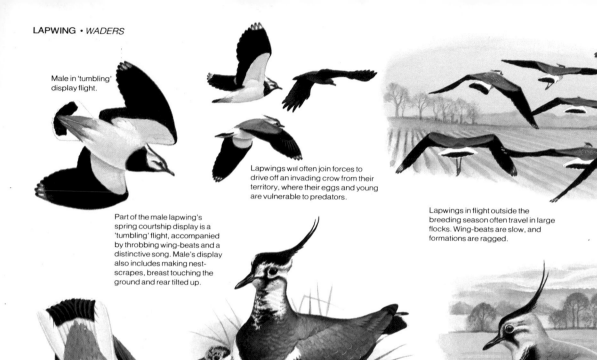

Male in 'tumbling' display flight.

Lapwings will often join forces to drive off an invading crow from their territory, where their eggs and young are vulnerable to predators.

Lapwings in flight outside the breeding season often travel in large flocks. Wing-beats are slow, and formations are ragged.

Part of the male lapwing's spring courtship display is a 'tumbling' flight, accompanied by throbbing wing-beats and a distinctive song. Male's display also includes making nest-scrapes, breast touching the ground and rear tilted up.

Female has more white on tail and throat.

Male making nest-scrape.

In winter, adult birds have white plumage on throat and upper breast. Plumage of birds in their first winter has a scaly appearance. During hard weather lapwings usually feed on farmland, though they are sometimes seen on seashore mud-flats. They feed in short runs alternating with pauses, during which they tilt forward to peck at food.

Adult male

Adult female

In flight, white underparts are conspicuous, and broad rounded wings are unlike those of any other wader.

Chestnut under-tail

Long crest

The lapwing's nest is a simple scrape in the earth, usually sited on slightly elevated ground and lined with grass. Eggs are well camouflaged against predators.

Present all year; in coldest winters most birds migrate.

Adult male in breeding plumage. Its long crest and striking plumage pattern of black, white and dark, iridescent green are very distinctive. 12 in. (30 cm).

Lapwing *Vanellus vanellus*

The male lapwing's territorial display flight is one of the most delightful sights of the countryside in spring. Rising from the ground on slowly beating wings it climbs steadily, then goes into a twisting, rolling dive which ends with an upwards twist and a flurry of rapid, buzzing wing-beats. The Anglo-Saxons used the word *hleapewince* – literally 'run' and 'wink' – to describe this twisting flight, and this is the origin of the bird's common name today.

The lapwing is one of the group of waders called plovers, and in some districts is known as the green plover because of its greenish, iridescent back plumage. Countrymen often know it as the 'peewit' call. At one time, lapwings were a common sight on ploughed fields and were welcomed by farmers because they devour many pests, especially leatherjackets and wireworms. But the use of insecticides and of farming machinery, which destroys nests, has driven them to meadows and marshes in summer.

In winter, lapwings gather in flocks, often of several hundreds, and move to warmer districts such as south-west England, Ireland or southern Europe.

125

Orange legs

In winter, upper parts are a dull black-brown and there is much less white on the head.

In summer, upper parts of adult bird appear tortoise-shell, while head is mainly white. Legs are orange, and bill is black. Sexes are alike. 9 in. (23 cm).

Mainly winter visitor; some non-breeders in summer.

Stones are turned over, and fine seaweed is rolled up with bill to locate food.

White head

In flight, the complex 'harlequin' pattern of black, white and brown in the turnstone's plumage shows clearly. It is unlike that of any other wader.

Rocks exposed at low tide are a common feeding ground for groups of turnstones, most numerous in autumn and spring.

Turnstone *Arenaria interpres*

This colourful black, white and chestnut wader quickly reveals the origin of its name as it walks across the sands and rocks at low tide in search of food. Not only stones but also seaweed, shells and driftwood are diligently lifted by its probing bill in the hope of finding sandhoppers and other small shore-life.

In Britain, the turnstone is a passage migrant in autumn and spring, on its way to and from its summer breeding grounds in the Arctic. It often winters in coastal areas, and some birds stay for the summer on the north-east coast of Scotland, though not to breed. Turnstones usually breed on islands, choosing rocky and stony ground for their nests which are no more than shallow scrapes in the ground lined with lichen, grasses and leaves. Three to five greenish eggs with blackish-brown spots are laid, and both parents share in the incubation. The eggs hatch after 22–23 days, and the chicks are able to feed themselves within a day. Young birds resemble winter adults, but are duller.

When feeding, the turnstone's back is an excellent camouflage against the background of stones and seaweed, but when disturbed it flies up showing its black-and-white wing pattern and emitting a twittering 'titititit'.

Seen from above in flight, adult in winter plumage shows dull whitish wing-bar.

Slate-grey above

Summer plumage is more variegated than winter, with some red-brown above.

The purple sandpiper is most commonly seen in northern Britain, searching for shellfish on offshore rocks.

Adult in winter plumage has slate-grey upper parts and breast, dull yellow legs, yellow base to bill and plump build. It feeds on shellfish found on seaweed-covered rocks; dog-whelks are a favourite food. Sexes are alike. 8¼ in. (21 cm).

Yellow legs

The purple sandpiper often swims for short distances; it frequently associates with the browner-coloured turnstones on rocky shores.

Mainly Sept.–May visitor to rocky coasts.

Purple sandpiper *Calidris maritima*

A purplish gloss on the plumage of its upper parts gives its name to the purple sandpiper, a passage migrant and a winter visitor to British coasts. It prefers rocky shores, but it is also seen on sand or shingle beaches. The pattern of its plumage makes it blend inconspicuously with beach boulders, but it is a tame bird that will also frequent the haunts of humans, such as harbours and weed-covered groynes and slipways, especially at high tide. If alarmed it will fly off silently, or with a low, piping cry.

This stockier relative of the dunlin feeds mainly on insects, crustaceans, spiders, molluscs and worms. It finds its prey by sight, rather than probing with its beak to find it by touch like some other waders. The bird's technique is to forage near the water's edge, advancing and retreating with the tide. It can be a remarkably fast feeder, sometimes picking up morsels of food at the rate of one every one or two seconds.

The purple sandpiper's principal breeding grounds – tundra, mountains and upland fells – are fairly close to Britain, in northern Scandinavia, the Faeroe Islands and Iceland. Indeed, since 1978, a few pairs are known to have nested annually on a Scottish mountain top.

127

Adult,
summer

In flight, the bird shows
a narrow white wing-
bar, and its rump
appears nearly white.

Adult,
winter

Grey above

Flocks in flight perform spectacular
co-ordinated evolutions, appearing
darker as upper parts show, then
silvery as they turn.

Adult bird in early autumn
has remains of brick-red
breeding plumage.

Adult in winter plumage:
a portly bird, with grey
upper parts, white underparts
and pale legs. Sexes are alike
10 in. (25 cm).

White
below

Pale
legs

Winter visitor to sandy
estuaries.

Juveniles have pale-edged
feathers on their upper parts.
Knots characteristically feed
in densely packed flocks.

Knots gather at their high-tide roosting
places on mud-banks, often with the
larger, longer-billed godwits.

Knot *Calidris canutus*

King Canute, the Viking who ruled England in the 11th century, is said to have been very fond of the wader known today as
the knot. The bird was later likened to a tiny Canute standing on
the shore and ordering the tide to go back as the monarch was
supposed to have done. According to a 17th-century work on
ornithology, Canute called the bird the 'knout'.

The 17th-century writer Sir Thomas Browne referred to the
bird as the 'knot', or 'gnatt', which could stem from the
similarity between a distant flock of knots and a swarm of gnats.
Less fancifully, the bird was probably named after its cry, a
low-pitched 'knut' – which, when uttered by a dense flock,
becomes a continuous low twitter. Another, mellower note is a
higher-pitched whistle-like 'twit-twit'.

Enormous numbers of knots pass through Britain in the
autumn and spring, and many of them winter on the west coast
of Africa. Some knots stay behind and provide one of the
winter's great bird spectacles – especially when they perform
their elaborate, group aerobatics. While on shore, they feed on
crustaceans, molluscs, worms and insects and roam rapidly over
the sand or mud, looking like dark, moving patches.

Adult, summer

Adult, winter

In flight, the sanderling is low, swift and direct. Both in winter and in summer plumage it displays a conspicuous white wing-bar.

Dark shoulder

Black legs

Adult sanderling in winter plumage is pale grey above, with dark shoulder mark. Legs are black. Sexes are alike. 8 in. (20 cm).

Plumage of young birds resembles winter garb of adults, but has a pinkish tinge.

Sanderlings usually feed in parties, sometimes mingling with other waders. They prefer sandy shores to mud.

Winter visitor to sandy coasts; a few inland on passage.

Adult bird in summer breeding season develops a chequered, reddish-black pattern on upper parts and breast.

Sanderling *Calidris alba*

With frenetic bursts of energy, flocks of sanderlings scurry along the seashore, their heads down in pursuit of retreating waves. They snatch a few morsels of food then race back in advance of the next wave to avoid getting washed off their feet. If disturbed they rise with a chorus of liquid 'twick, twick, twick' calls and move further along the beach to resume their feeding.

In winter, sanderlings can be seen on most sandy shores in Britain, but in the summer they are birds of the high Arctic where they breed. The nest is a neat and fairly deep cut, scraped in the ground near a clump of willow or other vegetation and lined with a deep layer of leaves. The usual clutch of eggs is four; coloured pale olive-green or sometimes brownish, with a sprinkling of fine, brown speckles and occasionally a few tiny black spots or streaks.

When danger threatens, one of the parents feigns injury, a common device among waders. The bird scuttles along the ground fluttering its wings as if they are broken, so distracting the predator from the nest. It flies up only if the predator approaches too close.

129

In juvenile, pale feather edges on back form two V-shaped marks.

Adult, winter

Narrow white wing-bar shows in flight. Outer tail feathers are grey, but hard to see.

Adult, summer

Mottled upper parts

Adult in breeding plumage. Upper parts mottled black and reddish-brown; legs black. Bill stouter than that of Temminck's stint. Sexes alike. 5¼ in. (13·5 cm).

Black legs

Aug.–Sept. passage migrant; may winter in Britain.

Adult in winter plumage is plain grey above. Underparts are whiter than in Temminck's stint. The breast is faintly streaked.

Little stints obtain their food on or near the surface of the mud, picking or probing for small shellfish and worms.

Little stint *Calidris minuta*

This little passage migrant is the smallest wader seen in Britain. From late summer to early November it passes through, between its breeding grounds in northern Russia and Siberia and its African wintering grounds, and inhabits inland lakes, marshes and sewage farms, and coastal sand and mud-flats.

Most little stints recorded in Britain in autumn are young birds, distinguished by two pronounced V-shapes on the back. The flocks perform aerial manoeuvres, twisting and turning in unison, showing first their upper parts and then their white underparts, the whole flock seeming to change colour. The diet consists of insects and their larvae, small shellfish, worms and some seeds. The call is a short 'chit, chit'.

A few adult birds in breeding plumage are sometimes seen in Britain, far from their breeding habitat in tundra or marsh. Towards the beginning of July a nest-scrape is made in a shallow depression in the ground and lined with dead leaves of plants like dwarf willow. Four eggs are usually laid; these are incubated chiefly by the male, which also takes the major share of caring for the young. The broods soon form into flocks, the young and old birds usually migrating separately.

In flight, adult in winter shows white outer tail feathers and narrow white wing-bar.

Slim dark bill

Birds in flight are less co-ordinated and more erratic in their movements than other waders.

The bird rises steeply and flies high on being flushed from cover.

The bird's call from its song perch on a rock near water is a short trilling 'ptirr', quite different from the little stint's call.

Adult in breeding plumage is plain greyish-brown above, with some red-brown feather edges. Bill is slim and dark, and legs olive or yellowish. Sexes are alike. 5½ in. (14 cm).

Yellow-green legs

Juvenile

Adult, winter

Rare passage migrant; has bred in north Scotland.

Adult is greyer, plainer in winter. Juveniles have pale feather edges.

Temminck's stint *Calidris temminckii*

Fewer than 100 Temminck's stints are recorded each year passing through Britain in autumn and spring on their way to and from their African winter quarters. It is therefore a much rarer visitor than the little stint, although some birds have bred in Scotland.

Temminck's stint is a greyer bird than the little stint and has more uniform, less mottled plumage. Unlike the little stint, Temminck's stint tends to rise steeply into the air on being flushed. It lives mainly on insects such as beetles and flies and their larvae and worms, which it usually gathers from the surface rather than by probing in the mud. Temminck's stint is much less prone to mix with other species than many other waders, including the little stint. Its call is a short, trilling 'ptirr'.

The breeding habitat of Temminck's stint is usually an inland or coastal area of low-lying ground near fresh water, with a low cover of grasses, sedges or scattered shrubs. The nest, a shallow hole in the ground, is built in late June and four eggs are laid. These are incubated for about three weeks, mainly by the male. The chicks are cared for by both birds, until the female loses interest and leaves the job to the male. The young birds become independent after two to two and a half weeks.

131

Unlike the dunlin, the curlew sandpiper tends to probe thoroughly in one area, then move on; thus tracks show clustered probe marks.

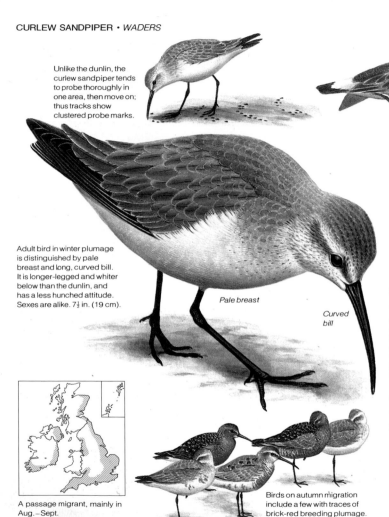

Adult bird in winter plumage is distinguished by pale breast and long, curved bill. It is longer-legged and whiter below than the dunlin, and has a less hunched attitude. Sexes are alike. 7½ in. (19 cm).

Pale breast

Curved bill

A passage migrant, mainly in Aug.–Sept.

Birds on autumn migration include a few with traces of brick-red breeding plumage.

In flight the white rump clearly distinguishes the bird from the dunlin.

The immature bird, with its pinkish-buff breast, is the curlew sandpiper most often seen in Britain in autumn.

Curlew sandpiper *Calidris ferruginea*

To a bird on migration, Britain represents a haven that provides resting sites, a supply of food and relative freedom from animal predators. So attractive are these islands that the curlew sandpiper, migrating from its breeding grounds high in Arctic Siberia to winter in equatorial and southern Africa, flies in a great half-circle to take in Britain on the way. It can be seen foraging on sand and mud-flats in creeks and marshes.

Most of the birds pass through the eastern side of the country as they travel southwards between late August and the end of September. At that time, the immature birds, with their pink-buff breasts, outnumber the adults. Much smaller numbers, however, pass through on their way northwards in the spring.

In flight the white rump of the curlew sandpiper distinguishes the species from the dunlin, with which it often associates; so does its call, which is less grating and more of a musical 'chirrup'. The bird's downward-curved bill resembles that of the much larger curlew, and gives the curlew sandpiper its name. With its bill it picks from the surface and probes in the mud for shrimps and sandhoppers, small molluscs, worms, insects and plant matter, such as tiny seeds.

Feeding birds leave a trail of probe marks, made with a rapid sewing-machine-like action of the beak while on the move.

At high tide, huge flocks fly along the shore, moving in unison and looking from a distance like clouds of smoke.

Winter plumage is brown-grey above, white below with darker breast. Juveniles are similar. Bill length varies but is usually shorter than in curlew sandpiper.

Red-brown and black back

Adult, winter

Adult, summer

In flight, at all seasons, wing shows white wing-bar; tail and rump dark with white edges.

In breeding plumage, adult's distinguishing features are black belly and red-brown and black back. Young are white below and brown and black above. Sexes are alike. 7 in. (18 cm).

Black belly

Present all year; mainly round coasts in winter.

Dunlin are the most abundant wintering waders to be found on British estuaries. They are augmented by passage birds.

Dunlin *Calidris alpina*

When crossing damp moors in the Pennines or upland Scotland, it is easy to overlook the unobtrusive dunlins that breed there in considerable numbers. Dunlins are never dense on the ground and tend to keep their distance, watching silently from afar.

A purring trill is often the first clue to the bird's presence. During its song the dunlin circles over its territory at heights of up to 200 ft (60 m), either gliding with wings partly raised, or else hovering, rising and falling as it does so. Sometimes several birds take part in aerial chases, darting rapidly about, and twisting and turning abruptly.

The dunlin's nest is a neat little cup, in a hollow in a grass tussock. Normally four eggs are laid, which vary in colour from pale greenish-blue to brown. The markings also vary, from tiny stipplings to heavy blotchings of chestnut or chocolate-brown. The eggs are incubated by both birds, and hatch after three weeks. In winter, dunlins often feed on coastal mud-flats, where they live on flies, molluscs, crustaceans and worms. With its head constantly bowed, the dunlin probes the mud with its bill for food. When it finds its prey it seizes and swallows it immediately, with little break in its insistent probing.

133

SMALL WADERS IN FLIGHT

The best way to identify these fast-flying and rather similar birds is by the presence or absence of white patterns and markings on their wings and rumps. Most species also have recognisable, short call-notes, which they constantly utter in flight. Other identification features are the flight patterns and habitats of the different groups.

For instance, although most small waders are found on shores and mud-flats, the snipe is an inland bird and is usually seen in marshy areas and on watersides. The common snipe is a long-billed bird that rises steeply in flight; it has some white on its outer tail feathers and its call is a harsh 'scarp'. The smaller jack snipe is a quieter bird, with a shorter flight.

Freshwater and coastal beaches

Three species of sandpiper are found beside fresh water, and of these, the common sandpiper tends to skim just above the surface. It has short, downward-flipping wing-beats and gives a shrill call of 'twee-wee-wee'. In contrast to this, the green and wood sandpipers rise steeply when disturbed; the green sandpiper has a sharp call of 'weet-a-weet', and the wood sandpiper utters a softer 'whit-whit-whit'. Another freshwater small wader is the tiny Temminck's stint which, when flushed, rises high with a startled, spluttering call. Plovers are short-billed birds with dark ear-patches and breast-bands. With its loud call of 'pee-oo', the little ringed plover occurs almost always beside fresh water. On the other hand, the ringed plover, with its musical 'thlu-i' call, mainly frequents coastal beaches.

Coastal waders tend to move in close, fast-manoeuvring flocks and are recognised by their calls. For example, the dunlin gives out a harsh 'treep'. The call of the longer-billed curlew sandpiper is a distinctive, liquid 'chirrip'; but the bird is usually first noticed by its white rump. A soft 'wee-whit' is the call of the purple sandpiper, which is usually seen on rocky shores. The turnstone is also found in rocky and pebbly places and its call is a rapid, staccato 'tuk-a-tuk'. But the small, plump sanderling prefers sandy regions and its flight call is a sharp 'twik'.

The remaining small waders are usually solitary visitors to shores or coastal marshes. Of these, the little stint is like a tiny version of the dunlin; but its call is a sharp 'chik', or a short trill. Both the phalaropes, grey and red-necked, have a soft 'twit' call-note, although that of the red-necked is more varied. In flight, the red-necked species is usually faster and more agile.

Turnstone
Arenaria interpres
Summer plumage
Page 126

Undersides of wings pale

Complex tortoiseshell pattern

Wood sandpiper
Tringa glareola
Page 150

White rump

Legs project beyond tail

Green sandpiper
Tringa ochropus
Page 150

Undersides of wings blackish

Bright white rump

Very pale plumage

Bold white wing-bar

Sanderling
Calidris alba
Winter plumage
Page 129

Long, straight bill

Pale stripes

Snipe
Gallinago gallinago
Page 138

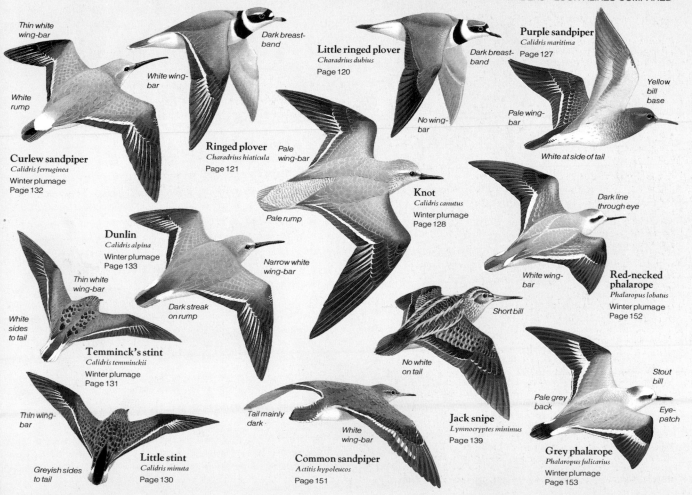

Thin white wing-bar

White rump

White wing-bar

Dark breast-band

Little ringed plover
Charadrius dubius
Page 120

No wing-bar

Dark breast-band

Purple sandpiper
Calidris maritima
Page 127

Yellow bill base

Pale wing-bar

White at side of tail

Curlew sandpiper
Calidris ferruginea
Winter plumage
Page 132

Ringed plover
Charadrius hiaticula
Page 121

Pale wing-bar

Pale rump

Knot
Calidris canutus
Winter plumage
Page 128

Dark line through eye

Dunlin
Calidris alpina
Winter plumage
Page 133

Narrow white wing-bar

Dark streak on rump

White wing-bar

Red-necked phalarope
Phalaropus lobatus
Winter plumage
Page 152

Thin white wing-bar

White sides to tail

Short bill

Temminck's stint
Calidris temminckii
Winter plumage
Page 131

No white on tail

Stout bill

Pale grey back

Eye-patch

Thin wing-bar

Tail mainly dark

White wing-bar

Jack snipe
Lymnocryptes minimus
Page 139

Greyish sides to tail

Little stint
Calidris minuta
Page 130

Common sandpiper
Actitis hypoleucos
Page 151

Grey phalarope
Phalaropus fulicarius
Winter plumage
Page 153

Satellite male

Wing-flashing display.

Satellite male

Dominant males on their communal display ground, or lek, perform bowing threat displays to one another: outsiders are warned off by wing flashing. White-ruffed satellite males may be tolerated.

Bowing threat

Appeasement posture by defeated bird.

Adult male, winter.

Adult male, summer.

Thickened neck of male in summer plumage shows in flight. All plumages show white wing-bar and white rump and tail patches.

Female

Male in winter.

Plumage of female, or reeve, is mottled buff; bill is pale, and legs yellowish, greenish or flesh-coloured. Plumage of male in winter is like that of female, though male bird is larger.

Ear-tufts

Ruff

Adult male in breeding display raises huge ruff and ear-tufts in varying colours, here black and reddish-brown. No two birds have an identical colour pattern. The bill is short, for a wader. 11½ in. (29 cm).

Present all year. Mainly autumn migrant; few breed.

Adult female

Even with its ruff lowered, a male in the breeding season is still easily recognised by its thick neck plumage and brighter colouring than female.

Ruff *Philomachus pugnax*

One of the most dramatic courtship displays of the bird world is that performed communally by male ruffs, on display grounds called 'leks'. Here the males gather to show off and fight in front of the females – called 'reeves' – and to defend the small patch of the lek that each has made its mating territory. The neck ruffs that they fluff out to intimidate one another, and that give the bird its name, can be plain black, red-brown, purple, white, creamy or buff, or else striped, barred or spotted. The females walk among the males and crouch to encourage them to mate.

In the breeding season the ruff is a bird of marshy grasslands, fens and flood meadows; at other times it also frequents lake margins, sewage farms and other inland waters, while on the coast it prefers muddy creeks in salt-marshes. Some birds winter in Africa. Because of the draining of its habitat and the activity of egg-collectors, the ruff had vanished from Britain by the end of the 19th century; but, helped by protection, a few have nested, albeit erratically, since the mid-1960s.

The nest is a shallow hollow in the ground, concealed in long grass or other vegetation not far from the lek. Four eggs are usual, greenish with small blackish or greenish-brown blotches.

137

Long
bill

When the bird dives,
air rushing over its tail
feathers makes a
bleating sound.

Adult bird is dark with contrasting
light stripes on the crown and back.
It has a very long straight bill. Its tail
is fringed with reddish-brown and
white. Sexes are alike. 10½ in. (27 cm).

When flushed, the snipe rises and
zigzags away with hoarse calls.

Snipe feed singly or in small groups, often
at the edges of pools or ditches; the birds'
diet consists largely of worms.

Snipe *Gallinago gallinago*

The most remarkable thing about the snipe is the length of its
bill, which is about a quarter of the bird's total length. The tip of
the bill is flexible and highly sensitive, and this enables the snipe
to detect and identify the worms and invertebrates on which it
mainly lives. But although it usually 'digs' for its food, it also
eats surface-living insects.

The snipe performs a spectacular courtship display. It climbs
on rapidly beating wings to heights of from fifty to several
hundred feet and then dives with its outer tail feathers spread.
The feathers vibrate in the airstream and give out a plaintive,
bleating sound. At the end of its shallow dive, the bird climbs
again and repeats the performance. When flushed, the snipe's
alarm call is a scraping 'scaaap', which it utters as it twists
alternately from left to right. The call in the spring is a hollow
'chippa–chippa–chippa'.

The snipe's nest is well hidden on the ground, and the clutch
is usually of four pale, greenish-brown eggs with grey and dark
brown blotches and speckles. The female incubates the eggs. At
first, both parents feed the young. But the chicks soon learn to
feed themselves and they can fly when about three weeks old.

Present all year; most numerous in winter.

Snipe nest in tussocks of
grass, rushes or other
marsh vegetation. The
chicks are dark with
white speckles.

The bird probes deep in the
mud of its marshy habitat for
much of its prey. Surface-
living insects are also eaten.

In flight, the shorter bill, rounder wings and lack of white in the tail distinguishes the jack snipe from the common snipe.

When flushed, the bird flies straighter than the snipe, and often drops back into cover after flying a short distance.

Jack snipe prefer to escape intruders by hiding among vegetation on the ground rather than by flying away.

Unstreaked crown

Adult bird is distinguished from the common snipe by its shorter bill and the dark, unstreaked crown. Sexes are alike. 7½ in. (19 cm).

Sept.–Apr. visitor; never in Britain in summer.

Jack snipe sometimes feed with the larger, slimmer common snipe.

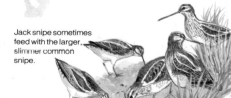

Jack snipe *Lymnocryptes minimus*

Our ancestors used the word 'jack' to denote something that was small or undersized. Hence, the jack snipe is smaller than its close relation the common snipe. Unlike the larger bird, it does not breed in the British Isles – although outside the breeding season its habitat is much the same as that of the common species. The jack snipe's nearest breeding grounds to Britain are the swamplands of northern Scandinavia.

Like the common snipe, the jack snipe probes in the mud for earthworms, molluscs and insect larvae. It has the peculiar habit of flexing its legs while feeding and so bobbing up and down. Generally, it is reluctant to fly; even when approached it takes to the air at the last moment and flies silently a short distance away before landing and resuming its feeding.

The jack snipe is far less sociable than the common snipe, and it is almost always seen singly. Even if several of the birds are flushed at the same time, they rarely gather in a flock or 'wisp'. The bird's display flight is a less flamboyant version of that of the common snipe, and its call in the mating season is a hard, reverberant 'lok-toggi . . . lok-toggi . . . lok-toggi', a sound that resembles tiny hoof-beats.

139

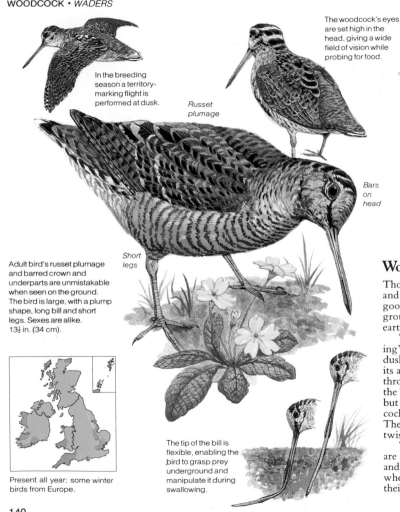

In the breeding season a territory-marking flight is performed at dusk.

Russet plumage

The woodcock's eyes are set high in the head, giving a wide field of vision while probing for food.

When flushed from cover, the woodcock takes to the air and swerves adroitly among the trees to evade enemies.

Bars on head

Short legs

Adult bird's russet plumage and barred crown and underparts are unmistakable when seen on the ground. The bird is large, with a plump shape, long bill and short legs. Sexes are alike. 13½ in. (34 cm).

Present all year; some winter birds from Europe.

The tip of the bill is flexible, enabling the bird to grasp prey underground and manipulate it during swallowing.

Blending with its surroundings, a parent woodcock tends its nest among the undergrowth of a forest floor.

Woodcock *Scolopax rusticola*

Though it is a wader, the woodcock has deserted open marshes and taken to damp woodland with open clearings and rides and a good growth of bracken and bramble. Woodcocks need soft ground in which to feed, probing with their long bills for earthworms, insects and their larvae, centipedes and spiders.

The territorial display flight of the woodcock, called 'roding', is very distinctive. The male bird flies over its territory at dusk, covering a wide area on slow-beating wings which belie its actual speed of flight. From time to time it utters two calls, a throaty 'og-og-og' with the bill closed and a 'chee-wick' with the bill open. The first call is barely audible except at close range, but the second carries for a considerable distance. The woodcock's escape flight, when flushed from cover, is very different. Then it moves rapidly among the trees with deftly executed twists and turns.

The nest is a leaf-lined scrape in the ground. The eggs, which are pale fawn speckled with brown and grey, take between 20 and 23 days to hatch. The chicks are tended by both parents, and when danger threatens the parent birds usually squat and rely on their natural camouflage to prevent discovery.

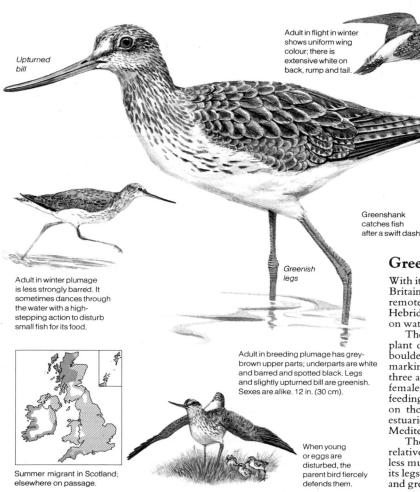

Upturned bill

Adult in flight in winter shows uniform wing colour; there is extensive white on back, rump and tail.

Greenshank catches fish after a swift dash.

Greenish legs

Adult in winter plumage is less strongly barred. It sometimes dances through the water with a high-stepping action to disturb small fish for its food.

Adult in breeding plumage has grey-brown upper parts; underparts are white and barred and spotted black. Legs and slightly upturned bill are greenish. Sexes are alike. 12 in. (30 cm).

When young or eggs are disturbed, the parent bird fiercely defends them.

Summer migrant in Scotland; elsewhere on passage.

Greenshanks nest in wild moorland, usually by a rock or piece of dead wood which is not too far from water.

Greenshank *Tringa nebularia*

With its long green legs and sleek body, the greenshank is one of Britain's most elegant waders. The species is a bird of wild, remote country, and breeds in the Scottish Highlands and the Hebrides. At dawn and dusk, greenshanks may be seen feeding on water insects on the shores of lochs.

The greenshank's nest is a hollow in the ground lined with plant debris, and is often close to some large object such as a boulder or dead branch. The eggs are creamy-coloured, with markings of dark brown or grey, and they hatch after about three and a half weeks. The chicks are generally brooded by the female for most of the first day; later, they are led to the nearest feeding area. Outside the breeding season the birds may turn up on the banks of rivers, and on marshes, sewage farms and estuaries. In winter they move south to the shores of the Mediterranean and beyond to south of the Sahara desert.

The call of the greenshank is similar to that of its close relative, the redshank, but it is a shorter call, more staccato and less musical – a ringing 'tew-tew-tew'. Apart from the colour of its legs, the greenshank differs from the redshank in being larger and greyer, and in lacking white wing-patches.

141

White wing-patches

Redshanks perform a characteristic 'alarm' flight when intruders threaten a nest or young in the area.

Young birds remain in dense marsh vegetation until old enough to fly. They are guarded by the mother.

Adult in breeding plumage has orange-red legs; in flight, large white wing-patch is conspicuous. Tail is barred black and white. Sexes are alike. 11 in. (28 cm).

Orange-red legs

Present all year; winters chiefly on coasts.

Adult winter plumage is less strongly streaked. Most food is obtained from estuary mud. When feeding, the bill tip just touches the surface.

Redshanks and dunlins frequently gather together on the tideline in winter to feed on small marine life such as shellfish.

Redshank *Tringa totanus*

Extreme alertness has earned the redshank the description of 'sentinel of the marsh'. A hysterical volley of harsh, piping notes sounds the alarm as soon as any intruder approaches. This piercing warning contrasts sharply with the bird's musical and liquid 'tew-ew-ew' call at other times.

During its display flight the redshank utters a fluting 'tee-woo-tee-woo-tee-woo' song or a long succession of 'teu, teu, teu' notes as it rises and falls on quivering wings. On alighting, the bird often leaves its wings stretched vertically over its back, displaying the white undersides. The redshank begins to breed from the middle of April onwards, nesting amongst the grass in a shallow, lined hollow in the ground. There it lays three or four darkly speckled, creamy eggs. Both adults incubate the eggs, which hatch after about three and a half weeks.

Redshanks inhabit a variety of grassy meadows, river meadows and marshes. When winter comes many move to the coast, especially to the salt-marshes where they often congregate in flocks many hundreds strong. The birds live off all sorts of invertebrates, some small fish and frogs, and a certain amount of seeds, buds and berries.

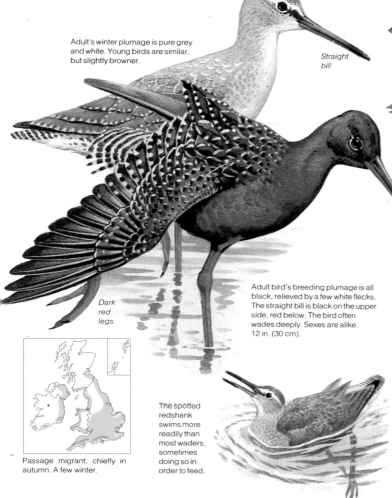

Adult's winter plumage is pure grey and white. Young birds are similar, but slightly browner.

Straight bill

Dark red legs

Adult bird's breeding plumage is all black, relieved by a few white flecks. The straight bill is black on the upper side, red below. The bird often wades deeply. Sexes are alike. 12 in. (30 cm).

Passage migrant, chiefly in autumn. A few winter.

The spotted redshank swims more readily than most waders, sometimes doing so in order to feed.

In flight, white rump and tail base are clearly seen.

Passage migrants in Britain may show plumages ranging from breeding plumage to winter colouring.

Spotted redshank *Tringa erythropus*

In winter it is easy to mistake the spotted redshank for the redshank at a distance. The birds have similar winter plumage, and the orange-red legs which give both species their name. The spotted redshank is, however, larger and usually greyer, with a longer bill and finely barred and speckled upper parts. It is not until the summer that the description of 'spotted' becomes appropriate; for then the bird wears black plumage, boldly spotted with white, which has earned it the alternative name of 'dusky redshank'.

Between April and mid-May and between mid-June and mid-October, spotted redshanks pass through south-east England. They are on their way to or from breeding grounds in the far north of Europe and winter quarters in central Africa.

Occasionally on coastal mud-flats and salt-marshes small parties of spotted redshanks can be seen mixing with other waders. Usually, however, the birds are seen in ones and twos around lakesides, freshwater marshes and sewage farms. In these watery haunts they live almost exclusively off animal matter such as water beetles and water-boatmen, small shellfish, worms, shrimps and small fish.

143

Adult in winter.

Adult in summer.

In flight, black and white tail and broad white wing-bar identify the bird in summer and winter.

Black tail

Adult in summer plumage. White under-tail coverts and black tail distinguish this bird from bar-tailed godwit in breeding season. Bill is straight; bird often wades deeply. Sexes are alike. 16 in. (40 cm).

Present all year. Some breed; most migrants or visitors.

Display postures of male during courtship include wing and tail spreading.

Adult bird in winter plumage. Upper parts are more uniform than in bar-tailed godwit, and legs are longer.

Straight bill

Black-tailed godwit prefers swampy inland grasslands as its breeding ground.

Flocks of black-tailed godwits are often seen in winter in estuaries on the south coast of England and Ireland.

Black-tailed godwit *Limosa limosa*

Along with the avocet and the ruff, the black-tailed godwit is one of the few species recently re-established in Britain as breeding birds. Until the beginning of the 19th century, the black-tailed godwit was widespread in East Anglia and parts of Yorkshire, but by 1830 it had almost disappeared because of extensive drainage and, probably, organised shoots and egg-collecting. In 1953 only four breeding pairs were recorded on the Ouse Washes. Thanks to the efforts of conservationists, the population had increased in the early 1970s to more than 60 pairs. At the same time, the winter migrant population rose to more than 4,000 birds; it now stands at more than 12,000.

Breeding males fly with rapid wing-beats to a height of about 200 ft (60 m), uttering a loud 'tur-ee-tur' that changes at the peak of the ascent to 'crrweetew . . . crrweetew'. At this point the wing-beats slow down and the bird twists from side to side before silently gliding downwards. It completes the display with a final steep dive, with wings almost closed, to the gound. The nest is in a hollow among thick grass; usually four light green eggs are laid, and both parents incubate them for about three weeks. The young fly at about one month old.

Flocks sometimes plunge down in erratic spirals, or 'whiffle', like pink-footed geese.

Adult in winter.

Adult in summer.

Russet underparts

In flight, bar-tailed godwit shows extensive white rump and barred tail, but no wing-bar. Slightly upturned bill is distinctive.

Bird often makes swift probe for food, walking on round its bill almost without pausing.

Passage migrant and winter visitor; a few in summer.

Barred tail

Adult male in summer. Russet underparts extending to under-tail coverts distinguish this bird from black-tailed godwit in breeding season. Tail is barred. Female is duller. 15 in. (38 cm).

Adult in winter plumage. Upper parts are more streaked than in black-tailed godwit, and legs are shorter. This bird wades less, walks more briskly.

In winter, bar-tailed godwits are often seen in large flocks on the tideline, in company with other waders.

Bar-tailed godwit *Limosa lapponica*

Anglo-Saxons appear to have regarded the godwit as a table delicacy, for the name they gave the bird, *god wiht*, meant 'good creature' and implies a respect for its eating qualities. Nowadays, however, the godwits have nothing to fear from man.

Unlike its close relative the black-tailed godwit, the bar-tailed godwit does not breed in Britain. Its nearest breeding grounds are in Scandinavia, beyond the tree line on the open swampy tundra, with scattered pools. Flocks of 'bar-tails' pass through Britain's mud-flats and estuaries in autumn and spring, but rarely venture inland. Some non-breeding birds stay for the summer, and many stay all the winter, when flocks may be seen probing for small crabs, shrimps, sandhoppers and marine worms. In summer, insects form a large part of the bird's diet.

Outside the breeding season, bar-tailed godwits are usually seen in flocks, when their medium size, long legs and very long, slightly upturned bills make them unmistakable for any other bird except the black-tailed godwit; however, 'black-tails' have a prominent white wing-bar, conspicuous in flight, which the bar-tail lacks. Flocks of bar-tails may sometimes be quite noisy, producing a chorus of reedy 'kirruc' calls.

145

In flight the whimbrel, like the curlew, shows its white rump, but its shorter bill is distinctive.

Like curlews, whimbrels often flock in line or V-formation; but they have a distinctive flight call and a quicker wing-beat.

Striped crown

Down-curved bill

The down-curved bill of the adult whimbrel is shorter than that of most curlews. A pale stripe runs across the centre of the bird's crown. Sexes are alike. 16 in. (40 cm).

The bird breeds chiefly on moorland in the Northern Isles of Scotland, especially the Shetlands and the Orkneys.

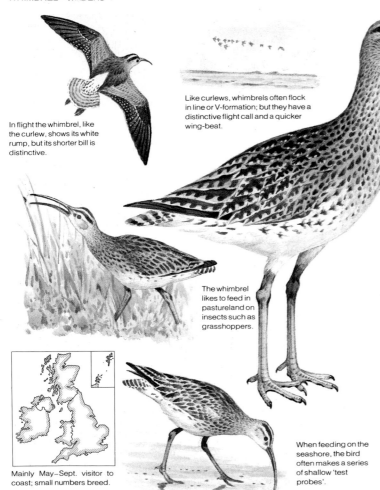

The whimbrel likes to feed in pastureland on insects such as grasshoppers.

When feeding on the seashore, the bird often makes a series of shallow 'test probes'.

Mainly May–Sept. visitor to coast; small numbers breed.

Whimbrel *Numenius phaeopus*

A high-pitched, rippling 'peepeepeepeepeepeepee' is often the first indication of a whimbrel's presence high overhead. This distinctive call is one of the features distinguishing the whimbrel from the larger and more common curlew; other differences are its shorter bill and its striped crown.

The whimbrel is one of Britain's rarest breeding waders and is confined to the Shetlands, the Orkneys and a few remote areas in the extreme north of mainland Scotland. There it generally lives in areas covered with cotton grass, feeding on insects, worms and molluscs. During its migration, however, it can be seen feeding on creatures which it catches along the seashore and mud-banks.

Arriving from its winter quarters in Africa in May or June, the bird builds its nest. Like other waders it makes a shallow hollow in the ground, which it lines scantily with plant material. It lays a clutch of three or, more usually, four eggs which are smaller and darker than those of the curlew. While one bird incubates, the other keeps watch and gives the alarm if danger approaches. After about 24 days, the well-camouflaged chicks hatch, and within five or six weeks they can fly.

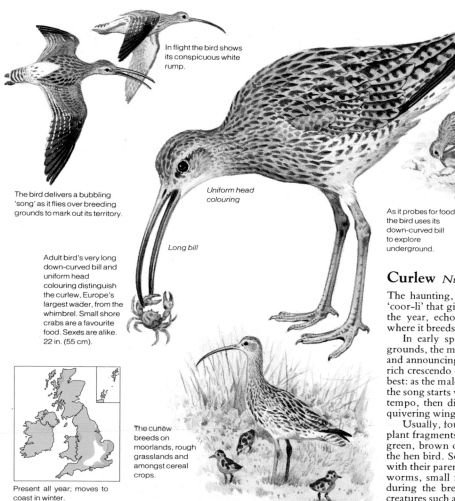

In flight the bird shows its conspicuous white rump.

The bird delivers a bubbling 'song' as it flies over breeding grounds to mark out its territory.

Uniform head colouring

Long bill

Adult bird's very long down-curved bill and uniform head colouring distinguish the curlew, Europe's largest wader, from the whimbrel. Small shore crabs are a favourite food. Sexes are alike. 22 in. (55 cm).

The curlew breeds on moorlands, rough grasslands and amongst cereal crops.

Present all year; moves to coast in winter.

As it probes for food, the bird uses its down-curved bill to explore underground.

Curlews gather at regular roosts on the shore, often in the company of other waders such as oystercatchers.

Curlew *Numenius arquata*

The haunting, melancholy call of the curlew – the plaintive 'coor-li' that gives the bird its name – can be heard for most of the year, echoing across windswept moors and marshlands where it breeds, or above the coastal mud-flats in winter.

In early spring, when the birds arrive at their breeding grounds, the males establish their territories, circling a wide area and announcing their presence loud and clear. This is when the rich crescendo of notes which is the curlew's song is heard at its best: as the male rises steeply into the air with rapid wing-beats, the song starts with low-pitched notes and rises both in tone and tempo, then dies away as the bird glides gracefully down on quivering wings.

Usually, four eggs are laid in a shallow depression lined with plant fragments. The eggs are pale green in colour, with darker green, brown or purple blotches, and are incubated mainly by the hen bird. Soon after hatching the young birds leave the nest with their parents. They fly when five or six weeks old. Insects, worms, small frogs and snails form most of the curlew's diet during the breeding season, but in winter it feeds on shore creatures such as crabs, shrimps and cockles.

147

LARGE WADERS IN FLIGHT

Waders are fast-flying birds and look rather alike. Usually there is opportunity to notice little more than a bird's general shape, a few conspicuous patches of contrasting colour, and distinctive flight calls and flight patterns. Habitat may help to identify some birds: the stone curlew, for instance, rises suddenly from open, stony areas on long, brown and white barred wings, and usually drops to run and hide after a short flight. The woodcock, with its short, broad wings and plumage patterned like dead leaves, flits like a great moth low among trees and scrub. Lapwings, with their broad, blunt, slowly flapping wings, appear dark above with white on their tails; just as easily recognised is the avocet, with its quick flickering flight and a 'klooit' call-note.

Other large waders have less obvious differences. The curlew and whimbrel are both large brown birds with white rumps and long, down-curved bills; but while the whimbrel has a pale-striped crown and repetitive trill, the curlew has plaintive whistling and bubbling calls. Godwits are a little smaller; they are straighter-billed, with yelping and whickering calls. The black-tailed godwit shows black and white patterns on wings and tail, and feet that in flight project well beyond the tail; the bar-tailed godwit has shorter legs, and a distinct white rump. The oystercatcher has a stout black body and white belly, and a loud, penetrating 'kleep' call.

Plumage and calls as identification

Three of the waders shown are smaller than the rest, with long bill and white rump and lower back. Of these, the redshank has prominent white trailing edges to its wings and a plaintive, piping 'tew-ew-ew' call. The greenshank and spotted redshank lack bold white wing marks, but the greenshank has an emphatic 'tew-tew-tew' call, while the spotted redshank gives a loud 'chi-weet', and its long legs project well beyond the tail. Ruffs, except for males in summer plumage, are duller, more silent birds of heavier build.

Apart from the lapwing, the plovers are inconspicuous as well as smaller than the others. Their heads are rounded and their bills stout and stubby. In winter the golden plover is golden above and whitish below, and has a clear, whistling 'thlui' call. The grey plover is similar but has a white rump and a black patch at the base of the under-wing, and a three-syllable 'tee-oo-ee' whistle. Both species are black on the belly and face in summer. The rare dotterel lacks bold markings.

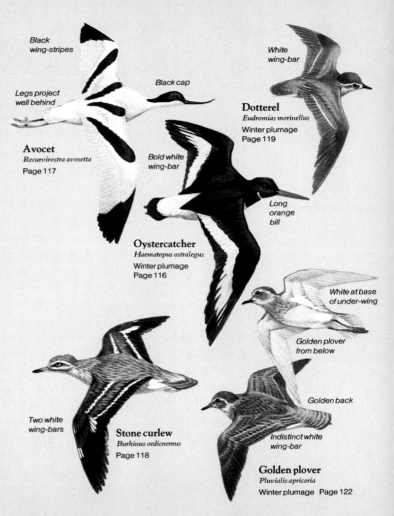

Black wing-stripes

Legs project well behind

Black cap

White wing-bar

Dotterel
Eudromias morinellus
Winter plumage
Page 119

Avocet
Recurvirostra avosetta
Page 117

Bold white wing-bar

Long orange bill

Oystercatcher
Haematopus ostralegus
Winter plumage
Page 116

White at base of under-wing

Golden plover from below

Golden back

Indistinct white wing-bar

Two white wing-bars

Stone curlew
Burhinus oedicnemus
Page 118

Golden plover
Pluvialis apricaria
Winter plumage   Page 122

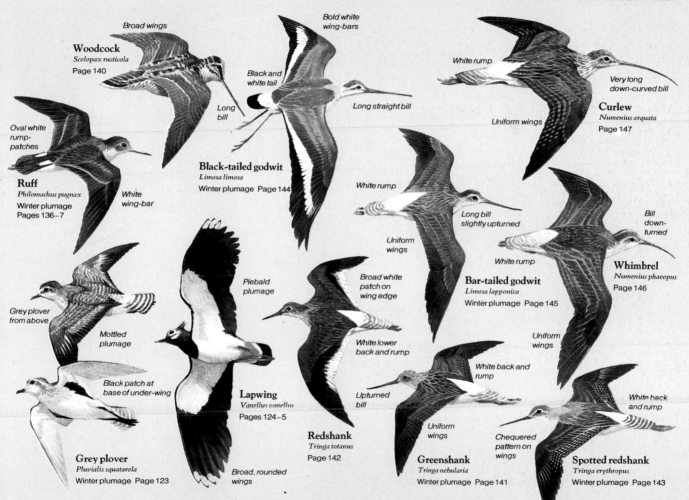

Broad wings

Woodcock
Scolopax rusticola
Page 140

Bold white wing-bars

Black and white tail

Long bill

Long straight bill

White rump

Very long down-curved bill

Curlew
Numenius arquata
Page 147

Uniform wings

Oval white rump-patches

Ruff
Philomachus pugnax
Winter plumage
Pages 136–7

White wing-bar

Black-tailed godwit
Limosa limosa
Winter plumage Page 144

White rump

Long bill slightly upturned

Uniform wings

White rump

Bar-tailed godwit
Limosa lapponica
Winter plumage Page 145

Bill down-turned

Whimbrel
Numenius phaeopus
Page 146

Grey plover from above

Mottled plumage

Piebald plumage

Broad white patch on wing edge

Uniform wings

White lower back and rump

Upturned bill

Redshank
Tringa totanus
Page 142

White back and rump

Uniform wings

Greenshank
Tringa nebularia
Winter plumage Page 141

Chequered pattern on wings

White back and rump

Spotted redshank
Tringa erythropus
Winter plumage Page 143

Black patch at base of under-wing

Lapwing
Vanellus vanellus
Pages 124–5

Grey plover
Pluvialis squatarola
Winter plumage Page 123

Broad, rounded wings

Green sandpiper

In flight, the underwing of the green sandpiper appears much darker than that of the wood sandpiper.

Wood sandpiper

White speckles

Adult in breeding plumage. The very dark upper parts are speckled with white. Despite the bird's colourful name, only its legs are green. Sexes are alike. 9 in. (23 cm).

Green legs

Passage migrant and winter visitor; has bred in Britain.

When flushed, birds shoot up almost vertically for about 10 ft (3 m), then fly on upwards to a great height. Their white rumps and upper tails tipped with black bars are then conspicuous.

Wood sandpiper
Tringa glareola

This species resembles the green sandpiper, but is smaller, paler above, and has paler legs; immatures have green legs. Sexes are alike. 8 in. (20 cm).

The green sandpiper is usually seen in or near water, alone or in pairs. It normally avoids open shores or mud-flats.

Green sandpiper *Tringa ochropus*

Often the first view of a green sandpiper is when it takes off steeply from a marshy pool. When flushed it usually gives a distinctive 'klee-weet-tweet' call. Green sandpipers are passage migrants that visit Britain mainly in spring and autumn, and winter here in small numbers. They breed very rarely in northern England and Scotland, preferring the mixed marsh and woodland country of northern Europe and Asia.

For a wader, the green sandpiper's choice of nest is unusual. Normally it is in a tree, on the old nest of some other species such as the song thrush, blackbird or jay, or in an old squirrel drey. Sometimes the species uses a chance accumulation of sticks and leaves on a branch, adding hardly any new material to it. The clutches it lays there are usually of four greenish or buff-coloured eggs, speckled sparsely with reddish-brown.

The wood sandpiper's call is a distinctive 'chiff-iff-iff'. In its song flight the bird flies round over its territory with occasional spells of quivering wing-beats, rising and then gliding down again on down-curved wings. Although the wood sandpiper sometimes nests in old thrush nests, it more frequently lays in a wader-like scrape in the ground.

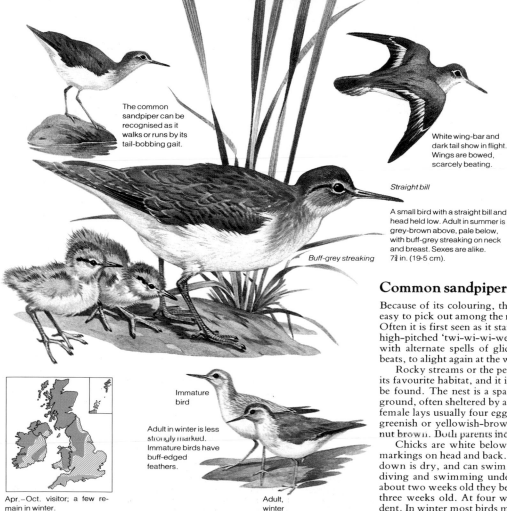

The common sandpiper can be recognised as it walks or runs by its tail-bobbing gait.

White wing-bar and dark tail show in flight. Wings are bowed, scarcely beating.

Straight bill

A small bird with a straight bill and head held low. Adult in summer is grey-brown above, pale below, with buff-grey streaking on neck and breast. Sexes are alike. 7¾ in. (19·5 cm).

Buff-grey streaking

Immature bird

Adult in winter is less strongly marked. Immature birds have buff-edged feathers.

Adult, winter

Apr.–Oct. visitor; a few remain in winter.

The long bill is used for probing in the mud beside water for small shellfish and worms. Insects and frogs are also eaten.

Common sandpiper *Actitis hypoleucos*

Because of its colouring, the common sandpiper is not always easy to pick out among the rocks and stones of a lake shoreline. Often it is first seen as it starts into flight with a loud, musical, high-pitched 'twi-wi-wi-wee', flying low just above the water with alternate spells of gliding and flickering shallow wing-beats, to alight again at the water's edge some distance away.

Rocky streams or the pebbly shore of a lake or reservoir are its favourite habitat, and it is often common where these are to be found. The nest is a sparsely lined hollow or scrape in the ground, often sheltered by a plant or bush. About mid-May the female lays usually four eggs, which vary from creamy-buff to greenish or yellowish-brown, stippled or speckled with chestnut brown. Both parents incubate them for 20–23 days.

Chicks are white below and buff above, with a few dark markings on head and back. They leave the nest as soon as their down is dry, and can swim and feed almost at once, including diving and swimming under water to escape enemies. When about two weeks old they begin flying, and are fully airborne at three weeks old. At four weeks they are completely independent. In winter most birds migrate south to Africa.

151

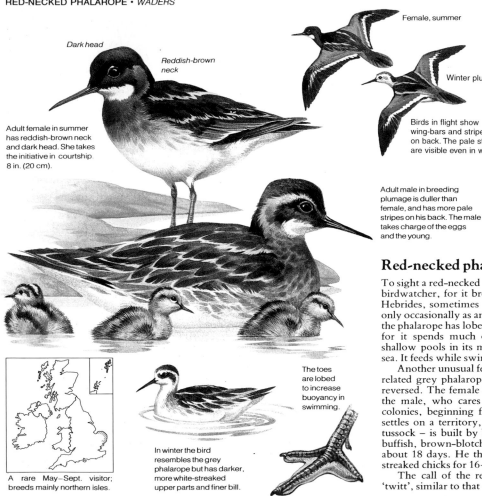

Dark head

Reddish-brown neck

Adult female in summer has reddish-brown neck and dark head. She takes the initiative in courtship. 8 in. (20 cm).

Female, summer

Winter plumage

Birds in flight show wing-bars and stripes on back. The pale stripes are visible even in winter.

Adult male in breeding plumage is duller than female, and has more pale stripes on his back. The male takes charge of the eggs and the young.

Migrant phalaropes in autumn may show traces of breeding plumage. They are blown in from the Atlantic by gales.

The toes are lobed to increase buoyancy in swimming.

A rare May–Sept. visitor; breeds mainly northern isles.

In winter the bird resembles the grey phalarope but has darker, more white-streaked upper parts and finer bill.

Red-necked phalarope *Phalaropus lobatus*

To sight a red-necked phalarope is a rare experience for a British birdwatcher, for it breeds only in the Shetlands and the Outer Hebrides, sometimes in Ireland. It visits other parts of Britain only occasionally as an autumn migrant. Unusually for a wader, the phalarope has lobed toes – an adaptation to its aquatic habits, for it spends much of its time swimming around in small shallow pools in its marshy breeding grounds, and winters at sea. It feeds while swimming, like the grey phalarope.

Another unusual feature of the red-necked phalarope and the related grey phalarope is that the usual roles of the sexes are reversed. The female has the brighter plumage, and she courts the male, who cares for the young. Breeding is usually in colonies, beginning from late May to late June. The female settles on a territory, and the nest – a grass-lined hollow in a tussock – is built by both sexes. The female lays usually four buffish, brown-blotched eggs and the male incubates them for about 18 days. He then cares for the yellowish-buff, brown-streaked chicks for 16–20 days until they become independent.

The call of the red-necked phalarope is a short 'witt' or 'twitt', similar to that of the grey phalarope but lower in pitch.

Adults' summer plumage is brick-red with a whitish face. The female is more strongly marked.

Male, summer

Female, summer

Dark eye-stripe

Stout bill

Female, summer

Female, summer

Winter plumage

In flight, birds show white wing-bar.

Grey phalaropes spend much of their time swimming, and often permit a close approach by humans.

Adult in winter plumage. It differs from the red-necked phalarope in having a stouter bill and lighter upper parts. 8 in. (20 cm).

Mainly Sept.–Oct. visitor; numbers vary year by year.

The birds winter at sea, where groups of them sometimes land on the backs of whales to catch hard-shelled parasites.

Grey phalarope *Phalaropus fulicarius*

Unlike the red-necked phalarope, the grey phalarope does not breed in the British Isles. It is a scarce passage migrant, appearing in very small numbers on its journeys between high Arctic breeding grounds in Greenland, Spitzbergen and northern Siberia and the wintering area at sea off West Africa.

Grey phalaropes eat small shellfish, insects, worms and other invertebrates. They feed while swimming, and often swim in tight circles in shallow water, apparently to create whirlpools and so suck up prey from the bottom. Like their red-necked relations, they have lobed feet similar to the coot – the name phalarope is from the Greek for 'coot-foot'. The birds are not very vocal, although flocks do keep up a continual twittering.

As with the red-necked phalarope, the normal roles of the sexes are reversed. The female establishes a territory in the Arctic tundra where feeding pools are plentiful and courts the male of her choice. The nest is a grassy tussock or a hollow in the ground and in it she lays usually four buffish, brown-blotched eggs in late June or early July. The male incubates them for about 19 days and tends the chicks for 16–20 days. The female may pair with more than one male each season.

153

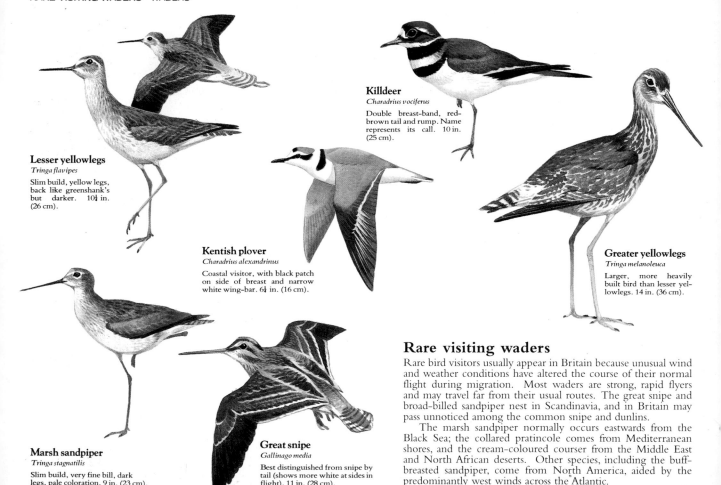

Lesser yellowlegs
Tringa flavipes
Slim build, yellow legs, back like greenshank's but darker. 10¼ in. (26 cm).

Killdeer
Charadrius vociferus
Double breast-band, red-brown tail and rump. Name represents its call. 10 in. (25 cm).

Kentish plover
Charadrius alexandrinus
Coastal visitor, with black patch on side of breast and narrow white wing-bar. 6¼ in. (16 cm).

Greater yellowlegs
Tringa melanoleuca
Larger, more heavily built bird than lesser yellowlegs. 14 in. (36 cm).

Marsh sandpiper
Tringa stagnatilis
Slim build, very fine bill, dark legs, pale coloration. 9 in. (23 cm).

Great snipe
Gallinago media
Best distinguished from snipe by tail (shows more white at sides in flight). 11 in. (28 cm).

Rare visiting waders

Rare bird visitors usually appear in Britain because unusual wind and weather conditions have altered the course of their normal flight during migration. Most waders are strong, rapid flyers and may travel far from their usual routes. The great snipe and broad-billed sandpiper nest in Scandinavia, and in Britain may pass unnoticed among the common snipe and dunlins.

The marsh sandpiper normally occurs eastwards from the Black Sea; the collared pratincole comes from Mediterranean shores, and the cream-coloured courser from the Middle East and North African deserts. Other species, including the buff-breasted sandpiper, come from North America, aided by the predominantly west winds across the Atlantic.

White-rumped sandpiper
Calidris fuscicollis

White rump, bill shorter and straighter than in curlew sandpiper. 7½ in. (19 cm).

Pectoral sandpiper
Calidris melanotos

Shows sharp division between dark-streaked breast and white belly. 8¾ in. (22 cm).

Wilson's phalarope
Phalaropus tricolor

Larger and longer-legged than other phalaropes, larger bill, white rump. Spends less time in water. 9 in. (23 cm).

Spotted sandpiper
Actitis macularia

Distinguishable from common sandpiper in summer plumage by underparts heavily spotted. 8 in. (20 cm).

Buff-breasted sandpiper
Tryngites subruficollis

Overall buff plumage with dark chequering. Short bill, yellow legs. 8 in. (20 cm).

Least sandpiper
Calidris minutilla

Finer bill than little stint, pale legs. Brownish outer tail feathers distinguish it from Temminck's stint. 5¼ in. (13·5 cm).

Broad-billed sandpiper
Limicola falcinellus

Short, pale legs, long bill drooping at tip, white eye-stripe. 6½ in. (16·5 cm).

Long-billed dowitcher
Limnodromus scolopaceus

Snipe-like, but plain grey and white plumage in winter, red-brown in summer. White rump. 12 in. (30 cm).

Cream-coloured courser
Cursorius cursor

Conspicuous head pattern, red-brown to buff upper parts, very long pale legs. 9 in. (23 cm).

Collared pratincole
Glareola pratincola

Short legs, buff throat with black border, long wings and tail. Swallow-like in flight; red-brown under-wings. 10 in. (25 cm).

155

Pale plumage

Immature, brown-streaked birds lack the adult's distinctive tail shape.

Kittiwakes are frequently pursued to obtain food, which they are forced to disgorge.

In flight, white wing-patches are less pronounced than in great skua. Dark-plumaged birds are much rarer than pale.

Dark plumage

Yellowish collar

Thick tail projection

Adult in pale plumage, with yellowish collar and cheeks. It is a smaller bird than the great skua, with a thicker tail. Stranded fish form part of its diet. Sexes are alike. 20 in. (50 cm).

The pomarine skua's diet includes carrion, such as dead seabirds washed up on the shoreline, and also live fish.

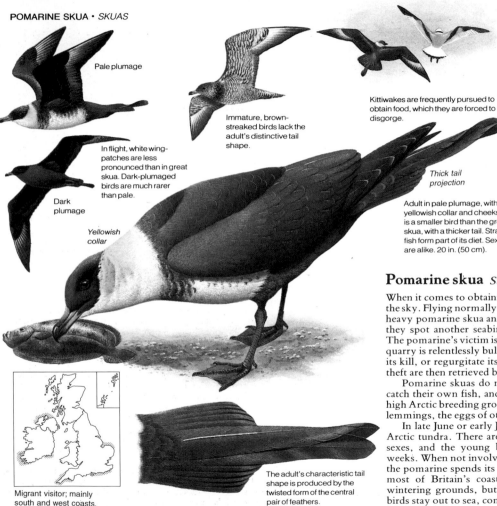

Migrant visitor; mainly south and west coasts.

The adult's characteristic tail shape is produced by the twisted form of the central pair of feathers.

Pomarine skua *Stercorarius pomarinus*

When it comes to obtaining food, the skuas are the plunderers of the sky. Flying normally on slow, powerful wing-beats, the big, heavy pomarine skua and its relatives accelerate suddenly when they spot another seabird that has been hunting successfully. The pomarine's victim is usually a hapless kittiwake or tern. The quarry is relentlessly bullied and chased until it is forced to drop its kill, or regurgitate its most recent meal. The proceeds of the theft are then retrieved by the robber.

Pomarine skuas do not rely entirely on larceny. They also catch their own fish, and eat carrion and ships' refuse. On their high Arctic breeding grounds, the pomarines extend their diet to lemmings, the eggs of other birds, and to small birds.

In late June or early July, the bird nests on the ground in the Arctic tundra. There are usually two eggs, incubated by both sexes, and the young become independent after five or six weeks. When not involved in producing its single annual brood, the pomarine spends its life at sea. It is a fairly regular visitor to most of Britain's coasts, on the way to its South Atlantic wintering grounds, but it is seen only in small groups. Most birds stay out to sea, coming inshore only during a storm.

Adult

On adult bird, the white wing-patch is prominent in flight, which is usually more ponderous than that of other skuas.

Skua harries other seabirds to steal food.

Kittiwake chicks often fall victim to the great skua's powerful bill.

Gannets are forced into the sea to disgorge their food.

Immature

White wing-patch

This fierce bird viciously attacks intruders in its nesting area, striking with its feet in a head-on swoop.

The great skua breeds in colonies on bare ground or moorland. The nest is a simple depression, lined with lichens.

Brown underparts

Mainly Apr.–Sept. visitor; occasionally in winter.

Adult in characteristic aggressive display posture, wings held up and back, beak wide open. Plumage is brown, with white wing-patches and pale streaking on upper parts. Sexes are alike. 23 in. (58 cm).

Great skua *Catharacta skua*

All skuas are pirates, and none is better equipped for the part than the great skua. This brute of a bird is not only sturdily built, aggressive and bullying, but is also the biggest of the skuas, well able to rob really large birds of their latest meals.

The great skua's favourite victim is the gannet, the large white seabird that nests on islands off the coasts of the British Isles. The skua seizes the gannet by the wingtip, so making it stall and fall into the sea. The gannet then disgorges its food and the spoils are snapped up by the waiting skua.

In the Shetland Isles, where the great skua has its main breeding grounds, the bird is known as the bonxie. The word is used by Shetlanders to describe a stout and bullying sort of person, and is so appropriate to the great skua that birdwatchers apply the term to the bird more and more widely. All intruders at a great skua's nest are 'dive-bombed' – buffeted with the bonxie's webbed feet and pecked viciously in repeated swoops. Bonxies will even land on the heads of trespassing sheep, battering them with their wings and driving them from the colony. At first the chicks are brooded by the female while the male brings food; later they are fed by both parents.

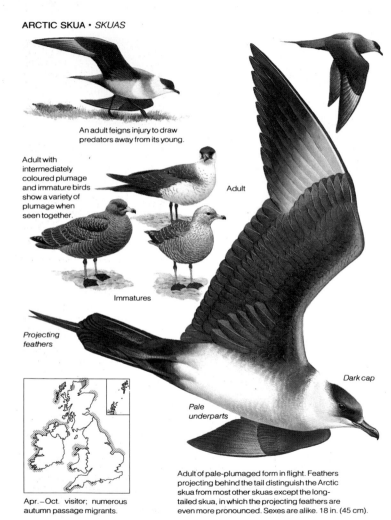

An adult feigns injury to draw predators away from its young.

Adult with intermediately coloured plumage and immature birds show a variety of plumage when seen together.

Adult

Immatures

Projecting feathers

Pale underparts

Dark cap

Adult of pale-plumaged form in flight. Feathers projecting behind the tail distinguish the Arctic skua from most other skuas except the long-tailed skua, in which the projecting feathers are even more pronounced. Sexes are alike. 18 in. (45 cm).

Apr.–Oct. visitor; numerous autumn passage migrants.

Dark-plumaged adults are a deeper brown, with dark underparts. They are smaller than the otherwise similar great skua, with less-prominent wing-patches.

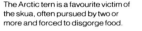

The Arctic tern is a favourite victim of the skua, often pursued by two or more and forced to disgorge food.

Arctic skuas breed in colonies on moorland, where they can be seen indulging in spectacular flights and chases.

Arctic skua *Stercorarius parasiticus*

No bird's nest is safe from the Arctic skua, which feasts on both eggs and young. It usually hunts alone, and is savage and determined enough to scare away birds much bigger than itself. But sometimes the male and female form a team, when one bird will fight off a pair of puffins or kittiwakes, for example, while its mate plunders the nest. Like other skuas, it will steal another seabird's most recent meal by forcing it to disgorge.

Unlike the long-tailed and pomarine skuas, the Arctic skua breeds in Britain. Its nesting grounds are mainly windswept moors in Orkney and Shetland, with smaller colonies in the Hebrides and on the northern tip of mainland Scotland. The nest is often placed near a rock, hillock or tussock which is used as a look-out. Like the nests of other skuas, it is often no more than a shallow depression in the ground – or vegetation on the ground – and is scantily lined with grass, heather, moss or lichen.

A single clutch, usually of two eggs, is laid in late May or early June. The eggs are greenish-brown or buff, and are spotted and blotched with various shades of brown and grey. Incubation takes 24–28 days. The chicks are tended by both parents. They fly after one month and are independent in about two months.

Though perhaps less piratical in its behaviour than other skuas, the long-tailed skua is just as agile in flight.

Immature birds lack the long tail, but can be recognised by their small size and graceful flight.

On the breeding grounds, lemmings are an important part of the diet.

An adult swims high in the water, tail pointed up.

This seldom-seen bird usually avoids the mainland in its long passage from the Arctic to winter quarters off West Africa.

These skuas are often seen in parties, with birds diving playfully at one another.

Pale under-parts

Scarce passage migrant; mainly off east coast, autumn.

Adult long-tailed skua is slimmer than the Arctic skua, with longer projecting tail feathers. The bird frequently hovers like a kestrel. Sexes are alike. 20–22 in. (50–55 cm).

Long tail

Long-tailed skua *Stercorarius longicaudus*

With its long, angular wings, elongated central tail feathers, and floating, easy flight the long-tailed skua is the most graceful and one of the smallest of the four species of skua. In most other respects it is typical of its family – for instance, it is a 'pirate' like other skuas, supplementing its diet by harrying other birds until they regurgitate food they have recently swallowed.

Small mammals, especially lemmings, and birds and fish are eaten too, as are insects: the sight of this big, predatory creature 'hawking' for flies, beetles, earwigs and butterflies makes an incongruous spectacle. It is hawk-like, too, in its flight, and is often seen hovering, and gliding and soaring at great heights.

The long-tailed skua is an Arctic species, breeding in Spitsbergen, northern Scandinavia and northern Russia in June. The eggs, usually two, hatch after 23 days and the young can fly at about three weeks old. In autumn, the long-tailed skua passes down the east coast of Britain on its way to warmer winter quarters, probably off the west coast of Africa. It is seldom seen on passage, for it generally prefers to keep well out to sea. On its way south, it sometimes pauses at the breeding grounds of the Arctic skua in Scotland's Western Isles.

159

Adult in winter: all that remains of the dark hood of its breeding plumage is a dark spot behind the eye.

Brown head

Dark red bill

Adult in breeding plumage. The 'black' head (in fact chocolate brown) is distinctive, as are the dark red bill and legs. Sexes are alike. 14–15 in. (36–38 cm).

Immature bird

Adult, winter

Wings have white fore-edge, black tips, all year. Immature birds have darkish band across wing.

Young birds have more grey in plumage than larger gull species at the same age.

In southern Britain, inland sites such as reservoirs are frequently homes for colonies of black-headed gulls.

Flocks of birds follow ploughs and harrows to capture insects exposed in the turned-up soil.

Present all year; many birds from Europe winter here.

Black-headed gull *Larus ridibundus*

Of all the British gulls, the black-headed gull least deserves the description of 'sea-gull'. A recent survey showed that out of a total British population of some 300,000 pairs, only about a quarter nested on the coast. Meanwhile numerous colonies, some numbering many thousands of birds, were found inland, particularly in the north, usually in boggy areas around lakes.

In the south a higher proportion of colonies are on the coast, especially on salt marshes or among sand dunes. But even in the south the black-headed gull sometimes nests inland, on gravel or clay pits or on sewage farms.

The voice of the black-headed gull consists of a series of extremely harsh and rasping notes, and the sound of a colony in full cry is overpowering. The nest is a slight platform of vegetation or a sparsely lined scrape in the ground. There are normally three eggs, laid daily from mid-April onwards. Both parents incubate the eggs, for a total period of slightly more than three weeks. If danger threatens, the adults give the alarm and the young hide in the nearest cover or flatten motionless on the ground. The black-headed gull will eat almost anything, from fish and worms to grass, seaweed and refuse.

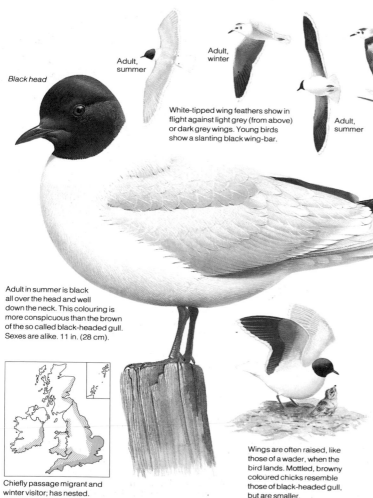

Black head

*Adult,
summer*

*Adult,
winter*

White-tipped wing feathers show in
flight against light grey (from above)
or dark grey wings. Young birds
show a slanting black wing-bar.

*Adult,
summer*

*Immature
bird*

Black markings dwindle in winter
to dark face-patches and a spot
on the crown.

Adult in summer is black
all over the head and well
down the neck. This colouring is
more conspicuous than the brown
of the so called black-headed gull.
Sexes are alike. 11 in. (28 cm).

Chiefly passage migrant and
winter visitor; has nested.

Wings are often raised, like
those of a wader, when the
bird lands. Mottled, browny
coloured chicks resemble
those of black-headed gull,
but are smaller.

Wintering birds are often seen singly, inland near lakes or reservoirs. Nests are
sited in tussocks of waterside vegetation.

Little gull *Larus minutus*

Unlike its larger cousin the black-headed gull, the little gull
really does have a black head rather than a brown one. Its
common name, however, describes its status as the smallest
species in the gull family.

The little gull very rarely breeds in the British Isles. When it
does, it builds a casually thrown-together platform of dead
water plants such as reeds, rushes and sedges. The nest is sited in
a tussock or among reeds in shallow water, or else on low islands
in marshy areas. There are usually three eggs, yellowish or
greenish-brown in colour, speckled with blackish-brown and
grey. Nesting colonies are often mixed with those of other
species such as terns. The chicks, which hatch after about three
weeks, can fly about three weeks later.

Outside the breeding season – when the black head plumage
is lost – little gulls wander from their favoured freshwater
marshes to a wide variety of inland and coastal waters. When
feeding they resemble black terns in their actions, flying
buoyantly over the water, dipping to the surface or alighting
from time to time to pick up a creature such as a stickleback or
small crustacean. Insects are often caught on the wing.

161

Adult bird in winter plumage has grey-brown streaking on head. Underparts are white, bill and legs yellow-green and wingtips black with white spots. Sexes are alike. 16 in. (40 cm).

Yellow-green bill

Black and white wingtips

Adult

Yellow-green legs

First-year birds

In flight, long and pointed wings typical of all gulls are conspicuous. Young birds have clear white tail with black band near tip.

The nest, always built on the ground, is usually sited on a marsh or moor near the sea, or on an islet or shingle beach.

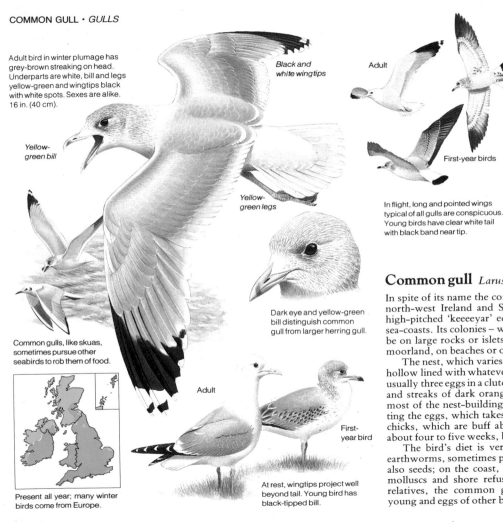

Dark eye and yellow-green bill distinguish common gull from larger herring gull.

Common gulls, like skuas, sometimes pursue other seabirds to rob them of food.

Adult

First-year bird

At rest, wingtips project well beyond tail. Young bird has black-tipped bill.

Present all year; many winter birds come from Europe.

Common gull *Larus canus*

In spite of its name the common gull is not common, except in north-west Ireland and Scotland. The common gull's shrill, high-pitched 'keeeeyar' echoes above inland waters as well as sea-coasts. Its colonies – which are seldom large or dense – may be on large rocks or islets in lochs, on boggy areas of grass or moorland, on beaches or on offshore islands.

The nest, which varies a great deal in size, consists of a small hollow lined with whatever plant material is available. There are usually three eggs in a clutch; they are olive-green, with blotches and streaks of dark orange-brown. Although the female does most of the nest-building, both sexes share the task of incubating the eggs, which takes three to three and a half weeks. The chicks, which are buff above and yellowish beneath, fly after about four to five weeks, but stay near the nest.

The bird's diet is very varied. Inland, it eats insects and earthworms, sometimes picked up from behind the plough, and also seeds; on the coast, crustaceans, marine worms, starfish, molluscs and shore refuse are eaten. Like many of its close relatives, the common gull also takes small mammals, the young and eggs of other birds, and even small adult birds.

In flight, kittiwakes are buoyant and graceful. Adults have solid black wingtips; juveniles show diagonal black wing-bars.

Yellow-green bill

Kittiwakes are not noisy birds away from their breeding grounds, but a pair at their nest will defy all comers with their cries.

Kittiwakes usually form large colonies on inaccessible cliff ledges.

The slenderly built kittiwake has dark eyes, a yellow-green bill and black legs. The inside of the mouth is bright red. Sexes are alike. 16 in. (40 cm).

Present offshore throughout year; rarely far inland.

Fish or fish remains are taken from the surface when the kittiwake is in flight or while swimming.

Black bars on the wings and a black half-collar distinguish juvenile birds.

Kittiwake *Rissa tridactyla*

No one visiting a colony of these gulls will be left in any doubt about the origin of their name, as the strident cry of 'kitti-wa-a-k' rises on all sides. Some half a million or so pairs of kittiwakes breed in Britain and Ireland, mainly along coasts in the north and west. There has been an enormous growth in the gull's population during this century, since it was given legal protection. Before that, the kittiwake was slaughtered for sport and to supply feathers for Victorian ladies' hats.

The birds usually make their homes on projecting ledges of rock on cliff faces. The nests are neat, cup-shaped structures of moss, seaweed and other plant material, cemented together with considerable quantities of droppings. The birds consolidate this with the constant paddling of their webbed feet. A typical clutch consists of two, or occasionally three, pale bluish-grey, brownish, or stone-coloured eggs with ash-grey and rich brown spots and blotches. The chicks are mainly creamy white, with greyish-brown upper parts. Both parents feed the chicks during the five to eight weeks that they spend in the nest.

The kittiwake spends its time outside the breeding season at sea, and lives on small fish, small squids, molluscs and shrimps.

In flight, lesser black-backed gulls show slender build and yellow legs.

Though closely related, herring gulls and lesser black-backed gulls stay in separate groups even in mixed colonies.

Dark grey upper parts

Yellow legs

Upper parts of the lesser black-backed gull are slightly paler than those of the great black-backed gull. Sexes are alike. 21–22 in. (53–55 cm).

Mainly summer visitor, but many winter in Britain.

Large winter roosts may form on reservoirs and other inland waters.

First-year bird is slightly darker than herring gull.

The parent birds have to be on constant guard against other gulls of their own species robbing them of their chicks.

Lesser black-backed gull *Larus fuscus*

This is a smaller bird than its heavyweight relative, the great black-backed gull, with a lighter coloured back and yellow legs. The lesser black-back has more in common with its closer relative, the herring gull. They are similar in size; both rob other birds of their chicks; both are scavengers that eat practically anything, from carrion to edible refuse at sea or on inland rubbish tips; and the two species very occasionally interbreed.

The habitat of the two birds is virtually identical, with the lesser black-back more partial to offshore waters and, curiously, more often breeding in inland localities on fresh water, such as upland moors, lowland mosses and bogs. The lesser black-back is mainly migratory, moving south in winter to warmer waters where it undergoes its annual moult.

Nesting usually takes place in colonies from early May onwards, after the birds have returned from north-west African, Spanish and French waters. The nest is a small accumulation of nearby plant material – seaweed, grass or moss – lining a shallow hollow in the ground. The usual clutch is three buff or greenish eggs, spotted with blackish-brown marks. Incubation, by both sexes, lasts for three and a half to four weeks.

Heavy bill

Young birds have whiter heads and underparts than young lesser black-backed gulls and herring gulls.

Heavy build and stout bill are conspicuous in flight. Young birds have white on tail, with a black band near the tip.

Young bird

This gull is a formidable predator, capable of swallowing an egg or gull chick whole.

Great black-backed gulls are less colonial than most gulls, building a typical gull nest of piled-up plant rubbish.

Pink legs

Like other gulls, these birds flock around coastal fishing craft throwing out fish waste.

Present all year; birds from Europe also winter in Britain.

The great black-backed gull has a heavy bill and darker upper parts than the lesser black-backed gull. Sexes are alike. 25–31 in. (64–79 cm).

Great black-backed gull *Larus marinus*

Nothing weak enough to be overpowered and killed by the great black-backed gull is safe while this butcher of the bird world is about. With its heavy, hook-tipped bill, it feeds voraciously on anything from crabs, molluscs and worms, to fish, mice and voles. Puffins, kittiwakes, Manx shearwaters and even sickly lambs are vulnerable. The bird is also a scavenger of carrion and edible refuse thrown from ships.

Breeding, either singly or in colonies, is confined to rocky coasts where cliffs, islets and offshore stacks offer refuge from mammal predators. Both sexes build a large nest on the ground, between May and early June, using seaweed, heather, grass and a few feathers. The usual clutch is three eggs, which are a pale buff or olive-brown, blotched and speckled with dark brown and grey. The greyish chicks, mottled with black, are hatched by both parents and fledge after seven weeks' feeding.

In spite of its omnivorous nature, this bird is the rarest of Britain's indigenous gulls, although its numbers have been increasing during the last century – possibly because of the gradual warming of the North Atlantic Ocean and an increase in the quantity of fish offal and edible refuse thrown away by man.

165

Herring gulls drop hard-shelled prey such as mussels from a height to smash them.

Heavy looking bill, grey upper parts and black wingtips with white spots or patches identify adults in flight. Brown first-year birds have speckled tail merging into black band near tip.

Red bill spot

Nestlings peck at the adult's red bill spot to solicit regurgitated food.

Herring gulls threaten other birds such as coots with a fierce and intimidating display if they come too close.

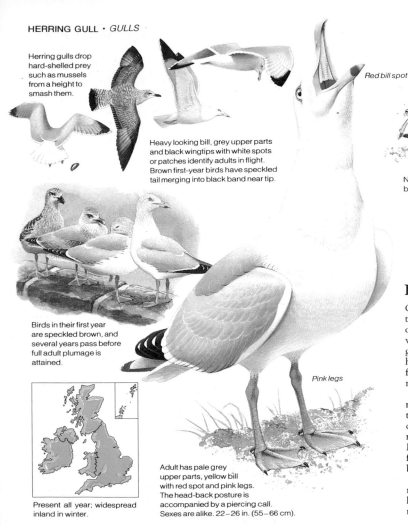

Birds in their first year are speckled brown, and several years pass before full adult plumage is attained.

Present all year; widespread inland in winter.

Pink legs

Adult has pale grey upper parts, yellow bill with red spot and pink legs. The head-back posture is accompanied by a piercing call. Sexes are alike. 22–26 in. (55–66 cm).

Herring gull *Larus argentatus*

One sound more than any other conjures up the atmosphere of the sea-coast – the yodelling 'kee-owk-kyowk-kyowk-kyowk' of the herring gull. This is one of a large vocabulary of mewing, wailing and choking noises characteristic of this bird. 'Herring' gull is not a particularly apt name, for although it will eat herrings, it will also eat almost anything else, particularly animal food – crustacea such as shrimps, prawns and crabs, small mammals and birds and edible rubbish.

The growing number and size of rubbish dumps, and of reservoirs where it can live, has encouraged the great increase in the herring gull population that has recently occurred. Some colonies have expanded so much, spilling over even on to rooftops, that noise and fouling have become major problems. More delicate species such as puffins and terns have been driven from cliffs, islands and coastal dunes, so that drastic culls have been necessary to reduce the gulls' numbers.

The herring gull can live long, occasionally for 30 years or more; it suffers from few predators once mature, and it has a high breeding rate. A single clutch of three eggs in a season is the rule, but if the eggs are lost more are laid.

Pale grey wings

White wingtips are noticeable in flight, distinct from the black wingtips of the herring gull.

White wingtips

In hard winters, this visitor from the Arctic can be found scouring the seashore for carrion, seaweed and other food.

Fully grown adult is a very large gull; it has pale grey wings and back, with white wingtips. Sexes are alike. 27 in. (68 cm).

Iceland gull
Larus glaucoides

Though similar to the glaucous gull, this bird can be identified by its smaller size and slighter bill. 21 in. (53 cm).

Scarce winter visitor, mainly to fishing ports.

Young bird has evenly speckled, brownish plumage, paler and less contrasting than that of herring or great black-backed gulls.

Glaucous gull *Larus hyperboreus*

This rare visitor to the British Isles is a bird of the extreme high Arctic, with its nearest breeding grounds in Greenland and Iceland. Its numbers here often increase during severe winters, and it may be seen on the east coast of Britain from Shetland south to Norfolk and in the north-west from the Outer Hebrides to Western Ireland.

In size the glaucous gull is similar to its cousin the great black-backed gull, the largest of our native gulls, but is distinguishable from it by the greyish-blue plumage on the back from which it takes its name. Like its cousin, the glaucous gull has a voracious appetite; it will eat fish, crabs, shrimps, carrion and seaweed, but it also eats birds, including such large species as eider ducks, fulmars and kittiwakes in addition to young birds and eggs. It is less noisy than some other gulls, and utters a variety of wailing notes similar to those of the herring gull.

The Iceland gull is like a miniature glaucous gull and breeds only in southern Greenland and a small part of Arctic Canada. It appears in Britain in small numbers from mid-October to mid-March, with a few birds occasionally staying on in this country into the summer months.

167

GULLS IN FLIGHT

Though all gulls are basically similar in appearance, each species has features which distinguish it from others when seen in flight. To confirm identification, it helps to be close enough to glimpse the bill and feet. Distinguishing features include differences in size and variations in marking, and it is helpful to compare an unidentified bird with a known species. The two commonest species – the herring gull and the black-headed gull – provide standards for comparison. The herring gull is a large species with an ash-grey back and the familiar nagging and yodelling calls, whereas the black-headed gull is a small, slender bird with a lighter flight and quicker wing-beat.

A number of large gulls have the identifying feature of a stout yellow bill with a red spot near the tip. Among these are the herring gull, lesser black-backed gull and great black-backed gull. All have black wingtips with white spots at the extreme tips, but they stand out more on the herring gull, which is pale grey on its upper back (mantle) and upper wings. The lesser black-backed gull has a dark grey or sooty mantle, and the much larger great black-backed gull, whose deep-toned call is unmistakable, has a sooty-black mantle. Leg colours vary; the British race of herring gull has pink legs, as has the greater black-backed gull, but the lesser black-backed gull has yellow or yellowish-grey legs. Glaucous and Iceland gulls both have ash-grey on mantle and wings, but lack black wingtips; the Iceland gull is the smaller of the two.

Identifying the smaller gulls

The common gull is between the herring gull and smallest gulls in size, with the quicker wing-beats typical of all smaller birds. Its wing colour is like that of the herring gull, but it has a much more slender, greenish-yellow bill lacking a red spot, and its legs are greenish-yellow rather than pink.

Characteristic of the small gulls is a dark head in summer and a white head with a dark spot behind the eye in winter. Helpful distinguishing features are the bill colour and under-wing colour. In summer, the black-backed gull, Bonaparte's gull, little gull and Mediterranean gull, for example, all have dark heads; but only Bonaparte's gull has a black bill. Viewed from below, in summer or winter, the little gull had dark under-wings, the Mediterranean gull light under-wings, the black-headed gull light under-wings with dark primaries, and Bonaparte's gull light under-wings with black at the rear edges.

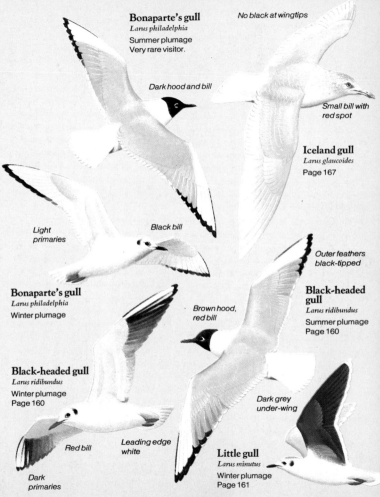

Bonaparte's gull
Larus philadelphia
Summer plumage
Very rare visitor.

Dark hood and bill

No black at wingtips

Small bill with red spot

Iceland gull
Larus glaucoides
Page 167

Light primaries

Black bill

Outer feathers black-tipped

Bonaparte's gull
Larus philadelphia
Winter plumage

Brown hood, red bill

Black-headed gull
Larus ridibundus
Summer plumage
Page 160

Black-headed gull
Larus ridibundus
Winter plumage
Page 160

Red bill

Leading edge white

Dark primaries

Dark grey under-wing

Little gull
Larus minutus
Winter plumage
Page 161

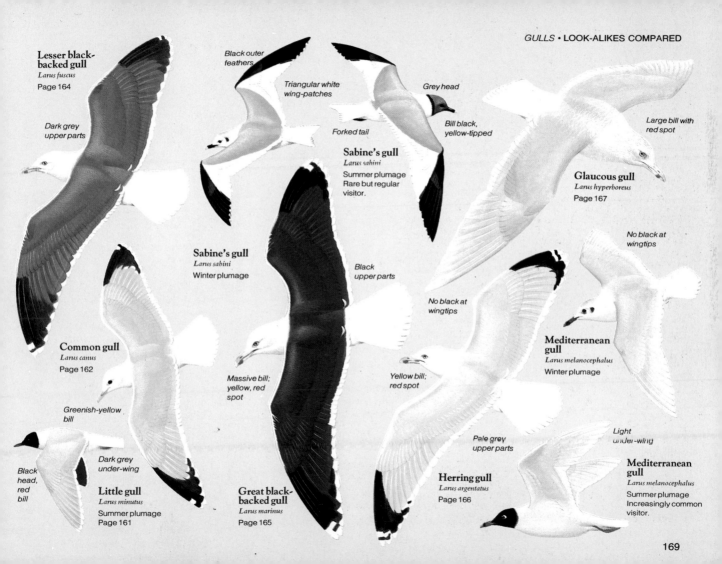

Lesser black-backed gull
Larus fuscus
Page 164

Dark grey upper parts

Black outer feathers

Triangular white wing-patches

Grey head

Forked tail

Bill black, yellow-tipped

Sabine's gull
Larus sahini
Summer plumage
Rare but regular visitor.

Glaucous gull
Larus hyperboreus
Page 167

Large bill with red spot

No black at wingtips

Sabine's gull
Larus sabini
Winter plumage

Black upper parts

No black at wingtips

Mediterranean gull
Larus melanocephalus
Winter plumage

Common gull
Larus canus
Page 162

Greenish-yellow bill

Massive bill; yellow, red spot

Yellow bill; red spot

Pale grey upper parts

Light under-wing

Black head, red bill

Dark grey under-wing

Little gull
Larus minutus
Summer plumage
Page 161

Great black-backed gull
Larus marinus
Page 165

Herring gull
Larus argentatus
Page 166

Mediterranean gull
Larus melanocephalus
Summer plumage
Increasingly common visitor.

169

IMMATURE GULLS

Immature gulls are very much harder to tell apart than adult gulls. Most of them are a dull, mottled brown with a dark tail band; glaucous and Iceland gulls share a similar pale colouring. Immature plumage lasts for two years among smaller species and for four years in the larger birds. Most species are best distinguished by comparing them with adults, or by the first signs of adult plumage.

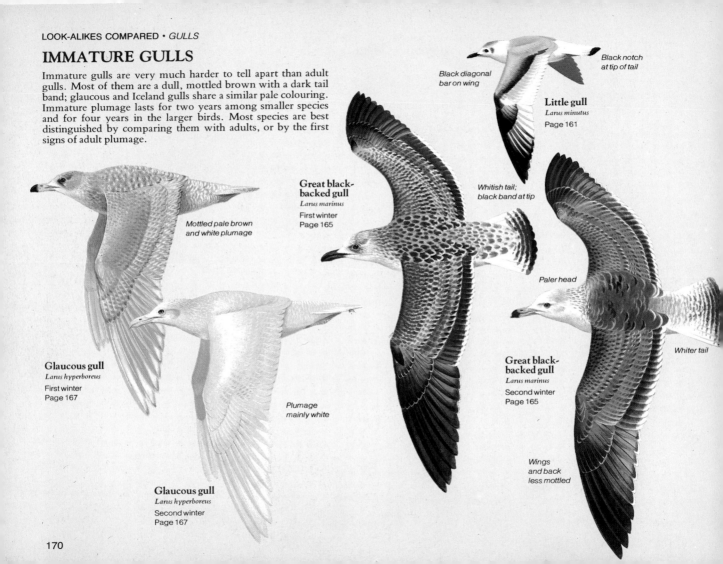

Black diagonal
bar on wing

Black notch
at tip of tail

Little gull
Larus minutus
Page 161

Mottled pale brown
and white plumage

**Great black-
backed gull**
Larus marinus
First winter
Page 165

Whitish tail;
black band at tip

Paler head

Glaucous gull
Larus hyperboreus
First winter
Page 167

Plumage
mainly white

**Great black-
backed gull**
Larus marinus
Second winter
Page 165

Whiter tail

Glaucous gull
Larus hyperboreus
Second winter
Page 167

Wings
and back
less mottled

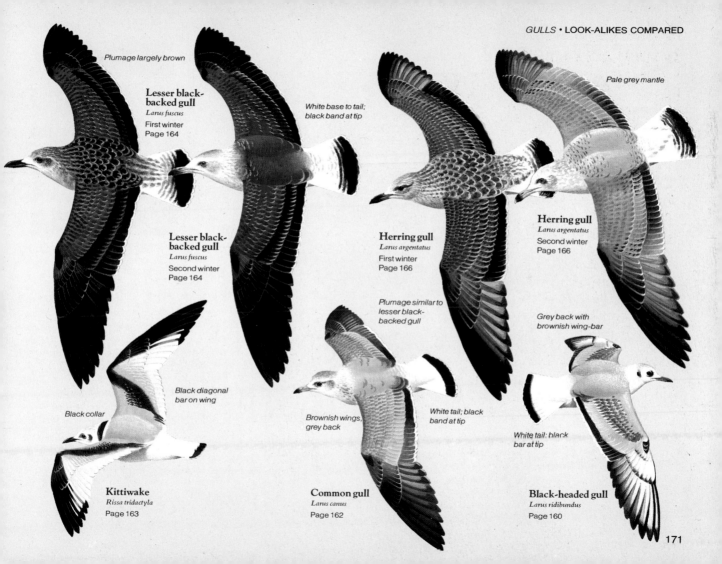

Plumage largely brown

Lesser black-backed gull
Larus fuscus
First winter
Page 164

White base to tail; black band at tip

Pale grey mantle

Lesser black-backed gull
Larus fuscus
Second winter
Page 164

Herring gull
Larus argentatus
First winter
Page 166

Herring gull
Larus argentatus
Second winter
Page 166

Plumage similar to lesser black-backed gull

Grey back with brownish wing-bar

Black diagonal bar on wing

Black collar

Brownish wings, grey back

White tail; black band at tip

White tail; black bar at tip

Kittiwake
Rissa tridactyla
Page 163

Common gull
Larus canus
Page 162

Black-headed gull
Larus ridibundus
Page 160

171

Shaggy crest

Black bill, yellow tip

Courtship behaviour includes 'fish-flight', when the male offers fish to the female in mid-air.

Adult, summer

Adult, winter

Heavy flight and dark bill are conspicuous at all seasons. In winter the forehead is white.

Adult in summer plumage has a black forehead and crown, a shaggy crest and a black, yellow-tipped bill. Sexes are alike. 16 in. (41 cm). Downy chicks have a characteristic 'spiky' plumage.

After fledging, young birds gather on sand-banks near the colony.

Some birds start to develop winter plumage, their foreheads streaked with white, before the breeding season ends.

Mar.–Sept. visitor; coastal, a few nest inland in Ireland.

In courtship displays on the ground, the neck and bill are stretched upwards and the wings held out from the body.

Sandwich tern *Sterna sandvicensis*

The surest sign that the breeding season of the sandwich tern has started is when two birds are seen conducting their 'fish–flight', in which one of the birds carries a fish. Early in the breeding season the two birds are not necessarily male and female, and either may carry the fish; but later the sexes pair off, and the male feeds its fish to its mate as part of the courtship ritual. This extra nutrient probably helps to strengthen the female while she is producing eggs.

It is in the breeding season that the terns are at their most quarrelsome, and the colonies resound with the harsh 'kirrick' that is their usual call. Both sexes incubate the eggs, for a period of three weeks. When the female is incubating, the male brings food in the form of marine worms, sand eels and other small fish. It catches these by making headlong plunges into the water. The chicks assemble with the young of other sandwich terns when one or two weeks old, but their parents are apparently able to distinguish them from the crowd. They fly at about five weeks. Juveniles lack a yellow tip to their bills.

The bird is called after the town in east Kent, the scientist who named the species having received a specimen from there.

Adult, winter

Adult, summer

Adult, summer

In flight, the roseate tern shows the longest tail streamers of any tern, and has a generally whiter appearance and a more slender build.

Adult, summer

Downy young are much smaller than those of sandwich tern, but have similar 'spiky' plumage.

Dark bill

Rosy breast

Adult in summer breeding plumage. At close range breast shows rosy flush. Dark bill turns red at base. Sexes are alike. 15 in. (38 cm).

Courtship display includes posture with wings drooped, tail and neck pointing upwards.

May–Sept. visitor; scarce and seen only rarely inland.

The roseate tern frequently lays only one egg. When the bird produces two, they are laid two or more days apart.

Roseate tern *Sterna dougallii*

The roseate tern is perhaps the most graceful and attractive of all the terns that visit Britain's shores. But it is also one of the country's rarest breeding seabirds, and the delicate rosy flush of the breast that gives the bird its name is visible for only a brief time during breeding – and even then only at close range.

There are only a few colonies in Britain and Ireland used regularly by the roseate tern – mostly on small islands and always coastal. Moreover the birds usually breed in mixed colonies with other species such as common or Arctic terns, which adds to the difficulty of spotting them. However, the roseate has a distinctive alarm call, a harsh, guttural 'ark ark', and another, rather softer 'chewic' note.

In flight the roseate's very long tail streamers, whiter colouring and more slender build single it out; so too does its dark bill, red at the base in summer. One or two eggs are laid from early June onwards in a shallow depression on the seashore, or a hollow in a rock. Creamy or buff, speckled and blotched reddish-brown, they hatch in three to three and a half weeks. Like other terns, the bird may hover in the air before plunging to catch small fish like sand eels just below the surface of the water.

173

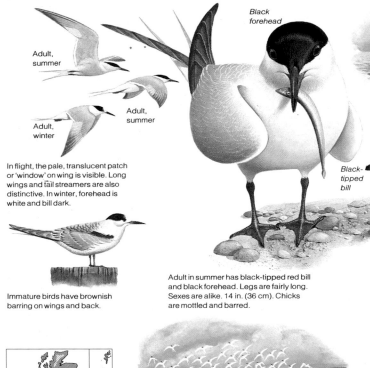

Adult, summer

Adult, summer

Adult, winter

In flight, the pale, translucent patch or 'window' on wing is visible. Long wings and tail streamers are also distinctive. In winter, forehead is white and bill dark.

Immature birds have brownish barring on wings and back.

Black forehead

Terns feed by plunging from the air to catch fish. They often hover as they seek prey.

Black-tipped bill

Adult in summer has black-tipped red bill and black forehead. Legs are fairly long. Sexes are alike. 14 in. (36 cm). Chicks are mottled and barred.

Unlike the Arctic tern, the common tern often makes its nest near inland stretches of water, particularly in Scotland.

Apr.–Sept. visitor; also passage bird. Mainly coastal.

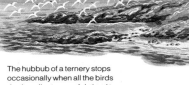

The hubbub of a ternery stops occasionally when all the birds rise in a silent, graceful cloud to sweep out over the sea for a minute or so, then return.

Common tern *Sterna hirundo*

In spite of its name this species is not Britain's commonest tern – a distinction that belongs to the very similar and closely related Arctic tern. But it is the most widely distributed tern, breeding around much of the Irish and Scottish mainland and island coastlines, and also in southern and south-eastern England.

The common tern frequently breeds in mixed colonies with other species of tern, some colonies numbering many hundreds of pairs. Visitors to the nesting area are certain to be 'dive-bombed' repeatedly; although the common tern is less inclined than the Arctic tern to press home its attack to the point of actually striking a blow, its bill does occasionally draw blood.

The nest is merely a scrape in the ground, either unlined or scattered with a few plant strands. Two or three eggs are laid from the end of May to early June. Most vary in colour from stone to brownish or yellowish, speckled and blotched with dark brown and ash-grey. The chicks hatch at intervals of one or two days and remain in the nest for several days more. During their time in the nest, the female normally broods and protects them while her mate fetches food. Common tern eat small fish, crabs and shrimps, marine worms, starfish and molluscs.

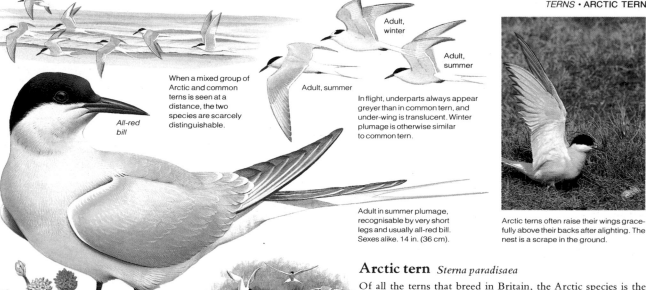

When a mixed group of Arctic and common terns is seen at a distance, the two species are scarcely distinguishable.

All-red bill

Adult, winter

Adult, summer

Adult, summer

In flight, underparts always appear greyer than in common tern, and under-wing is translucent. Winter plumage is otherwise similar to common tern.

Adult in summer plumage, recognisable by very short legs and usually all-red bill. Sexes alike. 14 in. (36 cm).

Short legs

Arctic terns often raise their wings gracefully above their backs after alighting. The nest is a scrape in the ground.

A fox intruding into a colony comes under fierce attack. Sometimes blood is drawn from human visitors.

Apr.–Sept. visitor; most numerous in northern isles.

Other birds, such as eiders, often nest in Arctic tern colonies, protected by the terns' aggressive reaction to intruders.

Arctic tern *Sterna paradisaea*

Of all the terns that breed in Britain, the Arctic species is the most numerous, with around 50,000 pairs nesting every year. Most are concentrated in the north, few pairs breeding south of a line from the Scottish borders to Anglesey. Nearly all colonies in the British Isles are on or very near the coast. In them, Arctic terns usually mingle with common terns, adding to the problems of identifying birds that are, in any case, much alike in appearance.

Arctic terns arrive from their southern-ocean wintering grounds in May, and many clutches are complete by the end of the month. They generally consist of two eggs – occasionally one or three – which are similar to those of the common tern. Both parents tend the chicks, which at first normally remain in or very near the nest; though they can, if need be, swim when only two days old.

The call of the Arctic tern is a harsh 'kee-yaar', like that of the common tern, but with a tendency for the emphasis to fall on the second syllable. When an attack on human intruders is being pushed home the calls may become more excited, with a harsh growling 'kaar' just as the bird strikes or passes close overhead.

175

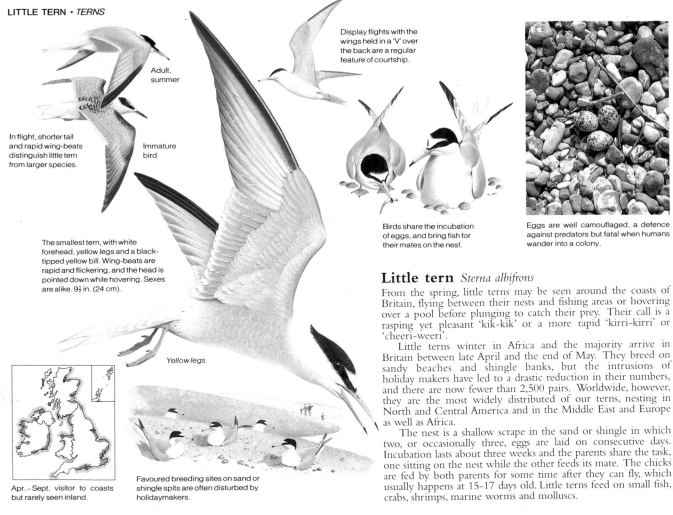

Adult,
summer

In flight, shorter tail
and rapid wing-beats
distinguish little tern
from larger species.

Immature
bird

Display flights with the
wings held in a 'V' over
the back are a regular
feature of courtship.

The smallest tern, with white
forehead, yellow legs and a black-
tipped yellow bill. Wing-beats are
rapid and flickering, and the head is
pointed down while hovering. Sexes
are alike. 9½ in. (24 cm).

Yellow legs

Birds share the incubation
of eggs, and bring fish for
their mates on the nest.

Eggs are well camouflaged, a defence
against predators but fatal when humans
wander into a colony.

Apr.–Sept. visitor to coasts
but rarely seen inland.

Favoured breeding sites on sand or
shingle spits are often disturbed by
holidaymakers.

Little tern *Sterna albifrons*

From the spring, little terns may be seen around the coasts of
Britain, flying between their nests and fishing areas or hovering
over a pool before plunging to catch their prey. Their call is a
rasping yet pleasant 'kik-kik' or a more rapid 'kirri-kirri' or
'cheeri–weeri'.

Little terns winter in Africa and the majority arrive in
Britain between late April and the end of May. They breed on
sandy beaches and shingle banks, but the intrusions of
holiday makers have led to a drastic reduction in their numbers,
and there are now fewer than 2,500 pairs. Worldwide, however,
they are the most widely distributed of our terns, nesting in
North and Central America and in the Middle East and Europe
as well as Africa.

The nest is a shallow scrape in the sand or shingle in which
two, or occasionally three, eggs are laid on consecutive days.
Incubation lasts about three weeks and the parents share the task,
one sitting on the nest while the other feeds its mate. The chicks
are fed by both parents for some time after they can fly, which
usually happens at 15-17 days old. Little terns feed on small fish,
crabs, shrimps, marine worms and molluscs.

Grey wings

In winter, birds are identified by black smudge at side of breast.

Chicks have downy plumage of gold, buff and black, with a pale ring round the eyes. Both the parents tend and feed them.

Black body

In summer, black terns of both sexes are easily recognised by their black bodies, grey wings and white coverts on underside of tail. 9½ in. (24 cm).

May–Sept. migrant, in some years more widespread.

Black terns fly low over the water, dipping rather than diving for food.

Nesting colonies are often situated among rushes that border muddy inland lagoons.

After the breeding season, black terns often have a patchy appearance as they moult to their winter plumage.

Black tern *Chlidonias niger*

Until the middle of the 19th century, the black tern was a regular breeder in east and south-east England. Today, although it is quite common as a summer migrant, it rarely breeds on these shores. Pairs were recorded breeding in 1966, 1969 and 1975, but with little success – only three birds fledged successfully in 1966, for example. The black tern prefers wetlands – fens, swamps, marshes – to the sea-coast, and it is probable that it has been deterred by the decline in breeding areas through drainage for agriculture.

The nest is generally a floating platform of water plants such as reeds, with a lining of finer stems. Sometimes it is just a lined hollow scraped in the ground on a drier marsh site. Eggs are laid from mid-May onwards, usually three in a clutch but sometimes two or four. They are brownish or greenish in colour, with blackish-brown speckling. The parents share in the incubation, eggs hatching after 14–16 days. Chicks leave the nest after two weeks, but it is another two weeks before they can fly.

Black terns eat mainly marshland and aquatic insects such as mayflies and dragonflies and their larvae, but spiders, leeches, tadpoles, frogs and small fish are all included in their diet.

TERNS IN FLIGHT

There are two distinct types of terns: the grey and white sea terns and the black terns of inland waters. The sea terns are sometimes mistaken for small gulls, but they can be distinguished by their faster flight with deeper wing-beats. Another characteristic is their habit of hovering over the water and then plunging in after a fish. Their bodies and bills are slender and their tails are forked. They have little black on their wings, but they have a neat black cap on their heads, which turns white at the front after the breeding season. In summer they breed along most parts of the British coastline.

Most of the grey and white sea terns are small in size. But the Caspian tern – with its stout, tapering red bill and slow, majestic flight – is the size of a large gull. The next largest is the Sandwich tern, which has a long, black, yellow-tipped bill; its grating cries can be heard over a great distance. Almost as big is the heavily built gull-billed tern, whose plumage is generally whiter than that of the two larger birds.

The smaller of the grey and white terns are often difficult to identify in flight. In particular, the Arctic and common terns are very much alike, especially when not breeding. When it is breeding the Arctic tern's body is distinctly grey, its bill is red and flight feathers are translucent. The common tern, by contrast, has a white body, a dark scarlet bill with black tip, and a small, translucent wing-patch. In a mixed flock, the roseate tern is told apart by its shorter wings, much whiter appearance, pink-tinged breast in spring and very long tail streamers. Its extremely harsh call-notes usually attract attention. Smallest of all is the little tern, a miniature species with rapid wing-beats.

Terns that fly inland

Black terns are mainly found beside lakes, lagoons and marshes. However, on spring or autumn migrations they may fly along the coasts. They usually feed by skimming over the water and swooping to snatch insects from the surface. Despite their name, they are not black all the time. In summer, the black tern itself (*Childonias niger*) is sooty-black with white on its under-tail feathers and wings; while the white-winged black tern (*Childonias leucopterus*) has white wings with black under-wing feathers, a white rump and tail and red bill. In winter, both birds are paler, with white beneath and mainly dark grey above. The black tern has a dark spot on the sides of its neck, forming a wedge, and the white-winged variety retains its white rump.

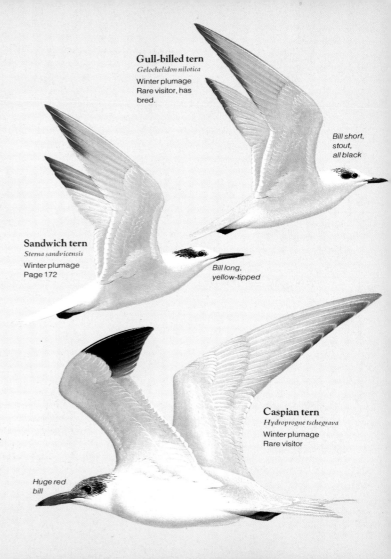

Gull-billed tern
Gelochelidon nilotica
Winter plumage
Rare visitor, has bred.

Bill short, stout, all black

Sandwich tern
Sterna sandvicensis
Winter plumage
Page 172

Bill long, yellow-tipped

Caspian tern
Hydroprogne tschegrava
Winter plumage
Rare visitor

Huge red bill

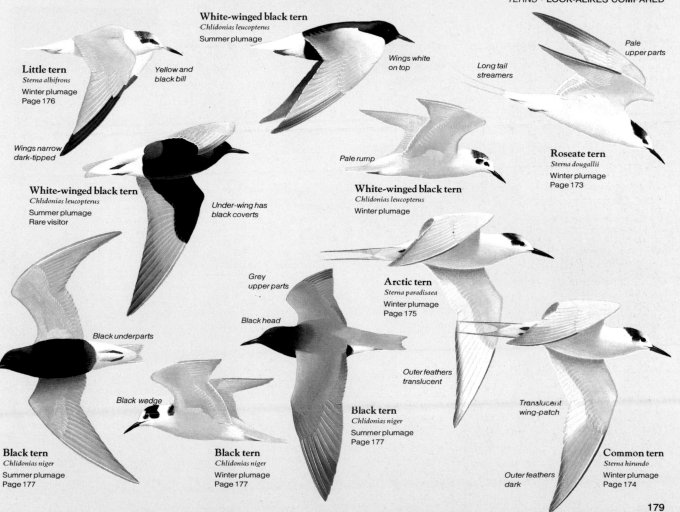

Little tern
Sterna albifrons
Winter plumage
Page 176

Yellow and
black bill

Wings narrow
dark-tipped

White-winged black tern
Chlidonias leucopterus
Summer plumage

Wings white
on top

Pale
upper parts

Long tail
streamers

Roseate tern
Sterna dougallii
Winter plumage
Page 173

White-winged black tern
Chlidonias leucopterus
Summer plumage
Rare visitor

Under-wing has
black coverts

Pale rump

White-winged black tern
Chlidonias leucopterus
Winter plumage

Grey
upper parts

Arctic tern
Sterna paradisaea
Winter plumage
Page 175

Black underparts

Black head

Outer feathers
translucent

Black wedge

Black tern
Chlidonias niger
Summer plumage
Page 177

Translucent
wing-patch

Black tern
Chlidonias niger
Summer plumage
Page 177

Black tern
Chlidonias niger
Winter plumage
Page 177

Outer feathers
dark

Common tern
Sterna hirundo
Winter plumage
Page 174

179

Slim pointed bill

Adult in breeding plumage. Upper parts are paler and browner than those of razorbill; bill is dagger-shaped. Sexes are alike. 16½ in. (42 cm).

Dark brown above

Adult in winter plumage has white face and breast, and fine black line behind eye.

Newly fledged young make their first journey down to the sea at dusk, to reduce danger from predators.

A few guillemots are 'bridled', having a white line behind the eye when in breeding plumage.

Breeds Apr.–July, but some return to colonies in winter.

A 'bowing' action is frequently seen among birds in a colony.

Guillemots nest in dense colonies on precipitous cliff ledges.

The guillemot's single egg is elongated and tapered, reducing the risk of it rolling off the rock-ledge breeding site.

Guillemot *Uria aalge*

When standing upright with its black-brown upper parts and pure white underparts fully visible, the guillemot is the nearest approximation to that feathered 'waiter' of Antarctic waters, the penguin, that exists in Britain. Another similarity is the way in which the breeding birds crowd together in vast colonies. Guillemots need breeding sites near their marine food supply that are as safe as possible from predators. The ledges of islands and offshore rock pillars provide these, but space is limited and the birds pack themselves on to whatever footholds are available, often having just room to stand.

Like many other seabirds, guillemots congregate well before breeding begins in late May. The single egg is strongly tapered; probably a natural adaptation which allows it to roll in a circle on the bare ledge on which it is laid, rather than fall off. Both sexes incubate the egg, balancing it on their feet and covering it with their belly plumage.

The chick is fairly helpless, and if undisturbed remains on its ledge for up to three weeks. Then, still only partly grown, it makes its way down to the sea, where it continues to develop until it flies, four to six weeks later.

Heavy bill

Mass diving by groups of birds is a feature of the pre-breeding ceremonial display activities.

Bird rises laboriously, pattering along the surface, but then flies strongly with rapid wing-beats.

Black upper parts

Adult, summer

Adult, winter

The bird's black throat and breast change to white in winter.

Colonies breed in remote, sheltered crevices in cliffs or on rocky foreshores. There is no nesting material.

Young flutter down to sea from nest site when 14-18 days old.

Present all year; breeding in colonies Apr.–July.

Adult in breeding plumage. Upper parts are blacker than those of guillemot, and bill much stouter. Sexes are alike. 16 in. (40 cm).

Razorbill *Alca torda*

Anyone handling a razorbill without thick gloves is likely to find out quickly how it acquired its common name. The bird's very sharp, hooked upper mandible, well suited to grasping the fish and marine invertebrates that make up its diet, also enables it to look after itself against many would-be predators.

From a greater distance, a watcher can see razorbills in 'rafts' or strings riding out the swell. In the breeding season courting couples may be striking the so-called 'ecstatic' pose, in which one bird stretches its beak upwards, emitting a grating noise with bill parted, while its mate nibbles its throat.

Razorbills tend to nest in the same area as guillemots, but choose more protected sites. Some breeding colonies may number many thousands of birds; one, at Horn Head in County Donegal, was estimated in 1969-70 to hold 45,000 pairs. Egg laying generally begins in early May. Both adults share the incubation duties, but only one feeds the young. The chick makes its way to the sea when about two weeks old, so continues to be tended by a parent. The journey to the water is undertaken under cover of darkness, to avoid the attentions of predatory gulls.

181

Group displays include formation swimming in line astern or line abreast.

Black body

White wing-patch

Perching attitude is usually more crouched than that of the guillemot. The black guillemot seldom roves as far out to sea as other guillemots.

Nestlings are mainly blackish-brown. They take to the water only when fully fledged, at five to six weeks old.

Summer plumage is completely dark except for white wing-patches. The posture is a pre-breeding display. Sexes are alike. 13½ in. (34 cm).

Upper parts in winter are barred black and white, with the head and underparts mainly white.

Present all year at breeding sites on north-west coasts.

Wings are used to aid underwater steering when the bird dives for fish, usually in shallow water.

Black guillemot *Cepphus grylle*

No other bird breeding in Britain can be confused with the black guillemot, for none has its uniformly black summer plumage, broken only by a prominent white wing-patch. Its red feet furnish a splash of colour in an otherwise sombrely attired bird.

The black guillemot resembles other auks in its upright stance, necessary because the legs are set far back for efficient swimming and in its pattering take-off, straight flight and rapid wing-beats, all of which are a result of the bird's small wing area in relation to its body weight. The bird's voice – a shrill and rather plaintive whistling – is, however, very different from the deep-toned barking and grunting calls of other auks. The black guillemot's call is a particular feature of the courting display, when a pair or several pairs of birds circle one another, opening their bills widely to show their bright vermilion gapes.

The black guillemot generally lays its one to three eggs in a crevice or rock-hole near the base of a cliff. The eggs are basically creamy or bluish-white, with spots of reddish-brown or black and pale grey. Incubation, lasting about 24 days, is shared, with the female apparently sitting on the eggs by day and the male taking over at night.

White face

Triangular bill

Flight is rapid, with whirring wing-beats.

Webbed feet are spread as 'air-brakes' when landing.

In winter the face is darker, the bill less colourful and the horny eye-patch is lost.

Breeding colonies dig nesting burrows in grassy cliff tops. Usually only one egg is laid each year, in early May.

Chick has long brown down and small bill. Plumage develops during seven weeks in burrow.

Juvenile birds have more slender bills than adults.

Present all year, mainly on north and west coasts.

A portly build and massive bill, vividly coloured in summer, make adult puffins, male and female, unmistakable. In breeding plumage the face is white, with a horny patch above and below the eye. 12 in. (30 cm).

Puffin *Fratercula arctica*

Its huge red, blue and yellow bill and its orange feet make the puffin one of Britain's more colourful birds, and distinguish it clearly from its close but larger relatives in the auk family, the razorbill and guillemot. This distinctive bill has given the bird its popular names 'sea parrot' and 'bottlenose'.

The puffin is a marine species, and is only rarely seen inland on fresh water when driven ashore by storms. It is a good diver, and thanks to the size of its bill can catch as many as ten small fish in succession without having to swallow, carrying them cross-wise. The bird breeds in colonies sometimes numbering thousands of pairs, which nest in shallow burrows that they dig in the soft turf on cliff tops and islands, or in burrows taken over from rabbits or shearwaters. The puffin's rare call, a deep growling 'arr', is heard near its breeding sites.

Parents share incubation, and both feed the chick for about 40 days, then desert it. The chick stays in its burrow for seven to ten days, without food, as its plumage develops. It then makes its way to the sea by night to avoid hungry gulls. The young puffin does not return to the colony for two to three years, and does not breed until it is four to five years old.

183

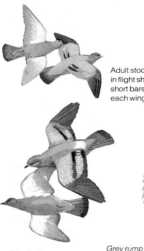

Adult stock dove in flight shows two short bars on each wing.

Grey rump

Rock dove
Columba livia

The rock dove in flight is distinguished from the stock dove by its bolder wing-bars, its white rump and its very long wings.

Stock doves (and rock doves) present all year.

Two pairs of stock doves may fight for possession of a desirable nest-hole.

The many varieties of domestic pigeons and the wild pigeons of city streets are descended from the wild rock dove.

Stock dove *Columba oenas*

Holes in trees and rock faces and, very occasionally, disused rabbit burrows are the stock dove's favoured nesting places. The bird is found in both coastal and inland habitats – in parkland, woodland, and farmland with old trees; and also on cliffs. The nest itself may be merely a few plant fibres, twigs or roots on the floor of the hole; sometimes there is no lining at all.

Two pure white, fairly glossy eggs are usually laid sometime between late March and July – although clutches have been recorded from the beginning of March to October. Starting with the first egg, incubation is shared by both adults and lasts for 16–18 days. The chicks, or squabs as they are called, have rather sparse, coarse tufts of yellowish-brown down. They feed on a milky secretion from the lining of the parents' crops called pigeons' milk – which they take by thrusting their bills into the adults' throats.

The birds have a distinctive display flight, with two or more doves flying in circles and loops, often with wings raised and sometimes punctuated with wing-clapping. The rock dove – similar in general appearance to the stock dove – is found mostly on the coasts of Ireland and northern and western Scotland.

The stock dove is a smaller bird than the wood-pigeon, lacking its white neck and wing markings. Each wing has two short bars; rump is grey. Sexes are alike. 13 in. (33 cm).

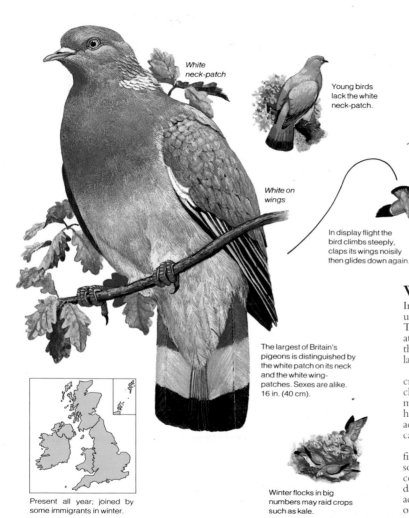

White neck-patch

Young birds lack the white neck-patch.

White on wings

In display flight the bird climbs steeply, claps its wings noisily then glides down again.

White wing-patches are conspicuous in flight. Take-off is marked by loud clatter of wings.

Newly hatched wood-pigeons in the nest are fed on a special secretion regurgitated from the stomach of a parent bird.

The largest of Britain's pigeons is distinguished by the white patch on its neck and the white wing-patches. Sexes are alike. 16 in. (40 cm).

Present all year; joined by some immigrants in winter.

Winter flocks in big numbers may raid crops such as kale.

Wood-pigeon *Columba palumbus*

In the eyes of farmers, the innocuous-looking wood-pigeon is undoubtedly 'public enemy number one' among British birds. Townsfolk find this hard to credit when they see the chubby, attractive bird quietly feeding in a local park. But in the country the wood-pigeon does immense damage to crops. It is particularly fond of cereals, potatoes, beans, peas and greens.

In winter, huge flocks of wood-pigeons feast upon root crops such as turnips, which are grown for animal feed, and clover, with which cereal crops are undersown. Without these modern 'additions' to the agricultural scene, the birds would have fallen back on their more traditional foods of ivy berries, acorns and weed seeds. Wood-pigeons are classified as pests and can be destroyed by the owners of the land where they occur.

The wood-pigeon's nest is a thin but well-built platform of fine twigs, through which the clutch of two pure white eggs can sometimes be seen from below. The newly born chicks are covered sparsely with yellowish down; but during their 29–35 days in the nest they develop their grey juvenile plumage. The adult bird's call is a delightful soft cooing, with the emphasis on the second of the usual five notes.

185

In flight bird looks grey above, with white tail edges. From below, wide white tail-band and dark wingtips show.

Neck mark is less apparent in young birds.

Black collar

In courtship display flight the collared dove rises steeply with strongly flapping wings, then glides down, often uttering a growling note.

Like all pigeons and doves, the collared dove drinks continuously without raising its head between sips.

The collared dove's nest, usually built in a tree, occasionally on buildings, is a thin, flat platform of twiglets and rootlets.

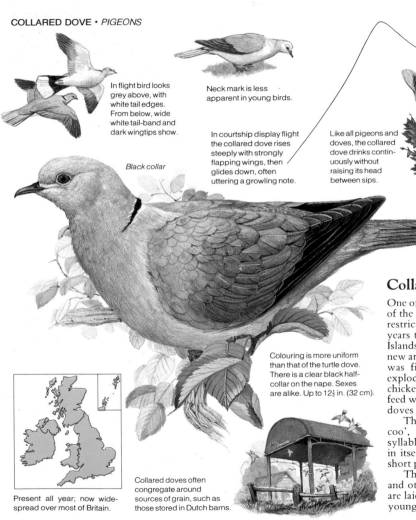

Colouring is more uniform than that of the turtle dove. There is a clear black half-collar on the nape. Sexes are alike. Up to 12½ in. (32 cm).

Present all year; now widespread over most of Britain.

Collared doves often congregate around sources of grain, such as those stored in Dutch barns.

Collared dove *Streptopelia decaocto*

One of the most dramatic success stories in the bird world is that of the collared dove. Before about 1930 its European range was restricted to parts of the Balkans, but during the following 40 years the whole of Europe was colonised, as far as the Faeroe Islands and Iceland. By 1955 the bird was nesting in Britain. The new arrivals seemed to find an ecological niche that no other bird was filling, and having little competition, their population exploded. Favourite habitats were in the vicinity of farms, chicken runs, corn mills and docks, where grain or other animal feed were often spilled. In some areas, there are so many collared doves that they are treated as pests.

The bird's song is a reedy, hoarse-sounding 'cooo-cooooo-coo', with the emphasis on the middle syllable and the last syllable almost an afterthought. Though quite a pleasing sound in itself, it is repeated so frequently and regularly, with only short pauses, that it becomes extremely monotonous.

The breeding season is lengthy, some pairs starting in March and others rearing young as late as September. Only two eggs are laid in a clutch, but five broods may be raised in a year. The young spend three weeks in the nest.

186

Courtship display postures include a bowing ritual performed in front of the female.

The frail nest of sticks is often built lower than those of other pigeons, and may be among brambles.

Reddish-brown upper parts are conspicuous in flight. From below, the tail appears black with a rounded white tip and the wings dusky.

Red-brown above

Black and white neck-patch

Pink breast

The turtle dove is a slender bird with chequered black and chestnut upper parts, and a black and white neck-patch. Sexes are alike. Up to 11 in. (28 cm).

Young bird is duller in colouring than adult, and lacks adult's neck-patch.

Like all young pigeons, the nestlings – called squabs – have a covering of coarse, hair-like, straw-coloured down.

Apr. – Sept. visitor; has bred in Ireland.

Though the turtle dove is shyer than the collared dove, it will enter farmyards where grain is scattered to share it with poultry.

Turtle dove *Streptopelia turtur*

One of the most endearing bird calls of high summer is the musical, throbbing, purring coo of the turtle dove – 'poooorrr-poooorrr-poooorrr', the syllables repeated continuously in groups of two to five. It is a lazy, soporific sound, appropriate to the hot, hazy days on which it is so frequently heard. An attempt to represent this sound in the Latin species name *turtur* is the origin of the common name 'turtle' dove.

Turtle doves arrive in Britain from their winter quarters in sub-tropical Africa in the latter part of April and May, along with a few destined to move through to breeding grounds further on in northern Europe; they depart again from early August to the beginning of October. In between, some pairs will have succeeded in raising two broods of young. The nest is a flimsy, flat platform of thin twiglets and roots.

Most clutches consist of two pinkish-white eggs, which are incubated by both male and female alternately for about two weeks. The chicks are fed by both parents with 'pigeons' milk', a soft, cheesy substance derived from the crop lining, and taken from the adults' throats by their offspring. Numbers have declined seriously since the 1980s, especially in the west.

187

CUCKOO

Angry reed warbler scares off cuckoo seeking nest.

Reed warbler feeds hungry young cuckoo.

Red-brown juvenile

Adult

Adult cuckoo in flight shows characteristic pointed wings; wing-beat is shallow. Wings of young cuckoos are rounded, like those of owls.

Juvenile

Cuckoos lay their eggs in the nests of other birds, especially meadow pipits, dunnocks and reed warblers. A newly hatched cuckoo pushes the eggs of the host bird out of the nest with its back, and soon fills the nest itself.

Cuckoo removes an egg from host's nest before laying her own.

New-born cuckoo ejects host bird's eggs.

Juvenile cuckoo may occur in red-brown plumage, with brown feathers. All young have white spot on nape of neck.

The cuckoo's song inspired the 16th-century poet Edmund Spenser to write of 'The merry cuckoo, messenger of Spring'. It favours wooded areas.

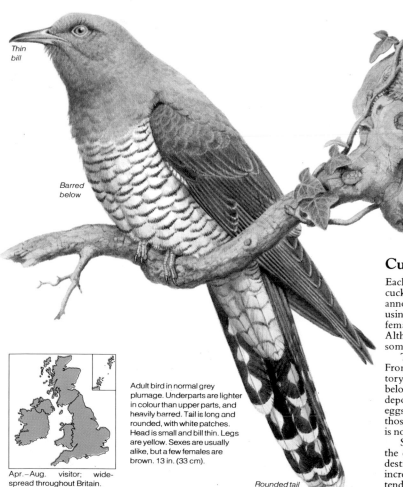

Thin bill

Barred below

Adult bird in normal grey plumage. Underparts are lighter in colour than upper parts, and heavily barred. Tail is long and rounded, with white patches. Head is small and bill thin. Legs are yellow. Sexes are usually alike, but a few females are brown. 13 in. (33 cm).

Apr.–Aug. visitor; widespread throughout Britain.

Rounded tail

Cuckoo *Cuculus canorus*

Each April the most eagerly awaited bird-call is that of the cuckoo, a sure sign that summer is on its way. The male bird announces his presence from a high perch and at great length, using the same monotonous but musical notes – 'coo-coo'. The female's call consists of an explosive, bubbling chuckle. Although mid-April is the likeliest time to hear the first cuckoo, some birds arrive from Africa towards the end of March.

The parasitic breeding habits of the cuckoo are notorious. From late May onwards the female flies over her chosen territory in search of foster-homes for her young. She selects a nest belonging to a pair of small birds – such as reed warblers – and deposits a single egg in it. Altogether, she may lay as many as 12 eggs in 12 different nests. Sometimes the eggs closely resemble those of the host bird: this is a natural adaptation and the female is not able to alter the colour and markings at will.

Since the mid-1940s there has been a widespread decrease in the cuckoo population. Reasons for this probably include the destruction of much of its habitat, including hedgerows; the increasing use of insecticides, which kill off its food; and the tendency towards colder, wetter, springs and summers.

189

When threatened, the adult bird flattens itself defensively on a barn floor, its wings spread horizontally. Its long-necked nestlings shelter behind it.

White face

Hollow elms are a favourite nest site with the barn owl, but they are fast disappearing from the countryside.

White underparts

Adult has white underparts, and golden-buff upper parts mottled with grey. It has a white heart-shaped face and long legs. Sexes are alike. 13½ in. (34 cm).

Present all year; scarce in parts of eastern Britain.

The barn owl systematically patrols fields at night in search of prey upon which to pounce.

The barn owl preys mainly on rats, mice and voles, which it usually hunts at night and carries off to its nest.

Barn owl *Tyto alba*

A barn owl's hoarse, eerie, prolonged shriek, often uttered in flight, still has the power to strike a chill into the hearts of those who recall the owl's reputation over the centuries as a bird of ill omen. Geoffrey Chaucer, in the 14th century, referred to the bird as a 'prophet of woe and mischance'.

Year after year many barn owls return to established roosts and breeding sites in old barns, ruins and exposed buildings such as church towers. The birds also inhabit natural holes in trees and cliffs. Often these sites are revealed by large accumulations of castings or pellets, the indigestible remains of prey.

The breeding season is long, starting in February or March. Sometimes there are two broods; though numbers of birds declined seriously in the mid-1980s. The size of each clutch of white eggs varies from three to 11, depending on the food available, but four to seven is the average. The male feeds the female during the 32–34 days of incubation. Young birds have two coats of down, the first white, the second, after 12 days, creamy. Like adult birds, the young make various hissing and snoring noises, but if disturbed in the nest they snap their bills together loudly. They fly at eight to ten weeks old.

Roosting and nesting places are on low hillocks above open ground.

The snowy owl's gliding flight action is like that of the buzzard, and is distinctive from a long way off.

The female bird's wings are spread and thrust forward as it defends its nest from attack by an Arctic skua.

Snowy owls have bred in the Shetlands, but are more often seen as rare winter visitors in the far north of Britain.

Snowy owl *Nyctea scandiaca*

For years the snowy owl was no more than a rare winter visitor to northern Britain. Then, in 1967, a nesting pair was discovered on the island of Fetlar in the Shetlands. At least 16 young birds have fledged since, but despite special protection the snowy owl has failed to establish itself as a breeding bird in Britain.

The pure white plumage of the male bird is adapted to the Arctic region where it usually breeds. In winter many snowy owls still wander southwards to escape the worst of the weather, and occasional birds are recorded in the Outer Hebrides, the Orkneys, the Shetlands and northern Scotland and Ireland.

The fortunes of the snowy owl depend very much on the availability of its prey: lemmings in the Arctic, and rabbits, mice and voles in Britain. For a nest, the female scrapes a hollow in the ground, which is sometimes lined with a few scraps of moss, grass or feathers. As soon as the first egg is laid, the female starts to incubate. Since the chicks hatch over a period of up to a fortnight, the first chick may be quite large by the time the last is hatched. The result is that the size of the eventual brood matches the food supply; because the weakest die when food is short, the welfare of the entire brood is not jeopardised.

Mainly Shetlands, where pair bred 1967–75.

Adult male is almost pure white, flecked with dark brown. It is a large bird, with yellow eyes and without ear-tufts. Its prey includes smaller birds such as the ptarmigan. 21–24 in. (53–60 cm).

The male bird is less strongly marked than the female, which has striking black or brownish bars.

The little owl's flight is low, swift and strongly undulating.

Yellow eyes

Fence posts and tree stumps are favourite day-time perches.

Its small size, yellow eyes and 'frowning' expression identify the little owl. Insects such as dor-beetles are its main prey. Sexes are alike. 8½ in. (22 cm).

The little owl prefers to nest and roost in a hole in an old orchard tree or pollarded willow. Both parents feed the young.

Fledgelings, when anxious, bob their heads in a comical manner.

Present all year; derived from 19th-century introductions.

Holes and crevices in old buildings are sometimes used as nesting sites. The eggs are incubated by the female.

Little owl *Athene noctua*

Warm spring evenings are the best time to listen for the call of the little owl: a long, musical but plaintive mewing 'kiew', repeated at widely spaced intervals. Occasionally the call is interspersed with a more excited, yelping 'werrrow'. The place to listen is on agricultural land where there are plenty of hollow trees and farm buildings, which provide nesting sites. Little owls can also be found in parkland, old orchards and quarries, and on sea cliffs.

The little owl was introduced to Britain from the Continent during the last century. By the early part of the 20th century it was widespread, breeding throughout most of England south of Yorkshire, except for the West Country. Wales was also partly colonised.

From mid-April onwards the single clutch of three to five eggs is laid on the bare floor of the nest cavity. The chicks hatch after about a month, and are at first clothed in thick, short, white down. Both adults feed them. They leave the nest often up to a week before they can fly well at five weeks old. The bird's diet consists largely of earthworms, molluscs and insects – particularly beetles – and some small mammals.

Small birds often mob a tawny owl discovered in daylight, though they seldom succeed in disturbing their victim.

Recently fledged young still retain much of their barred downy underparts.

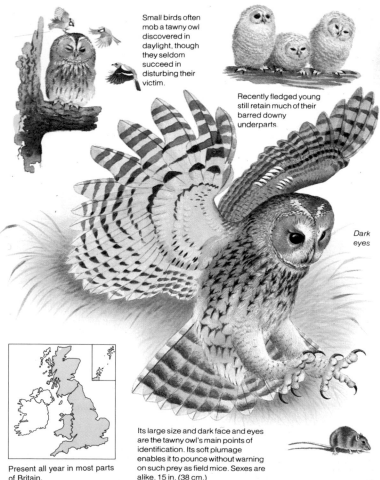

Dark eyes

Present all year in most parts of Britain.

Its large size and dark face and eyes are the tawny owl's main points of identification. Its soft plumage enables it to pounce without warning on such prey as field mice. Sexes are alike. 15 in. (38 cm.)

The owl watches for its prey from a tree perch, then swoops down in silent flight.

The tawny owl usually nests in a tree-hole, but will readily use a specially designed box. The young fly in about five weeks.

Tawny owl *Strix aluco*

The call of the tawny owl is one of the best known of all bird songs. The familiar hoot, often described as 'to-whit-to-wooo', is really 'hoo-hoo-hoo . . . hooooo': two or three short notes followed by a pause before the final quavering one. A less well-known call is the 'kee-wick' note, with a similar softer 'sheevick' uttered by the newly fledged young.

Owls are silent in flight because of their soft plumage and the comb-like leading edge to the wingtip. This allows the tawny owl to pounce from a perch, unheard by its prey. The bird's extraordinarily sensitive eyes and ears enable it to locate its prey in very dim light. Its diet consists largely of small mammals, but includes birds, frogs, fish, worms and large insects.

The tawny owl occurs in woodland and areas with scattered mature timber such as farmland, parklands and large gardens. Its nest is a shallow scrape in the bottom of a tree-hole or rock crevice, or very rarely a hole in the ground. Old nests of other birds are sometimes used. From about March onwards, the single clutch of one to seven rounded white eggs is laid at intervals of up to a week apart. Incubation starts with the first egg, so the young vary greatly in size.

193

In flight, the black patches on the wing 'wrists' are less strongly marked than those of the short-eared owl. The tail has tiny bars, and the underparts are darkish.

Ear-opening on left is slightly behind that on right. Sounds reach one ear before the other; time-lag enables owl to pin-point the source.

Present all year; local, and nowhere common.

Ear-tufts

The long-eared owl's ear-tufts and distinctive face pattern identify it when seen roosting by day. Sexes are alike. 13½ in. (34 cm.)

When anxious, the bird draws its body up into a stiff, slender posture.

To frighten off intruders at the nest, the brooding adult droops its wings and raises its back feathers to frame its head.

Long-eared owl *Asio otus*

Although the most conspicuous features of the long-eared owl are its 'ears', they are in fact no more than tufts of feathers; the actual ear openings are situated at the sides of the head. Active only at night, this owl spends the day roosting in dense tree cover, when it is easily overlooked by the casual observer. It lives in coniferous woodland, plantations, small copses and clumps of trees in farmland and moorland.

The bird's main call is a low, drawn-out 'oooo' repeated three times every few seconds. It has considerable carrying power, and can be heard up to half a mile away. The chicks have a curious call, like a creaking gate hinge.

Breeding begins at any time from late February onwards, and the courtship display involves wing clapping and flying with slow, exaggerated wing-beats. The pure white eggs – three to eight in number, but usually four or five – are laid on alternate days in an old nest of some other large bird, or in a squirrel's drey, or very occasionally on the ground at the foot of a tree or amongst heather. The female normally incubates the eggs for 25–30 days, and feeds the hatched young with food brought by the male. The chicks fledge at 23 or 24 days old.

Long, barred wings have dark patches at 'wrists' on both upper and lower surfaces, contrasting with the pale primary feathers.

Pale rear

A semi-horizontal stance is often adopted when perching.

Present all year; more widespread in winter.

Dark front

Display flight includes a loud clapping made as the wingtips meet below the body.

Underparts, seen in flight, are dark at the front and pale at the rear. Tail bars are fewer but bolder than those of the long-eared owl. Sexes are alike. 15 in. (38 cm).

The short-eared owl nests on the ground; the young move away before they can fly.

The number of short-eared owls in a district depends upon the availability of short-tailed voles, their main prey.

Short-eared owl *Asio flammeus*

The short-eared owl hunts by low–level searching, its sensitive ears enabling it to pinpoint the faintest rustle in the grass as it covers rough grasslands and other open country in search of prey. The bird is immediately identified by its wing-beats which are like those of an enormous moth, the wings passing through a large arc.

The bird hunts in daylight or at dusk in treeless country, chiefly in upland Wales, the Pennines and Scotland. Some breeding pairs occur in suitable country in Kent and East Anglia.

Breeding begins from April onwards. Three to eight white eggs are laid in a shallow, unlined hollow on the ground among long grass or heather. The eggs are laid at intervals of two days or more; incubation starts with the first egg laid and lasts for 24–28 days. The chicks, clad all over in thick creamy-buff down, are fed by the female with small rodents such as short-tailed voles, and also with shrews, small birds and insects brought by the male. The short-eared owl is usually silent except when the nest is approached too closely, when a shrill 'keeorr' may be heard. The British population is joined by migrant birds from the Continent.

195

Grey-brown plumage

Adult male has soft, grey-brown plumage. Slow beating of long wings is characteristic. Bill is small, but as it is opened, lower jaw becomes wider, giving wide gape for catching insects. 10½ in. (27 cm).

Wide gape

When perching, bird is usually aligned along the branch rather than across it.

Nightjars are usually seen in flight at dusk, gliding and banking erratically but buoyantly.

During the day nightjars lie motionless on the ground, their plumage blending with the dead vegetation around.

May–Oct. visitor; commonest East Anglia and the south.

Female lacks white wing-spots and tail-spots of male. The nest is no more than a scrape in the ground.

Nightjar *Caprimulgus europaeus*

Its extraordinary churring-jarring song, heard mostly at night, gives the nightjar its name. The sound is rather like that of a small engine revving rapidly for stretches of up to five minutes, with an alternating rise and fall in pitch. During this performance, the bird is usually perched lengthwise along a dead branch – though it sometimes delivers its song from a leafy branch, or even from the ground or in flight. By contrast, the call note is a simple 'cooic'.

On arriving from the southern half of Africa in the spring, the nightjar takes up territory in open woodland, heathland, moorland or coastal sand-dunes. During the day, the birds are almost invisible as they lie motionless on the ground and, from a distance, they are often mistaken for bunches of dead leaves. They lay their eggs on bare ground, often near dead wood, and this makes a sitting bird even harder to see.

The clutch of two eggs is laid from about mid-May onwards. Both parents take part in incubation, but the hen only does so during the day. Both birds feed the chicks until the female starts to incubate her second clutch, when the male manages alone. After dusk, the nightjar feeds on flying insects.

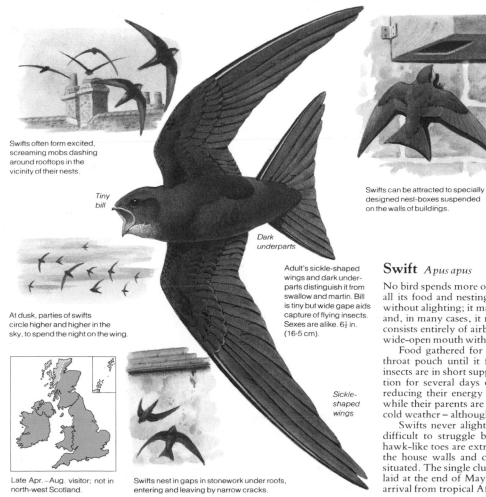

Swifts often form excited, screaming mobs dashing around rooftops in the vicinity of their nests.

Tiny bill

Dark underparts

At dusk, parties of swifts circle higher and higher in the sky, to spend the night on the wing.

Adult's sickle-shaped wings and dark underparts distinguish it from swallow and martin. Bill is tiny but wide gape aids capture of flying insects. Sexes are alike. 6½ in. (16·5 cm).

Sickle-shaped wings

Late Apr.–Aug. visitor; not in north-west Scotland.

Swifts nest in gaps in stonework under roofs, entering and leaving by narrow cracks.

Swifts can be attracted to specially designed nest-boxes suspended on the walls of buildings.

Young birds have pale feather edges. Their shallow nest is of fine plant material stuck together with parents' saliva.

Swift *Apus apus*

No bird spends more of its life in the air than the swift. It collects all its food and nesting material in flight; it drinks and bathes without alighting; it mates and can spend the night on the wing; and, in many cases, it manages to outfly birds of prey. Its food consists entirely of airborne insects which are funnelled into its wide-open mouth with the help of the surrounding stiff bristles.

Food gathered for the young is accumulated in the bird's throat pouch until it forms a large, compacted bulge. When insects are in short supply, the chicks can survive partial starvation for several days or even weeks by becoming torpid, so reducing their energy loss. Before their feathers develop, and while their parents are out hunting, they can even survive quite cold weather – although they become sluggish at such times.

Swifts never alight on the ground voluntarily, and find it difficult to struggle back into the air if they do. But their hawk-like toes are extremely strong, enabling them to cling to the house walls and cliff faces on which their nest holes are situated. The single clutch of two or three smooth, white eggs is laid at the end of May or the beginning of June, on the adults' arrival from tropical Africa.

197

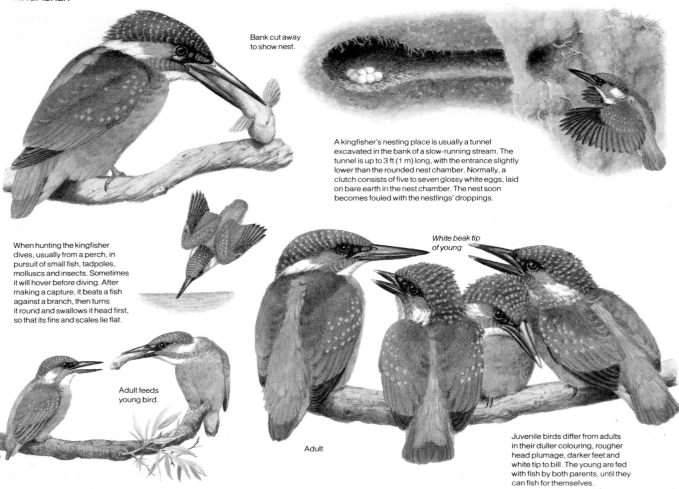

Bank cut away to show nest.

A kingfisher's nesting place is usually a tunnel excavated in the bank of a slow-running stream. The tunnel is up to 3 ft (1 m) long, with the entrance slightly lower than the rounded nest chamber. Normally, a clutch consists of five to seven glossy white eggs, laid on bare earth in the nest chamber. The nest soon becomes fouled with the nestlings' droppings.

When hunting the kingfisher dives, usually from a perch, in pursuit of small fish, tadpoles, molluscs and insects. Sometimes it will hover before diving. After making a capture, it beats a fish against a branch, then turns it round and swallows it head first, so that its fins and scales lie flat.

White beak tip of young

Adult feeds young bird.

Adult

Juvenile birds differ from adults in their duller colouring, rougher head plumage, darker feet and white tip to bill. The young are fed with fish by both parents, until they can fish for themselves.

In flight, short wings and tail and brilliant blue-green back are clearly visible. Flight is low, straight and swift, with rapid wing-beats.

Iridescent blue-green above

Adult male is a distinctive, stockily built bird with a large head, iridescent blue-green upper parts and orange-chestnut cheeks and underparts. It has a white throat and neck-patch, red feet and a long, dagger-like bill. Sexes are alike. 6½ in. (16·5 cm).

Orange-chestnut below

Red feet

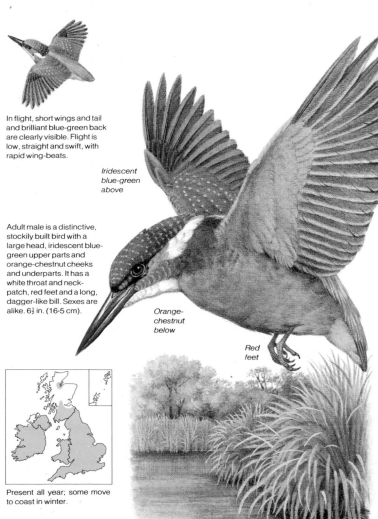

Present all year; some move to coast in winter.

A branch above the water provides the kingfisher with a perch from which to dive after its prey, and a post against which to kill the fish before eating it.

Kingfisher *Alcedo atthis*

Few birds are shyer than the kingfisher, so that birdwatchers rarely have a close view of it. The most that many people see of this beautifully coloured bird is a brief glimpse as it flashes past them – a swift arrow of colour speeding along the river bank. Frequently, the first indication of the bird's presence is its call: a loud, shrill, piping 'cheeeee' or 'chikeeee'.

The kingfisher spends all year in Britain, and suffers severely in cold winters when its food supply is literally cut off from it. Rivers and lakes ice over, and the bird cannot get at its usual diet of small fish and aquatic insects. At such times the kingfisher may move to coastal rock pools and creeks, where it has a better chance of survival.

Both male and female dig the burrow in which the nest is placed. The nest is gradually littered with an accumulation of regurgitated fish bones. Both birds incubate the eggs. The young are hatched after about three weeks and spend nearly four weeks in the nest. The adults get very dirty while moving in and out of the tunnel and frequently clean themselves by plunging into the adjacent stream. The kingfisher is seldom preyed upon by other birds, as its flesh has an unpleasant taste.

199

Male

Female

Golden oriole
Oriolus oriolus

Male is bright yellow, with black wings and black and yellow tail: female is yellow-green with darker green wings and tail, streaked with grey below. In spite of bright plumage, can be hard to see in favoured woodland habitat. 9¼ in. (24 cm).

Immature

Adult

Woodchat shrike
Lanius senator

Adult bird has red-brown crown and nape with black frontal band, white throat and breast, dark wings and distinctive white shoulder patches and rump. Immature bird is paler brown. Sexes are alike. 6½ in. (16·5 cm).

Rare summer visitors

In a good summer, some birds which normally migrate to southern and central Europe extend their journeys farther north-west and bring a dash of exotic colour to Britain. A few golden orioles now breed annually in East Anglia, and hoopoes sometimes nest. Despite the brilliance of their plumage, these birds are not always conspicuous: from a distance, the hoopoe's stripes, like those of the zebra, blend with a background of soil or rocks; and the golden oriole is hard to see among the green leaves where it usually hides. For the most part, the food of these birds consists of large insects.

Bee-eater
Merops apiaster

Upper parts are red-brown and
yellow, throat yellow. Bill is
long. In flight, blue-green breast
and belly, pale chestnut under-
wing and long central tail feathers are prominent. Sexes are
alike. 11 in. (28 cm).

Hoopoe
Upupa epops

Unmistakable features are black-
edged crest, pink-brown body, black
and white tail and wing-bars, and
long curved beak. Wings round and
barred; sexes alike. 11 in. (28 cm).

Roller
Coracias garrulus

Light blue plumage is relieved by
chestnut mantle; the greenish-
blue tail has brown central feathers. In flight, vivid blue wings
edged with black stand out.
Sexes are alike. 12 in. (30 cm).

201

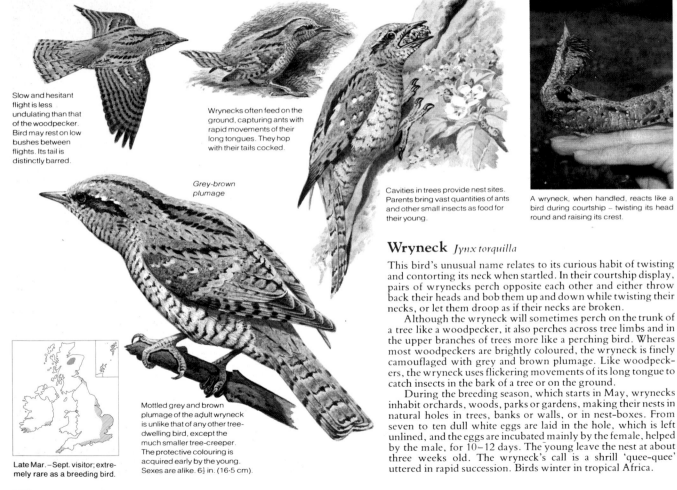

Slow and hesitant flight is less undulating than that of the woodpecker. Bird may rest on low bushes between flights. Its tail is distinctly barred.

Wrynecks often feed on the ground, capturing ants with rapid movements of their long tongues. They hop with their tails cocked.

Grey-brown plumage

Cavities in trees provide nest sites. Parents bring vast quantities of ants and other small insects as food for their young.

A wryneck, when handled, reacts like a bird during courtship – twisting its head round and raising its crest.

Late Mar. – Sept. visitor; extremely rare as a breeding bird.

Mottled grey and brown plumage of the adult wryneck is unlike that of any other tree-dwelling bird, except the much smaller tree-creeper. The protective colouring is acquired early by the young. Sexes are alike. 6½ in. (16·5 cm).

Wryneck *Jynx torquilla*

This bird's unusual name relates to its curious habit of twisting and contorting its neck when startled. In their courtship display, pairs of wrynecks perch opposite each other and either throw back their heads and bob them up and down while twisting their necks, or let them droop as if their necks are broken.

Although the wryneck will sometimes perch on the trunk of a tree like a woodpecker, it also perches across tree limbs and in the upper branches of trees more like a perching bird. Whereas most woodpeckers are brightly coloured, the wryneck is finely camouflaged with grey and brown plumage. Like woodpeckers, the wryneck uses flickering movements of its long tongue to catch insects in the bark of a tree or on the ground.

During the breeding season, which starts in May, wrynecks inhabit orchards, woods, parks or gardens, making their nests in natural holes in trees, banks or walls, or in nest-boxes. From seven to ten dull white eggs are laid in the hole, which is left unlined, and the eggs are incubated mainly by the female, helped by the male, for 10–12 days. The young leave the nest at about three weeks old. The wryneck's call is a shrill 'quee-quee' uttered in rapid succession. Birds winter in tropical Africa.

In flight, the green woodpecker's yellowish rump is its most striking feature.

Red crown

Juvenile

Green back

Adult bird's green back and red crown are distinctive. Male has a red moustache. Stiff tail feathers act as a prop while climbing. 12½ in. (32 cm).

Female

Adult female has black moustache. Juveniles have pale-spotted upper parts and streaked underparts.

The green woodpecker may sometimes perch on a branch in the water. It favours meadows, woods and parks.

Present all year; spreading in Scotland since 1951.

Green woodpecker *Picus viridis*

In some country areas the green woodpecker, largest of Britain's woodpeckers, is known as the 'yaffle' – an allusion to the bird's attractive, loud laughing call. This takes the form of a rapidly repeated 'kew-kew-kew . . .', fairly high-pitched at first, then falling. The green woodpecker seldom indulges in the 'drumming' action of the other species. It also feeds much more on the ground, for besides larvae of wood-boring insects, beetles, moths and flies, it is particularly partial to ants and their grubs. The bird has also been known to damage hives in search of bees and their grubs.

During courtship, the green woodpecker performs the same spiral pursuits round branches as the greater spotted woodpecker. However, the green species has one display all of its own; males fighting over a female sway their heads from side-to-side, with wings spread, tails fanned and crests raised. Only one brood is produced each year. Usually, five to seven eggs are laid in a bare nesting chamber, but clutches of up to 11 eggs have been known. Both sexes share in incubating the eggs for 18–19 days, and in feeding the young for 18–21 days by regurgitating a milky paste produced from their insect food.

Starlings often appropriate woodpeckers' nests.

In flight, the great spotted woodpecker's white shoulder patches are easily recognised.

The bird sometimes makes aerial sorties, like a flycatcher, to take insects on the wing.

Female

White shoulder

Juveniles have a red cap like the adult male lesser spotted woodpecker, and have white shoulder patches.

The great spotted, most widespread of the British woodpeckers, takes food put out for it in wooded areas.

A nest hole in a tree, usually at least 10 ft (3 m) above the ground, is excavated by the male and female together.

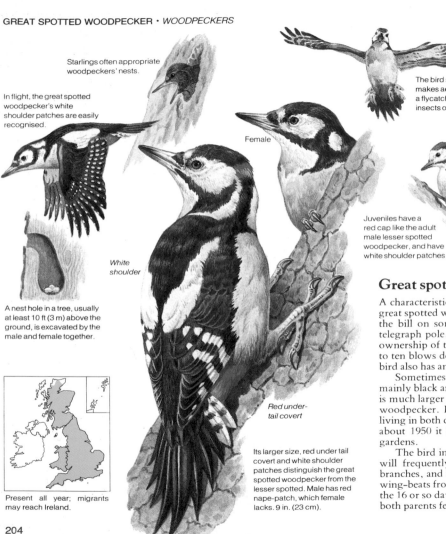

Red under tail covert

Its larger size, red under tail covert and white shoulder patches distinguish the great spotted woodpecker from the lesser spotted. Male has red nape-patch, which female lacks. 9 in. (23 cm).

Present all year; migrants may reach Ireland.

Great spotted woodpecker *Dendrocopos major*

A characteristic 'drumming' often gives away the presence of a great spotted woodpecker. The sound is made by rapid blows of the bill on some resonant surface such as a dead bough or a telegraph pole. Both sexes do this, as a means of proclaiming ownership of territory, and each 'drum' consists of some eight to ten blows delivered within the space of a single second. The bird also has an unmistakable call, a far-carrying 'tchick'.

Sometimes known as the pied woodpecker because of its mainly black and white plumage, the great spotted woodpecker is much larger than the lesser spotted but smaller than the green woodpecker. It is more a woodland bird than the other two, living in both coniferous and deciduous woods. However, since about 1950 it has spread into towns and suburban parks and gardens.

The bird indulges in elaborate courtship displays. The male will frequently make spiral pursuits of a female round tree branches, and a mutual display flight involves short, quivering wing-beats from tree to tree. The female does the major share of the 16 or so days' incubation of the pure white, glossy eggs, but both parents feed the chicks – on insects brought in the bill.

Red cap

In flight, the adult bird's barred back is noticeable.

Female

Juvenile

Adult bird is smaller than the great spotted woodpecker, and has no red under tail. It has barred upper parts, and face and underparts are whitish-brown with dark streaking. Male has a red cap. 5¾ in. (14·5 cm).

Barred back

Birds often forage on twigs and branches, as well as on trunks and major limbs of a tree. Juveniles have brownish-white foreheads; female has white cap.

A parent bird brings insect larvae to feed its young, sheltering deep within their tree-hole nest in open woodland.

The lesser spotted woodpecker often nests in orchards and gardens.

Present all year; uncommon; most numerous in south.

Lesser spotted woodpecker *Dendrocopos minor*

Barely larger than a sparrow, the lesser spotted woodpecker is the smallest of Britain's woodpeckers. It is an elusive bird, sometimes found in wooded gardens, old orchards, parkland and spinneys throughout much of England and Wales.

The lesser spotted woodpecker climbs up trees with the casual ease typical of the woodpecker family. February and especially March see the beginning of 'drumming' – the rapid hammering of a branch to establish territory. Each spell of drumming, which lasts for about two seconds, is usually longer and fainter than that of the great spotted woodpecker; the blows are struck at the rate of about 15 per second.

During courtship the male flutters moth-like from tree to tree, or sometimes both birds sit rigidly side by side on a bough. To make its nest, the lesser spotted woodpecker pecks a hole from the dead or rotting wood. The hole is then widened and deepened until it passes down inside the branch to the nest chamber itself. The breeding season is lengthy, and eggs, which are incubated for a fortnight, may be laid from April to June. Hatched naked, the young grow their juvenile feathers during the three weeks they spend in the nest.

205

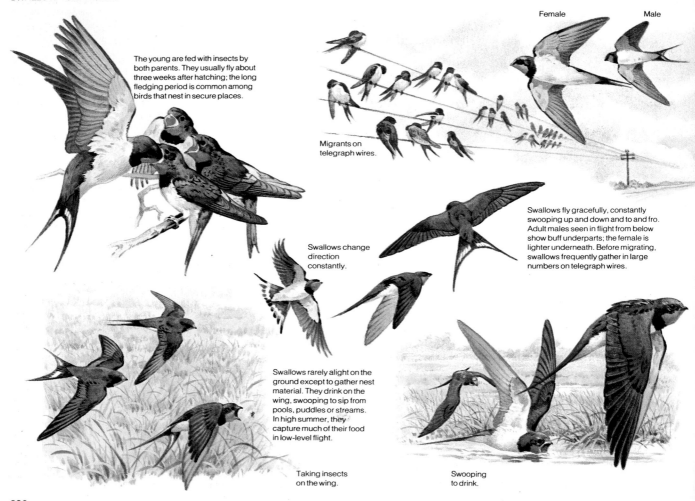

The young are fed with insects by both parents. They usually fly about three weeks after hatching; the long fledging period is common among birds that nest in secure places.

Female

Male

Migrants on telegraph wires.

Swallows fly gracefully, constantly swooping up and down and to and fro. Adult males seen in flight from below show buff underparts; the female is lighter underneath. Before migrating, swallows frequently gather in large numbers on telegraph wires.

Swallows change direction constantly.

Swallows rarely alight on the ground except to gather nest material. They drink on the wing, swooping to sip from pools, puddles or streams. In high summer, they capture much of their food in low-level flight.

Taking insects on the wing.

Swooping to drink.

Russet throat

Female

Male

Long tail streamers

Adult male's russet throat and long tail streamers are unmistakable. Upper parts are bluish-black, and there are white spots on the tail. Adult female has shorter tail streamers and is generally duller. 7½ in. (19 cm).

Mar.–Oct. visitor; widespread; none in cities.

The swallow's nest is a cup of mud with straw to bind it together, lined with feathers and placed on a ledge or against a roof beam or similar support.

Swallow *Hirundo rustica*

The old country saying that 'one swallow doesn't make a summer' is more justified than many of its kind. For although the swallow is popularly regarded as a harbinger of summer, the first birds may appear from their South African wintering grounds as early as the beginning of March. Adult birds usually return to the same locality where they bred the previous year – often to exactly the same site. Throughout the summer breeding season the swallow's pleasant twittering warble may be heard well before sunrise, from a bird in flight or from a perch.

When men lived in caves swallows probably did the same; nowadays they have adapted to nesting in buildings and under bridges. Usually, each of the two or three clutches produced in a year consists of three to six eggs, glossy white with a speckling of pinkish-brown or pale grey.

In autumn, adults and young birds head for the South African sun, feeding off insects caught on the wing. It was once thought that when swallows disappeared in autumn they had buried themselves in the mud of rivers and ponds: an idea doubtless fostered by the fact that the birds often congregate in such places just before they migrate.

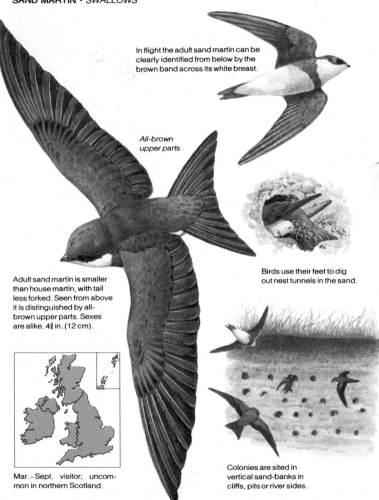

In flight the adult sand martin can be clearly identified from below by the brown band across its white breast.

All-brown upper parts

Adult sand martin is smaller than house martin, with tail less forked. Seen from above it is distinguished by all-brown upper parts. Sexes are alike. 4¾ in. (12 cm).

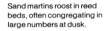

Birds use their feet to dig out nest tunnels in the sand.

Colonies are sited in vertical sand-banks in cliffs, pits or river sides.

Sand martins roost in reed beds, often congregating in large numbers at dusk.

Once they are well feathered, young sand martins scramble to the burrow entrance to clamour for food.

Sand martin *Riparia riparia*

Sand martins take their name from their nesting habits, for they scrape out horizontal tunnels 24–36 in. (60–90 cm) long in sand-banks and enlarge them at the end to form a nesting chamber. Industrialisation has provided them with plenty of nesting sites such as railway cuttings, or sand and gravel quarries; but lacking these they use river banks, soft sea-cliffs or ready-made holes.

The nesting chamber is lined with plant material and feathers picked up in flight. Breeding starts in mid-May in the south, and there are usually four or five eggs in a clutch; as with many hole-nesting birds, the eggs are pure white, probably so that they can be located in the dark. Both parents share incubation, which takes 12–16 days. The first chicks are fed by both adults in the nest itself, but later they come to the burrow entrance. After about 19 days they take to the air. Sand martins fly south to equatorial West Africa in August or September, where periodic droughts take a severe toll of their numbers.

Like swallows, sand martins feed on insects on the wing, often over water, but their flight lacks the swallow's easy grace. They have a hard, twittering call.

House sparrows often usurp a martin's nest.

Dense colonies may be found under sheltering roof eaves, the birds constantly coming and going with characteristic flicking of wings.

Young house martins remain in the nest for about three weeks until very fully developed. Both parents feed them.

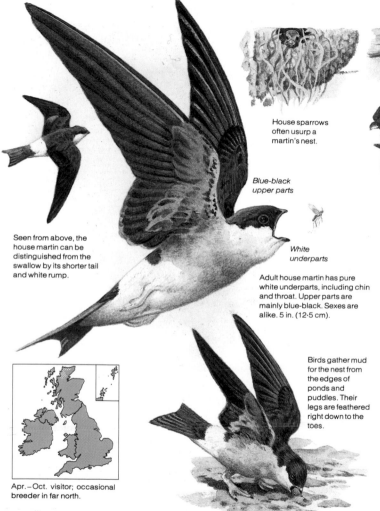

Seen from above, the house martin can be distinguished from the swallow by its shorter tail and white rump.

Blue-black upper parts

White underparts

Adult house martin has pure white underparts, including chin and throat. Upper parts are mainly blue-black. Sexes are alike. 5 in. (12·5 cm).

Birds gather mud for the nest from the edges of ponds and puddles. Their legs are feathered right down to the toes.

Apr.–Oct. visitor; occasional breeder in far north.

House martin *Delichon urbica*

A masterpiece in mud, the house martin's nest is snug and flask-shaped with only a small entrance near the top at one side. It is commonly built just under the eaves of a house. The mud pellets are taken up in beakfuls by both male and female and reinforced with plant fibres. Traditionally the house martin is a cliff-nesting species, and although there are still a few cliff colonies to be found, the bird has happily adapted itself to the convenient sites offered by man-made buildings.

Breeding starts towards the end of May, a few weeks after the birds arrive from their African wintering quarters. The nest is lined with dried grass, other plant material and feathers before the female lays a clutch of four or five glossy white eggs. These hatch in 13–19 days, and the young birds spend three or three and a half weeks in the nest before they are ready to fly from it. Two or three broods may be reared each year, and sometimes young birds from an earlier brood help feed later ones.

House martins feed on insects on the wing, swooping and wheeling in pursuit. Their call is a series of chirrups and twitters, with a 'tseep' alarm note. The song, like the quieter notes of a budgerigar, is uttered in flight, from a perch or inside the nest.

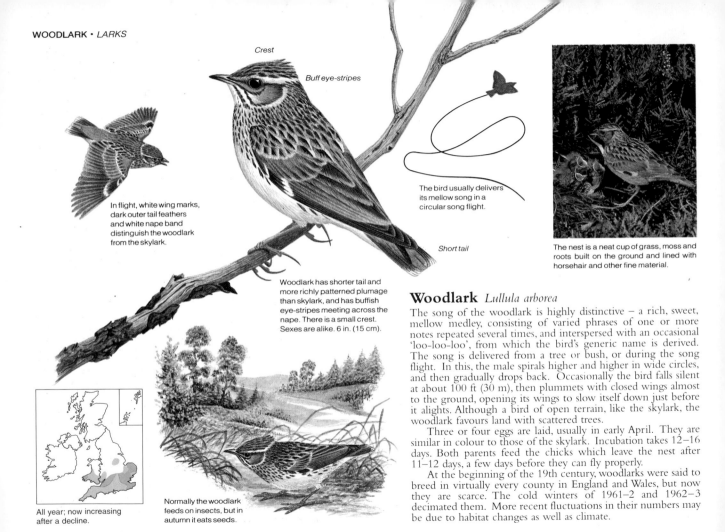

Crest

Buff eye-stripes

In flight, white wing marks, dark outer tail feathers and white nape band distinguish the woodlark from the skylark.

The bird usually delivers its mellow song in a circular song flight.

Short tail

The nest is a neat cup of grass, moss and roots built on the ground and lined with horsehair and other fine material.

Woodlark has shorter tail and more richly patterned plumage than skylark, and has buffish eye-stripes meeting across the nape. There is a small crest. Sexes are alike. 6 in. (15 cm).

All year; now increasing after a decline.

Normally the woodlark feeds on insects, but in autumn it eats seeds.

Woodlark *Lullula arborea*

The song of the woodlark is highly distinctive – a rich, sweet, mellow medley, consisting of varied phrases of one or more notes repeated several times, and interspersed with an occasional 'loo-loo-loo', from which the bird's generic name is derived. The song is delivered from a tree or bush, or during the song flight. In this, the male spirals higher and higher in wide circles, and then gradually drops back. Occasionally the bird falls silent at about 100 ft (30 m), then plummets with closed wings almost to the ground, opening its wings to slow itself down just before it alights. Although a bird of open terrain, like the skylark, the woodlark favours land with scattered trees.

Three or four eggs are laid, usually in early April. They are similar in colour to those of the skylark. Incubation takes 12–16 days. Both parents feed the chicks which leave the nest after 11–12 days, a few days before they can fly properly.

At the beginning of the 19th century, woodlarks were said to breed in virtually every county in England and Wales, but now they are scarce. The cold winters of 1961–2 and 1962–3 decimated them. More recent fluctuations in their numbers may be due to habitat changes as well as climate.

Parties of migrating birds are seen on open ground such as sand-dunes.

The skylark has a sustained song flight. The bird often delivers its song while hovering; but it may also sing as it rises, descends or perches.

Crest

The nest is always placed in a hollow on the ground; it is often partly concealed in a tussock of grass.

Shore lark
Eremophila alpestris

Yellow and black face pattern, black collar and black 'horns' of male distinguish the shore lark from other larks. It has a characteristic 'tseep' call.

Long tail

Present all year; common, but numbers declining.

Skylark is larger and browner than woodlark, with white outer tail feathers. It has a slight crest. Sexes are alike. 7 in. (18 cm).

Skylark *Alauda arvensis*

Though the skylark's plumage is sombre and its song not particularly fine, it is not hard to see why this bird became a favourite of poets and composers. As it performs its conspicuous flight above the open fields and downs, giving voice loudly and constantly, it is a difficult bird to ignore. It is very much identified with the countryside rather than with towns; moreover, it breeds more widely than any other bird in Britain, so is seen in all parts of the country that suit it – farmland, grassland, meadows, sand-dunes and commons.

The skylark rises several hundred feet vertically in hovering flight, sustaining its clear warbling song for several minutes at a time. Then the bird sinks down, singing until it is near the ground. Between three and five eggs are generally laid, in colour off-white or very pale green, heavily speckled with brown or olive. The chicks depend on camouflage and thick ground cover for protection, for they do not fly well until they are about three weeks old. Food is mainly seeds, insects and their larvae.

The shore lark, a visitor from Scandinavia, is a bird of dry, stony and sandy tracts in the Arctic and above the tree line in northern mountains.

The tree pipit usually feeds on the ground, where it seeks out insects, larvae and spiders.

The tree pipit is a plumper bird than the meadow pipit; its bill is stouter, legs pinker, and its breast yellowish. Tree pipits, unlike most pipits, habitually settle or perch on trees or bushes. Sexes are alike. 6 in. (15 cm).

Stout bill

Yellowish breast

Apr.–Sept. visitor; seen only as migrant in Ireland.

Male in song flight climbs steeply, then 'parachutes' down, floating with wings raised and tail spread.

Nests are usually well hidden in vegetation on the ground. They consist of dried grasses and hair on a foundation of moss.

Red-throated pipit
Anthus cervinus
In summer this non-breeding visitor has a rosy-coloured throat. In winter it is boldly streaked, but lacks the red throat.

Tree pipit *Anthus trivialis*

After a winter spent in central Africa, the tree pipit arrives in Britain in the spring to breed. From mid-April onwards the bird makes itself conspicuous by its song flight. It flutters up steeply from high in a tree and then, just before descending, starts to deliver its song: a loud, far-carrying phrase of a few repeated notes which ends in a shrill 'zeea-zeea-zeea'. The tree pipit continues to sing as, with wings and tail spread like a parachute, it floats down to alight on a tree or on the ground.

The tree pipit likes open countryside with low-growing vegetation, scattered trees and bushes; areas such as heaths, parkland, open woodland and pastures. Frantic chasing of the female by the male announces the beginning of the breeding season in May or early June. The eggs display a remarkable range of colours and patterns; they may be bluish-grey or hues of green, brown or pink, and speckled or streaked with brown, black, olive or chestnut.

The red-throated pipit, by contrast, does not breed in Britain. It has been seen, however, on passage between its breeding grounds in northern Scandinavia and Arctic Asia and its winter quarters in Asia and south of the Equator in Africa.

212

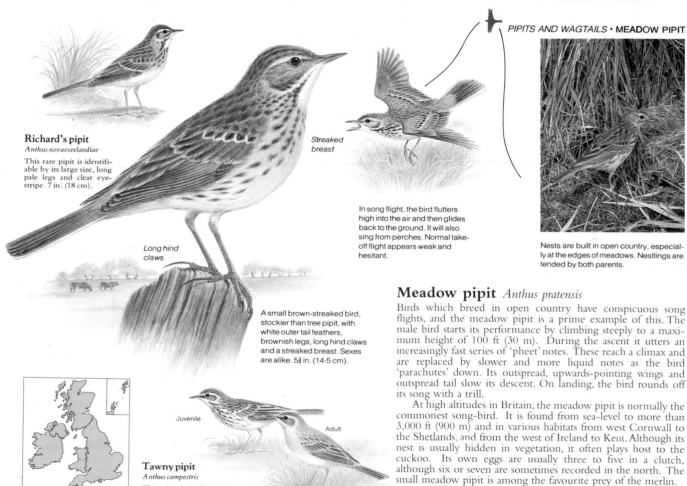

Richard's pipit
Anthus novaeseelandiae

This rare pipit is identifiable by its large size, long pale legs and clear eyestripe. 7 in. (18 cm).

Long hind claws

Streaked breast

In song flight, the bird flutters high into the air and then glides back to the ground. It will also sing from perches. Normal take-off flight appears weak and hesitant.

A small brown-streaked bird, stockier than tree pipit, with white outer tail feathers, brownish legs, long hind claws and a streaked breast. Sexes are alike. 5¾ in. (14·5 cm).

Nests are built in open country, especially at the edges of meadows. Nestlings are tended by both parents.

Present all year, but many winter on Continent.

Juvenile

Adult

Tawny pipit
Anthus campestris

This visitor is almost unstreaked in adult plumage; the juvenile is heavily streaked. 6½ in. (16·5 cm).

Meadow pipit *Anthus pratensis*

Birds which breed in open country have conspicuous song flights, and the meadow pipit is a prime example of this. The male bird starts its performance by climbing steeply to a maximum height of 100 ft (30 m). During the ascent it utters an increasingly fast series of 'pheet' notes. These reach a climax and are replaced by slower and more liquid notes as the bird 'parachutes' down. Its outspread, upwards-pointing wings and outspread tail slow its descent. On landing, the bird rounds off its song with a trill.

At high altitudes in Britain, the meadow pipit is normally the commonest song-bird. It is found from sea-level to more than 3,000 ft (900 m) and in various habitats from west Cornwall to the Shetlands, and from the west of Ireland to Kent. Although its nest is usually hidden in vegetation, it often plays host to the cuckoo. Its own eggs are usually three to five in a clutch, although six or seven are sometimes recorded in the north. The small meadow pipit is among the favourite prey of the merlin.

Richard's pipit usually arrives in small numbers from September to December. The tawny pipit is a rare migrant visitor from continental Europe.

213

The rock pipit is larger than the tree and meadow pipits. It has a more heavily streaked breast and dark olive-brown upper parts. In flight, dark legs and orange soles of feet may be seen. Sexes are alike. 6½ in. (16·5 cm).

Grey tail edges

Orange soles

Present all year; breeds on rocky coasts.

The rock pipit lives partly on insects living in rotting seaweed, such as kelp flies. It also eats seashore plant food.

Water pipit
Anthus spinoletta

The water pipit is the mountain cousin of the rock pipit. In winter plumage, its white outer tail feathers and clear white eye-stripe are distinctive. In summer, the breast is pinkish.

Both parents bring food to the young birds, whose nest is normally concealed in a hole or crevice in a cliff.

Rock pipit *Anthus petrosus*

A small, olive-brown bird flushed from rocks around Britain's coasts is very likely to be a rock pipit. It does not like very exposed places, and usually breeds in sheltered coves and gullies. As well as by its preference for rugged shorelines, it can be identified by grey outer tail feathers and by its alarm call – a thin 'phist'.

The female rock pipit builds a nest of grass, moss and fine seaweed, and lines it with finer material such as hair. Four or five eggs are normally laid; they are greyish or brownish in colour, similar to the eggs of the meadow pipit but larger. The female incubates the eggs for about two weeks, and both parents bring food to the young birds, which fledge after about 16 days. In winter, the rock pipit sometimes deserts the high cliffs and turns up on flat, sandy coastlines and inland at sewage farms, flood-lands and the borders of reservoirs. Insects such as small beetles, ants, flies and larvae form the bulk of the rock pipit's diet.

The water pipit is most commonly seen in Britain as a winter migrant, and may be found inland, particularly where there are watercress beds. It breeds in central and southern Europe, in mountainous areas with much running water.

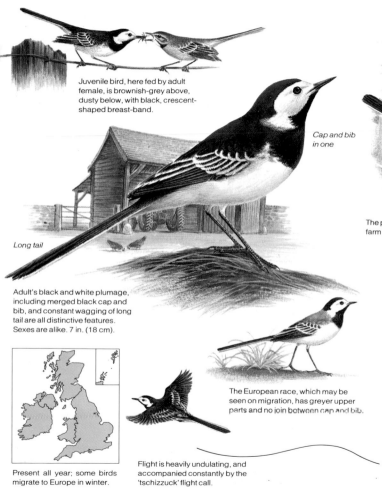

Juvenile bird, here fed by adult female, is brownish-grey above, dusty below, with black, crescent-shaped breast-band.

Cap and bib in one

Long tail

Adult's black and white plumage, including merged black cap and bib, and constant wagging of long tail are all distinctive features. Sexes are alike. 7 in. (18 cm).

Present all year; some birds migrate to Europe in winter.

Flight is heavily undulating, and accompanied constantly by the 'tschizzuck' flight call.

The European race, which may be seen on migration, has greyer upper parts and no join between cap and bib.

The pied wagtail often nests around farm buildings. Nest is built by female only.

Rivers and lakes provide a frequent background for the pied wagtail, which often nests by shallow streams.

Pied wagtail *Motacilla alba yarrellii*

In many parts of Britain the pied wagtail is called the water wagtail, for it is often seen near ponds, streams and reservoirs. But just as frequently it is found in open country, particularly in the vicinity of stables, farmyards and cultivated areas. These provide the bird with a plentiful supply of the flies and other insects that make up most of its diet, and suitable nest sites in the form of holes in buildings and walls. Cavities in cliffs, stream banks and trees, and even abandoned cars also furnish acceptable nooks and crannies.

In courtship, two or more males chase a female in an undulating, dancing flight. The nest is an accumulation of twigs and other plant stems, grass, roots, dead leaves and moss, with a lining of hair, wool and feathers. In it is laid a clutch of five or six pale greyish-white or bluish-white eggs, uniformly sprinkled with greyish speckles. The chicks are fed by both parents. A pied wagtail with a beakful of insects is usually a reliable clue to the whereabouts of a nest.

Once regarded as a species in its own right, the pied wagtail is now regarded by ornithologists as a race of the white wagtail of mainland Europe and Asia.

215

Grey crown

Black face-stripe

Juvenile birds are generally similar to females, but their plumage is more scalloped.

Adult male can be recognised by its erect posture, grey crown and chestnut back and black face-stripe. 6¾ in. (17 cm).

Adult male in flight shows pointed wings and white outer tail feathers. Its flight is gently undulating.

Adult female is dull brown above and scalloped buff-brown below.

The nest is made of grass stalks and moss, and lined with hair and roots. It is usually sited in a thorny bush.

May–Sept. visitor; no longer breeds regularly.

A bird sometimes impales its surplus food, such as insects, lizards and young birds, on thorns or barbed wire to be eaten later.

Red-backed shrike *Lanius collurio*

The shrike has been nicknamed the 'butcher-bird', because of its habit of storing its animal prey in 'larders'. The bird has a hawk-like hunting technique, and perches on top of a bush, fence or telegraph wire, watching for the slightest movement from insects or small reptiles, mammals and birds. When the prey is sighted, the shrike swoops down and snatches it up – and may impale it on a thorn or spike, to be eaten later.

The red-backed shrike population has decreased drastically both in England and Wales and on the Continent in the last 150 years or so. In the 1850s the bird was found as far north as the borders of Lancashire and Cumberland. But by 1950 it was mainly confined to England, south-east of a line from the Wash to the Severn estuary. The last 40 years have seen a further steep decline, and it is now effectively extinct as a breeding bird. The main reasons for the loss have been scarcity of food due to colder, wetter summers, the destruction of the bird's habitat and the harm done by egg collectors.

The birds usually have one brood a year, when five to six whitish eggs with dark markings are laid. The nestlings are fed by both parents and leave the nest after 12–16 days.

Black band

Juvenile lesser
grey shrike.

White underparts make bird
conspicuous when perching
against dark bushes.

Black, grey and
white plumage

Adult

Black, white and grey plumage and
broad black eye-band with a narrow
white stripe above are distinctive.
Sexes are alike. 9½ in. (24 cm).

The great grey shrike often returns to the
same perch with its kill, which may go into
a 'larder' for later consumption.

Lesser grey shrike
Lanius minor

Adult has pinkish breast and a
black eye-and-forehead band but
no white stripe above the eye. It
is smaller than the great grey
shrike, measuring about 8 in.
(20 cm). Juvenile bird has scalloped white and yellow-brown
feather pattern.

Great grey a winter visitor;
lesser a rare autumn migrant.

Great grey shrike pursues and kills
small birds and rodents. In flight, the
black and white wings stand out.

Great grey shrike *Lanius excubitor*

Like other shrikes, the great grey shrike is a lonely hunter and
'butcher bird'. Its prey consists mainly of small birds, insects and
small mammals. However, sometimes much larger birds, such
as blackbirds and thrushes, are killed. Usually great grey shrikes
are seen singly, but occasionally they are seen in small groups,
often in the vicinity of flocks of finches or buntings, their
potential prey.

The great grey shrike produces one brood each year. Parent
birds build nests of dry grass, moss and twigs, lined with roots,
wool and feathers, in thorny bushes and trees. The female is
largely responsible for the 15 days incubation of the five to seven
greenish-white, darkly marked eggs. Both parents look after the
chicks, which leave the nest at 19–20 days.

The lesser grey shrike is much scarcer in Britain than the
greater species, and lives mainly on insects. The calls of both
species are a harsh, chattering 'sheck, sheck', and their songs are
low-pitched warbles, interspersed with harsher notes and occasional imitations of other birds. Both species are extremely
aggressive, and will even drive away birds as large as buzzards if
they approach the nest too closely.

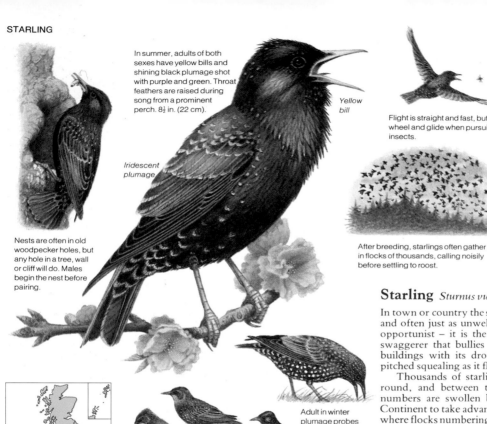

In summer, adults of both sexes have yellow bills and shining black plumage shot with purple and green. Throat feathers are raised during song from a prominent perch. 8½ in. (22 cm).

Yellow bill

Iridescent plumage

Nests are often in old woodpecker holes, but any hole in a tree, wall or cliff will do. Males begin the nest before pairing.

Flight is straight and fast, but birds wheel and glide when pursuing insects.

After breeding, starlings often gather in flocks of thousands, calling noisily before settling to roost.

Overhead power lines and telephone wires are favourite resting places for flocks of starlings.

Adult in winter plumage probes for food with open bill.

Present all year; migrants swell winter numbers.

Juveniles are mouse-brown. They slowly develop winter adult plumage – black with white spots, which are more pronounced in the female.

Starling *Sturnus vulgaris*

In town or country the starling is as familiar as weeds in a garden and often just as unwelcome. Brash, aggressive and a ruthless opportunist – it is the tearaway of the bird-world – a noisy swaggerer that bullies other birds on feeding grounds, fouls buildings with its droppings and fills the air with its high-pitched squealing as it flocks on ledges and in high trees.

Thousands of starlings are present in Britain all the year round, and between the end of September and April their numbers are swollen by millions more that come from the Continent to take advantage of the mild winter climate. In areas where flocks numbering hundreds of thousands congregate they can strip farmlands bare of corn; on the other hand, they also eat leatherjackets, wireworms and other agricultural pests.

Starlings start to breed from mid-April. The nest is an untidy accumulation of grass, straw and leaves in which are laid five to seven light blue eggs which take 12 to 15 days to hatch. The young are as noisy as adult birds, clamouring incessantly for food and pestering their parents for some time after leaving the nest. The starling's song is a jumble of squeaks and whistles, and it is an expert mimic of other birds.

Curved red bill

Juveniles are not as glossy as adult birds. Their bills are orange-yellow rather than red

Choughs feed in small flocks, often mixing with jackdaws.

The nesting site is a ledge or crevice in a cliff or quarry, or within a cave. The young hatch after 17–23 days of incubation.

In flight, choughs can be distinguished from jackdaws by their upturned wing-ends and musical 'keeaar' call. They glide, dive, roll and soar above the cliffs.

Red legs

Present all year; formerly more widespread.

A bird of mountain, crag and sea cliff, the chough is easy to recognise by its glossy purple-black plumage that contrasts with red legs and red, down-curved bill. Sexes are alike. 15½ in. (39 cm).

Chough *Pyrrhocorax pyrrhocorax*

Masters of aerobatics, choughs like to wheel and soar along the cliffs on broad, rounded wings, the tips spread out like fingers. The bird's name is pronounced 'chuff', but originally it was probably an imitation of its 'keeaar' or 'cheeow' call. Old alternative names were red-legged crow and Cornish chough or daw, 'choghe' also being an old name for the jackdaw. At one time the chough was abundant in Cornwall, and an old legend tells that King Arthur's spirit entered the bird after his death.

Although once widespread in Scotland, the north of England and the south coast, the chough is now found only on a few western coasts. A succession of cold winters during the 19th century may have started its decline. Birds begin breeding from late April, building a large, cupped nest of sticks bound with other plant stems and grass and well lined with wool or hair. The three or four eggs, pale greenish or creamy in colour and finely speckled with brown and grey, are incubated by the female. Both parents regurgitate food for the young.

The chough's down-curved bill is ideally suited for its diet of worms, caterpillars, ants and other insects such as beetles, particularly dung beetles. It also eats small shellfish.

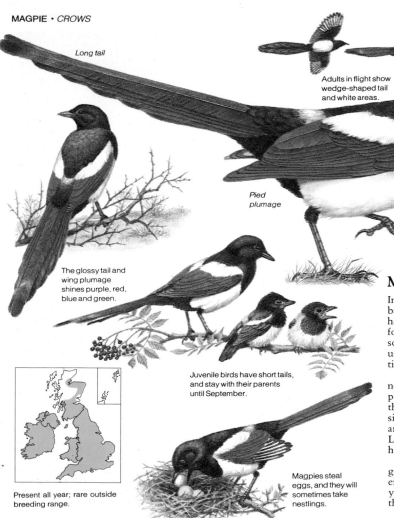

Long tail

Adults in flight show wedge-shaped tail and white areas.

Pied plumage

Adult bird has black and white plumage and a long tail. Flanks and belly are white and head dark. Sexes are alike. 18 in. (45 cm).

The glossy tail and wing plumage shines purple, red, blue and green.

Juvenile birds have short tails, and stay with their parents until September.

Magpies steal eggs, and they will sometimes take nestlings.

Present all year; rare outside breeding range.

The birds build large, domed nests of sticks in tall trees or thorn bushes. Only a single opening is left.

Magpie *Pica pica*

In much of Britain the magpie has long been regarded as a bird of bad omen. The most familiar superstition about sighting the handsome, black and white bird is expressed in the adage, 'One for sorrow, two for joy'. To protect themselves against the sorrow which the sight of a single magpie might bring, people used to cross themselves, raise their hats to the bird, or spit three times over the right shoulder saying, 'Devil, Devil, I defy thee'.

The magpie was originally a bird of rural areas – particularly neglected farmland with mature pasture and thick hedges. It was persecuted by humans, being wrongly regarded as a pest, and by the beginning of the 20th century the population was low. But since the 1940s magpies have increasingly bred in suburban areas and in gardens in large cities such as Glasgow, Manchester and London. Their presence is often first revealed by their call: a hoarse, laughing chatter, 'cha-ha-ha-ha-ha-hack!'

During the nesting season they often stay hidden in overgrown hedgerows and thickets. The normal clutch of five to eight bluish-green eggs is laid from April onwards. One brood a year is usual, and the young – fed by both parents – fledge after three to four weeks.

Nutcracker
Nucifraga caryocatactes

Another member of the crow family, this thin-billed bird has a brown body with bold white spots. In flight, its white under-tail and terminal band are conspicuous. 12¼ in. (32 cm).

Rump and wing pattern is conspicuous in the jay's wave-like flight. It usually stays near trees.

Streaked crest

The jay sometimes steals nestlings and eggs of other birds, such as blackbirds.

Adult bird has buff body with white rump, distinctive blue wing-patch, blue eyes and streaked crest. Sexes are alike. 13½ in. (34 cm).

Blue wing-patch

The jay is fond of acorns which it collects and buries among fallen leaves and twigs.

Present all year; sedentary, with some immigrants.

The jay's nest is usually situated in a tree, and is made of twigs bound with earth and lined with hair.

Jay *Garrulus glandarius*

As one of Britain's most wary birds, the jay is more often heard than seen. It greets woodland 'intruders' with a raucous, scolding call of 'scaaarg-scaaarg'. The jay is sometimes observed hopping along the ground and picking up seeds or acorns from under trees. When spotted in flight, it is usually flitting from one group of trees to another with distinctive, jerky beats of its rounded wings.

Jays depend heavily upon trees – especially oaks – for their existence. They bury acorns for their winter food and also store beech-nuts, peas, potatoes, fruit and berries. To a lesser extent, they eat small mammals, molluscs, earthworms, spiders and the eggs and young of other birds.

In the spring, the birds sometimes hold formal courtship ceremonies, in which groups of jays pursue each other with slow wing-beats and a great deal of calling. The ceremonies often speed up and reach their climax in an excited chase through the branches of trees, during which the male birds turn their bodies sideways to the females and raise their crest and body feathers. Usually five to seven eggs are laid and hatch in about two weeks. The young spend about three weeks in the nest.

223

Jackdaws sometimes hover in the air showing darkish bands under wings, and dark grey tail.

Grey nape

Dark grey underparts

Birds flock together, and have a liking for derelict buildings.

This small member of the crow family is easily identified by its grey nape and dark grey underparts. Other plumage is black. Sexes are alike. 13 in. (33 cm).

A jackdaw nesting in a chimneypot can be an unwelcome visitor; after years of use, the nest sticks may block the chimney.

Birds often gather in dozens, or even hundreds, in wooded areas such as parkland, and also on rocks and cliffs.

Jackdaw *Corvus monedula*

The thieving habits of the jackdaw were celebrated by the early 19th-century humorous poet Richard Harris Barham in *The Jackdaw of Rheims.* In the poem the bird – the most notorious robber in the crow family – steals the ring of the Cardinal Lord Archbishop of Rheims. 'The Devil,' wrote Barham, 'must be in that little Jackdaw.' Apart from snatching and hiding such inedible objects, the jackdaw occasionally steals young birds and eggs which it adds to its diet of seeds, fruit, insects and carrion.

As well as nesting in holes and chimneys, the jackdaw sometimes takes over the old nests of other birds, and occasionally even makes its nest in a rabbit burrow. The amount of nest material used depends very much upon the site. A large, exposed nest is usually lined with hair, fur, grass and wool – which the jackdaw sometimes plucks from the backs of sheep.

Late April sees the start of the breeding season, and three to seven eggs with black and grey speckles are laid. Incubation is by the female who is fed on the nest by the male. The young hatch in 17–18 days and are ready to fledge when about one month old. Usually, the jackdaw's call is a loud, explosive 'tchack'; occasionally this is expanded into a 'tchackertchack'.

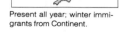

Present all year; winter immigrants from Continent.

A hole in a tree trunk is a favourite nesting place.

The jackdaw is a sociable bird, which often feeds with birds of other species.

Face-patch

A bare face-patch distinguishes the rook from the carrion crow, and gives a long-billed appearance. Plumage is black with a purple gloss; thigh feathers are thick. Sexes are alike. 18 in. (45 cm).

In breeding season, adults carry food to young in a throat pouch.

Thigh feathers

The bird has a sedate walk, and often follows farm ploughs picking up leather-jackets and other insects.

Rooks form large feeding flocks in winter, congregating with visitors from continental Europe on open inland or coastal sites.

Present all year; winter immigrants from Continent.

Young bird has no face-patch, but possesses baggy thigh feathers.

Rooks nest sociably in tall trees, often near farm buildings. Noisy, communal flight displays are common.

Rook *Corvus frugilegus*

Before the leaves are out in spring, rooks congregate in breeding colonies high up in tall trees, their nests standing out against the network of bare branches. This habit of breeding early in conspicuous 'rookeries' makes counting the species relatively easy. The British rook population has fallen recently, possibly because of the ploughing-up of permanent pasture in favour of temporary crops of grass and clover, where the soil does not harbour so many of the bird's favourite insect foods – leather-jackets and wireworms.

Even so, some rookeries may number several thousand pairs: at Hatton Castle near Aberdeen, more than 6,000 nests have been counted. In 1424 James I of Scotland decreed the extermination of the rooks in his kingdom, because of their practice of feeding on corn; but the damage done by the bird to crops may well be balanced by its liking for insect pests.

The rook's nest is a bulky cup of sticks consolidated with soil and lined with roots, leaves, moss or wool. The female builds the nest with materials brought by her mate. A clutch usually consists of three to five bluish-green eggs, with greenish-brown or blackish-green speckles.

225

Hooded crow
Corvus corone cornix

Adult hooded crow has grey back and underparts. It is common in Ireland and the north and west of Scotland. Where ranges overlap, it interbreeds with the carrion crow.

Heavy, rounded bill

Where trees are scarce, crows will nest on the ground.

Hybrids between carrion and hooded crows have some grey markings.

Adult carrion crow has glossy black plumage and a heavy, rounded bill. Its smaller size and squarer tail distinguish it from the raven. Sexes are alike. 18½ in. (47 cm).

Present all year; map only shows range of carrion crow.

Birds often feed on carrion such as dead rabbits. They sometimes take live prey, including chicks.

The carrion crow's nest is usually high in a tree fork. Its eggs, usually four to six, resemble those of the hooded crow.

Carrion crow *Corvus corone corone*

Dr Samuel Johnson described the carrion crow as 'a large black bird that feeds on the carcasses of beasts'. Its scavenging habits and harsh croaking call have never endeared it to man, and farmers and gamekeepers have persecuted it because of its liking for grain and root crops as well as for eggs and chicks. Intelligent, wary and difficult to approach closely, the crow ranges widely from mountain to moor and woodland to seashore, but is increasingly breeding closer to human habitation. The hooded crow is a race or sub-species of the carrion crow.

Both sexes build the nest, a large, bulky cup of sticks compacted with earth, moss and other material and usually lined with a thick layer of wool or hair. Eggs are laid during late March or April, and range from light blue to deep green with varied amounts of brown or grey blotching. The hen incubates the eggs for about 19 days, and she chiefly feeds the chicks.

Crows feed mainly on the ground, but will drop food such as a crab from the air in order to smash the shell, and also rob nests. They are sleeker than rooks, but less sociable and are usually seen singly or in pairs. The crow bows forward on its perch as it utters its 'kraaar' call.

Carrion, such as small mammals, form a major part of the raven's food. Occasionally it will feed on dead sheep and lambs.

When the raven croaks, the feathers on its crown and shaggy throat are raised.

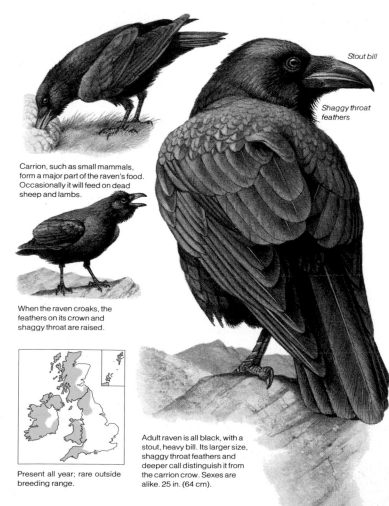

Stout bill

Shaggy throat feathers

Present all year; rare outside breeding range.

Adult raven is all black, with a stout, heavy bill. Its larger size, shaggy throat feathers and deeper call distinguish it from the carrion crow. Sexes are alike. 25 in. (64 cm).

Ravens fly higher than crows, often soaring or performing aerobatics. The heavy head, extended neck and diamond-shaped tail are prominent.

Occasionally the raven will nest in a tree, but it usually chooses a sheltered, rocky ledge in a crag or cliff.

Raven *Corvus corax*

For centuries the raven was regarded as a bird of ill-omen and a harbinger of death, probably because of its dark colouring and its habit of feeding on the corpses of victims of the gibbet. It was once common in Britain, but years of persecution by man have driven it to mountainous regions, and to cliffs, quarries, moors and windswept hills. The largest member of the crow family, renowned for its intelligence, the raven is also the largest species of perching bird in the world.

Ravens raise only one brood each year, starting very early in the spring, in February or March. Both sexes build the large nest of twigs, sticks, heather stalks and sometimes pieces of seaweed. It is reinforced with earth and moss, and the cup is thickly lined with grass, moss and an inner layer of hair and wool. There are usually four to six eggs, light blue or green with greyish or blackish-brown speckling. The male feeds the female on the nest while she incubates the eggs, which hatch in about three weeks. The chicks are five to six weeks old before they can fly.

Ravens have a varied diet. As well as eating carrion they kill their own prey – birds or small mammals such as meadow pipits or rabbits – and forage for eggs, reptiles, insects and seeds.

227

Waxwings fly swiftly and directly, gliding at intervals. The trilling call-note in flight is distinctive.

Crest

Waxwings are usually very tame, and it is possible to get close enough to identify them.

Bright wings

The bird derives its name from the unusual waxy-looking red tips to its upper flight feathers.

Waxwings are commonly seen feeding on the year's berry crop. Those that visit Britain are believed to breed in Finland.

The waxwing is the only buff-brown bird with a crest seen perching during autumn and winter months. Adults of both sexes have a black throat, brightly coloured wings and a yellow tail tip. 7 in. (18 cm).

Nov.–Mar. visitor; numerous only in occasional years.

Garden ponds, woodland pools or roadside puddles provide watering places for thirsty birds.

Waxwing *Bombycilla garrulus*

The waxwing derives its name from the blobs which look like red sealing wax at the tips of some of its secondary flight feathers. It does not breed in Britain, but every few years it erupts in large numbers and turns up in areas well away from its Arctic and sub-Arctic breeding grounds. The reason is not known, but may be connected with the availability of the rowan berry, one of the waxwing's favourite foods in northern latitudes. These invasions are erratic, but a 'waxwing winter' was recorded in Britain as early as 1679–80. The biggest invasion of all was in 1965–6, when more than 11,000 waxwings were recorded in this country.

Waxwings are very gregarious birds, flocking together in small parties to feed on the berries of shrubs such as dog rose, juniper, guelder rose, holly and hawthorn, as well as rowan. Flocks may invade city parks and gardens in search of berries when they become scarce in the countryside.

In the breeding season the waxwings chatter loudly, which led to the bird at one time being known as the 'Bohemian chatterer'. Outside the breeding season, however, it is generally rather a silent bird, occasionally uttering a faint trill.

Young birds lack the contrasting plumage of adults. They are grey-brown above, speckled white below.

Flight is direct and fast on whirring, short wings.

Dippers often prefer swimming to flying.

Short tail

Often seen perched on a boulder in a stream, the adult dipper has dark upper parts, white throat and breast and a chestnut waistband. Short tail and constant bobbing habit make it unmistakable. Sexes are alike. 7 in. (18 cm).

Continental black-bellied form, without chestnut band, occasionally appears in winter.

The young are fed by both birds. The nest is under a bridge or the overhang of a river bank, or behind a waterfall.

Present all year; some continental birds in winter.

The dipper has the remarkable ability to walk underwater up the beds of fast-flowing streams in search of food; it also dives into water from the air.

Dipper *Cinclus cinclus*

In contrast to all other birds, the dipper seeks its food by walking underwater on shallow river beds and the bottoms of streams. With its head down in search of water insects, tadpoles and worms, it may forge its way against the current, kept on its feet, probably, by the force of water pressing down on its broad back. Before submerging, the dipper often perches on rocks in the middle of rushing, tumbling water and repeatedly bobs up and down. Its legs flex, its wings quiver, its white eyelids blink, and its sweet, warbling song – which it maintains for most of the year – can be heard above the noise of the water.

The dipper is a plump, wren-like bird, with a distinctive, snow-white breast. Because of its feeding habits, it is mostly found in the uplands of western, central and northern Britain, where there are fast-running streams. A recent decline in numbers has been linked with water pollution.

The bird's low, rapid and direct flight usually follows the course of a river; and it often spends the entire year on the same stretch of water. The bulky, domed nest is built of moss, and the white eggs, usually five, are laid in late March. Nestlings hatch in 15–18 days and fly after about three weeks.

WREN

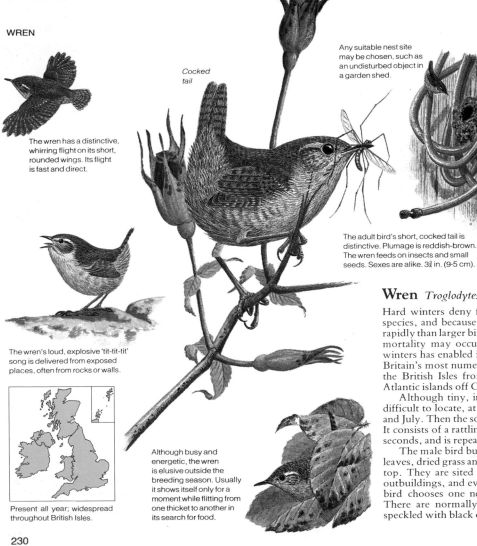

The wren has a distinctive, whirring flight on its short, rounded wings. Its flight is fast and direct.

Cocked tail

Any suitable nest site may be chosen, such as an undisturbed object in a garden shed.

The wren's loud, explosive 'tit-tit-tit' song is delivered from exposed places, often from rocks or walls.

Present all year; widespread throughout British Isles.

Although busy and energetic, the wren is elusive outside the breeding season. Usually it shows itself only for a moment while flitting from one thicket to another in its search for food.

The adult bird's short, cocked tail is distinctive. Plumage is reddish-brown. The wren feeds on insects and small seeds. Sexes are alike. 3¾ in. (9·5 cm).

An adult bird brings a beakful of caterpillars and insects to its nest. The male helps the female with feeding the young.

Wren *Troglodytes troglodytes*

Hard winters deny food to the wren, along with many other species, and because of its tiny size the wren chills much more rapidly than larger birds. In freezing weather, therefore, massive mortality may occur, as in early 1963. After a spell of mild winters has enabled it to multiply, however, the wren becomes Britain's most numerous breeding bird. It is found throughout the British Isles from Shetland to the Scillies, and from the Atlantic islands off County Kerry to Kent.

Although tiny, inconspicuous and skulking, wrens are not difficult to locate, at least when in full voice between February and July. Then the song is shrill, and delivered with much force. It consists of a rattling warble of clear notes that lasts about five seconds, and is repeated at intervals.

The male bird builds a number of ball-shaped nests, made of leaves, dried grass and moss, with an entrance at the side near the top. They are sited in hedges, ivy-covered walls, tree trunks, outbuildings, and even in the old nests of other birds. The hen bird chooses one nest, and lines it plentifully with feathers. There are normally five to eight eggs, white in colour and speckled with black or reddish-brown at the larger end.

The nest is normally built in a bush, hedge or pile of wood within 6 ft (1.8 m) of the ground. Birds breed from early April.

Grey head

Thin bill

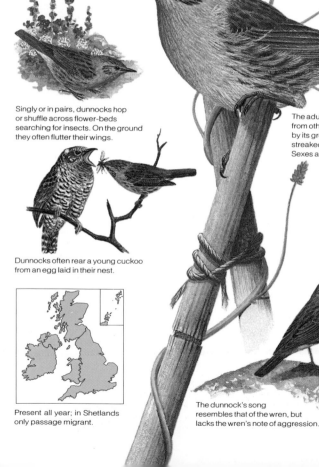

Singly or in pairs, dunnocks hop or shuffle across flower-beds searching for insects. On the ground they often flutter their wings.

The adult is distinguished from other small, brown birds by its grey head and underparts, streaked flanks and thin bill. Sexes alike. 5¾ in. (14·5 cm).

Juvenile birds are spotted, and resemble young robins.

Dunnocks often rear a young cuckoo from an egg laid in their nest.

Present all year; in Shetlands only passage migrant.

The dunnock's song resembles that of the wren, but lacks the wren's note of aggression.

Dunnock *Prunella modularis*

For many years the dunnock has been called the hedge sparrow, yet it is not related to the sparrow at all. It is a song-bird belonging to the accentor family, many of which live in high mountainous regions. It is widespread throughout Britain in gardens, spinneys, open woodland and wherever there are bushes, shrubs and low scrubby vegetation. It can also be found in open coastal and moorland areas if there is low scrub cover.

The nest, which is built by both birds, is a substantial cup of fine twigs, plant stems, leaves, rootlets and moss, neatly lined with hair, wool or feathers. From three to six, but usually four or five, bright blue eggs are laid. They are incubated for 12–13 days by the female, which leaves the nest frequently to feed. The newly hatched chicks have long black down on their heads and backs. They are fed by both parents, and when begging for food their wide-open beaks reveal bright orange inside the mouth and two black spots on the tongue.

After 12 days the fledglings leave the nest, although they are not very good at flying by then. Two or even three broods may be raised each year. The song is a high-pitched warbling refrain, lasting four or five seconds and repeated at intervals.

The bird is usually seen only briefly in flight as it flits from one bush or tussock to another.

The bird's streaked upper parts and rounded tail are clearly visible at close quarters.

Apr.–Sept. visitor; wide but thin distribution.

Long tail

Adult bird is brown with whitish-buff underparts and a long tail. A distinctive trilling song sometimes reveals the elusive bird's presence. Sexes are alike. 5 in. (12·5 cm).

The bird's long middle toe enables it to grasp two stems at once when moving among tangled vegetation.

Buff underparts

When disturbed, the bird usually creeps away through the grass rather than taking wing.

The nest, built from dead grass, leaves and sticks and lined with hair, is usually well hidden in a large grass tussock.

Grasshopper warbler *Locustella naevia*

A watcher could be forgiven for thinking that the high-pitched whirr that comes from an expanse of tangled grass, bushes and brambles is being produced by some tiny machine. In fact the source of the sound is probably the grasshopper warbler, so named because its song resembles the sound made by some grasshoppers. An attempt to catch sight of the songster, however, is likely to be defeated by its 'voice-throwing' as it turns its head from side to side, and by its shy, skulking habits.

The species arrives from winter quarters in north and west Africa between early April and the third week of May. The concealed, cup-shaped nest, approached from one way only, contains usually six creamy eggs, each so thickly speckled with fine purplish-brown spots as to appear dark. Both male and female incubate the eggs, which hatch after two weeks. Nestlings spend 10–12 days in the nest, fed by both parents.

Appetising morsels for grasshopper warblers are small insects and beetles, or spiders and woodlice. The nestlings also receive such succulent titbits as green caterpillars and aphids. By early August some birds will be flying south again, and by the end of September nearly all will have gone.

In courtship display flight male flies vertically upwards, singing, then descends with wings and tail spread.

Flights between patches of cover are low and direct; reddish-buff rump and spread tail are conspicuous.

Streaked back

Creamy eye-stripe

The head pattern, streaked back and more dumpy shape distinguish sedge warbler from reed warbler. Sexes are alike. 5 in. (12·5 cm).

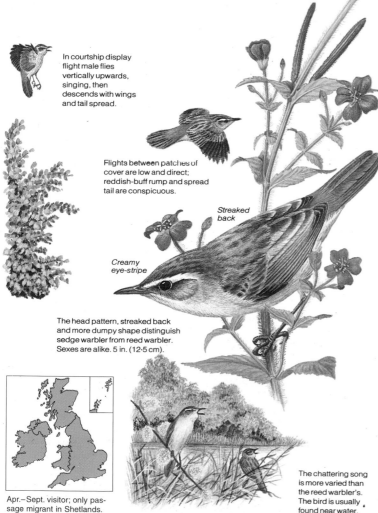

Apr.–Sept. visitor; only passage migrant in Shetlands.

The chattering song is more varied than the reed warbler's. The bird is usually found near water.

The bird spends much time skulking in cover to hunt for insects.

The nest has a bulkier foundation than that of the reed warbler, and is built near the ground in dense vegetation.

Sedge warbler *Acrocephalus schoenobaenus*

One of many species that have benefited from the increase in young forestry plantations is the sedge warbler. It adapts well to their dense, rank vegetation, although it is traditionally a bird of damper areas such as osiers or reed-beds; it also occurs sometimes in standing crops.

Its attractive song, occasionally performed at night, is similar to the reed warbler's but more varied – a continuous and hurried series of notes, some chattering, some musical, each variant usually being repeated several times. Its own song is interspersed with accurate mimicry of other birds' songs.

Although more widespread than the reed warbler, this elusive bird is hard to spot, as it hides itself in low vegetation, hunting insects; and when it does emerge it darts straight to the next patch of cover. But its identity will be revealed by even a brief glimpse. Its colour is creamier than the reed warbler's, with bold streaks of darker colour on the back and wings and a prominent, creamy stripe above each eye. Usually five or six eggs are laid in a nest hidden low down in dense vegetation. The young, which hatch after about two weeks, are fed on small insects such as crane-flies, midges, beetles and dragonflies.

233

Birds are usually found among mixed vegetation near water.

Supporting stems do not pierce the nest, but are encircled by a few 'basket handles' of nest material.

The marsh warbler often feeds among willows and osiers.

Flat head

Pink legs

Song, often from high perch, is more melodious and varied than reed warbler's.

A rounder shape and flatter head distinguish the marsh warbler from the reed warbler. Its plumage is generally more olive above and paler below, and its legs are pinker. Here it perches on meadowsweet. Sexes are alike. 5 in. (12·5 cm).

The nest is placed in a bush or among low plants such as nettles or willow-herb, often near standing crops.

Marsh warbler *Acrocephalus palustris*

A very rare bird, breeding in only a few areas of southern England, the marsh warbler would be almost indistinguishable from the more common reed warbler were it not for its remarkable song. This consists of long bursts of warbling with some canary-like twitterings, varied with mimicry of other birds. This mimicry will often betray the presence of the marsh warbler to the careful listener, for no bush could hold such a varied collection of birds as the marsh warbler's recital would suggest: it has been known to imitate more than 50 other species.

Unlike the reed warbler, which lives almost entirely among reeds and osier beds, the marsh warbler is more often found in drier, bushy areas, though usually near to water.

The marsh warbler is one of the latest summer visitors to arrive, in late May or early June. It builds a deep, cup-shaped nest of dry grass and fine stems, slung by 'basket handles' from stems of reed, willow-herb or nettles. Three to six eggs are laid, mainly in June. After about 12 days the young hatch and are fed with insects in the nest by both parents for 10–14 days before fledging. The marsh warbler leaves Britain again in early September, for East Africa.

234

The harsh, repetitive song is often heard when the reeds are disturbed.

Rounded head

Dark legs

The bird often flies from the reed beds to nearby trees or bushes for food.

The reed warbler is plainer and slimmer than the sedge warbler, and a warmer brown than the marsh warbler. Sexes are alike.
5 in. (12·5 cm).

Young often leave the nest before they can fly. They can move nimbly among the reeds.

The nest is woven round reed stems. Its deep cup retains the eggs even when the reeds bend over in the wind.

Apr.–Oct. visitor; recently spreading west and north.

Old nests are dismantled to make new ones, and material may even be filched from the nest of another pair.

Reed warbler *Acrocephalus scirpaceus*

Beds of the common reed are the favourite haunt of reed warblers, although they can also be found among osiers and occasionally in other dense vegetation or bushes near water. Their song is a flow of 'churr-churr-churr . . . . chirruc-chirruc-chirruc' notes.

Fairly common in East Anglia and south–eastern England, the reed warbler becomes much rarer away from this area. It is absent from Ireland, Scotland and most of Wales and much of northern and south-western England, despite the existence in these areas of plenty of common reeds and the accompanying marsh insects which are the bird's normal food.

The reed warbler's nest is a beautifully woven cup, slung between several reed stems and built extra deep to prevent the eggs or young from being tossed out in high winds. The reed warbler is a favourite victim of the cuckoo, which removes one of the three to five eggs, replacing it with one of its own. Like its relatives, the sedge warbler and marsh warbler, the reed warbler undertakes a long migration each year from Europe to spend the winter in tropical and southern Africa, where it moults before its next flight to the reed beds of the north.

Aquatic warbler
Acrocephalus paludicola

A buff central crown stripe and well-marked upper parts distinguish this bird from the sedge warbler. It also has a streaked rump. 5 in. (12.5 cm).

Savi's warbler
Locustella luscinioides

Similar to a large reed warbler, this bird is identifiable by its uniformly coloured, unstreaked upper parts, buff underparts and broad rounded tail. 5¼ in. (14 cm).

Cetti's warbler
Cettia cetti

A darkish-brown bird with pale chest and cocked tail. It resembles a small nightingale in colour, but lacks the nightingale's prominent rufous tail. It is a secretive bird, usually located by its loud, abrupt and repetitive song. 5¼ in. (14 cm).

Melodious warbler
Hippolais polyglotta

Combination of bright yellow and green plumage distinguishes this bird from most other warblers. Its legs are dark. Its 'melody' is a prolonged musical babbling. 5 in. (12·5 cm).

Rarer warblers

Only two of these warblers breed in Britain, Savi's warbler and Cetti's warbler. Both are secretive marshland species, and are resident mainly in the south-east; Cetti's warbler is also found in East Anglia. Another marshland bird, the aquatic warbler, is an autumn visitor from Europe to southern England.

The other warblers illustrated are all summer or passage visitors, and birds of scrub and woodland. The barred warbler prefers scrub, whereas the melodious warbler likes parks and lush vegetation. The remainder are leaf warblers, inhabiting trees, bushes and thickets. They are separated only by subtle differences in size, plumage, number of wing-bars and variations in eye-stripes.

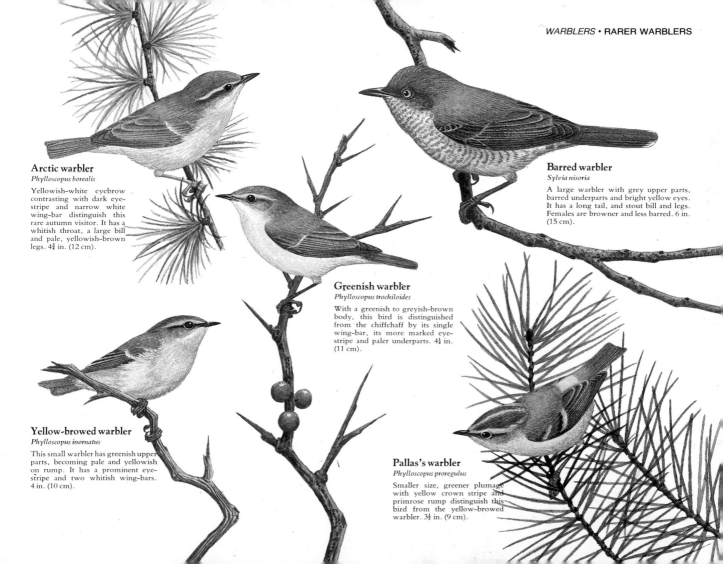

Arctic warbler
Phylloscopus borealis

Yellowish-white eyebrow contrasting with dark eye-stripe and narrow white wing-bar distinguish this rare autumn visitor. It has a whitish throat, a large bill and pale, yellowish-brown legs. 4¾ in. (12 cm).

Barred warbler
Sylvia nisoria

A large warbler with grey upper parts, barred underparts and bright yellow eyes. It has a long tail, and stout bill and legs. Females are browner and less barred. 6 in. (15 cm).

Greenish warbler
Phylloscopus trochiloides

With a greenish to greyish-brown body, this bird is distinguished from the chiffchaff by its single wing-bar, its more marked eye-stripe and paler underparts. 4¼ in. (11 cm).

Yellow-browed warbler
Phylloscopus inornatus

This small warbler has greenish upper parts, becoming pale and yellowish on rump. It has a prominent eye-stripe and two whitish wing-bars. 4 in. (10 cm).

Pallas's warbler
Phylloscopus proregulus

Smaller size, greener plumage with yellow crown stripe and primrose rump distinguish this bird from the yellow-browed warbler. 3½ in. (9 cm).

Dense plantations of young trees are a favoured habitat. The bird's behaviour much resembles the blackcap's.

During courtship the male turns towards the female with tail spread and fluttering wings.

A rather heavy-looking, short-billed bird; its brown and buff plumage lacks distinctive markings. Sexes are alike. 5½ in. (14 cm).

Apr.–Oct. visitor; rarer in Scotland and Ireland.

Like many warblers, the garden warbler feeds on berries before migrating in autumn, and its bill, vent and droppings become stained by purple fruit-juice.

Nesting material is carried to a bramble site; the nest is usually lower down than the blackcap's.

Nests are built in thick cover. The male may build several trial nests before deciding on the site.

Garden warbler *Sylvia borin*

From the middle of April, open woodlands, copses, thickets and areas of bushy undergrowth are enriched with the melodic song of the garden warbler, a sombre-plumaged summer visitor from tropical and southern Africa. Despite its name, this shy bird does not visit gardens unless there are tangled hedges or bramble thickets where it can breed undisturbed.

In appearance, the garden warbler is notably lacking in distinctive features. It is pale buff below and darker brown above with no speckles, streaks, eye-stripes or wing-bars.

The nest is built in thick cover, often in a fork and usually at a lower level than the blackcap's. Male and female build it together, using grass stems and some heavier material such as twigs. The cup is lined with finer grass, roots and, if available, hair. The normal clutch of eggs is four or five, and after 11 or 12 days' sitting the naked young are hatched. It takes a further nine or ten days of parental care before they can leave the nest, and when their tails have reached full length they look very much like their parents. Adult garden warblers distract predators threatening their young by spreading their tails and fluttering their wings, in a display similar to that of a courting male.

Some blackcaps winter in Britain and may visit gardens for scraps in the snow.

Male: black cap

Female: brown cap

A male with nest material. Males build several frail 'cock's nests' in addition to the main nest built by both sexes.

Apr.–Oct. visitor; some winter, mainly in south-west.

The striking black cap distinguishes the male from all other warblers. The female's brown cap is less striking. 5½ in. (14 cm).

A female feeds her chicks. Young birds all have brown caps.

Courting males assume extraordinary postures. Cap feathers are raised, wings drooped and tails spread.

The nest is sited in a bramble or other thick bush, just concealed from predators by the outer leaves.

Blackcap *Sylvia atricapilla*

Unless he can spot the characteristic jet-black crown, a bird-watcher may have difficulty in distinguishing the blackcap from the garden warbler. Both are shy, live in thick cover and greet the intruder with a loud, scolding 'tacc-tacc' like two stones struck together. The blackcap's rich song, however, most often heard from March to July, is usually more variable in pitch, and delivered in shorter bursts.

The blackcap nests in woods, tall hedgerows and gardens with plenty of brambles and briers. It can most typically be seen picking its way through the branches and stems, searching for insect food such as flies and caterpillars between bouts of singing.

The nests, hidden in bushes or undergrowth, are neatly built but flimsy cups of dry grass and roots, lined with finer strands of grass, roots and hair. The four to six eggs are incubated by both parents for 10–14 days. Most blackcaps leave for tropical Africa in August or September; unlike garden warblers, blackcaps complete their moult before migrating. In recent years a few blackcaps from Central Europe have taken to braving the English winter, visiting bird-tables for food.

A short, 'dancing' display flight often accompanies the song of the male bird.

White throat

White outer tail feathers of the whitethroat are noticeable in flight.

The song may be delivered from the top of a bush or hedge on heaths, on the edge of woodland, or on farmland.

Red-brown wings

Adult male has a grey head, with crown feathers often raised, white throat and reddish-brown wings. Adult female has brown head. 5½ in. (14 cm).

Whitethroats often skulk half-seen in cover, betraying their presence with a harsh, scolding song.

Apr.–Sept. breeding visitor; widespread in most areas.

The nest is frequently sited among stinging nettles; nestlings are tended for about 12 days.

Whitethroat *Sylvia communis*

Until 1968, a feature of the British summer was the brief, musical song of the male whitethroat, the commonest member of the warbler family. It would be delivered from the depths of a wild rose bush or overgrown hawthorn hedge, from the top of a shrub or telephone wire, or during a short, 'dancing' song flight before the bird dropped back into the cover of roadside brambles, hedge-parsley or nettles.

Then suddenly, in the spring of 1969, many birdwatchers found themselves waiting in vain for the spring arrival of this jaunty little summer visitor from Central Africa. They were soon to learn that almost four-fifths had failed to put in an appearance, and by 1974 the population had further dwindled to one-sixth of the 1968 level. The cause was probably drought in the whitethroat's winter home just south of the Sahara.

Even so, probably more than half a million breeding pairs still visit Britain. The breeding season begins with the male courting the female by dashing at her and swerving away at the last moment. He builds several nests, one of which may eventually be used. It is a deep cup of dead grasses and roots, lined with hair. Usually, two clutches of four or five eggs are laid.

240

The lesser whitethroat sometimes sings while flying.

The nest is neat but frail. Sometimes the eggs can be seen from beneath.

Dark cheek

Brown wings

The short, rattling song is often heard from the shelter of a bush or thicket.

The bird lacks the red-brown colour of the whitethroat and is shorter-tailed, with dark cheeks. Sexes are alike. 5¼ in. (13·5 cm).

Cobwebs may be collected to festoon the rim of the nest.

The nest is often sited higher than that of the whitethroat, and may be hidden away deep inside a hedge or bush.

Apr.–Sept. visitor; occasionally nests in Scotland.

The bird is less obtrusive than the whitethroat, with less jaunty movements.

Lesser whitethroat *Sylvia curruca*

Only by the narrow margin of a quarter of an inch is this bird 'lesser' than the common whitethroat, measuring up to 5¼ in. (13·5 cm) compared with the common whitethroat's 5½ in. (14 cm). At times the two species may share habitats, but the lesser whitethroat prefers areas with taller trees and shrubs, such as gardens and shrubberies, and avoids areas of sparse bushes. It is most easily distinguished by its brown wings, which lack the reddish tinge of the whitethroat's wings.

The bird's song often begins with an animated and attractive warble, then continues with a rattling note rapidly repeated five or six times, audible far away. Attempts to approach are usually thwarted by the bird's habit of moving long distances between snatches of song.

The nest, concealed amid thick vegetation, is a cup of dead grass and rootlets. When the young first leave the nest parents proclaim anxiety for their brood's safety with a loud and persistent 'tac–tac–tac' and a distinctive trilling call. Wintering mainly in East Africa, just north of the Equator, the lesser whitethroat escaped the fate of so many common whitethroats during the Sahara drought of 1968–9.

241

Bushy head

Long tail

Red-brown below

Song flight resembles that of whitethroat, but body is held more level.

Its long tail, held cocked, its reddish-brown underparts and bushy head make this bird unmistakable. Sexes are alike. 5 in. (12·5 cm).

Present all year, but scarce and local to southern counties.

Young birds have paler plumage than adults.

Birds behave furtively, and are usually seen only when flitting between bushes.

The nest is built low in gorse and is well concealed. Grass, roots and stalks are bound with cobwebs or insect cocoons.

Dartford warbler *Sylvia undata*

Unusual among British warblers in not migrating for the winter, the Dartford warbler runs the risk of starving to death in a period of severe frost, when it cannot find the insects and spiders on which it relies for food. Populations reduced by hard winters build up again in milder periods, but the heath areas that the bird can inhabit continue to shrink. As a result of careful conservation it now breeds in Hampshire, Dorset, Surrey, Sussex, Devon and Cornwall. But even there the dry, lowland heaths that it needs, with mature heather and plentiful gorse, are disappearing because of tree planting, mineral exploitation or fire.

A secretive bird, the Dartford warbler is most often glimpsed darting between bushes. If it is surprised while perching, its long tail jauntily cocked and flicking, it scolds the intruder with a harsh rattling call before it vanishes into cover. Its song, however, is a mixture of liquid tones and chattering notes, sometimes uttered in a dancing flight.

The compact cup-shaped nest is built 18 in. (45 cm) or so off the ground. Two clutches of grey-speckled white eggs, three or four each time, are laid in the same season. Chicks hatch in 12 days and leave the nest after a fortnight.

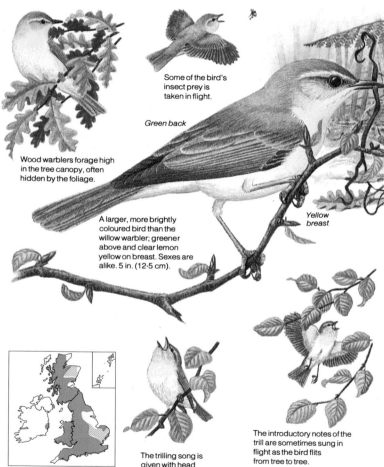

Some of the bird's insect prey is taken in flight.

Green back

Wood warblers forage high in the tree canopy, often hidden by the foliage.

A larger, more brightly coloured bird than the willow warbler; greener above and clear lemon yellow on breast. Sexes are alike. 5 in. (12·5 cm).

Yellow breast

The nest is built on the ground like the willow warbler's, but is usually less well concealed.

Apr.–Aug. visitor; commonest in west and north.

The trilling song is given with head thrown back and wings drooped.

The introductory notes of the trill are sometimes sung in flight as the bird flits from tree to tree.

Unlike the willow warbler, the wood warbler uses only grass, not feathers, to line its nest, built on the ground.

Wood warbler *Phylloscopus sibilatrix*

Unlike many warblers, the wood warbler has a name which accurately pinpoints its habitat – it confines itself to woodlands, especially those of sessile oak in western Britain, but occasionally also woods of beech, birch or pine. Flitting about in the tops of trees hunting insects, the bird betrays its presence with an unforgettable song, in two phases. The first is a series of single notes, which accelerate into a trill; this lasts about four seconds and is repeated regularly. Interspersed with it is the second phase of the song: a series of plaintive 'pew-pew-pew' notes, growing gradually fainter.

This elusive, handsome bird has yellowish-green upperparts and a sulphur-yellow breast and throat. It is noticeably bigger than the willow warbler or the chiffchaff.

Wood warblers arrive from equatorial Africa late in April and usually raise one brood of six to seven young before departing between late July and early September. The female builds the nest, a cup of dead leaves, bracken and grass placed on the ground with a domed roof and side entrance. The male does not help with nest-building, but he does help in feeding the young with insects.

243

Male in courting display rears up with its tail fanned out and makes its wings quiver.

Olive above

Yellowish below

Flights are usually short, from one tree to another near by.

Feeding bird darts restlessly about among foliage, seeking its insect prey.

Pale legs

Bird looks plumper than chiffchaff; underparts yellower, legs paler. Sexes alike; 4½ in. (12 cm).

Apr.–Sept. visitor, breeding in wood and shrubland.

Young birds have much stronger yellow tinge than adult.

The domed, feather-lined nest of moss and grass is usually on the ground – not just above it like that of a chiffchaff.

Willow warbler *Phylloscopus trochilus*

Filling the summer countryside with its sweetly wistful song, the willow warbler is the most widely distributed of all the birds that visit Britain in the breeding season. Almost any area of woodland or shrubs is suitable – the bird has no special preference for willow – as long as the foliage does not form a closed canopy. The total British Isles population is probably more than three million pairs.

When its cadence of soft, liquid notes can no longer be heard, early in autumn, this determined little bird has started its annual 2,500 mile (4,000 km) journey to tropical and southern Africa. The wear and tear of this taxing migration may account for the willow warbler's curious distinction among British birds: it moults completely, replacing all its plumage, twice a year. Even its close relative the chiffchaff moults only once. Nevertheless the willow warbler is able to produce two broods in most breeding seasons, while the chiffchaff manages only one.

The domed nest with its side opening usually contains six eggs, white with pinkish or reddish-brown speckles. The hen alone incubates them, taking about 13 days, but the male helps in feeding the chicks during the 13 days they spend in the nest.

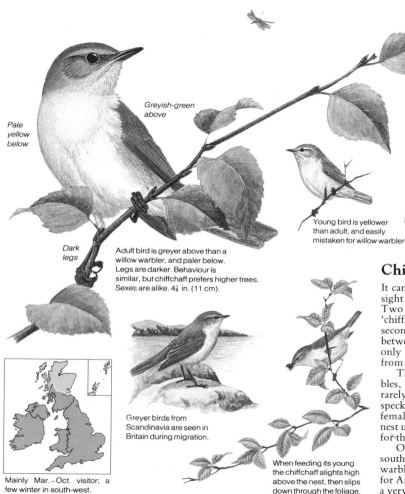

Pale yellow below

Greyish-green above

Dark legs

Adult bird is greyer above than a willow warbler, and paler below. Legs are darker. Behaviour is similar, but chiffchaff prefers higher trees. Sexes are alike. 4¼ in. (11 cm).

Young bird is yellower than adult, and easily mistaken for willow warbler.

Courting male 'floats' down to female on spread wings.

Chiffchaff's nest is similar to that of a willow warbler, but it has a narrower entrance, and is slightly above ground.

Greyer birds from Scandinavia are seen in Britain during migration.

When feeding its young the chiffchaff alights high above the nest, then slips down through the foliage.

Mainly Mar.–Oct. visitor; a few winter in south-west.

Chiffchaff *Phylloscopus collybita*

It can be difficult to tell a chiffchaff from a willow warbler by sight alone, but the chiffchaff's far-carrying song gives it away. Two notes are uttered in random order: one a high-pitched 'chiff' or 'tsip', the other a lower 'chaff' or 'tsap'. After 15 seconds or so the bird seems to fall silent, but in the intervals between songs it often gives a soft, chirring call that is audible only at close range. Unlike the willow warbler, it likes to sing from high in a tree.

The female chiffchaff hides its ball-shaped nest among brambles, nettles or other dense vegetation, near the ground but rarely on it. The six or seven white eggs have purplish-brown speckles. They are incubated for less than a fortnight by the female, which is sometimes fed by its mate but usually leaves the nest unattended when it is hungry. The male helps to bring food for the chicks during the two weeks they stay in the nest.

One of the hardier migratory warblers, the chiffchaff flies south for the winter two or three weeks later than the willow warbler, and usually returns a fortnight or so earlier. Most head for Africa, although some go only as far as southern Europe and a very few winter in south-west England.

245

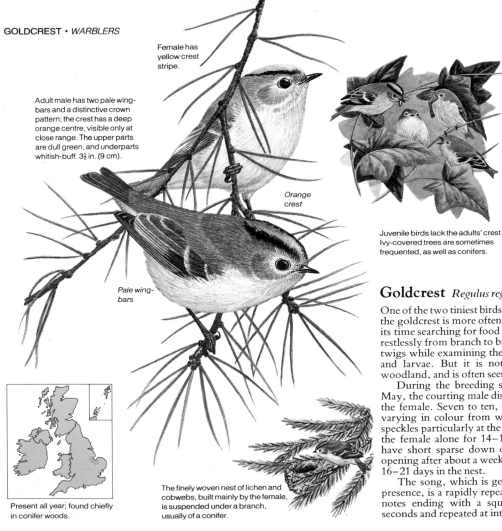

Female has yellow crest stripe.

Adult male has two pale wing-bars and a distinctive crown pattern; the crest has a deep orange centre, visible only at close range. The upper parts are dull green, and underparts whitish-buff. 3½ in. (9 cm).

Orange crest

Pale wing-bars

Present all year; found chiefly in conifer woods.

The finely woven nest of lichen and cobwebs, built mainly by the female, is suspended under a branch, usually of a conifer.

Juvenile birds lack the adults' crest. Ivy-covered trees are sometimes frequented, as well as conifers.

Goldcrests are tame birds, often allowing very close approach. Together with the firecrest they are Europe's smallest birds.

Goldcrest *Regulus regulus*

One of the two tiniest birds in Europe – the other is the firecrest – the goldcrest is more often heard than seen, as it spends most of its time searching for food in the tops of coniferous trees. It flits restlessly from branch to branch, often clinging upside-down to twigs while examining them for spiders, insects, and their eggs and larvae. But it is not entirely dependent on coniferous woodland, and is often seen elsewhere.

During the breeding season, which starts in late April or May, the courting male displays his orange-and-yellow crest to the female. Seven to ten, occasionally up to 13, eggs are laid, varying in colour from white to buff, with purple or brown speckles particularly at the larger end. The eggs are incubated by the female alone for 14–17 days. The hatched chicks, which have short sparse down on their heads, are blind, their eyes opening after about a week. Both parents feed them during their 16–21 days in the nest.

The song, which is generally the first hint of a goldcrest's presence, is a rapidly repeated series of extremely high-pitched notes ending with a squeaky twitter, lasting three or four seconds and repeated at intervals.

Juvenile lacks crest, but is identifiable by its eye-stripe.

The crest is raised and spread when the courting male is displaying.

Orange crest

Eye-stripe

In winter, firecrests and goldcrests may be seen with groups of tits.

The nest is similar to that of the goldcrest, but more compact. It is found mainly in spruce and larch woods.

Firecrest *Regulus ignicapillus*

Although very similar to the goldcrest, the firecrest can be identified chiefly by its black-and-white eye-stripes. The song also helps to distinguish the bird; it is similar in tone and pitch to the goldcrest's, but is simpler and lacks the squeaky twitter at the end. The call is a short 'zit-zit', rather harsher than the goldcrest's 'see-see'.

There are other slight differences between the two birds and their behaviour. The firecrest's nest tends to be slightly smaller and more compact, the breeding season begins a little later, and the eggs tend to be pink rather than buff. Despite these differences, however, there is often considerable rivalry between the two species.

Norway spruce forests are the bird's favourite habitat in England, but it can also be found in a variety of other conifer and deciduous woods. The firecrest is chiefly a passage migrant, seen mainly in southern England in autumn and winter, but it has bred in Britain. This fact first became evident in 1962, when fully fledged young were seen. There have been many other instances of likely breeding in Britain, though the number of sightings has dropped considerably in recent years.

Passage migrant; some breed or winter in Britain.

Adult bird is distinguished from goldcrest by its black-and-white eye-stripe, and a bronze tinge on the sides of the neck is visible at close quarters. Plumage in general is brighter than that of the goldcrest. Sexes are alike. 3½ in. (9 cm).

Spot above bill

Juvenile is speckled, like young spotted flycatcher, but has white wing-patches.

Pied flycatchers glean prey such as caterpillars from tree foliage, as well as catching insects in flight.

Wing-patch

Male, summer

Female, summer

Adult male is black above and white below, with a white wing-patch and a white spot above the bill. 5 in. (12·5 cm).

Adult female is distinguished from male by grey-brown upper plumage and lack of white spot above the bill.

Present Apr.–Oct.; passage migrants in autumn.

After catching an insect, the pied flycatcher often takes its prey to the ground.

The pied flycatcher is always on the look-out for insects; but after darting out in attack, seldom returns to the same perch.

Pied flycatcher *Ficedula hypoleuca*

During the last 50 years or so, the pied flycatcher has extended its breeding range from Wales to the valleys and foothills o upland England. This increase may have been assisted by the deliberate provision of nest-boxes by bird lovers in some areas. The bird is also found to a lesser extent in the Pennines, southern Scotland and the Scottish Highlands, but it does not nest in Ireland. Unlike the spotted flycatcher, male and female have different breeding plumage, although in autumn the male's black upper parts dull to the female's grey-brown colour.

The pied flycatcher needs a plentiful supply of caterpillars and other insects on which to feed. Tree-stumps and dead branches provide ideal song posts and holes for nesting. The nest site is chosen by the male when he arrives from Africa in the spring. The female follows a little later and builds the nest. She lines it with animal hair, wool and feathers.

The single, annual clutch usually consists of four to seven eggs. They are pale blue, and very occasionally have a few extremely fine reddish-brown speckles. The male feeds the female while she is incubating the eggs, which takes just under a fortnight. The young can fly after about two weeks.

Juvenile birds are grey-brown and prominently speckled.

The broad-based bill closes on an insect with an audible snap.

The spotted flycatcher's song is two or three notes resembling a squeaking, slow-turning wheel.

May–Sept. visitor; widespread but decreasing.

Head streaks

Breast streaks

After catching a flying insect, the bird usually returns to the same watching point.

Streaks mark the adult bird's crown and breast. The plumage is mainly grey-brown above and pale below. Sexes are alike. 5½ in. (14 cm).

The nest may be made in any sheltered place, even an old lamp. Both sexes build the nest and tend the nestlings.

Spotted flycatcher *Muscicapa striata*

While awaiting its prey, the spotted flycatcher sits upright on a low branch or other convenient perch, its head slightly sunk into its shoulders. Periodically, it darts out and snaps up flies which it either eats itself or takes to the nest for its mate or its young. Birds begin breeding in May, on arrival from their winter quarters in central Africa.

The nest is a neat cup of dried grass, twiglets, rootlets and lichen lined with small feathers, hair and dead leaves. It is usually in a protected place such as a ledge against a wall or a wound in a tree-trunk where a branch has been broken off. Open-fronted nest-boxes are also readily used if they are not too exposed.

A clutch usually consists of four or five blue-green or greenish-grey eggs with red-brown speckles. The speckles are often so dense at the broader end of the egg that they form a distinct colour cap. After 11–15 days the chicks emerge, and are fed in the nest for 12–14 days by both parents – although at first the female broods them and feeds them with the flies brought by the male. The young are dependent on their parents for food for about three weeks after leaving the nest. Usually there is only one brood a year, but two broods are occasionally reared.

249

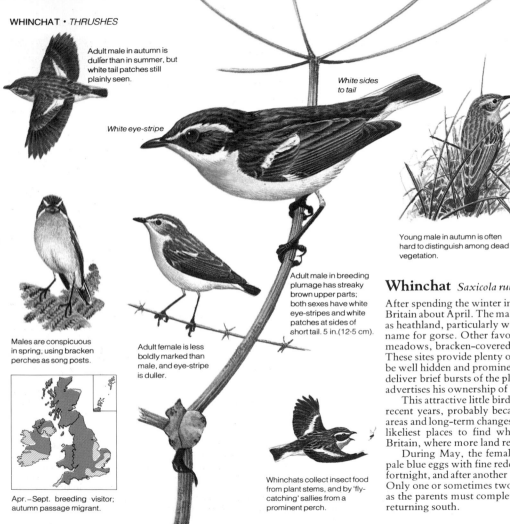

Adult male in autumn is duller than in summer, but white tail patches still plainly seen.

White eye-stripe

White sides to tail

Males are conspicuous in spring, using bracken perches as song posts.

Adult female is less boldly marked than male, and eye-stripe is duller.

Adult male in breeding plumage has streaky brown upper parts; both sexes have white eye-stripes and white patches at sides of short tail. 5 in.(12·5 cm).

Apr.–Sept. breeding visitor; autumn passage migrant.

Whinchats collect insect food from plant stems, and by 'fly-catching' sallies from a prominent perch.

Young male in autumn is often hard to distinguish among dead vegetation.

The nest of the whinchat is built of grass or moss and carefully concealed under thick grass or bracken.

Whinchat *Saxicola rubetra*

After spending the winter in tropical Africa, whinchats arrive in Britain about April. The males set up territory in open areas such as heathland, particularly where there is gorse: 'whin' is another name for gorse. Other favourite areas for whinchats are water-meadows, bracken-covered hillsides and young fir plantations. These sites provide plenty of ground cover in which the nest can be well hidden and prominent perches from which the male can deliver brief bursts of the pleasant, metallic, warbling song that advertises his ownership of the territory.

This attractive little bird has disappeared from many areas in recent years, probably because of the loss of suitable breeding areas and long-term changes in summer weather. Nowadays the likeliest places to find whinchats are in the upland areas of Britain, where more land remains unploughed.

During May, the female whinchat lays from five to seven pale blue eggs with fine reddish speckles. These hatch in about a fortnight, and after another 14 to 17 days the young are airborne. Only one or sometimes two broods can be raised each summer, as the parents must complete a moult of all their feathers before returning south.

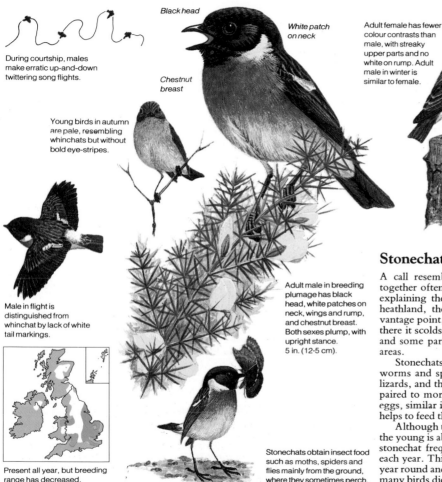

During courtship, males make erratic up-and-down twittering song flights.

Black head

White patch on neck

Chestnut breast

Adult female has fewer colour contrasts than male, with streaky upper parts and no white on rump. Adult male in winter is similar to female.

Young birds in autumn are pale, resembling whinchats but without bold eye-stripes.

Male in flight is distinguished from whinchat by lack of white tail markings.

Present all year, but breeding range has decreased.

Adult male in breeding plumage has black head, white patches on neck, wings and rump, and chestnut breast. Both sexes plump, with upright stance. 5 in. (12·5 cm).

Stonechats obtain insect food such as moths, spiders and flies mainly from the ground, where they sometimes perch.

The stonechat's nest of moss, grass and hair is well hidden, low down in bushes or thick grass.

Stonechat *Saxicola torquata*

A call resembling the sound of two pebbles being banged together often betrays the presence of a stonechat – as well as explaining the origin of its name. Primarily a bird of gorse heathland, the stonechat is usually seen perching on a high vantage point, such as the top of a bush or telegraph wire; from there it scolds intruders with its 'wee-tac-tac' alarm. In Ireland and some parts of Britain stonechats can be found in moister areas.

Stonechats feed mainly on small creatures such as insects, worms and spiders, but they have been known to take small lizards, and they also eat some seeds. A male stonechat may be paired to more than one female, each of which lays five or six eggs, similar in appearance to those of the whinchat. The male helps to feed the young until they become independent.

Although the length of time from egg-laying to the flying of the young is about the same for stonechats as for whinchats, the stonechat frequently manages to raise three broods of young each year. This is because most stonechats stay in Britain all the year round and do not migrate south for the winter. As a result, many birds die during severe winters.

251

The wheatear often chases insects upwards in vertical flight, with fluttering wing-beats.

Adult female is brown with buff underparts, but has the same tail pattern as the male.

White rump

Grey above

Black cheeks

Adult male in summer has grey upper parts, black cheeks and wings, white rump and black, inverted-T tail pattern. In autumn he resembles the female. 6 in. (15 cm).

Juvenile bird is brown like adult female, but also heavily speckled.

In flight, white rump and black, T-shaped tail pattern are conspicuous.

When the wheatears arrive, usually in March, they can be seen seeking insects, larvae and centipedes in ploughed fields.

Mar.–Oct. visitor, and also passage migrant.

Nests are built under stones or in crevices. Both parents feed the dark grey nestlings with insects.

Wheatear *Oenanthe oenanthe*

One of the first signs that spring is on its way is the arrival in Britain of the wheatear, among the earliest of the summer migrants. Normally, early arrivals from Africa are seen in southern England about the second week in March; most birds appear between the last week of March and mid-April.

The most noticeable feature of the wheatear is its white rump, visible as the bird flits low over the ground to perch on a prominent stone, clod of earth or other vantage point. The bird's common name comes from *hwit* and *oers*, Anglo-Saxon words for 'white' and 'rump'.

The wheatear is mainly a bird of upland Britain, and elsewhere occurs mostly on heathlands and coasts. It is in such areas that suitable nest sites in the form of holes in drystone walls or under large stones are most plentiful. The nest of loose grass, stems and leaves is built largely by the female. The four to seven pale blue eggs are laid in late March, or as late as June in the north. They hatch after 14 days and the young spend about two weeks in the nest. The wheatear is noted for its distinctive 'wee-chat-chat' call; its song is a vigorous, though brief, warble, intermingled with harsh rattlings and squeaky notes.

Scandinavian form

In flight, the black-eared wheatear's wings are conspicuously black.

In some males, the black cheek plumage extends to the throat as well.

Bluethroat
Luscinia svecica
Adult bird has tell-tale blue throat and red base to tail. Scandinavian form has red spot in centre of throat-patch.

Adult female is similar to the female wheatear, but has darker wings and a whiter tail.

A rock is this bird's favourite perch when it sings in the breeding season, though trees may be used where available.

Black cheeks

Black wings

Adult male in autumn is identifiable by its creamy buff-white back and black wings and cheeks. 5¾ in. (14·5 cm).

Black-eared wheatear *Oenanthe hispanica*

This extremely rare visitor has occasionally been sighted in Britain on its spring or autumn migration. It is a bird of Mediterranean lands with a range extending from north-west Africa and Portugal eastwards to Iran.

The bird's habitat is open, arid country with scattered timber and scrub, or mountain-sides with stony ground where there are plenty of holes among the rocks or in the walls for breeding. In timbered areas, the black-eared wheatear perches readily on trees. From such perches – or during a short display flight – it delivers its squeaky, warbling song. An unusual feature of the species is that the males occur in two forms: those with black throats and those with white throats. The birds exist almost entirely on insects.

The bluethroat is a scarce bird in Britain, and it is found mainly on the east and south coasts – again during the spring and autumn migrations. In 1968 a female bluethroat was discovered incubating six eggs in a nest in Inverness. No male parent was seen and the eggs – which were doubtless infertile – were taken by a predator. A shy and skulking bird, the bluethroat flies low, and prefers to stay in the cover of ground vegetation.

253

Adult male is sooty black, with a white wing-patch and rust-coloured tail. 5½ in. (14 cm).

White patch

Rusty tail

Adult female is less black than the male, and lacks the white wing-patch.

Wing-patches show prominently when the bird hovers to catch its insect prey.

The juvenile bird has speckled plumage but is otherwise similar to the adult female.

Breeding begins in late April. Nests, in crevices, are usually made of grass, moss and roots, lined with feathers.

Small numbers breed; a few winter in south.

Migrating birds are often seen on rocky beaches. They can be distinguished from redstarts by darker breasts and greyer upper parts.

Black redstart *Phoenicurus ochruros*

Until the Second World War, black redstarts were rare breeding birds in Britain. The rubble and broken walls of bombed sites, however, provided an environment similar to the rock-falls, screes and boulder-strewn hillsides which are the birds' natural habitat on the Continent, and their numbers increased considerably. Now an average of 50 pairs breed in Britain each year. As bomb damage was repaired after the war, some black redstarts moved to other nesting places, such as factory sites, gasworks and railway yards. Others occupy coastal cliffs.

The nest, normally built by the female alone, is a loose cup of dried grass, moss or rootlets, lined with hair, wool or feathers. It is built on a ledge or in a wall where a brick is missing, or in some other crevice; hollow trees are also sometimes used. The clutch of four to six white eggs is incubated for 12–16 days by the female, and young birds remain in the nest for 16–18 days. The female often produces two broods, and occasionally three. The male helps with the feeding, bringing beakfuls of insects.

The black redstart's song is distinctive: a fairly loud, brief, reedy warble, which can sometimes be heard from rooftops above the din of traffic.

Adult female can be distinguished from the nightingale by the dark centre of the tail, which is not rounded.

Adult female is brown above and paler below; she has a rusty tail, like the male.

Juvenile bird is brown and speckled.

Grey back

Redstarts commonly nest in drystone walls from early May, but holes in trees make acceptable building sites.

Adult male redstart has a rust-coloured tail (or 'start'), reddish belly, grey back, black throat and conspicuous white blaze on forehead. 5½ in. (14 cm).

Rusty tail

Apr.–Sept. visitor, which occasionally breeds in Ireland.

During migration birds may be found resting and feeding along the shoreline.

Redstart *Phoenicurus phoenicurus*

With its richly contrasting colours and distinctive markings, the redstart is one of Britain's handsomest small birds. Its most noticeable feature is its bright russet tail, and to this it owes its name: *steort* is Anglo-Saxon for 'tail'. The constantly flickering tail plays an important part in the bird's courtship ritual, during which the male splays its tail feathers to reveal the brilliant rust–coloured splash.

The bird commonly breeds in deciduous woodland, parkland, gardens or mature orchards; it also breeds in more open country if there are suitable nest sites, such as stone walls and tree holes. Nests, built by the female, are loosely constructed cups of dead grass, rootlets, moss and bark fragments, lined with finer materials such as hair and feathers. The usual clutch consists of five to seven eggs, which are incubated for about two weeks by the female alone. When the chicks are hatched the male helps to feed them for the 12–16 days they remain in the nest.

The alarm note of the redstart is an anxious 'wee-ticc-ticc'; its song is a brief but melodious warble terminating in a jingling rattle. Most of the breeding population depart in the autumn for winter quarters in tropical Africa.

255

Red
breast

The cock robin's pleasant warbling, heard all year except during late-summer moulting, is a reminder of claim to a territory.

Although regarded as tame and confident, robins sometimes behave secretively, especially during the late-summer moult.

Young birds have speckled plumage and look like juvenile nightingales, but their tails are darker and shorter.

Adult bird's red face and breast, with pale grey border, identify it easily. Upper parts and tail are brown and underparts whitish. Sexes are alike. 5½ in. (14 cm).

Present all year; Continental migrants in east and south.

Robins are generally pugnacious, and the male birds are vigorously aggressive in territorial disputes.

Any convenient hole or ledge – even an old container such as a tea-pot – may be chosen as a nesting place.

Robin *Erithacus rubecula*

For generations, the robin has earned its place as Britain's best-loved bird. It is noted for its tameness in town and city gardens, and often searches for food around the feet of gardeners who are turning over the ground. It will even eat meal-worms straight from the hand. Away from habitation, however, in woodland and other areas of countryside, the robin is more wary, and on the Continent it is a shy and retiring bird.

It is extremely possessive of its territory, and guards it fiercely from other robins. The nest is built entirely by the female and is usually hidden amongst thick ivy on trees or walls, or among roots or undergrowth on banks. Nests are also commonly found inside sheds and other buildings; and sauce-pans, old tins and the like are readily commandeered for nesting.

Breeding begins from late March in the south to June in the north. A clutch usually consists of five to six eggs, which are incubated by the female for 12–15 days. Young birds leave the nest after about two weeks. The male may take over the feeding and care of one brood if a second clutch follows quickly. The robin has a loud, penetrating 'tic-tic' alarm call and a thin, rather sad but sweet warbling song, consisting of short phrases.

Juvenile bird's tail colouring and paler underparts distinguish it from a young robin.

Chestnut tail is conspicuous on rare glimpse of nightingale in flight.

A chestnut tail is the only eye-catching feature of the adult bird, which is like an oversized robin in build and attitude. Seldom seen, it is usually identified by its song. Sexes are alike. 6½ in. (16·5 cm).

Chestnut tail

Apr.–Aug. visitor; rare outside breeding range.

A feeding bird may dart out of hiding to find insects.

The characteristic tail colour is usually all that is seen as the bird dives for cover.

The nest, of dead leaves lined with grass and hair, is hidden in brambles or nettles, on or close to the ground.

Nightingale *Luscinia megarhynchos*

Generations of poets have been inspired by the song of the nightingale. Milton, for instance, wrote of the 'nightingale, that on yon bloomy spray Warbl'st at eve, when all the woods are still'. The song, sometimes but not always delivered at dead of night, is remarkable for its tonal richness, variety and volume. It consists of a series of short phrases and single notes, usually repeated, often with increasing volume, some notes having a flute-like quality, others a more piping tone. The song period is short, lasting only from mid to late April until June.

The nightingale is a shy bird, generally to be found in open deciduous woodland where plenty of cover is provided by dense undergrowth of bramble, or by thickets of thorn bushes such as blackthorn. However, because the nightingale feeds largely on ground-living insects such as beetles, any site which has become too overgrown is deserted.

The four or five eggs laid in May are olive-green or olive-brown. Incubation takes about two weeks and is by the female alone. The young are fed for about 12 days by both parents. By the end of July many birds have started their journey back to Africa; and the stragglers have gone by the end of September.

257

White crescent

Adult female is a browner grey than the male, and the crescent on the breast is less clearly marked.

Juvenile lacks the white breast crescent of the adult. It resembles a young blackbird, but is more spotted.

Mar.–Oct. visitor; also a passage migrant.

Adult male has sooty black plumage, a white crescent on the breast, and pale wing-patches. In summer it is a bird of the uplands. 9½ in. (24 cm).

During their autumn migration, ring ouzels are often gregarious, and can be found together feeding on elderberries.

In flight, adult males can be distinguished by the pale edges of the flight feathers and by the white breast crescent.

The ring ouzel nests in a tree if one is available, but in open moors nests in a sheltered spot on the ground.

Ring ouzel *Turdus torquatus*

It can be as well for humans – and for predatory birds – to keep away from the nest of the ring ouzel at nesting time. It is then that this normally shy and nervous bird may become aggressive. It will vigorously defend its nest against such intruders as crows or buzzards, and some individuals will strike at the head of a human being who poses a threat.

The nest, built by male and female, is much like that of the ring ouzel's close relative the blackbird; it lacks an inner mud cup, though earth is sometimes used in the foundations. Heather from the bird's upland habitat is frequently used in the nest's construction. The eggs, numbering from three to five, are normally bluish-green with bold, reddish-brown blotches. They are incubated in turn by both parents for 13–14 days. The young are fed in the nest for about another fortnight with worms, flies, caterpillars and the like. Occasionally two broods are raised in one season.

Ring ouzels are mostly seen perched on far-off rocks. When disturbed they give a loud, rattling chatter of alarm; another call is a clear, shrill 'pee-u'. Most of the birds are migratory, and start to leave the breeding grounds in late summer.

Adult male is all black, with orange bill and yellow eye-ring. 10 in. (25 cm).

Orange bill

The plumage of a young bird resembles that of the female, but is more distinctly spotted.

Albino males, with white feathers, are often seen in town gardens.

A blackbird will stand with its head cocked on one side, listening for worms.

Adult female looks all brown at a distance, but has blurred spots on throat and breast.

The parents take turns to feed the nestlings with fruit, seeds and insects. The nests are often in a hedge or low tree.

Present all year; continental birds winter in Britain.

Young males, still with their first-winter black bill, are often seen feeding on hawthorn berries in winter, together with migrant thrushes such as redwings.

Blackbird *Turdus merula*

'I value my garden more for being full of blackbirds than of cherries, and very frankly give them fruit for their songs,' declared the 18th-century essayist Joseph Addison in *The Spectator*. Most people would agree with Addison. For the rich, short, fluty warbling, punctuated by pauses, that the blackbird delivers from any suitable vantage point – tree, rooftop or TV aerial – is a welcome herald of spring. When danger threatens, the blackbird gives a harsh, persistent 'pink-pink-pink-pink' call which is repeated until the peril has passed.

Blackbirds, among the commonest of British birds, eat fruit and berries in season and also feed on worms and insects. In the mating season, the black-plumaged male is conspicuous for its display, which involves much running about with rump feathers raised, tail fanned and wings drooped. Nest-building is left mainly to the female, which makes a solid cup of dried grass, rootlets, twigs and moss, lined with mud and dried grass.

The pale, blue-green, speckled eggs, usually three to five, are laid from March to April; they hatch in about a fortnight. The young leave the nest 14 days or so later, but can only flutter and depend on the parents for food for about another three weeks.

259

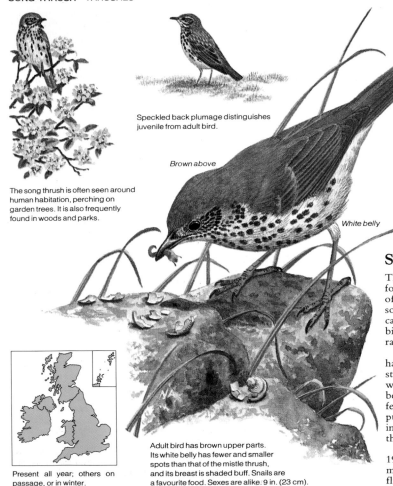

Speckled back plumage distinguishes juvenile from adult bird.

Brown above

The song thrush is often seen around human habitation, perching on garden trees. It is also frequently found in woods and parks.

White belly

In flight, yellow plumage under wing distinguishes song thrush from redwing.

The song thrush is an untidy eater, littering the ground around its favourite stone 'anvil' with broken snail shells.

Present all year; others on passage, or in winter.

Adult bird has brown upper parts. Its white belly has fewer and smaller spots than that of the mistle thrush, and its breast is shaded buff. Snails are a favourite food. Sexes are alike. 9 in. (23 cm).

Song thrush *Turdus philomelos*

The song thrush lives up to its name magnificently. Its song lasts for five minutes or longer, and consists of a loud, rich succession of musical phrases, some of which are repeated many times. The song is often delivered from a high perch such as a tree-top and can be heard at almost any time during the year on fine days. The bird's call, by contrast, varies from a thin 'tic' or 'sipp', to a rapidly repeated 'tchuck-tchuck' of alarm.

Its song apart, this thrush is probably best known for its habit of smashing open garden snail shells on suitable 'anvil' stones to get at the succulent contents. The bird often reveals its whereabouts by the noise it makes while hammering. Breeding begins from March in the south to May or June in the north. The female builds a nest of grass and twigs lined with mud or wood pulp, and lays usually four to six light blue speckled eggs. She incubates them for about two weeks, and the male helps to feed the young during their 12 to 16 days in the nest.

The song thrush suffers badly during harsh winters; in early 1963 its numbers declined by about 60 per cent. It is a partial migrant; some birds move to lower ground for the winter, some fly to southern Europe and others do not move at all.

Grey-brown upper parts and bold brown spots on a white breast distinguish the mistle thrush – the largest of the British thrushes – from the song thrush. Sexes are alike. 10½ in. (27 cm).

Grey-brown above

Large breast spots

Both wings are closed at regular intervals in flight, which is strong and direct.

In flight, its white underwing helps to distinguish the bird from other thrushes.

The plumage of juvenile birds is more speckled than adults'.

The hen bird builds a bulky, grass-lined nest of twigs, grass, earth and moss, usually in the fork of a high branch.

Present all year. Some birds winter on Continent.

Small family groups often move about together when the breeding season is over.

Mistle thrush *Turdus viscivorus*

The mistle thrush is also known as the 'storm cock', for it sings through the stormy days of winter as well as the fine days; indeed, its song was often believed to give warning of a coming storm. The song is a prolonged series of short fluty notes of varying pitch and considerable carrying power, sung usually from the topmost swaying twigs of high trees. In flight its call is a short rattling chatter, which becomes louder and more prolonged when the bird is alarmed.

Nest-building, by the female alone, takes place from February onwards. Three to five eggs, varying in colour from cream to turquoise, with purplish-brown spots, are usually laid. These are incubated by the female for 12–15 days. The male helps to feed the young in the nest for 12–16 days, and if the female has a second brood, the male alone feeds the fledged first brood until they become independent. The diet includes berries, slugs, small snails, earthworms and insects.

The species is widespread in areas with scattered trees. It is absent only from parts of northern Scotland and the northern and western isles. Some birds, especially the young, fly south to the Continent for the winter.

261

Noisy scuffles are common among flocks of fieldfares as they feed.

Fieldfares feeding on pastures often mingle with redwings and golden plovers.

Chestnut back

Grey head

Adult fieldfare has a grey head and rump, chestnut back, black tail and spotted underparts. Birds are fond of windfall apples. Sexes are alike. 10 in. (25 cm).

In flight, fieldfares look pale in colour from below; flashes of white appear beneath the beating wings.

The fieldfare rises into the air almost vertically. The unmistakable grey rump contrasts with the black tail.

Oct.–Apr. visitor; has begun to nest in Scotland.

The nest is a strongly constructed cup of dried grass, moss and rootlets, lined with mud and insulated with finer dried grass.

Fieldfare *Turdus pilaris*

Large, loose flocks of fieldfares are a common feature of the winter landscape in Britain. They are noisy, clamorous birds often seen in pastures searching for seeds and small creatures such as spiders or centipedes, or on thick hawthorns attacking the bright red berries. Alternatively they may be seen flying overhead, sometimes in large flocks on their way to a communal roost, when their chattering 'chack-chack-chack' and occasional squeaking 'weeek' calls may be heard.

Both fieldfares and redwings are northern species of thrush. Few breed in this country, but large numbers arrive in autumn to spend the winter in a less severe climate than that of their native land.

Fieldfares nest in a variety of European habitats, including farmland, woodland edges, forestry plantations and moorland valleys. The breeding season depends on the latitude, starting in April in the south of the bird's range and as late as June in the north. Two clutches of five to six eggs are laid each year. The eggs, which are glossy and light blue, with reddish-brown speckles, are incubated by the female. For their 12–16 days in the nest the chicks are fed by both adults.

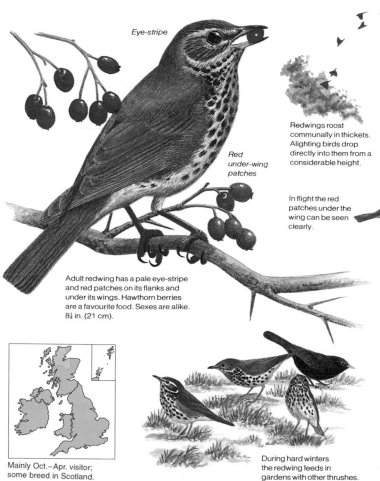

Eye-stripe

Red
under-wing
patches

Adult redwing has a pale eye-stripe
and red patches on its flanks and
under its wings. Hawthorn berries
are a favourite food. Sexes are alike.
8¼ in. (21 cm).

Redwings roost
communally in thickets.
Alighting birds drop
directly into them from a
considerable height.

In flight the red
patches under the
wing can be seen
clearly.

Rhododendrons are
a favourite home for
pairs nesting in
Scotland.

Like the song thrush, the redwing 'listens'
while searching on the ground for snails,
worms or insects.

Mainly Oct.–Apr. visitor;
some breed in Scotland.

During hard winters
the redwing feeds in
gardens with other thrushes.

Redwing *Turdus iliacus*

On clear, starry nights in September and October the careful
listener may detect a thin, hissing 'seeeeip'-like sound at intervals overhead. It is the sign that redwings are in flight, calling to
keep in contact with their fellows. They will have set out from
northern Europe, where they breed, some hours before. Some
will remain in Britain; others will continue further south. The
severe winters of their breeding grounds mean that they must
seek in warmer climes for their food – berries such as hawthorn,
yew, holly and mountain ash, and invertebrates like worms,
snails and spiders.

A few redwings breed in northern Scotland, in woodlands of
birch, alder or pine, in spinneys, valleys, gullies among mountains or even in gardens. The nest is usually in a tree, against the
trunk, or in a shrub; other nests may be in tree stumps or steep
banks. The female builds the nest – a firm cup of dried grass,
fine twigs and moss – between May and July.

The eggs are smooth and glossy, pale blue or greenish-blue
in colour with fine specklings of reddish-brown. Incubation
lasts for up to 15 days. The nestlings are fed by both parents for
about two weeks in the nest, and for some time after they fledge.

263

BEARDED REEDLING

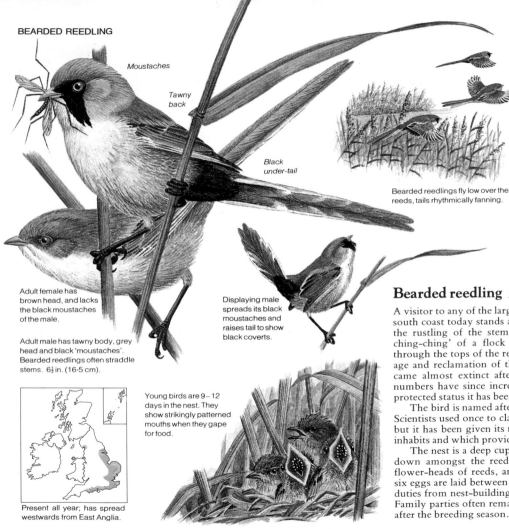

Moustaches

Tawny back

Black under-tail

Adult female has brown head, and lacks the black moustaches of the male.

Adult male has tawny body, grey head and black 'moustaches'. Bearded reedlings often straddle stems. 6½ in. (16·5 cm).

Displaying male spreads its black moustaches and raises tail to show black coverts.

Bearded reedlings fly low over the reeds, tails rhythmically fanning.

The bearded reedling is confined to reed beds, and conceals its nest low down at the base of a clump of reeds.

Present all year; has spread westwards from East Anglia.

Young birds are 9–12 days in the nest. They show strikingly patterned mouths when they gape for food.

Bearded reedling *Panurus biarmicus*

A visitor to any of the large reed beds in East Anglia or along the south coast today stands a reasonable chance of hearing, above the rustling of the stems, the far-carrying, bell-like 'ching-ching-ching' of a flock of bearded reedlings as they move through the tops of the reeds. Already threatened by the drainage and reclamation of the marshes, the bearded reedling became almost extinct after the severe winter of 1947; but its numbers have since increased, partly because of the specially protected status it has been given.

The bird is named after the black face markings of the male. Scientists used once to classify it as a member of the tit family, but it has been given its new name after the *Phragmites* reeds it inhabits and which provide its staple diet of seeds.

The nest is a deep cup of dead reeds and sedges, placed low down amongst the reed stems. It is lined with the feathery flower-heads of reeds, and occasionally some feathers. About six eggs are laid between April and July, the parents sharing all duties from nest-building onwards. Two broods are common. Family parties often remain together and group up with others after the breeding season.

264

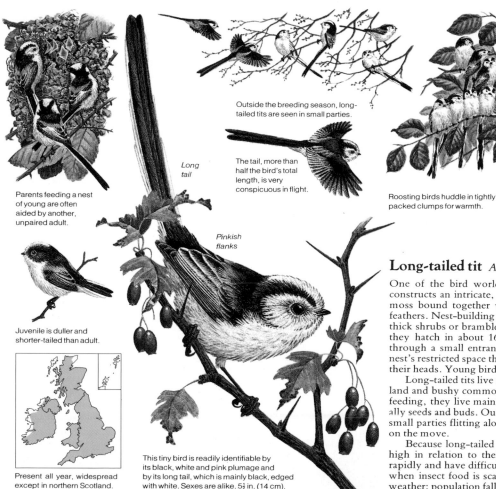

Parents feeding a nest of young are often aided by another, unpaired adult.

Outside the breeding season, long-tailed tits are seen in small parties.

Long tail

The tail, more than half the bird's total length, is very conspicuous in flight.

Juvenile is duller and shorter-tailed than adult.

Pinkish flanks

Roosting birds huddle in tightly packed clumps for warmth.

Present all year, widespread except in northern Scotland.

This tiny bird is readily identifiable by its black, white and pink plumage and by its long tail, which is mainly black, edged with white. Sexes are alike. 5½ in. (14 cm).

The long-tailed tit uses as many as 2,000 feathers to make the lining of its elaborate oval nest which it builds in early spring.

Long-tailed tit *Aegithalos caudatus*

One of the bird world's master builders, the long-tailed tit constructs an intricate, oval-shaped nest, consisting mainly of moss bound together with cobwebs and hair and lined with feathers. Nest-building starts in March, in the fork of a tree or in thick shrubs or brambles, and usually 8–12 white eggs are laid; they hatch in about 16 days. The adult birds enter the nest through a small entrance well up on one side, and inside the nest's restricted space they have to fold their long tails back over their heads. Young birds spend two to three weeks in the nest.

Long-tailed tits live mainly in fringes and clearings of woodland and bushy common or waste land. Active and agile when feeding, they live mainly on insects and spiders, and occasionally seeds and buds. Outside the breeding season they are seen in small parties flitting along hedges and woodland edges, always on the move.

Because long-tailed tits are small birds, their surface area is high in relation to their volume. As a result, they lose heat rapidly and have difficulty in keeping warm in winter, the time when insect food is scarce. Consequently, many die in severe weather; population falls of 80 per cent have been recorded.

265

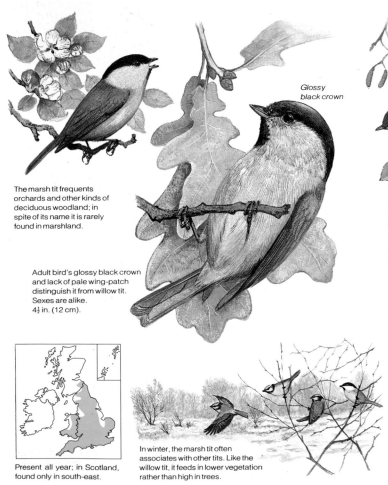

The marsh tit frequents orchards and other kinds of deciduous woodland; in spite of its name it is rarely found in marshland.

Adult bird's glossy black crown and lack of pale wing-patch distinguish it from willow tit. Sexes are alike. 4½ in. (12 cm).

Glossy black crown

Present all year; in Scotland, found only in south-east.

In winter, the marsh tit often associates with other tits. Like the willow tit, it feeds in lower vegetation rather than high in trees.

Juvenile bird has a browner crown than the adult; otherwise it is very similar to the young willow tit.

Unlike the willow tit, the marsh tit does not excavate its own nest-hole, but uses natural holes in trees or walls.

Marsh tit *Parus palustris*

From a distance, it is almost impossible to tell the marsh tit and the willow tit apart. On close inspection the marsh tit's black crown is glossy rather than sooty like the willow tit's. It also lacks the pale patch which the willow tit has on its wings. Yet no two British birds resemble each other more, and the only other way to distinguish them in the field is by their calls and songs.

The call of the marsh tit ranges from a distinctive 'pitchew' to a scolding 'chickabee-bee-bee-bee'. The willow tit has a loud 'tchay' and a high-pitched 'zee-zee-zee'. The marsh tit's song varies from a single note repeated over and over again, to a phrase such as 'pitchaweeoo'. One of the songs of the willow tit – 'chu-chu-chu' – is more melodious and warbling.

The marsh tit's mossy nest is built by the female, usually in a natural tree-hole, and forms a neat cup, lined with hair and a few feathers. Nesting usually begins in April or May and five to nine white eggs are normally laid. They are smooth, slightly glossy and have sparse purple-red or red-brown speckles. They take 13–17 days to hatch. Incubation is carried out by the female, fed on the nest by her partner. After fledging, the young remain dependent for a further week.

Matt black crown

Adult willow tit is identified by pale wing-patch and the sooty, matt black feathers of its crown. Sexes are alike. 4½ in. (12 cm).

Present all year; in Scotland, found only in south-west.

This species, like the crested tit, excavates its own nest holes, usually in the soft trunks of rotted alders, willows or birches.

The willow tit often hunts for food in the lower levels of vegetation, but rarely lands on the ground.

Once the nest hole is complete, the bird carpets it with wood fibre, rabbit-down and frequently a few feathers.

Willow tit *Parus montanus*

Until 1897, the willow tit was thought not to be present in Britain, although it was widespread on the Continent. Then two ornithologists, Otto Kleinschmidt and Ernst Hartert, found the skins of two willow tits in a tray marked 'marsh tits' in the Bird Room of the British Museum of Natural History. The two skins had come from Hampstead, in north London, where the willow tits had been nesting.

Later that year, the Rothschild Museum at Tring, in Hertfordshire, acquired two willow tits from Finchley. Gradually it was realised that the bird was almost as common as the very similar marsh tit. Both have recently declined and there are now less than 25,000 pairs of willow tits resident in Britain.

The willow tit favours damp woods with decaying trees such as the willow, the birch and the alder in which to build its nest. A normal clutch consists of six to nine smooth, glossy eggs. They are white with fine, red or reddish-brown speckles. The male feeds the female while she is incubating them. After about two weeks, the nestlings hatch and both parents tend them, bringing beakfuls of various insects, together with their eggs and larvae.

267

The crested tit, like the coal tit and treecreeper, moves along tree trunks picking insects from the bark.

Its pointed, black and white crest readily identifies this small bird. Sexes are alike. 4½ in. (12 cm).

Present all year; confined to Scottish pine woods.

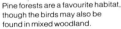
Crest

Pine forests are a favourite habitat, though the birds may also be found in mixed woodland.

In their first weeks of life the young in their tree-hole nest are fed by the male bird alone; later, both parents bring food.

Crested tit *Parus cristatus*

A distinctive soft, rattling trill in the tree canopy of pine forest or mixed woodland gives away the presence of a flock of crested tits. But the call is not heard outside a relatively small area of the central Scottish Highlands, focused on the Spey Valley. For a species which frequents so much of Europe from Spain and Greece north to central Scandinavia, it is remarkable that the crested tit is absent from such large areas of apparently suitable habitat in the British Isles.

Since the crested tit is a very sedentary species, the lack of suitable food in winter may be a crucial factor in restricting its range and preventing it from colonising the enormous areas of new pine plantation that have been established in Britain.

The nest is usually built in a hole in a tree stump excavated by the female. It is a cup of moss and lichen lined with hair, wool and sometimes spiders' webs. A clutch may vary in size from four to eight eggs, or occasionally more. They are white, speckled with various shades of red or reddish-brown, and are incubated by the female for two to two and a half weeks before they hatch. The bird's diet consists of insects and their larvae, as well as pine seeds and berries.

Coal tits are able to survive in prolonged periods of snow because they feed on insects living beneath the shelter of tree bark.

Black cap

White nape-patch

White nape-patch below a black cap distinguishes the coal tit, smallest of the seven tits breeding in Britain. It has greyish upper parts with a double white wing-bar and buff underparts. Sexes are alike. 4½ in. (12 cm).

Juveniles have yellow head patches and underparts. The nape-patch and lack of a belly-stripe distinguish them from young great tits.

Coal tits will use a hole in a tree to make a snug nest in which to raise a family. Both parents feed the nestlings.

Coal tit *Parus ater*

Coniferous woodlands are the favourite home of the coal tit. But it can also be seen in deciduous or mixed woods, in gardens, orchards and, outside the breeding season, in hedgerows.

The coal tit, which is the smallest of all British tits, eats beetles, flies, moths and bugs – whether as eggs, larvae or adults – and spiders. It also feeds on plant food, such as weed seeds and conifer seeds, nut kernels and beech-mast, and will take food such as meat and suet scraps from bird tables. Except during breeding time, coal tits often feed in flocks, sometimes mixing with other species of tit.

The bird's nest is almost always in a hole, in a tree or tree-stump, in a wall or in a bank. Both sexes build the nest, using moss with a thick lining of hair and often feathers to produce a neat cup shape. The male feeds the female on the nest during her 14–16 days' incubation of the seven to nine eggs. The chicks leave the nest 16–19 days after hatching. They swiftly acquire the acrobatic skills characteristic of the tit family, and become independent after about two weeks. The call notes of the fully grown coal tit are mostly musical, thin and high-pitched – the commonest a rather plaintive 'tsee' and a 'tsooee'.

Present all year, mainly in conifer woods.

Nesting coal tits may take over a disused rodent burrow as a site for building.

269

Blue
crown

White
face

Adult bird is identified by its bluish
upper parts and yellow underparts.
White face and bright blue crown are
also distinctive. Sexes are alike.
4½ in. (12 cm).

Blue tits readily use
nest-boxes, from
which they
immediately remove
the droppings of
their young.

Present all year; familiar and
widespread in Britain.

Brighter-coloured Continental birds
may reach southern Britain in
sudden migratory movements.

Young birds have yellow faces, and
remain together in groups for some time.

Birds are noisy and aggressive,
and may threaten each other
in squabbles over food.

The blue tit displays great resource in
finding food, and is known for its habit of
pecking through milk-bottle tops.

Blue tit *Parus caeruleus*

Although the blue tit is chiefly a woodland bird – and feeds in the
tops of trees – it will visit garden bird-tables and amuse onlook-
ers with its lively, acrobatic behaviour. It is able to cling on to a
piece of suspended food at any angle, and eats a wide variety of
titbits. It may breed wherever there are areas of trees with holes
in which it can make its nest. The bottom of the nest-hole is
filled with moss, dried grass, dead leaves and wool, and the
nest-cup itself is lined with hair, feathers or down. Nest-boxes
can be put out for the blue tit, but the entrance hole should be too
small to admit the acquisitive house sparrow.

A clutch of usually 7–12 eggs is laid from mid-April to early
May. As the eggs are laid at daily intervals, and incubation
begins only when the clutch is almost complete, the hen bird
usually covers them with some nest lining if she has to leave
them for a while. The young are fed largely on caterpillars, and
remain in the nest for two to three weeks.

The blue tit has a large vocabulary of calls, though less so
than that of the great tit. Its song consists of two or three notes
followed by a rapid trill, which sounds like 'tee-tee-tee-
tississississississi'.

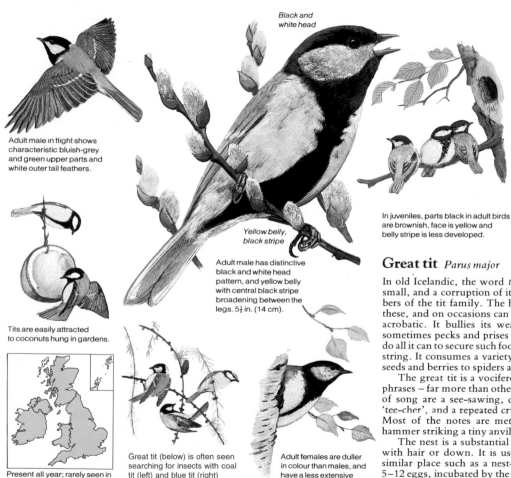

Black and
white head

Adult male in flight shows
characteristic bluish-grey
and green upper parts and
white outer tail feathers.

Tits are easily attracted
to coconuts hung in gardens.

Yellow belly,
black stripe

Adult male has distinctive
black and white head
pattern, and yellow belly
with central black stripe
broadening between the
legs. 5½ in. (14 cm).

Great tit (below) is often seen
searching for insects with coal
tit (left) and blue tit (right)
outside the breeding season.

Adult females are duller
in colour than males, and
have a less extensive
belly stripe.

In juveniles, parts black in adult birds
are brownish, face is yellow and
belly stripe is less developed.

Great tits start to breed in late March, in
time for nestlings to be fed mainly on
newly hatched moth caterpillars.

Great tit *Parus major*

In old Icelandic, the word *tittr* meant a small bird or anything
small, and a corruption of it provided a fitting name for members of the tit family. The handsome great tit is the largest of
these, and on occasions can be among the most aggressive and
acrobatic. It bullies its weaker relatives; like the blue tit, it
sometimes pecks and prises the tops off milk bottles; and it will
do all it can to secure such food as a nut suspended from a piece of
string. It consumes a variety of food, from spring buds, fruits,
seeds and berries to spiders and household scraps.

The great tit is a vociferous bird and has scores of calls and
phrases – far more than other tits studied. Its commonest forms
of song are a see-sawing, double-noted 'tee-cher', 'tee-cher',
'tee-cher', and a repeated cry of 'pee-too', 'pee-too', 'pee-too'.
Most of the notes are metallic and sound rather like a tiny
hammer striking a tiny anvil.

The nest is a substantial cup of moss and a little grass lined
with hair or down. It is usually sited in a tree or a wall, or a
similar place such as a nest-box, letter-box or drainpipe. The
5–12 eggs, incubated by the female, hatch in a fortnight. Young
birds are independent by about four weeks old.

271

In winter the nuthatch often associates with tits, especially the great tit and blue tit.

The nuthatch places nuts such as acorns in cracks in the bark; it then hammers them open with its bill.

Blue-grey upper parts

Adult bird is plump and short-tailed, with blue-grey upper parts, buff underparts and reddish flanks. It has a strong, pointed bill and black eye-stripe. Sexes are alike. 5½ in. (14 cm).

By adding mud to the entrance the adult bird adjusts the size of its nesting hole.

Present all year in areas where there are large trees.

The bird hops obliquely up and down a trunk, gripping with one foot and bracing itself with the other.

A nuthatch emerges cautiously from its nesting hole in a tree trunk; the bird also nests in boxes and walls.

Nuthatch *Sitta europaea*

A loud 'chwit', repeated many times as the bird scrutinises a tree-trunk, or a rapid trilling 'chirirriri', can be the first clue to the presence of a nuthatch. It is the only member of its family to breed in Britain, and inhabits deciduous woodland, large gardens and parkland.

The original name for the nuthatch was 'nut-hack', derived from the bird's habit of fixing nuts in a crevice of the tree's bark and hacking them open with its bill to find the kernel. It eats hazel and beech nuts, acorns, seeds and also insects that it picks from the bark. The nuthatch is the only bird that can hop down tree trunks as easily as it hops up.

Nuthatches breed in holes in trees or walls, or in nest-boxes, from late April to early May. They make the entrance and any neighbouring cracks smaller by filling them with mud which hardens to a rock-like consistency. The bottom of the hole is usually lined with small fragments of bark or dried leaves which are used to cover the eggs. The average clutch, laid at daily intervals, numbers six to nine white eggs. These are boldly blotched, especially at the larger end, with reddish or purplish spots. The female incubates the eggs for about two weeks.

The search for bark-dwelling insects begins low on the trunk. Birds climb spirally up one tree, then fly down to the base of a neighbouring tree to begin the process again.

In winter, treecreepers searching for insects can frequently be seen mixing with tits.

Present all year in most parts of Britain.

Down-curved bill

Its small size and long, down-curved bill identify the treecreeper. Both sexes are mottled brown above with a buff wing-bar, and have silky white underparts and a white eye-stripe. 5 in. (12·5 cm).

The flight is slightly undulating, usually over short distances only. The long tail, divided into points at the end, shows up clearly.

Nests are usually sited behind loose bark or ivy on old trees, or in large cracks in the trunk. Two broods are reared each year.

Treecreeper *Certhia familiaris*

Large claws and a stiff, fairly long tail enable the treecreeper to creep jerkily up tree trunks. It makes short hops with both feet at once, and uses its tail as a prop. As the central pair of tail feathers are not moulted until all others have been renewed, there is always sufficient support for climbing. Because it cannot descend in the same way, the bird flies from the upper trunk down to the base of the next tree.

Weevils, beetles, earwigs, small moths, woodlice, spiders and their eggs – all these form part of the treecreeper's diet. Its nest is a loose cup of moss, roots and dried grass on a base of small twigs, and is lined with feathers, wool and bark fragments. Here the female lays three to nine, but most often six, white eggs, speckled red at the large end. Once the chicks hatch, both parents feed them for 14–16 days. On leaving the nest they can climb competently, but are weak fliers at first.

The song of the treecreeper is thin and high-pitched, the note sequence starting slowly and accelerating to a flourish. Its call note is a shrill 'tseee'. The rare short-toed treecreeper, common on the Continent, is distinguished by its light brown flanks and less-distinct white eye-stripe.

273

The female house sparrow is a duller brown than the male, and lacks the grey crown and black bib. The white wing-bars are less distinct.

Young birds beg for food from their parents by holding their bodies low and quivering their wings.

Grey crown

The streaked brown back of the adult house sparrow is a familiar sight around most cities, towns and villages. Its grey crown distinguishes the male from the more lightly built tree sparrow. 5¾ in. (14·5 cm).

Birds often dust-bathe in suitable spots on open ground in high summer.

In winter, house sparrows and finches sometimes mingle as they seek food.

Present all year; common but recently declining.

Nests are domed structures of straw and feathers when built in hedges; but in cities and towns an untidily lined hole in a building or tree may suffice.

House sparrows love to splash and bathe in any available water, and do so regularly – often in groups.

House sparrow *Passer domesticus*

Ever since man began to build houses, this sparrow has partly depended upon him and his settlements for food and shelter. It is an intelligent bird and has adapted to major changes in the environment; for example, feeding off man's large grain fields and searching out nesting places in warm, sheltered hollows and ledges of his buildings. But not all nests are in buildings, occasionally they are found in hedges or ivy-clad trees.

Although the house sparrow is possibly the most familiar of British birds, it is not as numerous as the chaffinch, blackbird or wren. From March to August, three broods of from three to five young are quite frequent. The greyish-white eggs are covered with dark grey and greyish-brown speckles. The chicks hatch after 11–14 days and can fly reasonably well in another two weeks or so.

The most common call of the house sparrow is a rather persistent, rattling 'chissup' or 'chee-ip', repeated endlessly on rooftop, guttering, or garden trellis. A noticeable feature of the bird's courtship display is when several males, chirping noisily, crowd round a female who raises her bill and tail, droops her wings and pecks at them.

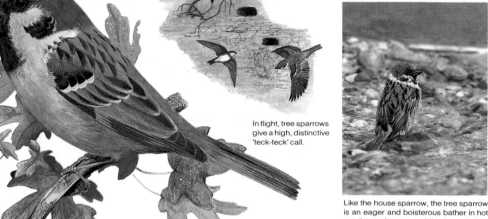
Chestnut crown

Like the house sparrow, the tree sparrow is an eager and boisterous bather in hot weather, using any puddles it can find.

Holes in old fruit trees are popular nesting sites. Nest-boxes may be used.

In flight, tree sparrows give a high, distinctive 'teck-teck' call.

After the breeding season, tree sparrows may search for food with finches and house sparrows.

Its all-chestnut crown and the black patches on its cheeks distinguish the tree sparrow from the male house sparrow. It is also slightly smaller. Males, females and juveniles are similarly marked. 5½ in. (14 cm).

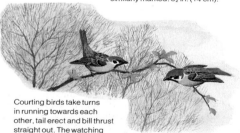
Present all year. Birds from Continent also winter here.

Courting birds take turns in running towards each other, tail erect and bill thrust straight out. The watching bird 'bows' to its partner.

Tree sparrow *Passer montanus*

Country cousin to the house sparrow, the tree sparrow is a bird of open woodlands and orchards, feeding mainly on weed seeds. Its distribution is dependent to some extent on the availability of suitable nesting sites. It is rare in some parts, including, surprisingly, the New Forest, Hampshire. In most of Britain it is quite common, although populations fluctuate mysteriously, building up over a few years and then rapidly decreasing. In recent years there has been a considerable and widespread decline.

Breeding, usually in colonies, begins any time from late April to late May, or even June in the north. Both birds build an untidy nest of dried grass or straw, forming a deep cup, and if the site is open they may add a domed roof. The hen usually lays four to six eggs, white or pale grey and boldly speckled with purplish-brown or grey.

The parent birds take turns to incubate the eggs, which hatch after 11–14 days, and both feed the chicks during their two weeks or so in the nest. They may raise two or three broods each season. The tree sparrow is one of the few species in which juveniles progressively moult all their plumage, including the flight feathers, in late summer.

275

Slate-blue crown

In flight, white wing-bar and shoulder-patch are distinctive.

Pink-brown below

In winter, chaffinches often flock with other finch species such as bramblings and greenfinches.

Females lack males' bright colours, but have same wing pattern.

Chaffinches nest in hedgerows, bushes or tree-forks, building a neat cup of grass, moss and lichens, lined with hair.

Adult male is unmistakable, with slate-blue crown and neck, chestnut back, pinkish-brown underparts and greenish rump. 6 in. (15 cm).

Present all year; joined by winter migrants.

Birds display aggression when food is short.

Chaffinch *Fringilla coelebs*

It is estimated that there may be as many as seven million pairs of chaffinches in the British Isles, making it one of our most widespread and common birds. Even so, the chaffinch population has gradually decreased since the 1950s, due partly to the increasing use of toxic seed dressings and perhaps partly also to the disappearance of hedges in some areas. The bird exists mainly on weed seeds taken from the ground, and insects.

Chaffinches are mostly found in mature, deciduous woods; but they also abound in gardens, parks, orchards and farmland where there is scrub and bushes. Breeding starts in April or May. Usually four to five bluish or browny-white eggs, sometimes spotted, are laid and incubated by the female for 11–13 days. Both birds tend the young, which fly in 12–15 days.

The song is a loud, jangling affair which starts slowly, accelerates down the scale, and usually ends with an exuberant flourish of notes. The actual detail of the song varies greatly from bird to bird, and there are even distinct regional 'dialects' in different parts of Britain. The entire song normally lasts for about four or five seconds and is repeated up to five or ten times a minute. The alarm call is a loud and persistent 'pink, pink, pink'.

Black head

Orange-
buff breast

Female is similar to male, but
colours are duller and black
markings are lacking.

Male in winter may
resemble female, but
usually keeps some black
markings on head and back.

Adult male in breeding
plumage, which may still be
seen in early autumn or late
spring. Head and back are
black; breast and
shoulders orange-buff.
Black bill turns yellow in
winter. 5¾ in. (14·5 cm).

In flight, bird is
identified by white
rump and orange-buff
leading edge of wing.

A very small number of bramblings have
bred in Britain, where they may make
their nests in birch trees.

Mainly Oct.–Apr. visitor;
others rest during migration.

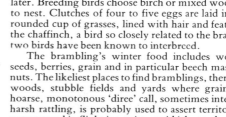

Bramblings often flock with
other species such as
chaffinches and greenfinches
in winter, seeking nuts and seeds.

Brambling *Fringilla montifringilla*

Isolated cases of the brambling breeding in England and Scotland have been recorded, but this bird is for the most part only a
winter visitor to Britain from breeding grounds in Scandinavia
and northern Russia. The number of visitors that come varies
widely, depending on the amount of food available in their cold
northern latitudes, and on the severity of the winter there.

Immigrants normally arrive from the end of September to
the middle of November, and stay until March, April or even
later. Breeding birds choose birch or mixed woodland in which
to nest. Clutches of four to five eggs are laid in a nest that is a
rounded cup of grasses, lined with hair and feathers like that of
the chaffinch, a bird so closely related to the brambling that the
two birds have been known to interbreed.

The brambling's winter food includes weed seeds, pine
seeds, berries, grain and in particular beech mast – fallen beech
nuts. The likeliest places to find bramblings, therefore, are beech
woods, stubble fields and yards where grain is stacked. A
hoarse, monotonous 'diree' call, sometimes interspersed with a
harsh rattling, is probably used to assert territorial rights. The
note uttered in flight is a quiet, rapid 'chucc–chucc–chucc'.

277

Male in song flight display flits and weaves erratically among tree-tops.

Wing and tail patterns are distinctive in flight.

Juvenile bird, more heavily streaked than adult female, receives food regurgitated by parents.

Yellow tail edge

Adult male has bright yellow wing-patch and tail edges. Seeds are cracked with characteristic pink bill. 5¾ in. (14·5 cm).

Pink bill

Adult female is duller in colour, with faintly streaked underparts. Bird collects nesting materials of twigs, moss or roots.

Vigorous bathers, greenfinches flock to urban gardens where there is water, particularly in dry summer conditions.

Present all year; sedentary, near human settlements.

Serin

Serinus serinus

This bird has bred in Britain on rare occasions since 1967. It is smaller than the greenfinch – about 4¾ in. (12 cm) long – and its plumage is much yellower and more streaked.

Greenfinch *Carduelis chloris*

Almost any area with trees and bushes, except dense woodland, will harbour greenfinches. In gardens, woodland edges, copses and plantations their olive-green plumage can be seen, set off admirably by bright yellow wing and tail flashes.

While hardly the star of any dawn chorus, the greenfinch's song is nonetheless pleasant: a loud, rapid twittering on one note, followed by four or five musical notes – 'tew, tew, tew, tew, tew' – then a pause sometimes followed by a single 'greeee'. The song may be delivered from a bush or tree-top perch, or during a display flight high in a floppy, bat-like flight with slow, exaggerated wing-beats. When disturbed the bird flies off with a quiet 'chi-chi-chi-chi'.

Greenfinches start to breed in late April or early May. The nest is a bulky cup of twiglets, plant stems and moss, lined with rootlets, hair, fine stems and occasionally a few feathers. Several nests sometimes appear in one bush. The eggs, usually four to six, are greyish-white to pale greenish-blue with a sparse speckling of reddish-brown, black or lilac. They hatch in two weeks and the young spend about two weeks in the nest. With two or three broods a year, nestlings may be seen as late as September.

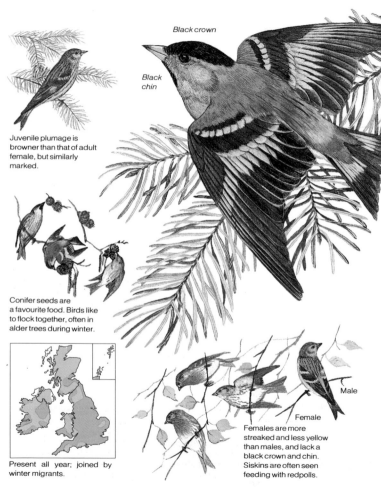

Juvenile plumage is browner than that of adult female, but similarly marked.

Black crown

Black chin

Conifer seeds are a favourite food. Birds like to flock together, often in alder trees during winter.

Present all year; joined by winter migrants.

Adult male has yellow-green rump and yellow tail-patch, like greenfinch. But it is smaller, and differs in having black crown and chin and different wing pattern. 4½ in. (12 cm).

Male

Female

Females are more streaked and less yellow than males, and lack a black crown and chin. Siskins are often seen feeding with redpolls.

Nesting site is usually in a conifer tree, towards the end of a branch and at least 15 ft (4·5 m) above the ground.

Siskin *Carduelis spinus*

The 20th-century practice of pine-planting in Britain has greatly benefited the siskin, which depends heavily upon the seeds of pines and spruce for food in spring and early summer. At one time the species was confined to the pine forests of the Scottish Highlands, but during the last 130 years it has spread widely.

The bird's flight calls are a high-pitched and squeaky 'tsys-ing' and a wheezy 'tsooeet'. The song is a sweet, musical and varied twittering refrain. It is delivered from a tree or during song flight, when the male slowly circles the tree tops on slow, deliberate wing-beats, with plumage fluffed-up and tail fanned. Both partners take part in a fast-moving display flight, in which the male rises to a considerable height with tail spread and wings quivering rapidly, and the female follows close behind.

The siskin's nest usually consists of small, lichen-covered twigs bound with grass, moss, plant fibres and wool. It is lined with finer materials such as hair and thistledown. In April or May the female lays usually three to five very pale blue speckled eggs, which hatch in two weeks. The young spend about two weeks in the nest, fed by the male for the first week, after which the female shares in collecting food for the chicks.

279

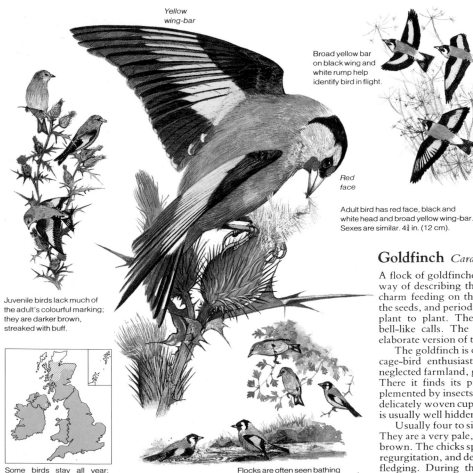

Yellow wing-bar

Broad yellow bar on black wing and white rump help identify bird in flight.

Red face

Adult bird has red face, black and white head and broad yellow wing-bar. Sexes are similar. 4¾ in. (12 cm).

Orchards are favoured as breeding areas. The female sits on the eggs in the nest for about two weeks.

Juvenile birds lack much of the adult's colourful marking; they are darker brown, streaked with buff.

Some birds stay all year; others go south in winter.

Flocks are often seen bathing together in summer.

Goldfinch *Carduelis carduelis*

A flock of goldfinches is called a 'charm', and there is no better way of describing these delightful birds. It is a joy to watch a charm feeding on thistles or groundsel, delicately picking out the seeds, and periodically moving – with dancing flight – from plant to plant. The pleasure is enhanced by their tinkling, bell-like calls. The song is a pretty, liquid twittering – an elaborate version of the flight notes.

The goldfinch is one of the most popular small birds among cage-bird enthusiasts and birdwatchers alike. It is found in neglected farmland, gardens and open areas with scattered trees. There it finds its preferred diet of annual weed seeds, supplemented by insects. The nest, built by the female, is a neat and delicately woven cup of plant material, including thistledown. It is usually well hidden in the upper branches of small trees.

Usually four to six eggs are laid from late April to early May. They are a very pale, bluish-white with a few streaks of reddish-brown. The chicks spend about two weeks in the nest, are fed by regurgitation, and depend on their parents for about a week after fledging. During that time they make a constant twitter of contact calls with the adult birds.

In flight, the male twite shows its pink rump and notched tail. The flight is fast and undulating.

Pink rump

Adult male has nondescript, streaky brown plumage, except for buff throat and pink rump. Paler wing areas resemble wing-bar of linnet, but are far less distinct. 5¼ in. (13·5 cm).

Female twite is drabber than male, with greyish rump. Her darker, unstriped throat distinguishes her from the female linnet.

The nest is a bulky grass cup lined with wool and sometimes feathers. It is built on the ground among heather or scrub.

Mainly resident; but some winter on coasts.

In winter, twites mix with other finches, such as linnets and greenfinches, but can be identified by their all-brown plumage.

Twite *Acanthis flavirostris*

According to some ornithologists, the name twite comes from the bird's nasal call note which sounds rather like 'twa-it'. The song, heard on the breeding-ground, is a pleasant twittering. It is similar to the somewhat faster song of the linnet, but has a more metallic and resonant quality. The twite breeds on moorland edges, rough pastures and bracken-clad hillsides; but in winter it deserts the high ground for stubble fields, salt-marshes and coastal areas where it is usually seen in flocks feeding on or near the ground. Its food is mainly vegetable matter such as weed seeds, and it will also eat insects.

Breeding is also a social affair, and the nests are often in loose-knit colonies. They are built by the females, with the males in attendance. Clutches of usually five or six eggs are laid in April or May. They are pale blue with a variety of purple, red-brown, pink or lilac speckles and spots, which are mainly grouped on the larger end.

Incubation is carried out by the female and lasts for 12 or 13 days. Both parents provide food by regurgitation, and after 15 days of parental attention the chicks leave the nest. They remain dependent for a further two weeks.

Red
forehead

Chestnut
back

Red
breast

Male in flight. Both
sexes show white-
edged wing and
tail feathers.

In late summer, some males
develop a gold breast and
forehead in place of red.

Male

Female

Female lacks red colouring
and is more streaked. Linnets
like bushy country and prefer
low perches.

Adult male in summer has
grey head, red forehead
and breast, and chestnut
back; but is grey in breeding season, and tail is
forked. 5¼ in. (13·5 cm).

Most birds stay all year; some
migrate in autumn.

In winter, large flocks search on
the ground for weed seeds.

The linnet's nest is usually built within a
few feet of the ground. Gorse and bramble bushes are favoured sites.

Linnet *Acanthis cannabina*

Flax seeds were once considered to be the linnet's favourite food,
so its name is a diminutive of *lin*, the Old English word for flax.
It eats many other plant seeds, however. In the 19th century,
linnets were often kept as cage birds because of their musical
song, and this led to a decline in their population. Legal protection in the early part of this century brought about a recovery,
but now the population is again reported to be declining,
probably because the increased use of weed-killers has depleted
the food supply.

Linnets breed from mid-April, often in small colonies. The
female builds the nest, a rather ragged cup of plant stalks, grass
and moss with a nest lining of hair and wool. She alone incubates
the four to six bluish-white, purple-speckled eggs for 10–14
days. The male helps to feed the grey nestlings for their fortnight
or so in the nest, the diet of seeds being well supplemented with
small moths, caterpillars and other insects.

The linnet's twittering song is usually delivered from an
exposed spray of a bush, sometimes by several males in chorus.
It can be heard at any time from January to October, but most
often between the end of March and late July.

Juvenile birds lack any red colouring and have yellower bills than adults.

Red forehead

Black chin

Pink breast

Redpolls are often seen by ponds, where they like to drink and bathe.

Adult male in summer plumage has red forehead, black chin and pink breast and rump. Adult female generally lacks pink breast and rump. 4½–6 in. (12–15 cm).

Most birds stay all year; some migrate, others visit.

Native bird

Northern visitor

Larger, paler redpolls from northern Europe and Greenland may visit Britain in winter.

In winter, males have less pink on breast and rump. Birds feed in flocks on alder and birch seeds, often mixing with siskins.

Redpolls eat tree and plant seeds. Both sexes have buff-coloured double wing-bars.

Silver birch trees and gorse bushes are popular nesting sites. Redpolls often nest in loose-knit colonies.

Redpoll *Acanthis flammea*

Conifers, alders and birches are the favourite habitat of the redpoll. The population has generally increased in the last 40 years with the spread of conifer planting, and often overflows from woodlands to hedgerows and gardens with suitable vegetation.

Usually, the first indication of the redpoll's presence is its distinctive flight call, a rattling, bell-like 'ching, ching, ching'. Like most finches, its flight is undulating. It also has an unusual display flight – a series of loops and circles with slow wing-beats and occasional glides – sometimes performed by several males together. The alarm call is a musical, plaintive 'tsooeet'.

Redpolls start to breed at the end of April in the south. Nesting sites vary from low bushes to high tree branches, and the nest is a small, rather untidy cup of twigs, dried grass and plant stems neatly lined with hair, thistledown and occasionally feathers. The four or five eggs are whitish-blue, finely speckled with lilac and purple-brown, and the female incubates them for 10–13 days. Both parents tend the downy, dark grey nestlings for about a fortnight until they are fledged, and then for a short while afterwards. The redpoll's diet of seeds is sometimes supplemented by small insects and their larvae.

283

Female, green

Crossed bill

Forked tail

Adult male has brick-red or orange-red plumage. Adult female has yellow-green plumage. Both sexes have a forked tail, and large crossed bill to extract seeds from pine cones. 6½ in. (16·5 cm).

Male, red

Present all year; Continental migrants swell numbers.

Crossbills are grègarious birds that often drink in family groups.

Juveniles are heavily streaked, and for the first three weeks after leaving the nest their bills are not crossed.

Two-barred crossbill

Loxia leucoptera

This rare migrant is identifiable by its two white wing-bars and its smaller, thinner bill. 5½ in. (14 cm).

The crossbill builds its nest in a coniferous tree. The female alone incubates the eggs, but both parents feed the young.

Crossbill *Loxia curvirostra*

This odd-looking bird owes its name to its peculiar bill, one mandible of which is crossed over the other. This 'double hook' helps the crossbill to extract seeds from the cones of pine, spruce, larch and other conifers. These seeds form the bulk of its food, but it also eats the seeds of rowan, ivy, hawthorn, weeds, grasses and thistles, as well as insects such as flies and beetles.

Different populations of crossbills have different-sized bills. Those feeding mainly in Scots pine areas have larger and stouter bills – to deal with the harder cones – than those existing in the spruce forests of central Europe and Asia. The birds have an emphatic and persistent call of 'chip-chip-chip'.

Breeding may occur at any time from early in the year until July. Normally, only one brood is raised. The nest has a strong foundation of pine twigs, with grass, wool, moss and lichen on top, and a shallow, inner cup of hair, rabbits' fur, or feathers. The clutch of three or four bluish-white eggs with purplish markings is hatched by the female after 13–16 days of incubation. The young leave the nest when two and a half to three weeks old, but they are dependent on their parents for up to a month afterwards.

Black cap

In flight the male's black cap, white rump and white wing-bar are conspicuous.

White rump

Adult male is unmistakable with its red underparts, black cap, grey upper parts and striking white rump. 6 in. (15 cm).

Adult female has the same basic plumage as the male, but underparts are dull salmon-pink. Bullfinches are notorious for attacking flowering fruit trees.

Like other finches, bullfinches can sometimes be seen bathing in rivers and pools during hot summer weather.

Present all year; absent from extreme north and north-west.

Juveniles are mostly brownish, but have the adult's white rump.

Bullfinch *Pyrrhula pyrrhula*

Although one of Britain's prettiest birds, the bullfinch can also be one of the most destructive. It attacks the buds of fruit trees and flowering shrubs, and at times the damage is so costly that fruit growers are permitted to destroy the birds by shooting or trapping.

The nest, a distinctive structure of fine twigs, moss and lichen lined with black or blackish-brown rootlets, varies in size from a shallow platform to a bulky cup. The four or five eggs are pale greenish-blue with dark purplish-brown spots and streaks. They are incubated for 12–14 days mainly by the female, which is fed during this time by the male. Both parents feed the hatched young in the nest by regurgitation from special throat pouches. Young birds fly after 12–18 days. Two and sometimes three broods may be raised each year.

The call note, often the only clue to a bullfinch's presence, is a soft, piping 'dew', repeated at intervals. It has considerable carrying power but is often difficult to locate. The fledged young have a similar call though less pure, louder and more persistent. The bullfinch does not have a proper song, though at close quarters a faint, creaky warble can be heard.

285

Large head

Large bill

Birds in flight appear large-headed and short-tailed. Wing and tail pattern is prominent.

Juveniles are yellower than adults, lack a black bib, and have a yellow throat-patch. Birds of all ages visit ponds regularly.

Aggression is frequently displayed while feeding.

Adult male appears heavy-headed, and has a mainly chestnut body, with black and white wings. The powerful bill is used to open seeds. 7 in. (18 cm).

Female

The bird raids vegetable gardens in early morning to tear open pea-pods and feed on the peas.

Male

Hawfinches are frequently seen in small parties feeding in hornbeams. Females are duller than males.

Present all year; sometimes seen outside breeding range.

The nests are bulky, made from twigs and moss lined with roots and grass. They are often placed high in fruit trees.

Hawfinch *Coccothraustes coccothraustes*

Any ornithologist, who, during bird-ringing studies, is lucky enough to catch a hawfinch will handle the bird with considerable respect. It is quite capable of removing a neat chunk from his finger, in much the same way as an apple–corer removes the core from an apple. The heavy, conical bill of the hawfinch is designed to crack open such hard seeds as cherry stones, to get at the edible kernel inside. The bones of its bill and palate and its jaw muscles are especially powerful.

An abrupt, explosive 'tik' is occasionally a clue to the bird's presence high overhead. The hawfinch, however, is a shy bird and is difficult to find. The species is mainly confined to England and a few places in Wales, where it favours deciduous or mixed woodlands, old, well-wooded parks and gardens, and bushy areas scattered with trees. These places provide a wide variety of seeds and kernels, including beechmast, maple, hawthorn, yew, pea and sloe. The bird supplements its diet with buds in the spring and insects in the summer.

In late April or early May the hawfinch begins to breed. It usually lays a single clutch of five greenish or bluish eggs, finely stippled with black. They hatch after 9–14 days of incubation.

Heavy
head

Streaked
plumage

During its display flight
the male bird leaves its
legs dangling.

This bird will nest among dense ground
vegetation, but may also choose a higher
site in a hedge.

Little bunting
Emberiza pusilla

A small, rare migrant distinguished by its black-bordered chestnut crown and cheeks. It may be seen near water.

Adult bird's streaked brown plumage, large size and heavy-looking head and bill are the corn bunting's main distinctive features. Sexes are alike. 7 in. (18 cm).

Present all year; numbers declining seriously.

Corn buntings often feed around farm buildings in winter, in the company of other seed-eating birds such as the house sparrow.

Corn bunting *Miliaria calandra*

As well as being the largest of British buntings, the corn bunting is also the drabbest. It is a gregarious bird, often found in the company of other buntings outside the breeding season. As its name suggests, one of its favourite haunts is the cornfield, but it also frequents other open, lowland areas with few trees.

The song, a rapidly repeated note ending with a flourish and repeated regularly six to eight times a minute, is usually delivered from a hawthorn bush, fence post or telegraph wire. The male's display consists of a series of short upward flights, then hovering low, legs dangling, over the female on the ground before alighting.

The nest, a fairly loose cup of grasses and plant stems, lined with finer grasses, rootlets and animal hair, is usually built on the ground in grassy areas with thistles or other tall plants, or up to 5 ft (1·5 m) above the ground in a hedge. The eggs, usually three to five, are whitish with bold blackish-brown lines and spots. These are incubated for 12–13 days by the female, which also mainly feeds the hatched young; they spend about ten days in the nest. The diet consists mainly of fruits and seeds, supplemented by insects and a few molluscs and worms.

287

White tail sides show up in flight. Its chestnut rump distinguishes the bird from the cirl bunting.

Females are duller in colour than males, and more streaked. Juveniles are very similar to females.

Bright yellow head

Yellow breast

Adult male has bright yellow head and breast, and sings lustily. Upper parts are chestnut streaked with black. 6½ in. (16·5 cm).

Present all year. Sedentary; widespread in open country.

Yellowhammers feed on the ground. In winter they are often seen feeding in flocks, in the company of finches and other buntings.

The nest is built by the female, and is usually low down. Young birds spend about two weeks in the nest.

Yellowhammer *Emberiza citrinella*

Countrymen say that the yellowhammer's song is 'a-little-bit-of-bread-and-no-cheese'. It requires a little imagination to relate this phrase to the bird's simple repetition of a single note – 'chiz-iz-iz-iz-iz-iz-zeee' – or to any of the several variations.

Yellowhammers are common in areas of grassland, fields with hedgerows, allotments and commons – in fact almost any open area with low cover but few trees. Like other buntings they feed mainly on the ground, but perch on bushes and telegraph wires to deliver their song at intervals from February to the end of August. Breeding starts from the end of April; the courtship is a boisterous, madcap affair with the male hotly pursuing the female in a headlong, twisting flight that often ends with both birds tumbling through the branches in a flurry of feathers.

The nest, built by the female, is a neat cup of grasses, moss and plant stems lined with grass and hair. It is built on the ground in cover and concealed by overhanging plants, but occasionally it is built a few feet up in a thick bush. The three or four eggs are white or purplish-white with bold scribblings; these have given rise to the alternative name of 'scribble lark' for the bird in some country areas.

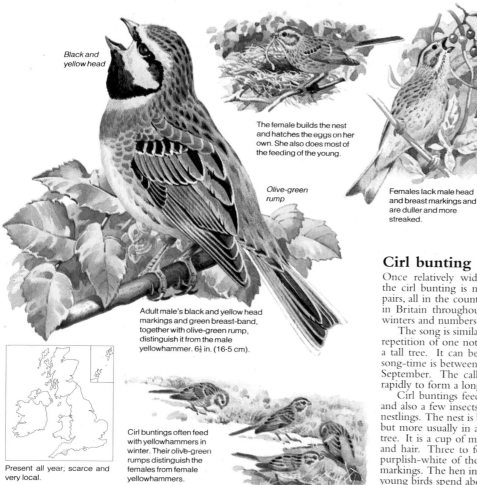

Black and yellow head

The female builds the nest and hatches the eggs on her own. She also does most of the feeding of the young.

Olive-green rump

Females lack male head and breast markings and are duller and more streaked.

Adult male's black and yellow head markings and green breast-band, together with olive-green rump, distinguish it from the male yellowhammer. 6½ in. (16·5 cm).

Present all year; scarce and very local.

Cirl buntings often feed with yellowhammers in winter. Their olive-green rumps distinguish the females from female yellowhammers.

Nest sites vary more than those of the yellowhammer, and may be at ground level or in tree branches.

Cirl bunting *Emberiza cirlus*

Once relatively widespread in southern England and Wales, the cirl bunting is now restricted to some 300–400 breeding pairs, all in the county of Devon. Although the bird is resident in Britain throughout the year, it suffers considerably in cold winters and numbers become depleted.

The song is similar to that of the lesser whitethroat, a rattling repetition of one note delivered from a bush, telegraph wire or a tall tree. It can be heard throughout the year, but the peak song-time is between the end of February and the beginning of September. The call note is a short 'sit', sometimes repeated rapidly to form a longer 'si-si-si-si-sit'.

Cirl buntings feed mainly on grass seeds, corn and berries, and also a few insects, which form the bulk of the food for the nestlings. The nest is built by the hen, sometimes on the ground, but more usually in a thick bush or in the lower branches of a tree. It is a cup of moss, grass and rootlets lined with fine grass and hair. Three to four eggs are laid, similar in colour to the purplish-white of those of the yellowhammer but with bolder markings. The hen incubates them for about two weeks, and the young birds spend about two weeks in the nest.

289

Pairs of reed buntings are often found in drier areas, but, never far from water.

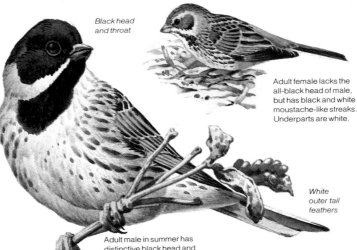

Black head and throat

Adult female lacks the all-black head of male, but has black and white moustache-like streaks. Underparts are white.

White outer tail feathers

Adult male in summer has distinctive black head and throat with white, moustache-like streak and nape. The upper body is rich brown streaked with black. White outer tail feathers are conspicuous. 6 in. (15 cm).

Male in winter lacks most of its black plumage. The male bird frequently flicks its wings and tail, or spreads its tail showing white outer feathers.

The nest is usually well hidden and built close to or on the ground. Reed-beds and sewage farms are popular sites.

Reed bunting *Emberiza schoeniclus*

With its white collar and moustachial streak and black head, the male reed bunting is reminiscent of a Victorian Guards officer. Clinging to a swaying reed, the bird delivers its chirruping song, a simple 'cheep-cheep-cheep-chizzup', with an occasional flick of the tail before flying jerkily to another clump of reeds.

The reed bunting is less appropriately named than it once was, for in recent years it has extended its range from the reed beds of fenland and river bank to drier places such as farm hedgerows, downland scrub and forestry plantations. In some areas it has been seen visiting gardens to feed along with house sparrows and greenfinches. Its favourite breeding grounds, however, are still the marshy places and riversides, where the female builds her nest in a tussock of rush or among dense vegetation close to the ground.

The nest is a cup of grass and moss lined with fine grasses, reed flowers and hair. A clutch usually numbers four or five eggs, brownish-olive or buff with a few streaks and spots of blackish-brown. The chicks hatch in two weeks and spend about two weeks in the nest, tended by both parents. Two, or occasionally three, broods may be raised each year.

Present all year; Continental birds on passage.

Reed buntings often associate with other birds such as yellowhammers in stubble fields while searching for winter food.

Black and white head

Chestnut nape

Adult males in moult have duller plumage and a variable extent of black on the head.

Male

Female

Male

In flight the Lapland bunting may be identified by its chestnut nape, but more often by its call of 'ticky-tick-teu'.

Adult male in breeding plumage is distinguished by its yellow bill, black and white head pattern, chestnut nape and long hind claw. 6 in. (15 cm).

Females and juveniles lack the prominent black markings of the male.

Chiefly autumn migrant; has bred in Scotland.

The Lapland bunting searches for food on the ground, sometimes together with skylarks and finches.

In autumn and winter, the Lapland bunting lives on coastal moors and fields, and is seen along the seashore.

Lapland bunting *Calcarius lapponicus*

A brownish, sparrow–sized little bird looking rather like a hen reed bunting, seen busily running about stubble fields and marshes near the eastern coast of England with skylarks and finches, may well be a Lapland bunting. It is hunting for its winter food, the seeds of grasses and other plants. Like the skylark, it has a long claw on its hind toe – probably an adaptation to spending so much time on the ground – and this accounts for its North American name of Lapland longspur. In common with many of its relatives, such as the snow bunting, the Lapland bunting also roosts on the ground.

In summer, Lapland buntings breed in more northerly climes; most birds seen in Britain are on autumn migration, some of them staying for the winter. The handsome spring plumage of the male is not, therefore, often seen. The call most often heard in autumn is a musical 'ticky-tick-teu'.

Although in summer the Lapland bunting is found in the region after which it is named, it also occurs much further south in Norway and Sweden, and ranges east and west from Arctic Asia to Greenland and Canada. It nests in creeping birch scrubland and marshes in open tundra.

291

Almost entirely white wings of the adult male are unmistakable in flight.

White head

Black back

Pairs of snow buntings usually nest in a cranny between rocks. The nest is made of moss and grasses, and is sometimes lined with wool, fur or feathers.

Adult male has black and white plumage in summer. 6½ in. (16·5 cm).

In winter, male birds' black and white plumage is replaced by brown on back and head, with red-brown patches on head and breast and white on underparts.

Female bird is brown and white in summer, and has less white on its wings than the male.

Snow buntings flock together in winter, and large numbers can sometimes be seen feeding on the seashore.

Chiefly winter visitor, but a few breed on Scottish mountains.

Snow bunting *Plectrophenax nivalis*

Only a small number of snow buntings have been seen nesting in Britain since the first to breed there was recorded in Scotland in 1886. The species usually breeds in the Arctic, further north than any other perching bird; but summers there are very fleeting, and so the snow bunting visits Britain between September and April to enjoy the milder climate. Even in Britain the bird does not forsake the snowy regions after which it is named, but lives on high mountains such as the Cairngorms.

The snow bunting delivers its song – a brief, fluting 'turee-turee-turee-turiwee' – either in flight or from the ground. During courtship the male sometimes displays with its song flight, rising 20–30 ft (6–9 m) into the air; at other times it walks away from the female with wings and tail spread, showing off its prominent back, wings and tail patterns. Then it turns round and runs back before repeating the performance.

Fine materials such as hair, wool and feathers line the grassy nest, which is usually concealed in a crevice or amongst rocky scree. The bird lays from four to six eggs, pale blue and speckled with brown. It feeds on insects for the most part, but in autumn and winter the diet is supplemented by reeds.

Greyish-green head and breast

Eye-ring

Yellow throat

Adult male is mainly pinkish-brown, with a greyish-green head and breast, yellow throat, pink bill and a clearly defined eye-ring. 6½ in. (16·5 cm).

Scarce passage migrant, chiefly in autumn.

Small parties of migrant buntings may be seen feeding on seeds on cultivated land.

The ortolan bunting makes an occasional appearance in British gardens; it may also occur in widely varied countryside.

Females and young birds have paler, browner, less striking plumage than the adult male, with dark streaks on their underparts, but have the pink bill and eye-ring.

Ortolan bunting *Emberiza hortulana*

In France the ortolan bunting has been served to diners as a popular delicacy for years; but in Britain, where the bird is quite scarce, it has nothing to fear from the traps and nets of the bird-catcher. In the spring and autumn small numbers of ortolans reach Britain, off course during migration between their winter quarters in Africa and their breeding grounds; which are spread widely across continental Europe from Scandinavia and northern Russia south to the Mediterranean.

Ortolans usually appear in the eastern counties, and as far north as the Shetlands. They live on a variety of seeds such as those from grasses, and insects such as grasshoppers, beetles and caterpillars – all of which they can find on farmland and scrubland, and also in gardens. Abroad they inhabit a very varied range of country, from barren, stony ground to vineyards, the edges of woods and birch woods.

The song of the ortolan bunting, a 'zew-zew-zew-zew-zeee-zeee', is generally delivered from a perch on a bush, tree or telegraph wire. It is similar to the song of the yellowhammer, but much more varied and musical in tone, with the higher-pitched notes at either the beginning or the end.

293

FINCHES AND BUNTINGS IN FLIGHT

Plumage, flight pattern and habitat all help to distinguish these birds, shown here in breeding plumage. Wing, rump and tail patterns usually identify the finches; buntings differ only slightly in head, rump and outer tail feathers. The flight of most finches is strongly undulating; that of smaller birds is jerky and dancing. Linnets, twites and goldfinches frequent open, weedy places, while redpolls, siskins and serins flit between trees. Bullfinches skulk in woodland and scrub; hawfinches, when disturbed, take refuge high in trees. Crossbills are birds of conifer woods; snow and Lapland buntings keep to bare shores and high moors. The reed bunting breeds in marshes or other damp spots. The corn bunting has an abrupt 'quit' call-note.

Orange forewing
White rump

Brambling
Fringilla montifringilla
Male Page 277

Black back and head
Green rump
White outer tail feathers
White forewing, wing-bar

Chaffinch
Fringilla coelebs
Male Page 276

Yellow wing flashes
Yellow tail flashes

Greenfinch
Carduelis chloris
Male Page 278

Yellow rump
Yellow wing-bars

Serin
Serinus serinus
Male Page 278

Buff wing-bars
Red forehead, black chin
Pink rump

Redpoll
Acanthis flammea
Male Page 283

Greyish bill
Pink rump
Buff throat

Twite
Acanthis flavirostris
Male Page 281

Green rump
Yellow wing-bars
Yellow tail flashes

Siskin
Carduelis spinus.
Male Page 279

Scarlet face, black and white head
White rump
Broad yellow wing-bar

Goldfinch
Carduelis carduelis
Page 280

Crimson crown, breast
Pale rump
White wing flashes

Linnet
Acanthis cannabina
Male Page 282

Short tail, white band

Hawfinch
Coccothraustes coccothraustes
Male Page 286

Female

Crossed bill

Red rump

White rump

Black cap

Pink underparts

White wing-bar

White outer tail feathers

Heavy head, pale bill

White nape, moustache

Crossbill
Loxia curvirostra
Page 284

Bullfinch
Pyrrhula pyrrhula
Male Page 285

Male

Black head, bib

Reed bunting
Emberiza schoeniclus
Male Page 290

Bright yellow head, and underparts

Greenish-grey head

Red-brown rump

Large white tail-patches

Pink bill

Brown rump

Yellowhammer
Emberiza citrinella
Male Page 288

Ortolan bunting
Emberiza hortulana
Male Page 293

Large white wing-patches

Snow bunting
Plectrophenax nivalis
Male Page 292

All-brown wings

Black and yellow face

Olive-brown rump

All-brown tail

Black throat

Stubby bill

Yellow bill

Rusty nape-patch

Lapland bunting
Calcarius lapponicus
Male Page 291

Cirl bunting
Emberiza cirlus
Male Page 289

Corn bunting
Miliaria calandra
Page 287

BIRDWATCHING
AS A HOBBY

Techniques and equipment

Birdwatching is a hobby which quickly becomes a habit, with the rare merits of being simple to indulge, satisfying and healthy. In the beginning, you require nothing more than a sharp eye and an inquiring mind. As you go on, you will need more equipment – binoculars, notebooks, and waterproof clothing, perhaps even a camera or tape-recorder. Common sense will soon teach you the basics of field craft – how to move without being seen, how to make use of cover, how to approach birds without alarming them. From the initial satisfaction of being able to name different species correctly, you can progress to understanding their behaviour, or to spotting rarities. From making lists of the birds you have seen, you can move on to studying one species in detail, or even one individual within a species. The better you understand the lives of birds, the more you will find their lives enrich your own.

The keys to success in birdwatching are stealth, patience and quietness – in short, the ability to make yourself as inconspicuous as possible. Some birds, of course, are more easily alarmed than others: birds in towns, for instance, are generally much easier to come close to than their counterparts in the country, simply because they are more used to the presence of human beings. But wherever you are, remember that any sudden noise or movement – the crack of a dry branch underfoot, the unexpected raising of

a hand – can easily frighten birds away. By making the best use of hedges, shrubs, shadows and other forms of cover, and by moving at a steady pace, you can frequently come close to even the shyest of birds. The clothes you wear may also help to conceal you, so always choose quiet colours. And make certain that your clothes are warm, well-fitting and weatherproof.

Binoculars and telescopes

There is no harm in starting out as a birdwatcher without using binoculars; in fact, it may help you to develop a keen eye for the features which distinguish one species from another. But in the end, a pair of binoculars is an essential item of equipment for any serious birdwatcher; and choosing them requires great care.

There are three main factors which need to be considered: the magnification power of the binoculars, their weight, and the diameter of the object-lens. All binoculars carry two numbers – for instance, 7 x 50 or 8 x 30. The first number describes how many times the image is magnified, the second is the diameter of the front lens (called the object-lens) in millimetres. Higher magnifications give you a larger image, but they make focusing more difficult, and it is harder to pick up the object and keep it steadily in view. A large object-lens gathers more light than a small one – particularly impor-

tant when watching birds in dark or overcast conditions – but at the same time it increases the weight of the binoculars.

The binoculars most often used by birdwatchers are 8 x 30, 8 x 40 and 10 x 40; but the only way to find out which one suits you best is by trying out as many pairs as you can before making your choice. Ask if you can try the binoculars belonging to fellow birdwatchers; borrow them from friends; or obtain them on approval from shops.

For watching birds on reservoirs, marshes and estuaries, a telescope is often an advantage, as binoculars are rarely powerful enough. The old type of telescope, heavy and consisting of many sections, has now been superseded by single-draw tubes or prismatic types which allow magnifications of up to x 60.

When selecting a telescope, check that the object-lens measures no less than 60 mm; anything smaller will mean that not enough light will enter the telescope in poor conditions, and the image you see will show no detail. As with binoculars, always compare types before making your choice, as the different makes vary considerably in quality, weight and robustness.

Keeping records

To become a really proficient birdwatcher, it is important to keep a field notebook, and to keep a logbook at home in which to write up your notes in greater detail. Your notebooks will soon become an invaluable memory bank and fund of knowledge.

When you spot an unfamiliar bird, make a quick sketch, however rough, of its silhouette, and note down around the sketch as many features as possible of its plumage, anatomy or behaviour. Every entry in your notebook should also include the date when the bird was seen, the place, the time of day and the weather conditions. Give details of other species seen at the same time – how many there were, whether they were male or female and so on.

At the end of each year, check through your notes to see if they are worth sending to the records committee of your local bird-watching society. The annual bird reports of these societies, combined on a national level, often form the basis on which professional ornithologists establish the current status of a species.

If you think you have spotted a rarity, first write up your notes in detail, then try to obtain a second opinion. Then pass on a copy of your notes to your local society, which will decide whether or not to submit them to the Rarities Committee of the national journal, *British Birds*.

Taking part in a census

Once you have become experienced at bird-watching you may wish to take part in a detailed census, organised at a local or national level. A census can take the form of a monthly count of birds at a reservoir or estuary, to check on the numbers of wild-fowl or waders, for instance; or in the spring and summer months it may entail finding out the breeding population of a particular area. One such census is the Nest Record Scheme, co-ordinated by the British Trust for Ornithology, which aims to establish the exact breeding status of all British birds. If you wish to join this scheme, contact the BTO at their Norfolk address given on page 303.

Alternatively, you may prefer to start your own project. This could take the form of a census of the birds seen in your garden at different times of the year, or you could study the change in the type and number of birds on land undergoing development. Bird populations are always fluctuating, and keeping track of the changes taking place around you can be a fascinating pastime.

Bird ringing

The method of catching birds and ringing them – putting a light metal band on one leg – has been in use since the end of the 19th century, as a way of studying bird behaviour and migrations and to help in the conservation of particular species. Ringing birds has enabled conservationists to find out where certain species stop to rest while on migration; and international agreements between governments have made some of these stop-over points into nature reserves, to help to ensure the survival of the species.

The most common way of trapping birds in order to ring them is by using mist-nets – black nylon or terylene nets which are almost invisible to a bird in flight. The ringer quickly and carefully removes the trapped bird from the net, then fits the ring on its leg. The ring carries the address of the BTO, and a number which is unique to that bird. Before being released, the bird is identified and weighed and full details are taken of its age, sex and condition. The records are then sent for processing and storage to the BTO. If you wish to become a ringer yourself, you must be trained by a recognised expert and obtain a permit from the BTO. As co-ordinators of the ringing scheme in this country, the BTO will supply any information which you may require.

If you ever find a dead, ringed bird, remove the ring and send it to the BTO, with details about when and where you found the bird and, if you can tell, what may have caused its death. They will then send you all the information gathered about the bird when it was originally ringed. Never attempt to remove a ring from the leg of a living bird, as birds' bones are very fragile and can easily be broken.

Photographing and recording birds

Bird photography requires great patience, as well as expensive equipment and considerable technical skill; but, if you can afford it, it is one of the most satisfying activities which an amateur birdwatcher can perform.

The most suitable camera is a single-lens reflex camera, with interchangeable lenses and a through-the-lens metering system. At least one telephoto lens of not less than 200 mm focal length is essential; this will enable you to photograph birds in close-up without alarming them. A tripod and cable release will help to eliminate blurred pictures caused by camera shake.

Remember how easily birds can be disturbed, and never do anything which threatens their welfare. Disturbing birds in the breeding season often causes them to desert their eggs or young, and for certain species the law requires that you have a licence before photographing them at the nest. The Royal Society for the Protection of Birds publishes a booklet, *Wild Birds and the Law*, which lists all the protected species.

Many species of birds are heard more often than they are seen, and in recent years recording bird-song has become an increasingly popular hobby among birdwatchers. As with photography, it is necessary to choose your equipment with great care, and preferably with expert guidance; but even with inexpensive tape-recorders it is possible to achieve many interesting results.

Societies and journals

The best way to make contact with other birdwatchers is to join your local birdwatching society. These societies often organise weekend excursions to nature reserves and sanctuaries, and also have occasional films and lectures presented by experts. These meetings are excellent opportunities to discuss any problems you may have with bird identification or understanding individual bird behaviour, as well as for gaining advice on the purchase of equipment. The annual bird reports which they publish will give you much useful information about the birds in your own area. Most public libraries can tell you the addresses of local societies, and how to join them.

There are also several national ornithological societies, some of which you may wish to join. The major societies are listed below, together with a selection of their journals about birdwatching.

BRITISH ORNITHOLOGISTS' UNION *c/o Zoological Museum, Akeman Street, Tring, Herts HP23 6AP*. One of the world's foremost ornithological societies, chiefly for professional ornithologists, or advanced amateurs. It holds occasional meetings, with lectures on any aspect of world ornithology. Publishes *Ibis*, a quarterly journal covering a wide range of subjects to do with birds.

BRITISH TRUST FOR ORNITHOLOGY *The Nunnery, Nunnery Place, Thetford, Norfolk IP24 2PU*. Similar to the BOU, but deals solely with British Birds. Runs the national ringing scheme, the Common Birds Census, and various other educational or research projects. Publishes *BTO News*.

IRISH WILDBIRD CONSERVANCY *Ruttledge House, 8 Longford Place, Monkstown, Co. Dublin, Ireland*. The Irish equivalent of the BTO.

ROYAL SOCIETY FOR THE PROTECTION OF BIRDS *The Lodge, Sandy, Bedfordshire SG19 2DL*. Owns and manages some of the most important nature reserves in Britain. Runs courses for beginners in many parts of the country, and publishes *Birds*, a quarterly magazine dealing with all aspects of birdwatching.

SCOTTISH ORNITHOLOGISTS CLUB *21 Regent Terrace, Edinburgh, Scotland*. Similar aims to the BTO, with particular reference to birdwatching and birdlife in Scotland.

THE WILDFOWL AND WETLANDS TRUST *Slimbridge, Gloucestershire*. Mainly concerned with the conservation of wildfowl. Manages several important sanctuaries where wild ducks, geese and swans can be observed at close quarters. Publishes *Wildfowl*, an annual report containing articles about wildlife, and information about the Trust's collection.

ROYAL SOCIETY FOR NATURE CONSERVATION *The Green, Witham Park, Lincoln LB5 7JR*. Parent body of the Nature Conservation Trusts, which manage more than 1,500 reserves, many of which provide facilities for birdwatchers.

The birdwatcher's code

Whatever you choose to do as a birdwatcher – whether you prefer travelling widely to watch birds, or setting up a hide in one place, whether you are photographing, recording or counting birds – there is a code of conduct which should always be observed.

Never cause undue disturbance to birds, especially in the breeding season.

Always obtain permission before venturing onto private land.

Keep to paths as far as possible.

Never park so as to block the entrance to a field.

Leave gates as you find them.

Leave no litter.

In mountainous districts, always tell someone where you are going, and when you intend to return.

In marshes and coastal areas, make certain that you know the time of the high tide.

When you have finished watching a bird, leave quietly in order not to frighten it.

A garden for birds

Whether you live in the town or the country, you can easily turn your garden into a private bird sanctuary; and by making sure there is a plentiful supply of food and water, as well as places for birds to nest and roost, you can attract to your garden a great variety of different species. If you plant the right flowers and shrubs, you can expect to see not only familiar garden birds such as robins, wrens, dunnocks, tits and sparrows, but also less common species such as flycatchers and goldcrests. In the spring and autumn, migrant birds may use your garden as a resting place on their long and often dangerous journeys.

The birds which feed in your garden eat mainly seeds, fruit and insects. Plants such as sunflowers, antirrhinums, forget-me-nots and Michaelmas daisies will attract finches, tits and other seed-eating birds, especially if they are not cut down after they have flowered, but are left to go to seed. If you are willing to leave part of your garden to grow wild, weeds such as thistles, knapweed and teasel are also very attractive to birds, partly because of their seeds, but also because insect-eating birds thrive on the varied insect life which they support.

Berry-bearing shrubs provide birds with a rich source of food, particularly in winter when there is little else to eat. Blackbirds and other thrushes, together with finches, tits and starlings, feed on a great variety of berries, including holly, rowan, barberry, hawthorn and cotoneaster. These plants may even bring migrants such as redwings, fieldfares and waxwings to your garden.

The more variety you can bring into the design of your garden, the better birds will like it. An open lawn will attract birds foraging for worms and grubs; a pool and a small rockery will provide a rich supply of food for insect-eating birds. If your garden is large enough, trees offer shelter for roosting and nesting birds, as well as food. Even dead trees are attractive to birds, for insects breed in the rotting bark, and there are plenty of holes and crevices where birds can make their nests.

Feeding birds on a bird-table

By putting out food on a bird-table you can increase the number of birds visiting your garden, and bring many of them out into the open where they are easier to watch. But once you start feeding birds you must do so regularly, particularly in winter. Otherwise you will upset the balance between the number of birds in your garden and the amount of food they need in order to survive, and some birds will starve. You will also have to be careful that cats do not prey on the birds.

Most kitchen scraps are suitable food for birds. Bacon rind, meat bones and fat are always popular, as are stale biscuits, cake, bread and cheese. Thrushes are very partial to fruit, however rotten, and many birds will eat boiled rice, potatoes and suet. Only put out as much food as the birds can eat before nightfall, otherwise rats and mice may come scavenging. Also, spread the food about as much as possible, and shred or crumble it so that it is not all eaten by starlings, gulls, crows and other large, aggressive species.

Although tits are basically insect-eaters, they also like nuts, particularly coconuts and peanuts. These also attract jays and many finches, and sometimes even woodpeckers. Only use fresh coconuts cut in half, because birds cannot digest dried or shredded coconut and they may die if they eat too much of it. In the breeding season it is best to avoid coconut altogether, since parent birds may feed it to their nestlings, which cannot digest it at all.

One way of making sure that the smaller birds have their share of food is by making bird-food cake, and pressing portions of it into crevices in trees and other places which large birds cannot easily reach. Make the cake by mixing together ingredients such as seed, crumbs, currants, rice and even a few meat scraps. Then cover the mixture with melted fat and allow it to set.

There are also several feeding devices, which you can buy or make, from which only smaller birds can take food. Feeding baskets made of small-mesh wire netting and filled with nuts and scraps can be suspended below the bird-table. Seed and nut-hoppers can be attached to the post, or even placed at the foot of the table for species such as the dunnock which prefer to eat on the ground. If you fix a sloping roof onto the table, only the smaller birds will be able to feed under the lower parts of it.

There are many sorts of bird-table which you can buy, or you may prefer to make your own. Use 2 × 2 in. (5 × 5 cm) wood for the post, and exterior-quality plywood for the top. You can fix the top to the post with metal angle-brackets. A wooden lip around the table prevents too much food from falling to the ground, where it may rot and attract vermin. Do not place the table too close to shrubs or trees, for these will provide cover for lurking cats. A funnel-shaped collar of netting around the post will prevent cats from climbing it.

Water for drinking and bathing

Even in the coldest weather birds continue to bathe, for it helps them to keep their feathers in prime condition; and they always need water to drink. So an all-the-year-round supply of water is just as important as a regular source of food.

The ideal way to provide water is by having a small pond. Parts of the pond should be shallow enough to allow birds to bathe, with gently shelving sides where they can stand to drink. The pool, and the plants which grow in it, will attract aquatic insects, and these in turn will attract insect-eating birds such as flycatchers and wagtails.

If you do not have the space for a pond, a small bird-bath serves the same purpose. Many different sorts of bird-bath can be bought from pet shops or garden centres; or you can easily make your own, using a shallow bowl or even an upturned dustbin lid. To prevent the water from freezing in winter, raise the bath on bricks and then place a nightlight in a flowerpot or tin be-neath it. Never add glycerine or any other sort of anti-freeze to the water, as these may cling to the birds' bills or damage their feathers.

Places to nest and roost

Many of the trees and shrubs which provide food for birds also offer sheltered places for birds to nest and roost. But few gardens are wild enough to offer many natural nest-sites, and the best way to compensate for this is by putting up nest-boxes.

Some 30 different species of British birds can be tempted to use nest-boxes, from common garden birds such as tits, wrens and robins, to rarer species such as owls, woodpeckers and flycatchers. The design of

House sparrow

Great tit

Greenfinch

Great tit

Blue tit

A bird-table may greatly increase the number of birds visiting a garden. Tits like a fresh coconut, and many birds will eat from a hanging basket.

the nest-box – particularly the size and shape of the entrance – and its position in the garden determine which species are most likely to use it. The British Trust for Ornithology, The Nunnery, Thetford, Norfolk IP24 2PU publishes a booklet which lists types of box and the species they attract.

There are two basic sorts of nest-box – those with a hole entrance, which are used most often by tits and sparrows, and those with an open front, favoured by robins, spotted flycatchers and wagtails. The diameter of the hole determines which birds are most likely to use the nest-box. A box with a hole measuring $1\frac{1}{8}$ in. (2.8 cm) will be used most often by species such as blue tits, great tits, nuthatches and tree sparrows, or by coal tits if it is fixed on or near coniferous

trees. Redstarts and house sparrows prefer a box with a $1\frac{1}{2}$ in. (4 cm) hole.

Nest-boxes should be securely fixed to trees and walls no later than the middle of March, for birds start searching for nest-sites well before they actually begin to build their nests. If the box is tipped slightly forwards, this will help to keep out direct sunlight and driving rain. Avoid placing nest-boxes so that they face south, as the mid-day sun in summer will be too hot for the nestlings inside.

Nesting birds should never be touched, and they should be disturbed as little as possible. Otherwise the parent birds may desert their eggs or young. Even when the young birds are well grown it is dangerous to go too close to them, or to look at them too often, for you may cause them to leave the nest before they are ready, when they will fall easy victim to predators. Only when the nesting season is over is it really safe to visit the nest-box. Then you should clean it in order to eliminate parasites. Take away the remains of old nests, for these may discourage other birds from using the box when the next breeding season comes.

Dangers from chemicals

Pesticides should always be used with great care in the garden. Many, of course, are designed to kill insects or weeds, which means they reduce the main natural food sources of garden birds. Fortunately, DDT and other persistent chemicals which poisoned so many birds in the 1960s have been withdrawn from use.

Mistle thrush

Goldfinch

Allowing the right plants to grow – even weeds such as thistles – attracts birds that feed on their seeds and fruit, and on the insects they harbour.

303

Where to see birds

The following gazetteer of nature reserves in Britain is highly selective – a comprehensive list would probably cover over 1,000 sites, and such is the success of the wildlife conservation movement that the number of reserves grows monthly. Nature reserves cover only a tiny fraction of Britain, but they contain a large part of the breeding population of a number of British species.

Before visiting any nature reserve, check whether you need permission; access to some of them is by permit only. Details about the ownership of reserves are given immediately after the name of the reserve. The following abbreviations are used:

CCW: Countryside Council for Wales, Plas Penrhos, Ffordd Penrhos, Bangor, Gwynedd LL57 2LQ www.ccw.gov.uk

EN: English Nature, Northminster House, Peterborough PE1 1UA www.english-nature.org.uk

NT: National Trust, 36 Queen Anne's Gate, London SW1H 9AS www.nationaltrust.org.uk

NTS: National Trust for Scotland, 28 Charlotte Sq., Edinburgh EH2 4ET www.nts.org.uk

RSPB: The Royal Society for the Protection of Birds, The Lodge, Sandy, Beds. SG19 2DL www.rspb.org.uk

SNH: Scottish Natural Heritage, 12 Hope Terrace, Edinburgh EH9 2AS www.snh.gov.uk

WT: The Wildlife Trusts, The Kiln, Waterside, Mather Road, Newark, Nottinghamshire NG24 1WT. www.wildlifetrust.org.uk

WWT: The Wildfowl and Wetlands Trust, Slimbridge, Gloucestershire GL2 7BT www.wwt.org.uk

Arne Dorset. RSPB
One of the finest remaining examples of the heathland that once covered much of south Dorset and south Hampshire. The Arne peninsula lies 2 miles (3 km) east of Wareham, just into Poole Harbour, and in addition to extensive heather with gorse and Scots pine, the reserve contains saltings, grazing marshes, mud-flats and a freshwater reed-bed. Breeding birds include buzzards, sparrowhawks, stonechats, Dartford warblers, nightjars and shelduck. Many species of wintering and migrating wildfowl can be seen, including black-tailed godwits, spotted redshanks, hen harriers and avocets.

Aylesbeare Common Devon. RSPB
One of the best heathland areas in south-east Devon, north of the A3052, 8 miles (13 km) east of Exeter, with mature heather and gorse, some birch, oak and Scots pine woodland, valley bogs and streams. The reserve is one of the top sites in Europe for biodiversity, and is important for Dartford warblers, nightjars and stonechats.

Balranald North Uist, Western Isles. RSPB
Sand, lagoons, marsh and machair (chalky, sandy lowlands). The reserve is one of the last British strongholds of the corncrake, and nesting waterfowl include lapwing, snipe, oystercatchers, ringed plovers, dunlins, shoveler, little grebes and tufted duck. Whooper swans and greylag geese visit the island in winter and there are many birds of passage in spring and autumn.

Bardsey Island (Ynys Enlli) Gwynedd
CCW and BARDSEY ISLAND TRUST
An island at the tip of the Lleyn Peninsula, with cliffs, farmland and scrub. It is the site of a bird observatory. Many warblers, thrushes, starlings and other migrating birds pass over the island in spring and autumn. About 2,500 pairs of Manx shearwaters nest on the island, and among the other breeding birds are a few pairs of choughs. On the migration route of many birds, the island is an important research site and a large number of migrants are ringed here each year.

Baron's Haugh North Lanarkshire. RSPB
A marsh beside the River Clyde, ½ mile (0.8 km) south of Motherwell, with nesting redshanks, and sedge and grasshopper warblers. Common sandpipers and kingfishers frequent the river. Wigeon, teal and whooper swans visit in winter.

Bass Rock East Lothian. PRIVATE RESERVE
Rocky, cliff-bound island, rising to over 300 ft (90 m), 3 miles (5 km) north-east of North Berwick. From April to September boats cruise round Bass Rock and Craigleith, and landing is permitted on special days, depending on weather and sea conditions. It is notable as the site of a colony of some 40,000 pairs of gannets. Other nesting birds include large numbers of guillemots, puffins, kittiwakes and fulmars. Remote cameras have been installed on the island, which can be operated by visitors to the Scottish Seabird Centre in North Berwick, giving an intimate view of the bird life of the Rock.

Beinn Eighe Highland. SNH and NNR
A rugged mountain range rising to over 3,000 ft (900 m), near the village of Kinlochewe, at the southern end of Loch Maree. The reserve consists mainly of high moorland and mountain peaks, but also contains an area of Scots pine forest on the southern side of Loch Maree. In the glens and woods, breeding birds include buzzards, sparrowhawks, Scottish crossbills, siskins, redpolls, redstarts, long-tailed tits, wood warblers and dippers. Ptarmigan and ring ouzels nest higher up in the mountains, and golden eagles and snow buntings may also be seen.

Bempton Cliffs East Yorkshire. RSPB
Impressive chalk cliffs, 4 miles (6 km) north of Bridlington, rising over 400 ft (120 m) from the sea. They are famous as the site of the largest colony – more than 200,000 – of cliff-nesting seabirds in England, including kittiwakes, guillemots, razorbills, puffins, fulmars and several pairs of shags. The cliffs are also the site of the only mainland gannetry in Britain, with more than 2,500 pairs.

Birsay Moors and Cottasgarth Orkney. RSPB
Almost 6,000 acres (2,430 ha) of moorland in north-east Mainland. The reserve is chiefly noted for its nesting hen harriers, short-eared owls and other birds of prey. There are also colonies of great and Arctic skuas, and great and lesser black-backed gulls.

Blacktoft Sands East Yorkshire. RSPB
Tidal reed-swamps, salt-marsh, mud-flats and brackish lagoons on the south bank of the Humber estuary. Breeding birds include avocets and several ducks on the lagoons, and bearded

tits, water rail and warblers in the reeds. The lagoons attract large numbers of waders in passage, including ruff, black-tailed godwits, curlew and sandpipers. Many other birds visit on migration in spring and autumn, and hen harrier and merlin roost in winter.

Bridgwater Bay Somerset. EN
A large area of mud-flats, called Stert Flats, at the mouth of the River Parrett. The reserve is a wader and wildfowl feeding and roosting area, and it is also one of the few places in Britain where moulting shelduck go in autumn. Large numbers of waders visit the reserve in winter, including dunlin, curlew and oystercatchers. Other wintering birds include white-fronted geese, wigeon, pintail and other ducks, merlins, short-eared owls and occasional peregrines. It is best to visit the estuary at high tide.

Caerlaverock Dumfries and Galloway. SNH, WWT and NNR
Of its 19,000 acres (8,000 ha), 1,400 acres are managed by The Wildfowl and Wetlands Trust. Merse (salt-marsh), extensive mud-flats and sandy foreshore, on the Upper Solway, 8 miles (13 km) south-east of Dumfries. Thousands of barnacle geese winter on the reserve, together with large numbers of shelduck, wigeon, pintail, scaup, teal and other ducks, and many waders such as oystercatchers, knot and dunlin. The reserve also provides an important roosting site for pink-footed and greylag geese. Other birds found include whooper swans, hen harriers, peregrines and merlins.

Cairngorms Highland, Moray and Aberdeenshire. SNH and NNR

At 94,000 acres (38,000 ha), this is by far the largest terrestrial reserve in Britain, with the most extensive mass of really high land – four summits reach over 4,000 ft (1,220 m), the highest being Ben Macdui. At lower altitudes there is much Scots pine and other woodland. The reserve contains the greatest variety of mountain-dwelling and northern birds in the country. Mountain species include dotterels, ptarmigans, snow buntings, golden eagles, golden plovers, dunlin and peregrines. The birds of the lower moors are red and black grouse, hen harriers, merlin and curlews. The woodland contains Scottish crossbills, crested tits, capercaillie, redpolls, siskins, redstarts, wood warblers and great spotted woodpeckers.

Chapel Wood Devon. RSPB
Small, mixed woodland in an attractive north Devon valley, 2 miles (3 km) north of Braunton. The woods contain a good cross-section of common birds – nuthatch, tree-creeper, redstart, various warblers and tits and, in some years, raven and buzzard.

Cley Marshes Norfolk. NORFOLK WT
A reserve on the coast of north Norfolk, 6 miles (10 km) west of Sheringham, between Salthouse and Cley next the Sea, within the most 'birdwatched' parish in Britain. Marshland lies behind a shingle seashore, with reed-fringed scrapes and areas of low, damp meadows. In summer, bitterns, bearded reedlings, garganey, avocets and black-tailed godwits are among the rarer species. In winter there are wigeon, shoveler and other duck; brent geese, hen harriers, shore larks and large flocks of snow buntings. But it is mainly for its autumn migrants, including frequent

rarities, that Cley Marshes are most famous. Regular visitors include wood and curlew sandpipers, little stints, spotted redshanks, black terns, little gulls, bluethroats, marsh and Montagu's harriers, barred warblers and waxwings. Offshore, a variety of seabirds can be seen on migration. They include skuas, shearwaters, terns and little auks.

Coombes Valley Staffordshire. RSPB
A long, wooded valley and a clear, fast-flowing stream, 12 miles (20 km) north-east of Stoke-on-Trent. The woodland is mainly oak, birch, rowan and ash. Breeding birds include all three woodpeckers, dippers, redstarts, pied flycatchers, wood warblers, tree pipits and grey wagtails.

Copinsay Orkney Islands. RSPB
Island reserve, 2 miles (3 km) south-east of Point of Ayre on Mainland, established as a memorial to the ornithologist James Fisher, seabird specialist. The red sandstone cliffs rise to about 200 ft (60 m) and provide breeding sites for many birds. Among them are some 30,000 guillemots, 10,000 kittiwakes and smaller numbers of razorbills, puffins, black guillemots, fulmars, shags, great and lesser black-backed gulls, and Arctic terns. There is a good variety of passage migrants in spring and summer. The island is reached by a boat from Skaill.

Cors Caron (Tregaron Bog) Ceredigion. CCW
Marshes, pools and bogs – one of the finest raised-bog systems in Britain – 12 miles (20 km) north-east of Lampeter and to the north of Tregaron. A wide variety of wildfowl visits the reserve in winter, including wigeon, teal, pintail, tufted duck, goldeneye and whooper swans.

Buzzards, curlews, grasshopper warblers, redshanks and snipe are among the many breeding species. Hen harriers, red kites and a variety of other birds of prey can be seen. Public access is by permit from the warden (tel. 01974 298480).

Culbin Sands Highland. RSPB
On the south side of the Moray Firth, this reserve consists of shingle foreshore and one of the largest sand-dune systems in Britain, which is almost entirely forested, backed by an extensive salt-marsh. There is a wide variety of breeding birds, including oystercatchers, ringed plovers and occasional terns. In the pine woods near by, Scottish crossbills, crested tits and capercaillie nest. Large numbers of waterfowl arrive in autumn and winter, including common scoter, greylag geese, long-tailed duck and several species of wader.

Dinas Carmarthenshire. RSPB
An area of wooded valleys and hilly upland 10 miles (16 km) north of Llandovery. Most of the typical birds of mid-Wales can be seen on the reserve. They include buzzards, ravens, pied flycatchers, redstarts, wood warblers, dippers, grey wagtails and occasionally red kites, for which there are special viewing facilities.

Dungeness Kent. RSPB
The huge shingle beach of the Dungeness promontory is a unique habitat in Britain. Successive shingle ridges indicating the site of former beaches shelter patches of gorse and other low scrub. There are many pools, and several flooded gravel pits which have important breeding colonies of black-headed, Mediterranean and common gulls, and common and

Sandwich terns. Other nesting birds include wheatears and great and little crested grebes. Many migrating song-birds make their landfall here in spring and autumn – whitethroats, willow warblers and wheatears are among the most common. Other regular visitors include black terns, firecrests and little gulls. Increasing numbers of duck winter on the gravel pits, including smew, gooseander and goldeneye, and both Slavonian and red-necked grebe.

Elmley Marshes Kent. RSPB
Mostly reclaimed marshland, on the south side of the Isle of Sheppey, bordering the muddy shores of the Swale estuary. The main concentrations of breeding waders occur on Spitend, an area of rough, undulating grassland, and include lapwings, redshanks, pochards, with some avocets and little terns. The Swale is an important wildfowl refuge – as many as 30,000 birds gather there at once, chiefly mallard, teal and wigeon. About 20,000 waders winter on the estuary: knot, dunlin, curlew, golden and grey plovers and oystercatchers are among the most numerous. Other wintering birds include brent geese and white-fronted geese, bar-tailed godwits, short-eared owls and hen harriers.

Exe Estuary Devon. RSPB and LOCAL COUNCILS
Extensive mud and sand-flats at low tide; freshwater marshes at Exminster; sand-dunes and some saltings at Dawlish Warren. The RSPB has 237 acres (96 ha) of grazing marshes near Exminster and Bowling Green Marsh near Topsham. Lapwings and redshanks breed in the meadows at Exminster, with sedge, reed and the rare Cetti's warblers along the canal banks. In winter there are thousands of roosting and

feeding curlews, lapwings and wigeon, with flocks of avocets and dark-bellied brent geese. The reserve at Dawlish Warren is known for attracting rarities, as well as hosting hundreds of ringed plovers.

Fairburn Ings West Yorkshire. RSPB

Shallow lakes, marshes and wet meadows in the Aire Valley, just north of Castleford. Formerly the biggest spoil-heap in Europe, this reserve was created in 10 years and is now host to more than 40 breeding species of bird – the highest number recorded anywhere in inland Britain. These include lapwings, redshanks, snipe, great and little crested grebes, little ringed plovers, snipe and several species of duck. There is a colony of black-headed gulls. In autumn the pools attract huge numbers of swallows which roost in the reed-beds with yellow and pied wagtails. The reserve is of principal importance for wintering wildfowl, including whooper swans and golden plovers. A visitor centre opened in 2000.

Fair Isle Shetland Islands. NTS

A remote island, 24 miles (40 km) south-west of Sumburgh Head at the southern tip of Mainland, and the site of Britain's most famous bird observatory. It has a rugged, cliff-bound coastline, and the interior is a mixture of moorland and crofts, with little cover except drystone walls. Breeding birds include large numbers of guillemots, razorbills, puffins, kittiwakes and fulmars; and also storm petrels, great and Arctic skuas and twites. In late spring, a wide variety of migrant birds visits the island, including many rarities from northern and eastern Europe, Asia and North America. Huge numbers of wheatears, redwings, snow buntings and many

307

other song-birds can also be seen, and annual rarities include scarlet grosbeaks, barred and icterine warblers, red-breasted flycatchers, bluethroats, short-toed larks and Richard's pipits. The bird observatory is open from mid-April to October. Two-star accommodation can be booked through the Warden on 01595 760258.

Farne Islands Northumberland. NT
A group of 28 rocky islands, 2-5 miles (3-8 km) off the Northumberland coast opposite Bamburgh. Only Inner Farne and Staple Island can be visited and are reached by boat from Seahouses harbour between April and September. The islands provide nesting sites for many seabirds, including cormorant, shag, guillemots, razorbills puffins, kittiwakes and eider as well as common, Arctic, Sandwich and roseate terns.

Fetlar Shetland Islands. RSPB
A reserve on the north coast of the most fertile islands of the Shetlands. The area became famous for the pair of snowy owls which nested there from 1967 to 1975. But in recent years, only female birds have been recorded. There are many other interesting birds, including 90 per cent of the British population of red-necked phalaropes, whimbrels, great and Arctic skuas and red-throated divers. Other birds that breed on Fetlar include curlew, golden plovers, dunlin, black guillemots, storm petrels and Manx shearwaters.

Fore Wood East Sussex. RSPB
Mixed woodland, 4 miles (6 km) north-west of Hastings, containing oak, with coppiced sweet chestnut and hornbeam. Birds that breed here include great and marsh tits, nightingales, black-

caps, garden warblers, nuthatches, treecreepers; great and lesser spotted woodpeckers.

Fowlsheugh Aberdeenshire. RSPB
Cliffs overlooking the North Sea about 3 miles (5 km) south of Stonehaven. Innumerable holes and ledges provide ideal nesting sites for over 70,000 pairs of seabirds. Kittiwakes, guillemots and razorbills are the most numerous species.

Gayton Sands Cheshire. RSPB
Salt-marsh, reed bed and tidal flats on the upper Dee estuary. Good views can be obtained from the car park north of the Boathouse Restaurant, Parkgate, on the Wirral, 11 miles (18 km) north-west of Chester. The whole area is a wintering ground for waders and wildfowl, with large flocks of pintail, teal and other ducks. Water rails, short-eared owls, twites and bramblings can also be seen, with peregrines, merlins and hen harriers hunting along the foreshore.

Gibraltar Point Lincs. LINCOLNSHIRE WT and NNR
An extensive reserve at the north-west corner of The Wash comprising sandy and muddy shores, sand dunes, salt and freshwater marsh and some woodland. Breeding birds to be seen here include shelduck, skylarks, ringed plovers and little terns. Lagoons and areas of scrub provide shelter for migrant waders and song-birds in spring and autumn. There is a good variety of wintering birds including divers and sea ducks offshore, waders and wildfowl, hen harriers, snow buntings, shore larks and short-eared owls.

Gower Coast Swansea. CCW and NT
The limestone cliffs at Worms Head support small breeding colonies of guillemots, razorbills

and kittiwakes. Choughs and peregrines can be seen on cliffs to the east. Shearwaters, gannets and terns are seen offshore occasionally, and common scoters gather in Rhossili Bay in winter.

Handa Highland. SCOTTISH WT
Island reserve just off the north-west coast of Scotland, 43 miles (69 km) north of Ullapool, and reached by boat from Tarbet, near Foindle, daily in summer except Sunday. Cliffs on the west of the island rise to 460 ft (140 m) and contain huge numbers of breeding guillemots, razorbills and kittiwakes, with smaller populations of fulmar, puffin and shag. Great and Arctic skuas are colonising the moorland in increasing numbers and there are red-throated divers on the moorland pools. Other nesting birds include skylarks, wheatears and meadow pipits.

Havergate Island Suffolk. RSPB
Island reserve in the River Ore estuary, behind Orford Ness. The water levels in the bare, muddy lagoons are artificially maintained to provide the correct depth of water for Britain's oldest and largest breeding colony of avocets – over 100 pairs. Colonies of black-headed gulls. Sandwich and common terns are also present, and a pair of short-eared owls nest occasionally. Other breeding birds include shelduck and redshanks. In winter the island provides a refuge for many waders and ducks. Many species of waders visit the reserve as passage migrants.

Hayle Estuary Cornwall. RSPB
With intertidal mud-flats and two seawater lagoons, the area is important for wintering and migrating wildfowl and waders. Passage birds include wigeon, teal, dunlin and greenshanks,

and rare migrants have appeared, among them spoonbill, the North American ring-billed gull and white-rumped sandpiper.

Hermaness Shetland Islands. SNH
Moorland, sea-cliffs and off-shore stacks. More than 100,000 breeding seabirds nest on the cliffs and stacks, including 16,000 pairs of gannets, 25,000 puffins and 15,000 guillemots. Inland, the moorland hosts the world's third-largest colony of great skuas, with a sprinkling of Arctic skuas, golden plovers, dunlin and red-throated divers.

Hickling Broad Norfolk. NORFOLK WT
Hickling Broad holds the most extensive area of reed swamp on the Norfolk Broads. The reserve, 14 miles (22 km) north-east of Norwich, is of outstanding importance for its marshland birds, notably bearded reedlings, bitterns and marsh harriers. Breeding birds include water rails, kingfishers, common terns and various warblers, such as Savi's and Cetti's. The grazing marshes and open water attract many migrating and wintering waders and wildfowl. Montagu's harriers and garganeys pass through as migrants.

Hobbister Orkney Islands. RSPB
Coastal moorland, sandflats, saltmarsh and sea cliffs, 4 miles (6.5 km) south-west of Kirkwall. The reserve has breeding hen harriers, short-eared owls, merlins, red-throated divers, curlews, red-breasted mergansers, together with small cliff colonies of black guillemots and fulmars.

Hornsea Mere East Yorkshire.
A shallow lake behind Hornsea, surrounded by reed-beds and some woodland and only 1 mile (1.6 km) from the sea. The lake attracts a great variety of passage migrants and winter visitors, including mallard, teal and other ducks, black terns, mute swans and great crested grebes. It is a very important site for little gulls in August and September. Breeding birds include tufted duck, water rail and nine species of warbler.

Insh Marshes Highland. RSPB
Marshes, lying near Kingussie in the flood plain of the River Spey, and forming the largest tract of natural fen in northern Britain, one of the most important wetlands in Europe. The breeding birds include many species of wader and duck, including approximately half of all British goldeneyes. Lapwings, redshanks and curlews nest here, as well as oystercatchers, snipe and wigeon. Migrant waders and birds of prey visit the area in autumn, and in winter the flooded marshes attract flocks of whooper swans and greylag geese.

Isle of May Fife. SNH
Rocky island in the Firth of Forth, noted for its breeding seabirds and for the large numbers of migrants which it attracts in spring and autumn. Cliff ledges on the west side of the island offer nesting sites for large numbers of guillemots and razorbills. Several thousand puffins nest, and their numbers are increasing. There are also large colonies of herring and lesser black-backed gulls, and Arctic tern. The island is Scotland's oldest bird observatory. Migrants include thrushes, warblers, chats and flycatchers, chiefly in autumn. Rare visitors include blue-throats, ortolan buntings and barred warblers.

Isles of Scilly. DUCHY OF CORNWALL
There are several small islands in Scilly with important breeding colonies of seabirds, with at least 15 species breeding annually, including storm petrel, shag, roseate tern, kittiwake, guillemot, razorbill, fulmar and cormorant. Manx shearwater numbers have declined since 1996. Most of these islands are closed during the breeding season, and landing is difficult at any time, but throughout spring and summer, launches provide transport between the islands and it is possible to see birds at close range. The islands also have large numbers of song thrush, wren, robin and dunnock, and are famous for numbers of rare migrants which appear each spring and autumn.

Lake Vyrnwy Powys. RSPB
A 24,000 acre (9,700 ha) reserve in the Berwyn hills, centred on a large reservoir and containing coniferous and deciduous woodland, streams and much open, high moorland. A variety of woodland and upland species nest here, including buzzards, sparrowhawks, goosanders, dippers, ring ouzels, grey wagtails, wheatears and redstarts. There is an information centre near the dam.

Langstone Harbour Hampshire. RSPB
Large tidal basin, 6 miles (10 km) east of Portsmouth, part of which is an RSPB reserve. Farlington Marshes, on the northern edge of the harbour, is a Hampshire and Isle of Wight Wildlife Trust reserve. The extensive mud and sand-flats contain large beds of eel-grass, which support several thousand brent geese in winter. Considerable numbers of other wildfowl are present, especially in winter, including shelduck, teal, wigeon and goldeneye. Black-necked grebes, red-breasted mergansers and green-shanks appear regularly outside the breeding

season, and the islands are the site of one of Britain's largest little tern colonies. Curlews and dunlin are the most numerous of the large variety of wader species which occur each year.

Leighton Moss Lancashire. RSPB
Shallow water and reed marsh, with patches of willow, 2 miles (3 km) north of Carnforth. This is an important northern outpost for several pairs of bitterns and bearded tits – species whose main British breeding grounds are in East Anglia. Other breeding birds include a large population of reed warblers, as well as shoveler, teal, garganey, water rails and grasshopper warblers. Many different species of duck are present in winter, and regular passage migrants include black terns and marsh harriers.

Lindisfarne Northumberland. EN and NNR
Some 9,000 acres (3,600 ha) of sand and mud stretching from south of Berwick-upon-Tweed to Budle Bay. The reserve attracts large flocks of wildfowl and waders in winter – including 75 per cent of the wintering population of the pale-bellied brent geese, and whooper swans, bar-tailed godwits, knot and dunlin. Eider nest on Holy Island, which is also a good place to see migrant song-birds in spring and autumn.

Loch Druidibeg South Uist, Western Isles. SNH
A National Nature Reserve stretching across the island of South Uist, encompassing shore, dunes, coastal grassland, croftland, moorland, and nutrient-rich and nutrient-poor lochs. Breeding wildfowl include mute swans, tufted duck, shelduck, mallard and teal. A small population of Scottish greylag geese is resident throughout the year. Other nesting birds

include ringed plover, dunlin, redshank, lapwing, corncrake and golden plover.

Loch Fleet Highland. SCOTTISH WILDLIFE TRUST
Tidal basin 4 miles (6.5 km) north of Dornoch. At low tide the reserve is used as a feeding area by shelduck, oystercatchers, little tern and ringed plovers throughout most of the year, and by a variety of waders in winter and on spring or autumn migration. Breeding birds include Arctic terns and eiders. A large flock of long-tailed ducks is present on Loch Fleet in winter, when the other wildfowl present include considerable numbers of common scoter offshore.

Loch Garten Highland. RSPB
Forming part of the RSPB's massive Abernethy Forest Reserve, Loch Garten is 2 miles (3 km) east of Boat of Garten and is famous for its pair of breeding ospreys, which nest in the top of a tall Scots pine. Ospreys have used this eyrie since 1959, and have been viewed from the special observation hide by well over a million visitors. The reserve is also home to Scottish crossbills, crested tits, siskins, capercaillie and other birds of the Caledonian pine forest.

Loch Gruinart Islay, Argyll and Bute. RSPB
4,100 acres (1,660 ha) of saltings, grass and moorland at the head of Loch Gruinart, a 4 mile (6.5 km) estuary which almost divides the western third of the Islay from the rest. The island is famous as a staging post for large numbers of barnacle and white-fronted geese, over-wintering en route for Greenland. In spring it is home to hundreds of breeding waders, including lapwings, redshank and snipe, and the corncrake can be heard calling at night. Terns

and gulls nest by the loch, and on the moorland, hen harriers, red and black grouse, twites and stonechats are to be found breeding. Golden eagles and peregrines hunt all year round.

Loch Leven Perthshire and Kinross. SNH
Large, shallow loch on the east side of Kinross, surrounded by farmland. It holds the largest inland population of breeding ducks anywhere in Britain. Mallard and tufted duck are the most numerous, and there are also smaller numbers of gadwall, wigeon, shoveler, shelduck and teal. In autumn up to 20,000 pink-footed geese fly in from their northern breeding grounds. Large numbers of greylag geese also winter here, and other wildfowl which can be seen include whooper swans, tufted duck, pochard and goldeneye. Access to the loch shore is limited to three sites; the RSPB reserve and educational centre at Vane Farm on the south shore offer the best viewing.

Loch of Kinnordy Angus. RSPB
Shallow, nutrient-rich loch 1 mile (1.6 km) west of Kirriemuir, with lush emergent vegetation ideal for nesting wildfowl. It is one of the best places in Scotland for seeing black-necked grebes, which nest in the midst of a large colony of black-headed gulls. Thousands of greylag geese, teal, shoveler and gadwall roost on the loch in winter, and ospreys visit regularly in summer.

Loch of Strathbeg Aberdeenshire. RSPB
Shallow, freshwater lake north-west of Rattray Head, separated from the North Sea by sand-dunes. The loch and its shores are included in a nature reserve. Many species of wildfowl winter on the loch, including large numbers of pink-

footed geese, whooper swans and a wide variety of ducks, including goosanders and goldeneye.

Lochwinnoch Renfrewshire. RSPB
Shallow lochs, wet meadows and woodland west of Glasgow. Great crested grebes, tufted duck and black-headed gulls are among the birds which breed here. Good numbers of wigeon, teal and other wildfowl are present in winter. A large information centre is provided for visitors.

Lundy Devon. NT and LANDMARK TRUST
Rocky island with cliffs rising to 400 ft (122 m), 11 miles (18 km) north-west of Hartland Point. It can be reached by boat from Bideford. Apart from small areas of cultivation and trees and shrubs, the island consists mostly of windswept moorland. Breeding birds on the sea-cliffs include large numbers of auks, fulmars, shags and kittiwakes, as well as Manx shearwater and ravens. The island is named after the old Norse word for 'puffin', a few of which breed there. Many birds on migration, especially small songbirds, visit the island in spring and autumn. Information can be obtained from the Warden on 01237-431831 and www.lundyisland.co.uk

Marwick Head Orkney Islands. RSPB
Old red sandstone headland on the north-west corner of Mainland. Huge numbers of guillemots, kittiwakes and other seabirds nest on the cliffs, which also provide nest-sites for ravens.

Minsmere Suffolk. RSPB
The great variety of carefully managed habitats at Minsmere, 6 miles (10 km) north of Aldeburgh, provide a shingle seashore, low sand-dunes, a brackish lagoon with islands, extensive fresh-water reed-marsh, wet grazing meadows, open sandy fields, scrub, mixed woodland and heath – the nesting habitat of over 100 species of bird: a greater variety than can be found in any area of comparable size in the country. Breeding birds at Minsmere include marsh harriers, reed and sedge warblers, bitterns, gadwall, shoveler; common and little terns; avocets, nightjars, kingfishers, nightingales, and various species of tit. Regular visitors include spoonbills, purple herons, spotted redshanks and many other waders. Autumn migrants from Scandinavia sometimes include bluethroats, wrynecks and pied flycatchers. Bewick's swans and other wildfowl occur in winter.

Morecambe Bay Lancashire. RSPB
Sand-flats between the high and low tidelines. The bay supports one of the biggest wintering populations of waders anywhere in Europe. Around a quarter of a million waders are present at peak times each winter, including great numbers of oystercatchers, ringed plovers, curlews, bar-tailed godwits, redshanks, knot, dunlin and sanderlings. Adjoins Leighton Moss.

Mull of Galloway Dumfries and Galloway. RSPB
Sea-cliffs beside and just north of the lighthouse. There are several colonies of breeding seabirds. Guillemots, razorbills and kittiwakes are the most numerous, and there are also shags, fulmars, gulls and a few black guillemots.

Nagshead Gloucestershire. RSPB
Deciduous woodland, chiefly oak but with some sweet chestnut, beech and birch, in the Forest of Dean, 2 miles (3 km) south-east of Coleford. It contains a large population of pied flycatchers, and other breeding birds to be seen there include nightjars, redstarts, wood warblers, and green, great spotted and lesser spotted woodpeckers.

Northward Hill Kent. RSPB
Mixed woodland and wet grassland 4 miles (6.5 km) north-east of Rochester, situated on rising ground on the edge of the High Halstow marshes. Many nightingales, woodpeckers and other typical woodland birds breed there, but the reserve is noted chiefly for containing the largest heronry in Britain, with over 150 nests. Visits to the heronry by prior arrangement only. There are breeding waders on the marshes, including lapwings and redshanks, and waders and wildfowl visit in winter.

Noss Shetland Islands. SNH and NNR
Island 4 miles (6.5 km) east of Lerwick, reached by ferry from Noss Sound. During the summer the narrow ledges of the tall sandstone cliffs are packed with nesting seabirds. Some 12,000 pairs of gannets nest on the Noup on the east coast, and there are also thousands of guillemots, razorbills, puffins, kittiwakes and fulmars. Other breeding birds include black guillemots, eider and Arctic terns. The rough, hilly moorland supports colonies of great and a few Arctic skuas.

Noup Cliffs Westray, Orkney Islands. RSPB
These sandstone cliffs offer one of the largest seabird nesting sites in Britain, with at least 50,000 pairs of guillemots and kittiwakes. There are also large numbers of other cliff-nesting species, and puffins on the cliff tops.

Old Hall Marshes Essex. RSPB
A stretch of coastal fresh marsh and adjoining

salt-marsh with a network of pools which attract both wintering and breeding wildfowl. Terns nest, and marsh harriers and short-eared owls are seen. In winter, waders and brent geese pasture beside the nearby Blackwater estuary.

Ouse Washes Cambridgeshire and Norfolk. RSPB, WWT and WT
A 20 mile (32 km) long series of meadows on the west side of the Great Ouse river. The meadows flood regularly each winter and form one of the outstanding inland sites for wildfowl in Europe. Waterfowl concentrations are spectacular with large numbers of wigeon, Bewick's swans, pintail, shoveler, mallard, teal, pochard, coots, gadwall and whooper swans. During the summer the wet meadows attract many breeding birds – notably snipe, redshanks, lapwings and nine species of duck. This is a nesting place for black-tailed godwit, if conditions are right, and occasionally for ruffs. Rare species such as spotted crakes have nested or summered here.

Radipole Lake Dorset. RSPB
A series of freshwater or brackish, reed-fringed lagoons lying within the town of Weymouth. Breeding birds include great-crested grebes, bearded tits, Cetti's warblers and large numbers of grasshopper, reed and sedge warblers. In autumn large numbers of swallows and yellow wagtails gather to roost in the reed-beds. Regular migrants include little gulls, black terns, garganey, pochards, and many other waterfowl. Large numbers of mute swans inhabit the lakes.

Rostherne Mere Cheshire. EN
The largest of the Cheshire meres, 4 miles (6.5 km) south-west of Altrincham, fringed by

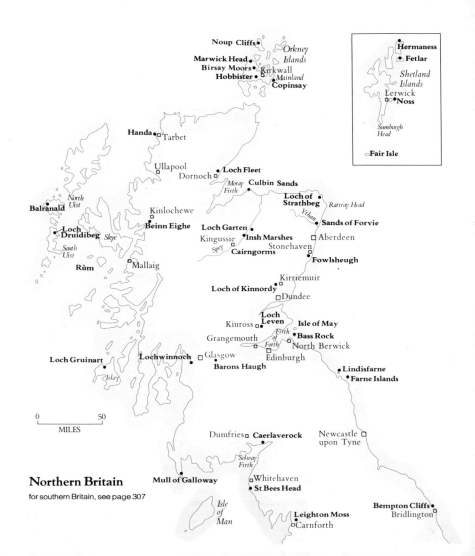

Northern Britain

for southern Britain, see page 307

reeds and woodland. Mallard are the most numerous birds in this important wildfowl refuge, but wigeon, teal, shoveler, pochard, tufted duck and Canada geese also occur. Up to 20,000 gulls roost on the lake, and black terns are frequent visitors in spring and autumn.

Rùm Highland. SNH and NNR
Mountainous island in the Inner Hebrides, south of Skye, with a rugged coastline and some woodland. The birdlife includes resident golden eagles, merlins, ravens, red-throated divers, golden plovers and large colonies of seabirds. A large colony of Manx shearwaters nests on the mountain from 2,500 ft (760 m) upwards. The reserve is also the site of a successful attempt to reintroduce the white-tailed eagle to Britain. More than 90 young birds were brought from Norway and released on the island from the mid-1970s to the mid-1980s. Day visits are possible and accommodation is available. Ring 01687 462026 for details.

St Bees Head Cumbria. RSPB
High sandstone cliffs 3½ miles (6 km) south of Whitehaven. Many seabirds nest on the cliffs, including guillemots, razorbills, kittiwakes and fulmars, and smaller numbers of puffins and a few black guillemots.

Sands of Forvie Aberdeenshire. SNH
Dunes 13 miles (21 km) north of Aberdeen, lying between a sandy foreshore and the Ythan estuary. They contain large colonies of common, Arctic, little and Sandwich terns and some 2,000 pairs of eiders, the largest concentration in Britain. Shelduck are also common. The estuary itself is an important waterfowl

refuge and feeding area. Many pink-footed and greylag geese roost here in winter, together with long-tailed duck and a wide variety of other wildfowl and waders.

Skomer Pembrokeshire.
CCW and WILDLIFE TRUST, WEST WALES
Island nature reserve south of St Brides Bay, open to visitors from 1 April to 31 October (not Mondays), and reached by boat from Martinshaven near Marloes. Farming was abandoned many years ago, and the heather and bracken-covered interior is now the home of wheatears, stonechats, and a large colony of lesser black-backed gulls. Choughs, ravens and buzzards nest on the cliffs, and there are large colonies of seabirds – guillemots, razorbills, kittiwakes, puffins, fulmars and the mainly nocturnal storm petrels and Manx shearwaters.

Slimbridge Gloucestershire. WWT
This is the headquarters of The Wildfowl and Wetlands Trust, 11 miles (17 km) south-west of Gloucester on the upper Severn Estuary. It contains the largest collection of captive waterfowl in the world. In winter it is a sanctuary for more than 20,000 wildfowl and waders, and is known for its over-wintering population of Bewick's swans. It is also Britain's main wintering area for the European white-fronted goose, and the most likely place to see the lesser white-fronted goose. The salt-marshes, meadows, lagoons and tidal flats of the Severn estuary also support many other waterfowl, most notably wigeon, pintail, shoveler and gadwall.

Snettisham Norfolk. RSPB
The Wash is one of the most important areas in

Europe for wintering waterfowl. At high tide, roosts of waders occur at several points. At Snettisham, on the east shore, thousands of oystercatchers and knots roost on the islands in the flooded gravel pits. The saltmarsh and mud-flats of the rest of the reserve attract thousands of other waders in winter, including knot, dunlins, bar-tailed godwits, curlews and grey plovers. From November to Febraury up to 40,000 pink-footed geese roost on the reserve, together with brent geese, tufted duck, pochard and gadwall on the gravel pits. Snow buntings winter on the beach, and sanderlings occur on migration.

South Stack Cliffs Anglesey. RSPB
Coastal moorland and sea-cliffs, on Holy Island on the most westerly point of Anglesey. Guillemots, razorbills, puffins, fulmars and kittiwakes nest in summer, and choughs are resident throughout the year.

Stodmarsh Kent. EN and NNR
Shallow wetland in the Stour valley, 4 miles (6.5 km) north-east of Canterbury. The extensive reed-beds, open water and wet meadows support a breeding community similar to that of the Norfolk Broads, including bearded tits, bitterns, garganey, gadwall and water rails. Visitors include marsh harriers. Reed and sedge warblers and bearded reedlings are numerous, and there are small numbers of Cetti's warblers. Large numbers of ducks spend the winter in the reserve.

Strumpshaw Fen Norfolk. RSPB
A typical area of Broadland fen, 6 miles (10 km) east of Norwich, on the banks of the River Yare. Its extensive reed-beds and willow and alder

woods support many breeding sedge, reed and grasshopper warblers, and several bearded tits and Cetti's warblers. One or two pairs of marsh harrier nest. In winter the grazing meadows at Buckenham Marshes attract Britain's main flock of bean geese.

Tamar Estuary Cornwall. CORNWALL WT
Mud-flats and salt-marsh on the west shore of the Tamar, north of Saltash. It is a nationally important reserve for passage and wintering waders, especially avocets and snipe, black-tailed godwit, redshanks, greenshanks, dunlin, curlew and whimbrel.

Tetney Marshes North East Lincolnshire. RSPB
Foreshore and saltings on the south side of the Humber estuary. The reserve contains a small colony of little terns in the summer and large numbers of waders in winter, especially at high tide. Brent geese and snow buntings are among the other species that winter here.

The Wetland Centre London. WWT
On the site of four disused Victorian reservoirs in Barnes, this site was opened in 2000, and already 130 species of bird have been recorded.

Titchwell Marsh Norfolk. RSPB
One of the most visited of all RSPB reserves, 5 miles (8 km) east of Hunstanton, with a variety of habitats including woodland, reedbed, freshwater and brackish lagoons, salt-marsh and beach. A wide range of species breed, including marsh harrier, avocet and bearded tit. There are many passage and wintering species, including golden plover, brent goose, shorelark and hen harrier. Barn owls occur throughout the year.

Tring Reservoirs Hertfordshire.
EN, HERTFORDSHIRE AND MIDDLESEX WT and THAMES WATER
Four reservoirs, just north of Tring, part banked with concrete and the rest more natural, with marshy edges. Wilstone reservoir, managed by the local Wildlife Trust, has a large heronry and is the best place to see hobbies in the summer. Breeding birds in the area include water rail, great crested grebes, sedge and reed warblers. Many wildfowl, including goosanders, spend their winter on the Tring reservoirs. Black terns, little ringed plovers, black-necked grebes, common and green sandpipers, greenshanks and other waders occur regularly as passage migrants, with the occasional smew.

West Sedgemoor Somerset. RSPB
A reserve, 6 miles (10 km) east of Bridgwater, one of the few areas of poorly drained grazing meadows now remaining on the Somerset Levels. Here lapwings, redshanks and snipe breed in good numbers. Winter flooding brings an abundance of dabbling ducks and also Bewick's swans. There is a heronry beside the visitors' car park.

Wicken Fen Cambridgeshire.
NATIONAL TRUST and NNR
An 850 acre (340 ha) remnant of the ancient peat fens of East Anglia, lying 9 miles (14 km) south of Ely. Areas of reed, sedge, willow and alder copse (or carr) support a varied population of song-birds, including large numbers of willow and sedge warblers. Grasshopper warblers, redshank and lapwing also nest. Winter visitors include bittern and hen harriers as well as small numbers of wildfowl.

Wolves Wood Suffolk. RSPB
Mixed woodland about 8 miles (13 km) west of Ipswich, consisting mainly of oak, hazel and birch, with some hornbeam coppice and hawthorn scrub. The reserve supports a varied bird population, which includes nightingales, garden warblers, blackcaps, willow and marsh tits, and great and lesser spotted woodpeckers.

Wyre Forest Hereford and Worcester.
FOREST ENTERPRISE/EN and NNR
Mixed deciduous woodland, with some areas of planted conifers, 4 miles (6.5 km) west of Kidderminster. Only part of the forest is a reserve, an area south of the village of Buttonoak. It contains an outstanding variety of woodland and stream-side birds, such as sparrowhawks, woodcock, wood warblers, pied flycatchers, redstarts, kingfishers, dippers and grey wagtails.

Yarner Wood Devon. EN and NNR
Upland oak woodland, with Scots pine, rowan and holly, on the east side of the Dartmoor National Park and 2 miles (3 km) north-west of Bovey Tracey. Breeding birds include wood warblers and pied flycatchers. Many other typical woodland birds can be seen, including the lesser spotted woodpecker.

Ynys-hir Ceredigion. RSPB
Salt-marsh, mixed woodland, bracken-covered slopes and brackish pools, on the edge of the Dyfi estuary. Breeding birds include buzzards, pied flycatchers, redstarts, wood warblers and nuthatches. The estuary attracts numbers of wildfowl and waders on migration and in winter, including many wigeon, pintail and Greenland white-fronted geese.

Glossary

Accidental Uncommon visitor, arriving only when blown off course or disorientated; same as VAGRANT.
Adult Bird with fully developed final plumage.
Albino Bird with partial or total absence of dark pigment, giving it a white appearance. In a true albino, dark pigment is completely absent from the beak, eyes and legs, as well as from the plumage.
Axillaries Feathers in the axilla, or 'armpit'.

Barb Branch of the central shaft of a feather.
Barbule Branch of the BARB of a feather.
Bastard wing Group of feathers at first digit of wing from tip, or 'thumb'.
Blaze Coloured patch at base of bill.
Breeding plumage Plumage developed during the breeding season.
Brood patch Area of featherless, thickened skin on abdomen developed as an aid to incubating eggs.

Call Brief sound used for contact within a species, to warn of danger, and so on. Same throughout the year.
Carpal joint Forward-pointing joint of the wing when closed: the 'wrist'.
Cere Fleshy covering at base of bill found in hawks, pigeons and other birds. Often distinctively coloured.
Colony Gathering of some species

of birds, to breed or roost.
Contour feathers Feathers lying along the body, streamlining it and insulating it against cold.
Coverts Feathers overlying the bases of the tail feathers or major wing feathers; for example tail covert, wing covert, under-wing covert. Also the area of feathers covering a bird's ear (ear covert).
Crepuscular Active only at dusk and dawn.

Dialect Local variation in the song of a bird population.
Display Posturing, usually by male bird to attract female during breeding season; also to warn off rival males, and to defend TERRITORY.
Diurnal Active only in daylight hours.
Dorsal Belonging to a bird's back.
Down First feather covering of young birds of some species.

Eclipse Post-breeding moult, characteristic of ducks, during which, for a short time, males become flightless, lose their bright plumage and come to resemble females.
Egg-tooth Horny protuberance at tip of upper MANDIBLE of a chick, used to crack shell when emerging.
Eruption Mass movement of birds, occurring at irregular intervals.
Escape Species or individual bird escaped or liberated from captivity.
Exotic Term describing a species foreign to an area.
Eye-stripe Distinctively coloured

stripe of feathers leading back from or through the eye.

Feral Term describing wild bird population that originated in captivity.
First year Period between the time a bird leaves the nest and the following breeding season.
Fore-edge, fore-wing Leading edge of wing.

Gape Angle of bill opening.

Hawking Capture of flying insects while bird is on the wing.
Hood Area of contrasting plumage covering most of head.

Immature Bird in plumage indicating lack of sexual maturity.
Introduced Term describing birds captured in one area and released in another.
Invasion Sudden mass arrival of birds not usually seen in an area.

Juvenile Bird in its first covering of true feathers.

Lek Place where males of some species, for example black grouse, display communally prior to breeding.
Lore Area between base of upper mandible and eye.

Mandible Upper or lower part of bill.
Mantle Back.
Melanistic Term describing a bird with an abnormally large amount of dark pigment in its plumage.

Migrant Species that does not remain on its breeding grounds throughout the year.
Mob Aggression, usually directed by a number of birds against a predator.
Morph Same as PHASE.
Moustachial stripe Streak of contrasting feathers running back from the base of the bill.

Nail Shield or horny plate at tip of upper mandible, found in some geese and ducks.
Nidiculous Term describing young that are hatched helpless and blind, and stay in nest for a considerable time.
Nidifugous Term describing young that are hatched with eyes open, covered with down and able to leave nest almost immediately.
Nocturnal Active only during darkness.

Oceanic Another word for PELAGIC.
Orbital ring Fleshy ring around the eye.

Partial migrant Species of which some individuals migrate, but others remain on their breeding grounds.
Passage migrant Bird usually breeding and wintering outside an area, but regularly seen on migration.
Pelagic Term describing seabird that seldom or never visits land except in breeding season.
Phase Distinctive variation of plumage within a species.

Preen gland Gland on rump that exudes oil as an aid to preening.
Primary feathers A bird's main flight feathers, attached to 'hand'.

Race Term used to describe a subspecies of a bird which inhabits a different region and has slightly different physical characteristics, as for example, plumage pattern.,
Raptor Bird of prey, excluding owls.
Resident Bird present throughout year.

Scapulars Feathers above the shoulders of a bird.
Secondary feathers Flight feathers attached to 'forearm'.
Sedentary Term describing species that does not migrate or move far from its breeding ground.
Song Language of a bird, intended to identify its TERRITORY to other birds and attract females to intended breeding area.
Speculum Contrasting patch of SECONDARY FEATHERS in wing, usually in ducks.
Spinning Action of some water birds, for example phalaropes, swimming in tight circles to bring food to the surface.
Stoop Term describing dive of a raptor, especially peregrine falcon.
Sub-song Subdued song outside period of full song, or by young males.
Subspecies See RACE.
Superciliary stripe Streak of contrasting feathers above a bird's eye.

Tarsus Part of a bird's leg from directly above the toes to the first joint.
Territory Part of a habitat defended by the bird or group of birds occupying it against other birds.

Vagrant Uncommon visitor, arriving only when blown off course or disorientated.
Ventral Belonging to a bird's underside or belly.

Wattles Fleshy protuberances on head.
Web Flesh between toes of water birds.
Wing-bar Conspicuous stripe across the wing, formed by tips of feathers of contrasting colour.
Wing linings Under-wing COVERTS.
Winter plumage Plumage developed outside breeding season, by male or female bird.
Winter visitor Bird that usually breeds outside the area in which it is seen in winter.

Index

Page numbers in **bold type** denote full-page entries; those in roman type denote additional references, or shorter entries on rarer birds.

Acknowledgments

Artwork in *Birds of Britain* was supplied by the following artists:

3, 8–17 John Busby · 18–23 Norman Arlott, Hermann Heinzel, Patrick Oxenham · 24–25 Jim Russell · 26–33 John Francis · 34–39 Trevor Boyer · 40–41 Tim Hayward · 42–45 Robert Gillmor · 46–49 Robert Morton · 50–51 Sean Milne · 52–57 Stephen Adams · 58–81 Robert Morton · 82–99 Ken Wood · 100–13 Tim Hayward · 114–19 John Francis · 120–37 Trevor Boyer · 138–41 Tim Hayward · 142–7 Robert Morton · 148–55 John Francis · 156–83 Trevor Boyer · 184–7 Tim Hayward · 188–9 Peter Barrett · 190–5 Trevor Boyer · 196–7 Robert Morton · 198–9 Peter Barrett · 200–9 Robert Morton · 210–11 Norman Arlott · 212–19 D. W. Ovenden · 220–7 Peter Barrett · 228–65 Norman Arlott · 266–83 Ken Wood · 284–93 Robert Morton · 294–5 Norman Arlott · 296–7 Jim Russell · 302–3 Mick Loates

Photographs in *Birds of Britain* were supplied by the following photographers and agencies. Names of photographers are in roman type and those of agencies in capital letters. The following abbreviations are used:

NHPA – Natural History Photographic Agency.
NSP – Natural Science Photos.
OSF – Oxford Scientific Films.
RSPB – Royal Society for the Protection of Birds.

26 BRUCE COLEMAN/G. Ziegter · 27 NSP/D. M. Turner-Ettlinger · 28 ARDEA/J. B. & S. Bottomley · 29 ARDEA/J. A. Bailey · 30 Eric Hosking · 31 ARDEA/J. A. Bailey · 32 BRUCE COLEMAN/S. C. Porter · 33 ARDEA/S. Fatras · 34 Brian Hawkes · 35 ARDEA/R. Vaughan · 36–37 BRUCE COLEMAN/R. K. Murton · 38–39 RSPB/M. Richards · 40 ARDEA/C. K. Mylne · 41 NHPA/J. Good · 42 BRUCE COLEMAN/M. F. Soper · 43 John Buckingham · 44 BRUCE COLEMAN/J. Markham · 46 ARDEA/J. P. Laub · 47 WILDFOWL TRUST/J. B. Blossom · 48 BRUCE COLEMAN/J. Markham · 49 BRUCE COLEMAN/Leonard Lee Rue · 50 BRUCE COLEMAN/N. Williams · 51 BRUCE COLEMAN/D. & H. Urry · 52 ARDEA/M. D. England · 53 NHPA/S. Krasemann · 54 NHPA/P. Scott · 55 ARDEA/R. J. C. Blewitt · 56 NATURFOTO/N. Christiansen · 57 AQUILA/M. C. Wilkes · 60 BRUCE COLEMAN/L. R. Dawson · 61 AQUILA/P. T. Castell · 62 ARDEA/G. K. Brown · 63 AQUILA/P. T. Castell · 64 BRUCE COLEMAN/P. Dermid · 65 BRUCE COLEMAN/J. van Wormer · 66 BRUCE COLEMAN/J. & D. Bartlet · 67 ARDEA/R. F. Porter · 68 RSPB/M. Richards · 69 Philippa Scott · 70 JACANA/G. Ziesler · 71 NATURFOTO · 72 Brian Hawkes · 73 BRUCE COLEMAN/G. Langsbury · 74 NATURFOTO/B. Gensbol · 75 WILDFOWL TRUST/J. B. Blossom · 78 ARDEA/G. K. Brown · 79 NHPA/P. Scott · 82 BRUCE COLEMAN/H. Reinhard · 83 AQUILA/P. T. Castell · 84 Frank V. Blackburn · 85 Eric Hosking · 86 NHPA/E. Martomäki · 87 ARDEA/R. J. C. Blewitt · 88 AQUILA/P. T. Castell · 89 Frank V. Blackburn · 90 NHPA/J. Jeffery · 91 RSPB/M. Richards · 92 AQUILA/M. C. Wilkes · 93 BRUCE COLEMAN/D. Green · 94 AQUILA/F. V. Blackburn · 95 Brian Hawkes · 100 NSP/A. W. Cundall · 101 BRUCE COLEMAN/C. Ott · 102 AQUILA/P. T. Castell · 103 AQUILA/P. T. Castell · 104 John Buckingham · 105 NHPA/D. N. Dalton · 106 AQUILA/M. C. Wilkes · 108 BRUCE COLEMAN/H. Reinhard · 109 Eric Hosking · 110 ARDEA/A. Fatras · 111 BRUCE COLEMAN/H. Reinhard · 112 Eric Hosking · 113 ARDEA/J. A. Bailey · 116 JACANA/R. Volot · 117 BRUCE COLEMAN/A. J. Deane · 118 ARDEA/C. Knights · 119 AQUILA/D. Green · 120 Frank V. Blackburn · 121 NSP/E. H. Herbert · 122 ARDEA/R. Vaughan · 123 ARDEA/R. Vaughan · 125 Brian Hawkes · 126 BRUCE COLEMAN/G. Langsbury · 127 BRUCE COLEMAN/L. R. Davidson · 128 FRANK LANE/G. J. H. Moon · 129 JACANA/Varin · 130 BRUCE COLEMAN/A. J. Deane · 131 BRUCE COLEMAN/L. R. Dawson · 132 AQUILA/S. Welch · 133 BRUCE COLEMAN/J. van Wormer · 136 BRUCE COLEMAN · 138 NATURFOTO/T. Schmidt · 139 OKAPIA/H. Zettl · 140 BRUCE COLEMAN/S. C. Porter · 141 NHPA/S. Dalton · 142 Eric Hosking · 143 AQUILA/T. Andrewartha · 144 JACANA/Varin-Visage · 145 ARDEA/R. J. C. Blewitt · 146 BRUCE COLEMAN/J. & D. Bartlett · 147 AQUILA/C. Smith · 150 JACANA/A. Rainon · 151 ARDEA/C. R. Knights · 152 Philip Burton · 153 NATURFOTO/M. H. Jensen · 156 BRUCE COLEMAN/J. J. Tulloch · 157 BRUCE COLEMAN/F. Erize · 158 Eric Hosking · 159 AQUILA/E. Soothill · 160 ARDEA/C. K. Mylne · 161 ARDEA/J. A. Bailey · 162 AQUILA/S. C. Brown · 163 Philip Burton · 164 BRUCE COLEMAN/D. & K. Urry · 165 AQUILA/H. A. Hems · 166 BRUCE COLEMAN/L. R. Dawson · 167 BRUCE COLEMAN/L. R. Dawson · 172 BRUCE COLEMAN/U. Hirsch · 173 John Buckingham · 174 BRUCE COLEMAN/D. Middleton · 175 Brian Hawkes · 176 OSF/Graham J. Wren · 177 ARDEA/J. A. Bailey · 180 John Buckingham · 181 Philip Burton · 182 AQUILA/P. T. Castell · 183 Brian Hawkes · 184 BRUCE COLEMAN/S. C. Porter · 185 ARDEA/R. J. C. Blewitt · 186–7 ARDEA/R. T. Smith · 187 NHPA/D. N. Dalton · 188–9 Frank V. Blackburn · 190 NHPA/S. Dalton · 191 Eric Hosking · 192 NHPA/S. Dalton · 193 BRUCE COLEMAN/E. Breeze-Jones · 194 BRUCE COLEMAN/J. Burton · 195 BRUCE COLEMAN/E. Breeze-Jones · 196 AQUILA/F. V. Blackburn · 197 ARDEA/U. Bergrens · 198–9 ARDEA/J. Daniels · 202 Philip Burton · 203 ARDEA/R. J. C. Blewitt · 204 AQUILA/M. C. Wilkes · 205 NHPA/S. Dalton · 206–7 AQUILA/J. A. J. Bond · 208 Frank V. Blackburn · 209 BRUCE COLEMAN/S. Dalton · 210 ARDEA/J. A. Bailey · 211 OSF/G. Wren · 212 BRUCE COLEMAN/J. Markham · 213 ARDEA/J. A. Bailey · 214 ARDEA/R. Vaughan · 215 BRUCE COLEMAN/J. Burton · 216 NSP/C. A. Walker · 217 NHPA/S. Dalton · 218 AQUILA/F. V. Blackburn · 219 BRUCE COLEMAN/G. Ziesler · 220 WILDFOWL TRUST/J. B. Blossom · 221 AQUILA/J. Lawton Roberts · 222 Brian Hawkes · 223 ARDEA/J. A. Bailey · 224 JACANA/Nardin · 225 ARDEA/R. F. Porter · 226 AQUILA/P. T. Castell · 227 Frank V. Blackburn · 228 JACANA/A. Ducrot · 229 BRUCE COLEMAN/S. Dalton · 230 BRUCE COLEMAN/S. Dalton · 231 Eric Hosking · 232 Frank V. Blackburn · 233 BRUCE COLEMAN/D. Middleton · 234 ARDEA/P. Laub · 235 NHPA/S. Dalton · 238 Frank V. Blackburn · 239 ARDEA/J. A. Bailey · 240 Frank V. Blackburn · 241 Philip Burton · 242 AQUILA/P. T. Castell · 243 BRUCE COLEMAN/S. C. Porter · 244 ARDEA/M. D. England · 245 BRUCE COLEMAN/J. Markham · 246 BRUCE COLEMAN/H. Reinhard · 247 ARDEA/R. T. Smith · 248 Eric Hosking · 249 NHPA/J. Good · 250 ARDEA/P. Laub · 251 AQUILA/D. Green · 252 AQUILA/S. C. Brown · 253 ARDEA/M. D. England · 254 BRUCE COLEMAN/H. Reinhard · 255 John Buckingham · 256 AQUILA/E. A. Janes · 257 FRANK LANE/D. Zingel · 258 NSP/A. W. Cundall · 259 NATURFOTO/E. Hanson · 260 David Hosking · 261 NHPA/S. Dalton · 262 ARDEA/K. J. Carlson · 263 FRANK LANE/N. Duerden · 264 BRUCE COLEMAN/J. Markham · 265 ARDEA/I. Beames · 266 Frank V. Blackburn · 267 NHPA/S. Dalton · 268 ARDEA/R. T. Smith · 269 BRUCE COLEMAN/J. Markham · 270 BRUCE COLEMAN/E. Breeze-Jones · 271 ARDEA/J. Daniels · 272 NHPA/S. Dalton · 273 BRUCE COLEMAN/R. & A. Clare · 274 NSP/F. Greenaway · 275 AQUILA/M. C. Wilkes · 276 AQUILA/J. A. Bailey · 277 Eric Hosking · 278 Brian Hawkes · 279 AQUILA/R. Foster · 280 Frank V. Blackburn · 281 NSP/D. M. Turner-Ettlinger · 282 BRUCE COLEMAN/R. K. Murton · 283 NATURFOTO/B. Gensbol · 284 AQUILA/T. Andrewartha · 285 BRUCE COLEMAN/L. R. Dawson · 286 ARDEA/M. D. England · 287 NATURFOTO/B. Gensbol · 288 BRUCE COLEMAN/J. Markham · 289 ARDEA/B. Bevan · 290 BRUCE COLEMAN/S. C. Porter · 291 JACANA/R. Volet · 292 BRUCE COLEMAN/C. J. Ott · 293 ARDEA/J. B. Bottomley

The publishers also acknowledge their indebtedness to the following books and journals which were consulted for reference:

The Atlas of Breeding Birds in Britain and Ireland by J. T. R. Sharrock (T. & A. D. Poyser) · *The Bird Table Book* by Tony Soper (David & Charles) · *The Birdlife of Britain* by Philip Burton and Peter Hayman (Mitchell Beazley) · *Birds* (Magazine of the Royal Society for the Protection of Birds) · *The Birds in Your Garden* (RSPB) · *The Birds of Britain and Europe* by Hermann Heinzel, Richard Fitter and John Parslow (Collins) · *Birds of Mountain and Moorland* edited by John Gooders (Orbis) · *Birds of Ocean and Estuary* edited by John Gooders (Orbis) · *Birds of the Atlantic Ocean* by T. Stokes and Keith Shackleton (Country Life) · *The Birds of the British Isles* by D. A. Bannerman (12 volumes, Oliver & Boyd) · *Book of British Birds* (Reader's Digest/AA) · *Book of the British Countryside* (Drive Publications) · *British Birds* magazine (Macmillan Journals) · *The Dictionary of Birds in Colour* by Bruce Campbell (Michael Joseph) · *Discover Birds* by Ian Wallace (Whizzard Press/Andre Deutsch) · *A Field Guide to the Birds of Britain and Europe* by Roger Peterson, Guy Mountfort and P. A. D. Hollom (Collins) · *A Field Guide to the Nests, Eggs and Nestlings of British and European Birds* by Colin Harrison (Demeter Press) · *A Field Guide to the Seabirds of Britain and the World* by Gerald Tuck and Hermann Heinzel (Collins) · *The Hamlyn Guide to Birds of Britain and Europe* by Bertel Bruun and Arthur Singer (Hamlyn) · *The Handbook of British Birds* edited by H. F. Witherby (5 volumes, Witherby) · *Handbook of the Birds of Europe, the Middle East and North Africa: The Birds of the Western Palearctic Vol. I* edited by Stanley Cramp (Oxford University Press) · *Handbuch der Vögel Mitteleuropas* by K. M. Bauer & U. N. Glutz von Blotzheim (Akademische Gelagsgesellschaft, Frankfurt am Main) · *A New Dictionary of Birds* edited by Sir A. Landsborough Thomson (Nelson) · *The Oxford Book of Birds* by Bruce Campbell (Oxford University Press) · *The Penguin Dictionary of British Natural History* by Richard and Maisie Fitter (Penguin Books) · *The Popular Handbook of British Birds* by P. A. D. Hollom (Witherby) · *Rare Birds in Britain and Ireland* by J. T. R. and E. M. Sharrock (T. & A. D. Poyser) · *R.S.P.B. Guide to British Birds* by David Saunders (Hamlyn)

Typesetting: VANTAGE PHOTOSETTING CO. LTD, EASTLEIGH
Separations: MULLIS MORGAN LTD, LONDON
Printer/Binder: MILANOSTAMPA, ITALY

400-079-03